We Are What We Sell

We Are What We Sell

How Advertising
Shapes American
Life ... and Always Has

Volume 3: Advertising in the Contemporary Age

Danielle Sarver Coombs and
Bob Batchelor, Editors

PRAEGER

AN IMPRINT OF ABC-CLIO, LLC
Santa Barbara, California • Denver, Colorado • Oxford, England

Library of Congress Cataloging-in-Publication Data

We are what we sell : how advertising shapes American life . . . and always has / Danielle Sarver Coombs and Bob Batchelor, editors.
    volumes ; cm
    Includes bibliographical references and index.
    ISBN 978–0–313–39244–3 (hardback) — ISBN 978–0–313–39245–0 (ebook)
    1. Advertising—Social aspects—United States—History. 2. Branding (Marketing)—United States—History. 3. Consumer satisfaction—United States. I. Coombs, Danielle Sarver, editor. II. Batchelor, Bob, editor.
HF5805.W394   2014
302.23—dc23   2013019253

ISBN: 978–0–313–39244–3
EISBN: 978–0–313–39245–0

18 17 16 15 14   1 2 3 4 5

This book is also available on the World Wide Web as an eBook.
Visit www.abc-clio.com for details.

Praeger
An Imprint of ABC-CLIO, LLC

ABC-CLIO, LLC
130 Cremona Drive, P.O. Box 1911
Santa Barbara, California 93116-1911

This book is printed on acid-free paper ∞

Manufactured in the United States of America

Contents

Acknowledgments

I've had the great pleasure of getting to know some truly wonderful scholars and writers during this process, and I'd like to thank each of our contributors for their hard work and dedication. Thanks to all of you, we have a wonderful set here. Our ABC-CLIO/Praeger editor, James Sherman, was an active source of knowledge and wisdom; James, your advice was both useful and valued. Much appreciation to my coeditor Bob Batchelor for bringing me on board—I've learned much from this experience, so thanks for that. In terms of actual execution of these volumes, I need to thank Norma Jones, graduate assistant extraordinaire, for always being willing to jump in and help, and always knowing when to bring coffee!

Working on projects like this takes a toll on everyone around you, and I could not have finished this without my academic support network: Amy Wilkens, Jan Leach, Fran Collins, Wendy Wardell, David LaBelle, Barb Hipsman, Ann Schierhorn, Michele Ewing, Jacquie Marino, and Gary Hanson. An extra-big expression of gratitude needs to be issued to the people who have suffered through every bump in the road with grace and humor, making me laugh at the height of my stress: Mark Goodman and Norman Mallard and Marianne and Mark Warzinski. Thanks, pals.

Finally, I'd like to thank my family for reminding me about what really matters, including my wonderful parents, William and Patricia Sarver; my patient and loving husband, Lindsey Coombs; and my beautiful daughters, Alexandra and Genevieve. Much love, always and forever.

—Danielle Sarver Coombs
Kent, Ohio

When my friend and former editor Dan Harmon asked me if I knew anyone who might want to edit a collection of essays inspired by the hit TV series *Mad Men*, I told him that if he did not let me do it, I would never forgive him. Thankfully, he said, "That is exactly what I hoped you'd say." Within a couple weeks, he and I hammered out the structure of *We Are What We Sell* and began searching for a team to make the collection a success.

Thanks to the team at Praeger for bringing this anthology to life, including editors James Sherman, Erin Ryan, and Mark Kane, and to the great designers who created the book covers. Unlimited thanks also go out to the team of scholars who worked so diligently on the collection. Danielle and I pulled from a cast of amazing writers across the academic and professional spectrum and benefited from their expertise.

Personally, I have a group of wonderful friends and mentors who serve as the wind to my writing sail. Many are scholarly role models, like Don Greiner, Gary Hoppenstand, Jim Plath, Lawrence Mazzeno, and Keith Booker. Others, like Phillip Sipiora and Lawrence S. Kaplan, have taken a more hands-on approach in teaching me what it means to be a writer and teacher. Other friends offered cheer along the way, including Chris Burtch, Larry Z. Leslie, Kelli Burns, Thomas Heinrich, Anne Beirne, Gene Sasso, Bill Sledzik, George Cheney, Josef Benson, Ashley Donnelly, Peter Magnani, and Tom and Kristine Brown. Thanks to my popular culture scholarly teammates: Brendan Riley, Brian Cogan, and Leigh Edwards!

I would like to thank my Thiel College colleagues, particularly President Troy VanAken and Dean Lynn Franken. In addition, I appreciate the support of Laurie Morocco and Victor Evans in the Department of Communication, as well as other members of the Thiel family. The great James Pedas endowed the chair I now hold at Thiel College, which I do with what I hope is the honor and grace it deserves.

My family is incredibly supportive, particularly considering that writing books necessitates long hours of writing and thinking time. Thanks to my parents, Jon and Linda Bowen, for everything they do to make our lives better. My wife Kathy, an amazing teacher and scholar in her own right, teaches me a little more each day about what life is meant to be. Finally, our daughter Kassie is simply the most wonderful person in the world! My love for her is endless and always abides.

—Bob Batchelor
Munroe Falls, Ohio

Advertising in the Contemporary Age

Bob Batchelor

Advertising is the educational program of capitalism, the sponsored art of capitalism, the language of capitalism, the pornography of capitalism. Most of all ... advertising is the culture developed to expedite the central problem of capitalism: the distribution of surplus goods.

—James B. Twitchell, *Adcult USA*

The eminent historian Warren I. Susman spoke of American culture and its multiple dualities as producing "tensions" that "provide both the necessary tensile strength to keep the culture stable and operative and the dynamic force that may ultimately bring about change or complete structural collapse." These warring factions inherent in Susman's definition of culture might be most evident in contemporary advertising and its curious grip on the modern world. Few topics exude such intense dichotomies.[1]

For example, think of the way television ads can bring viewers to tears by exploiting emotions on one hand and then, in the very next 30-second space, be utterly hilarious or completely factual. The spot showing abused puppies and caged kittens in an attempt to solicit donations for an animal shelter may be followed by the randy, middle-aged man playfully interacting with his wife, demonstrating the potency of the latest erectile dysfunction pill.

Advertising is also used for good and evil by organizations inside and outside the mainstream, thus the seemingly crazy idea that a fringe group could purchase ad time from the kind of utterly capitalistic company that it despises or hopes to eradicate. Here, advertising's central role in solidifying and simultaneously poking at the fusion of capitalism and a democratic society is evident and essential in comprehending the discipline's significance. Susman explains that groups or factions "seize and manipulate all the possible instruments of persuasion the culture provides: symbols, central icons, devices to achieve laughter and those to create tears, rhetorical flourishes of all kinds including the enormously effective use of key words or phrases." From this vantage point, one clearly identifies the tasks that advertising, public relations, and marketing perform in creating culture via communications.[2]

In the late twentieth century and now into the twenty-first, the role Susman advocated in the early 1980s is broadened based on the technology now available. Technology is at the center of a fundamental transformation in the way organizations and consumers communicate. Social media, for example, has deepened and expanded interactions, profoundly changing conversations on one hand and, on an even deeper level, revolutionizing the way individuals think about organizations.

In this new environment, for example, businesses and corporations take on human traits because consumers demand that the enterprise interact with them via the channel they desire. These exchanges could be over mobile devices, like an iPad or cell phone, or through tweets, instant messaging, or e-mail. Under any circumstances, the opportunity for interaction has expanded geometrically.

For organizations, the increase in both symmetrical and asymmetrical communication has revolutionized the language employed in discussing the many disciplines now conveniently placed under the "marketing" umbrella. In the early 1980s, communications experts and scholars dubbed the move to pull together marketing functions "integrated marketing communications" (IMC) or simply "integrated communications." In the contemporary world, technology has further blurred the lines between these disciplines—advertising, product marketing, public relations, and market research—creating a marketing-based ecosystem that enables organizations to get closer to consumers and vice versa. Other meta-nomenclatures have been used to describe the marketing-based system, including branding, reputation management, strategic communications, and others.

The overarching goal across this new world order is for all communications-related disciplines to work together toward the organization's goals and aspirations. As such, the name does not mean that much, rather that the work is integrated. Social media shapes the ecosystem by blurring the distinctions between fields at warp speed. For example, Target chief marketing officer Jeff Jones explained the company's strategy, telling *Advertising Age*, "The lines between products, services and marketing continue to blur. We will keep pushing ourselves to think in terms of content, not just campaigns."[3] Professionals, then, must keep up through a willingness to adapt to each new technology and then find methods for pulling the various pieces together into a unified campaign.

When one looks at the myriad of interactive channels available to today's marketers, the idea that blurry or essentially nonexistent lines separate many of the disciplines that were formerly distinct. Where, one might ask, does a corporation website reside? Is the news section the domain of public relations and the photos and images that adorn the page part of advertising? Does a tweet or Facebook status update belong to marketing, PR, or an executive being "ghosted" by one of these?

The essays that comprise Volume 3 address the multifaceted and wide-ranging consequences of advertising on American life and culture from the mid-1970s to our current, technology-dominated world. Since the world of 1975 seems so incredibly foreign to one's eyes in the midst of the twenty-first century, the chapters run the gamut from addressing the impact of industry legends such as David Ogilvy, and iconic campaigns like Nike's "Just Do It," to technology-based influences, such as marketing and advertising via mobile and handheld devices and the ubiquity of web ads.

For example, the debate about privacy centers primarily on technology companies such as Google and Facebook, which have mastered secretive methods of collecting consumer information or at least been able to create a master narrative that leads people to believe that their personal data is safe and secure. Applying this idea to Susman's notions of culture's tensions, one readily identifies with the ubiquity of the technology that people essentially trade in exchange for the information that makes them easier targets for marketing and advertising efforts. People recoil at face-to-face interactions that they deem too personal or that ask for specific details that they have been taught to protect, yet they drop their guard when at the laptop or on a mobile device. The idea that marketing efforts are not only selling the idea of web security and Internet privacy, but at the same time selling products via these channels, is a vicious cycle that resides at the heart of democratic capitalism.

Consumerism

In terms of marketing brilliance, Disney sits among the small number of top corporations in the world based on selling the idea of happiness to consumers eager to buy into the notion. One needs to look no further than the attendance figures at Walt Disney World Resort's Magic Kingdom Park to see the power of selling happiness. The busiest days of the year at the park include Christmas, Thanksgiving, and New Year's Eve, holidays usually associated with mental images of close family and loved ones. Rather than spend time with the family on these ultra-nostalgic holidays, about 90,000 to 100,000 people cram into Magic Kingdom, stuffing it so full that park officials have to block admittance to the park or close off Main Street USA.

Another example of Disney's advertising and marketing brilliance is the way the company revolutionized its business practices by mass-marketing its famous Princess characters. The Disney Princess merchandising line has grown into a $4 billion franchise since 2000, which is in itself larger than some global corporations. According to the Disney website, the consumer products division "has grown the global reach of Disney's girls franchises through an array of imaginative and compelling products. Sales of licensed _Disney Princess_ merchandise have ballooned and products are now available globally."[4]

The worldwide success of the line caused the _Economist_ to wonder whether the princesses would topple Barbie as the "world's favorite doll," given that its sales already pushed "Disney's Consumer Products division away from its reliance on Mickey Mouse and Winnie the Pooh."[5] In contrast, Mickey Mouse merchandise and licensing accounted for annual revenues of $6 billion in 2007. Because Disney Consumer Products is constantly on the search for new items, it will not be long before Disney Princess surpasses the iconic Mickey Mouse due to the whole plethora of items available for the continual expansion of the Disney Princess brand.

Princess material is no longer limited to dolls, jewelry, makeup, and costumes. Electronics, dinnerware, sleepwear, and bedding are all a part of the franchise. Today, it seems as if anything one can purchase can be created in the image of one of the Disney Princesses. A trip through any local grocery store, Walmart, or Target shows how thoroughly "princess-fied" consumer goods have become, with dozens of products sporting the now-famous Disney Princess logos. According to the Disney site, the Princess line also includes: "more than 142 million books, 81 million sticker packs and 16 million Disney Princess magazines sold."[6]

After so many years of keeping the characters under wraps, the natural question is, what is it that makes the Disney Princess brand so successful? First, the Disney Princess line works because the princesses are timeless. According to scholar Rebecca-Anne C. Do Rozario, much of the brand power is derived from the Magic Kingdom, both "detached from social progress" and like another world "caught in a perpetual time loop."[7] The same stands true for the fairytales themselves. Each fairytale basically tells a similar story of a young girl eagerly waiting for a prince to save her from all her potential troubles. Although each tale is reinvented to incorporate current-day values, thus piquing the interest of little girls, the same foundational idea is found across narratives.

The princess, Do Rozario claims, represents the nostalgia of the industry because she is "continuously updated and reinvented," keeping her "young and forever available."[8] As a result, the Princess is always accessible due to a cyclical rerelease system. Each character basically occupies center stage for one year. Then, the crown is passed on to another princess the following year.

One insider notes, "We release one of our platinum titles only once every few years. They're the crown jewels."[9] The princesses are also kept interesting for a modern audience as Disney improves and updates the quality of the movies. Snow White, in the 2001 rerelease, for example, received a major makeover—transformed from a "coquettishly curtseying princess" into a bedazzled diva. "Disney . . . maintains her contemporaneity in its dual aspects, maintaining the original design, while successively renewing its appeal by re-rendering her in her release, marketing and merchandising."[10] Bringing the Princesses into the twenty-first century serves as a bridge to selling more consumer product goods directly and the continued licensing of the Princess images to outside vendors.

Shifting cultural norms between parents and children and grandparents and grandchildren also play in Disney's favor. The brand remains popular because today's children are treated as royalty by families that have more disposable income and many that grant a sense of entitlement based on their parents' reaction to growing up in divorced families. At the beginning of the twentieth century, one scholar explains, children were removed from the workforce and "sacralized."[11] The idea that children should have activities and entertainment transformed the relationship between children and consumer culture. Also aiding in the transformation was the fact that the United States simultaneously shifted toward a consumer-oriented society. Thus developed the modern child.

As kids' influence on the family budget grew stronger and ideas defining childhood evolved, the children's market became more lucrative. The child consumer market grew around the idea that products "teach children good habits" and "facilitate wholesome play or foster creativity."[12] Today, according to writer Martha Irvine, Disney marketers aim to create products to help children engaged in fantasy play, which is normal for children beginning at age three. The Disney Princess, therefore, "constitutes a brilliant marketing move that targets a normal stage of child development."[13] While Disney Princess products are found at all age ranges, those aimed at girls from ages two to five are most ubiquitous.

This $4 billion industry is large enough to bring out the jealousy in Barbie, who is also popular among girls for fantasy play. But Barbie, known for her high fashion, stiletto heels, and endless accessories, is quite the controversy; critics of Barbie argue she makes girls grow up too fast and causes them to be weight conscious. In contrast, some argue, Disney focuses on letting little girls be little girls. Cindy Rose, head of Walt Disney in Britain, says the main characteristic of a princess is that she can "captivate, inspire and transport young girls into a fantasy world."[14]

The Disney Princess line is an important aspect of the company's revenue generation, which topped $42 billion in 2012. Perhaps more significant, however, is the role the characters hold in making the company a part of American girlhood in contemporary society. By democratizing access to the Princesses, the corporation ensured that a large generation of females would have them as mainstays, which only naturally will lead to them buying Princess products when they become mothers. Turning consumer products into significant cultural influences does not happen often or for long periods. The Disney Princesses, particularly as they are refined, added to, and adapted for current eras, show signs of continued growth and influence.

Technology

Pundits and commentators imagined a time when the Internet—like television—would be dominated by video and filmed content. It took some time for the technology and home computing power to catch up with this vision, but by the mid-to-late 2000s, the Web finally transformed into a kind of transportable television or movie house. Another decade later, and viewing a TV series or film via a handheld device or smartphone is commonplace. The only limitation seems to be the size of the screen people are willing to employ in their search for entertainment.

Looking back, the transformation from video-based pipedream to the smartphone reality took place fast. Spurred by technology, such as wider access to broadband Internet connections, and the popularity of social media networks and an ever-growing demand for content, the Web moved from a primarily text-based mass media channel into one dominated by video. If a single entity can be credited for this shift, it is YouTube, an independent entity later gobbled up by search engine and online advertising powerhouse Google.

The pervasiveness of online video is demonstrated by its astronomical growth. In November 2007, for example, more than 75 percent of Web users in the United States watched a video online, averaging 3.25 hours per person during the month. Powered by YouTube, Google is the dominant force in the video market. The company increased its market share in this category to 31 percent. In total, U.S. Internet users viewed approximately 9.5 billion videos in November, with 2.9 billion of this figure watched at YouTube.[15]

Interestingly, when a writer's strike crippled television in late 2007, statistics revealed that Americans turned to the web to fulfill their viewing needs, with 141 million people watching more than 10 billion videos in December alone. Without television, consumers quickly moved to the Web, resulting in the heaviest month of online video consumption to that point in Internet history. Market leader Google accounted for 3.3 billion videos, or nearly 33 percent of the total. The time spent watching videos also increased in December, reaching 3.4 hours (203 minutes) per person over the course of the month.

In early 2008, the Pew Internet & American Life Project survey examined web video consumers from a demographic viewpoint. The "typical" online video consumer was a male (53 percent versus 43 percent female), aged 18 to 29 (70 percent), with at least some college education (54 percent). Interestingly, about 60 percent of online video watchers claim household income exceeding $75,000, while another 53 percent fall in the $50,000–$75,000 segment. Investigating race/ethnicity, users break down as follows: English-speaking Latino (55 percent), African American (46 percent), and white (45 percent).[16]

The results of this survey confirm many preconceived notions of who uses the Web most often and frequently visits sites such as YouTube: young, white males with disposable income. However, there are other interesting aspects of the survey that show the true pervasiveness of online video. Some 30 percent of those 50 to 64 years old said they visited video sites, and 16 percent of those older than 65. The findings regarding household income show that either viewers themselves are well off, or that the children of upper-middle-class families are the most likely to go to these sites. The large number of English-speaking Latinos who visit YouTube and other video pages confirmed research that revealed extensive Web usage growth in the Hispanic community.[17]

Jumping ahead to January 2013, statistics reveal that the number of unique viewers has grown over time, but the actual number of videos and time spent watching these clips has skyrocketed. According to comScore, some 180 million Internet users in the United States watched 36.2 billion online videos that month. This viewership total included the 9.1 billion video ad views that consumers endured in the month's time.[18]

Not surprisingly, YouTube powered Google's dominance in online video viewership and ad displays, which totaled 150 million viewers and 12.3 billion videos. Facebook ranked second with 56.9 million viewers and 425 million videos. Overall, online ads were viewed by half the total U.S. population in January 2013 alone, with each viewer seeing some 58 ads in that timeframe. The comScore statistics reveal that online ads were driven by popular culture events, such as CBS broadcasting both the _Victoria's Secret Fashion Show_ and the _People's Choice Awards_ show. Online video segments also provided programming for other TV networks, like the series _Tosh.0_, hosted by comedian Daniel Tosh. The cross-platform use of online video helped ignite some to "viral" status, with word of mouth driving clip views into the millions or tens of millions. One simply needs to search for "cute cats" on YouTube to see the outcome of the video rage. About 2.6 million hits turned up, with the top-viewed clips exceeding 85 million views.[19]

Artistry

Standing off-center, hands in his pockets, halfway between radiance and shadow as the light moves behind him, a well-coifed actor with shoulder-length hair and a smartly trimmed goatee looks directly into the camera and murmurs in a low voice: "It's not a journey / Every journey ends, but we go on … / … Chanel No. 5 / Inevitable." A bottle of the perfume is superimposed over a shot of the earth at night, dots of glimmering humanity and sunlight bouncing off the northern horizon. The product is only shown for a moment. Then, in a tight close-up, the actor delivers the final line, his brow furrowed, suggesting intensity and thoughtfulness.

After such a hodge-podge of odd lines and the jostling camera and blinking lights, one might be more inclined to laugh than meet the actor's smoldering passion, but this is no ordinary pitchman. Instead, Chanel went directly to the stratosphere, hiring film icon Brad Pitt for a reported $7 million to shill the famous women's fragrance. In the world of celebrity advertising, few names are bigger than Pitt's. He is instantly recognizable across the globe.

Whether using the male Pitt to sell a female product works or not, Chanel certainly received more than $7 million in publicity in return. The YouTube version of the ad drew some 7.8 million views through early 2013, and thousands of articles talked about the work. Although Pitt recites his lines with a straight face, _Saturday Night Live_ spoofed the ad, as did countless people on the Web. More than 12,000 spoofs representing countless views ensured that people were talking about (and laughing at) the Pitt/Chanel ad long after it initially aired on television.

One imagines that Chanel and Pitt meant the commercial to be taken seriously. Regardless, though, the outcome beckons questions about the value of the YouTube views on the original and many satirical clips that resulted in response. An argument could be made that the ability of something to go viral (should we call this "virality"?) is the only thing that matters in today's culture, which leans so heavily on the Web. Even the spoofs kept both Pitt and the perfume on people's minds.

While the return on investment for such commercials will remain hotly debated among advertisers, brands, and other interested stakeholders, one thing that can be convincingly deduced is that the bond between advertising and celebrity is so solid that a celebrity selling goods and services via ads now seems mandatory. Therefore, even a star of Pitt's stature can now use his celebrity status as a selling point, whereas in the past, he might have shied away from such overt marketing efforts. In contemporary America, there seems to be no limit to how a star can market her image—particularly when the tradeoffs more or less benefit both sides.

Any examination of advertising history reveals the depths of the bond between celebrities and advertisers. However, advertising exec Harmish Pringle sees the contemporary use of celebrities running deeper today and having a more significant consequence. He explains that seeing celebrities in ads helps noncelebrities determine the traits they desire in a potential mate, whether this is based on looks, personality characteristics, or some combination. Given this role, Pringle says, there is clear rationale for the media scrutiny that celebrities face. People want to find out everything about them to use as a kind of research tool for thinking about their own lives and the lives of those around them.[20]

Like the Internet, the ubiquity of celebrity is in full display in contemporary America. The Faustian bargain that celebrities seem to make on their climb to the top includes that once they become famous, no aspect of their lives is off limits. In this equation, then, it makes perfect sense to reap the benefits of fame. "[T]he trend has slowly shifted from using models to celebrities to endorse products because regardless of what's going on in the world of luxury, celebrities sell," explains Ryan Schinman, president of Platinum Rye Entertainment, a firm that negotiates talent buys for companies and advertising agencies. "Of course, each celebrity has their own characteristics, so their image and lifestyle has to be in tune with the brand. Some are hits, some are misses."[21]

Examining another Chanel spokesperson, Nicole Kidman, demonstrates the way a celebrity can transform a brand. The company made the actress the face of the fragrance in 2004 for $12 million. She later starred in a commercial directed by filmmaker Baz Luhrmann, shot for an estimated

$46 million, making it one of the most expensive ads in history. The gamble paid off, however, when revenues jumped 16 percent. Her appeal as a celebrity opened the fragrance to a younger demographic, which then translated into sales. According to journalist Nicola Ruiz, "Endorsement money is key to a star's bank account. Celebrities, many of whom make between $10 million and $20 million for months of work on a movie set or while on a yearlong concert tour, are cashing in on ad campaigns that can pay as much as $3 million for a day's work."[22]

For advertisers using celebrities as spokespeople, the hard work of establishing character is already complete. A company may want to draw out a certain characteristic that equates to its brand, like Pitt's intensity, but it does not have to start from scratch, as it would if it pulled out an unknown model or actor, regardless of his handsomeness. Pitt and Kidman are already known entities. Corporations like Chanel that owe so much to brand and consumer loyalty realize this, which makes campaign worthwhile.

* * *

Advertisers have to work harder and work differently than they did in the past. Technology necessitates that they adapt to different levels of consumer interest and apathy. Many potential buyers are simply worn out by the pervasive presence of marketing, while others look to the industry for clues about how to live their lives. Perhaps the critical issue contemporary consumers must confront is what it all means, which necessitates that one use every ounce of critical and contextual thinking skills that can be mustered.

Based on the idea that advertising has always had multiple veiled agendas, such as creating a psychological setting where consumers conflate needs and wants, one could certainly argue that the industry is sinister. The degree of its insidiousness is derived from one's own sense of how tacitly corporations and their ad agencies worked to dupe or confuse consumers. For example, one needs to look no further than the way the industry misused and mangled the idea of "green" products to see how a good idea —that companies should produce environmentally safe products—can be used against consumers by diluting its meaning.[23]

There is also a public education aspect of marketing, public relations, and advertising that is essential within a democratic society, regardless of its coziness with capitalism. Based on technological innovations that have driven consumers and businesses closer, corporations and stakeholders essentially communicate via public relations, advertising, and marketing. This exchange helps people build their personal value systems and determines how organizations will continue to interact with consumers in the future.[24]

A theme running throughout Volume 3 is the way advertising has infiltrated every nook and cranny of people's daily lives. Readers might not find this a stretch, given the pervasiveness of advertising across the twentieth century—our lives have always seemed dominated by ads. However, the new twist to this narrative is the way consumers have opened up to advertising in a whole new way, literally handing over personal information on numerous fronts that allows marketers to then exploit that information. These important changes in the advertising industry will continue to both confront us as consumers and citizens as the world grapples with technological innovation.

Notes

1. Warren Susman, *Culture as History: The Transformation of American Society in the Twentieth Century* (New York: Pantheon, 1984), 288.

2. Ibid.

3. Natalie Zmuda, "Target CMO Shares Vision for Advertising, Media Agencies," *Advertising Age*, October 19, 2012, http://adage.com/article/agency-news/target-cmo-shares-vision-advertising-media-agencies/237849/?utm_source=mediaworks&utm_medium=newsletter&utm_campaign=adage.

4. Disney Corporation, "Disney Consumer Products," 2010, https://www.disneyconsumerproducts.com/Home/display.jsp?contentId=dcp_home_ourbusinesses_company_overview_us&forPrint=false&language=en&preview=false&imageShow=0&pressRoom=US&translationOf=null&region=0 (accessed January 24, 2013).

5. "A Challenge to Barbie," *Economist*, April 19, 2003, 54, Academic Search Complete, EBSCOhost (accessed August 29, 2010).

6. Disney, "Consumer Products."

7. Rebecca-Anne C. Do Rozario, "The Princess and the Magic Kingdom: Beyond Nostalgia, the Function of the Disney Princess,"*Women's Studies in Communication* 27, no. 1 (2004): 36. Academic Search Complete, EBSCOhost, http://search.ebscohost.com/login.aspx?direct=true&db=a9h&AN=13143218&site=ehost-live (accessed September 15, 2010).

8. Quoted in Do Rozario, "Princess and the Magic Kingdom."

9. James Quilter, "Bensons Banks on Disney Magic," *Promotions and Incentive*, October 2008, Academic Search Complete, EBSCOhost Connection (accessed December 14, 2010).

10. Do Rozario, "Princess and the Magic Kingdom," 36–37.

11. Julia L. Mickenberg, "American Studies and Childhood Studies: Lessons from Consumer Culture," *American Quarterly* 58, no. 4 (December 2006): 1217–27, Academic Search Complete, EBSCOhost (accessed March 30, 2012).

12. Ibid.

13. Martha Irvine, "Princess Pedestal: How Many Girls Are on One?" Associated Press, May 24, 2009, http://www.highbeam.com/doc/1A1-D98BEK3O0.html (accessed December 1, 2010).

14. Quoted in "A Challenge to Barbie."

15. Gavin O'Malley, "YouTube Continues to Grow Video Share," *Online Media Daily*, January 18, 2008, http://publications.mediapost.com/index.cfm?fuseaction=Articles.showArticle&art_aid=74597 (accessed January 18, 2008).

16. "Video Sharing Web Site Audience Doubles in a Year," *Research Brief*, Center for Media Research, January 22, 2008, http://www.mediapost.com/publications/article/74687/#axzz2auUPFDM7 (accessed February 1, 2008).

17. Ibid.

18. "comScore Releases January 2013 U.S. Online Video Rankings," *comScore Insights*, February 21, 2013, http://www.comscore.com/Insights/Press_Releases/2013/2/comScore_Releases_January_2013_U.S._Online_Video_Rankings (accessed February 21, 2013).

19. Ibid.

20. Hamish Pringle, *Celebrity Sells* (New York: Wiley, 2004), xxii–xxiii.

21. Quoted in Nicola Ruiz, "Can a Star Sell You Style," *Forbes*, April 18, 2008, http://www.forbes.com/style/2008/04/18/style-star-ad-forbeslife-cx_nr_0418style.html (accessed April 21, 2008).

22. Ibid.

23. Gina Anne Conley, "The Tension between Capitalism and Corporate Social Responsibility: A Case Study of Strategic Ambiguity in Clorox Environmental Communication, 1970–Present" (MA thesis, Kent State University, 2012).

24. For a more detailed examination, see Bob Batchelor, "Advertising, Marketing, and Public Relations in a Changing World," in *Popular Culture Values and the Arts: Essays on Elitism versus Democratization*, ed. Ray B. Browne and Lawrence A. Kreiser Jr. (Jefferson, NC: McFarland, 2009), 176–88.

Bibliography

Batchelor, Bob. "Advertising, Marketing, and Public Relations in a Changing World." In *Popular Culture Values and the Arts: Essays on Elitism versus Democratization*, edited by Ray B. Browne and Lawrence A. Kreiser Jr., 178–88. Jefferson, NC: McFarland, 2009.

"comScore Releases January 2013 U.S. Online Video Rankings." *comScore Insights*, February 21, 2013. http://www.comscore.com/Insights/Press_Releases/ 2013/ 2/comScore_Releases_ January_2013_U.S._Online_Video_Rankings (accessed February 21, 2013).

Conley, Gina Anne. "The Tension between Capitalism and Corporate Social Responsibility: A Case Study of Strategic Ambiguity in Clorox Environmental Communication, 1970–Present." MA thesis, Kent State University, 2012.

Disney Corporation. "Consumer Products: About Us." Disney Consumer Products, 2010. https://www.disneyconsumerproducts.com/Home/display.jsp?content Id=dcp_home_ourbusinesses_company_overview_us&forPrint=false&language =en&preview=false&imageShow=0&pressRoom=US&translationOf=null &region=0 (accessed January 24, 2013).

Do Rozario, Rebecca-Anne C. "The Princess and the Magic Kingdom: Beyond Nostalgia, the Function of the Disney Princess." *Women's Studies in Communication* 27, no. 1 (2004): 34–59. Academic Search Complete database, http://search .ebscohost.com/login.aspx? direct=true&db=a9h&AN=13143218&site=ehost -live (accessed September 15, 2010).

Irvine, Martha. "Princess Pedestal: How Many Girls Are on One?" Associated Press, 2009. http://www.highbeam.com/doc/1A1-D98BEK3O0.html (accessed December 1, 2010).

Mickenberg, Julia L. "American Studies and Childhood Studies: Lessons from Consumer Culture." *American Quarterly* 58, no. 4 (2006): 1217–27. Academic Search Complete database, http://search.ebscohost.com/login.aspx?direct =true&db= a9h&AN= 23575681&site=ehost-live (accessed March 30, 2012).

Quilter, James. "Bensons Banks on Disney Magic." *Promotions and Incentive*, October 1, 2008, Academic Search Complete, EBSCOhost Connection (accessed December 14, 2010).

Pringle, Hamish. *Celebrity Sells*. New York: Wiley, 2004.

Susman, Warren. *Culture as History: The Transformation of American Society in the Twentieth Century*. New York: Pantheon, 1984.

Zmuda, Natalie. "Target CMO Shares Vision for Advertising, Media Agencies." *Advertising Age*, October 19, 2012. http://adage.com/article/agency-news/target -cmo-shares-vision-advertising-media-agencies/237849/?utm_source=media works&utm _medium=newsletter&utm_campaign=adage (accessed October 19, 2012).

CHAPTER ONE

Mad Men: Framing Advertising History

Bob Batchelor and Norma Jones

Mad Men is about advertising, which means it's about the American Dream, in a period in which the American Dream was being assembled and yet already starting to change. Advertising is a fascinating industry, an intriguing window into our society and ourselves . . . *Mad Men* examines what is real, what is artifice, and whether there is any real difference in modernized society.[1]

"Nostalgia . . . it's delicate . . . but potent," Don Draper explains to the huddled Kodak executives sitting in the dark at an agency pitch. "It's not called 'The Wheel,' it's called 'The Carousel.'"

Draper's command performance selling his vision to Kodak in the season one finale served as the climactic event in a season that would set the tone for *Mad Men* and the show's relationship to advertising history. The Kodak scene showcased several related ideas that have served as the foundation for *Mad Men*, from Draper's immense charm and flair under pressure to the roles nostalgia and the American Dream would play for both the characters on the show and the audience.

The notions of history, nostalgia, and the American Dream are so pervasive, it seems as if *Mad Men* creator Matthew Weiner demands that the viewer understand two related viewpoints: first, that the characters hold both historical and nostalgic perspectives in portraying advertising professionals in the era; and second, that viewers are supposed to assess that worldview while also looking at the series as an interpretation of today's world. The levels of discourse taking place on *Mad Men*, therefore, are intricate and intertwined. Perhaps Draper's quote about nostalgia's delicacy should be changed to "but difficult."

As a matter of fact, the brilliance of Draper's speech actually serves as a glossy sheen over the character's failing marriage and wrecked home life. On *Mad Men*, viewers must always be cognizant of what is presented on the surface and what is roiling just beneath. For the *Mad Men* franchise, the carousel scene symbolizes the zenith of powerful writing, direction, style, and setting, culminating in overt audience outreach by appealing to viewers' nostalgic notions of the JFK-inspired Camelot era. Simultaneously, however, the show asks that we probe the motivations of the people behind the ads, and even the ads themselves, when these people use their creativity to dupe consumers into desiring certain products or goods. This perception of advertising history certainly meets F. Scott Fitzgerald's dictum that true genius is when one can hold two opposed viewpoints at the same time, in this case, that good people can create advertising meant to mislead consumers into purchasing things they do not actually need or do not fully understand. On the other hand, *Mad Men* also complicates ad history by tying it to a specific era, longing for a nostalgic vision of the past, and locating the show within the lives of compelling (fictional) characters.

This chapter examines how *Mad Men* frames advertising history through nostalgia, notions of the American Dream, and authenticity. We contend that the series asks viewers to reimagine ad history and advertising's central role in contemporary American society by using history as a kind of recurring character. Our focus is on each year's season finale, which Weiner and his team of creators use as both a summary of their work and as a point of departure, particularly since the show does not usually run in a strict chronological order like many others. This facet enables *Mad Men* to pick and choose start dates and end dates around major American historical moments, such as season two ending in the midst of the Cuban Missile Crisis, which heightens the show's ties to history and nostalgia.

Nostalgia

Nostalgia usually gets a bum rap in popular culture and academic studies. It is often viewed as simply romantic visions of the past or fanciful beliefs in earlier and better times. One of the reasons nostalgia is viewed negatively is that, over and over again, commentators, historians, and others reveal that memories of the past often do not hold up under further scrutiny. Scholar Michael Janover explains, "Nostalgia is the pain of homesickness." Developing this idea further, however, he creates the new term "nostalgias," which he defines as "the pangs of longing for another time, another place, another self . . . almost certainly romantic in seed and, potentially, corrosively decadent in growth."[2] Janover's perception of nostalgia contrasts with Draper's from the first season finale, where he defines it simply as an "ache," which causes psychological pain, but has a positive outcome by returning one to a better place—"where we know we are loved." In the carousel speech, nostalgia is heart-wrenching, but with a happy ending. Ironically, Draper's understanding of nostalgia as a tool to win an account is crystal clear, yet the concept is neglected in his own life.

For *Mad Men* viewers, nostalgia may also provide the tools for comparing and contrasting today's world with the fictional vision of 1960s America. According to scholars Jason P. Leboe and Tamara L. Ansons, "Nostalgic experiences represent a distortion of both the past and the present. The 'good old days' may not have been as good as they seem in retrospect. In turn, the present is only as bad as it seems when compared against an unrealistic ideal."[3] Given *Mad Men*'s focus on booze, cigarettes, sexism, and other decadent behaviors, today's audience may stand in triumphant judgment; but the contrast is that we still see all these personal and societal ills at play in contemporary America. Could the good old days really have been much better or worse?

The conflicting ideas at the heart of *Mad Men* provides viewers with multiple interpretations as they deconstruct the signs and symbols within the show and bounce these notions off of today's world. For example, the viewer who prides herself on condemning the harsh sexism and other shortcomings of the mid-1960s can simultaneously wrap herself in the romantic or glamorous visions the show portrays. *Mad Men* is unflinching in portraying life's dark side, but the power of the representation appeals to the audience. Thus, what could be considered pretty dour, or perhaps even depressing, programming is elevated to hit status. For all the dark events on *Mad Men*, like Lane Pryce's suicide and the subsequent removal of his body from his office in season five, the show retains an aura of hope amidst the carnage. Nostalgia plays a critical role in building this perception.

What viewers understand is that life is complicated and messy and sometimes can dip into immoral or unethical behavior. Sometimes people are caught in these webs and others not. Lane's suicide is an example of a character paying for his sins, but his embezzlement seems rather paltry in light of others who do not face the music for their own evils. Weiner intentionally presents this paradox of life as lived in the 1960s as represented by Camelot-style grandeur on one hand, and life's messy grind on the other. "I was interested in writing something about American men and their complexity, some of which is ugly," he explains. "There are two conflicting drives: one, to be an ideal father on the PTA . . . and, two, to get drunk, laid and smoke as much as possible."[4] Nostalgia is one of the primary tools viewers use to bridge the gap between the good and evil that Weiner outlines.

From the first season and through season five, Weiner and his writing and production teams have used nostalgia as a central theme. Characters entwine nostalgia and personal history to construct real and imaginary narratives that enable them to move closer to their goals and aspirations. Although the characters on *Mad Men* work in the forward-looking world of advertising and are on the cutting edge of technology by exploiting television for their clients, most of them hold sentimental notions of the past.

Interestingly, placed in the backdrop of an early 1960s advertising agency, the self-created stories and roles the employees play in and out of the workplace expose the real power of image. For example, senior partner Bert Cooper plays the role of eccentric, punctuating important decisions by pruning his bonsai tree, rather than raising his voice and referencing Ayn Rand. Viewers do not see the "real" Cooper, how he got to his powerful position or pieces of his personality that might counteract the image he crafts. However, one does get the sense that things like the Japanese art and asking that people take their shoes off in his office are props in Cooper's self-creation.

As is often the case in *Mad Men*, Draper's interaction with nostalgia is more complicated. While most of the key figures reveal some degree of romantic yearning for the past, such as a drunken Roger Sterling regaling Don and Betty with war stories in "Red in the Face" (season one, episode seven), all of Don's memories are negative. From a narrative perspective, the lead character's antinostalgia accomplishes two related tasks: as Don's story develops, the viewer recognizes that his adult discretions are derived from a violent youth, in some ways softening them or providing some bit of justification. Also, exposing Don's past in snippets enables Weiner to give the character an aura of mystery and danger. Even when we think we know everything about Draper, new bits of the past are exposed.

The American Dream

One interpretation of Don Draper would anoint him an Alger Hiss–type example of the success one can have in achieving the American Dream. Yet, from another viewpoint, Draper is little more than a con man, faking his way into a life that he does not deserve by stealing the identity of a man he barely knew. This conflicting image heightens the show's mystery, because the viewer knows so much more about Draper than the other characters do. We see him through multiple lenses hinging on his secret identity, a narrative trope that fills popular culture from the time of Homer's *Odyssey* to the comic book pages of Superman, Batman, and Spiderman.

Portraying Draper as a mystery also makes a statement about his quest for the American Dream. Once the viewer finds out that "Don Draper" is actually Dick Whitman and realizes the lengths he journeyed to erase his past life, one might assume that he did so to establish his shot at a normal life, filled with a quest for consumer goods that defined the American Dream in the late 1950s and 1960s.

In many instances, however, Don is shown to have little care for money. A blatant example comes at the end of "The Hobo Code" (season one, episode eight). Although Midge Daniels refuses his offer to run off with him to Paris, Don gives her his $2,500 bonus while she sleeps and slips out of the apartment unseen. Later, in season five, after acquiring a swank, Manhattan apartment with a killer view for he and new wife Megan Calvet, Don resists the trappings of luxury, showing little care for such things. In contrast, in season four, on his own as a newly divorced man, Don eventually rents a small, dark apartment, more like a modern man cave than the glamorous residence he gets after remarrying. The apartment's spartan furnishings are spruced up just a bit for the weekends his children come to visit, not because Draper needs to be surrounded by consumer society's baubles.

Dick risks everything to become Don, yet avoids the consumerism that drives most of his colleagues and competitors. His pursuit is more self-centered, hurtling toward some skewed vision of freedom. The viewer sees that young Dick learns at the knee of a hobo who stays overnight at his family's farm. From this odd mentor, the displaced youngster—a self-described "whore child," with no strong ties to home—learns that "I had a family once; a wife, a job, a mortgage. I couldn't sleep at night tied to all those things. Then, death came to find me . . . One morning I freed myself, with the clothes on my back . . . Goodbye . . . Now, I sleep like a stone." The message stays with Dick as he transforms to dapper Don. But, dapper Don is also dour Don, a man perpetually in fear that he will be unmasked.

Authenticity

Authenticity is an essential facet of *Mad Men*. For viewers, one of the show's primary attractions is its commitment to capturing its 1960s in minute detail, from the cut of Joan's dress to the décor of the Draper homes. Many early commentators applauded the way Weiner and his team captured the look and feel of the era. There are occasional slips, but the setting, props, and even the actors' speech and body movements are calculated to stimulate a response on the part of the audience. As a result, *Mad Men*'s historical accuracy and representation of "the good old days" becomes a kind of character itself. Included in Weiner's obsessive commitment to detail is the way he uses music to accentuate each episode's aura and themes. Both the recognizable jazz tune at the beginning of the show—with its vivid black-and-white depictions of Don falling—and the song played as the credits roll at the end are important facets of creating *Mad Men*'s authenticity with the audience.

Yet, despite the commitment to authenticity, some famous, real-life "mad men" (and women) criticized the show for focusing on negative, sensational aspects of agency life. For example, George Lois, who created the legendary Xerox commercials that featured a monkey using the copier to show its simplicity, explained, "It has nothing to do with the creative evolution. It was really obnoxious, the whole thing. I guess the world can watch it and say, 'That's exciting; that's wild.' But I was throwing up watching it. I kept moaning."[5]

For viewers, though, the use of nostalgia to sell *Mad Men* overwhelmingly counteracts this dissent. The series capitalizes on the nation's love affair with the Camelot era—Draper may be the prototype anti-Kennedy, but his rugged good looks remind viewers of JFK. The show's style, therefore, creates an atmosphere that triggers the audience's nostalgic feelings about the early 1960s, even if these memories are fanciful. Leboe and Ansons explain, "Many instances of nostalgic experience represent distorted perception, leading to an appreciation of the past that is more fantasy than reality. Out of this bias to distort the past in the positive direction emerges a biased characterization of contemporary circumstances."[6] Fantasy, then, is a tool that Weiner wields in telling the story, while simultaneously using nostalgia to market the show as a financial entity.

The commitment to authenticity and its resulting influence on viewers is critical in creating an atmosphere in which the audience can root for often-vile characters. Comparable to motion picture cinematography, every aspect of what would normally be considered background comes alive in *Mad Men*. Writer Barbara Lippert explains, "The rich cinematography, evocative lighting and fantastic devotion to period furnishings and wardrobe could make a mid-century fetishist out of anyone watching. The fact that Draper looks perfectly appointed and dashingly handsome in the midst of all his inner turmoil is part of the appeal."[7] As such, careful viewers recognize nostalgia's role in both creating and propelling the story.

Contemporary audiences are used to commercials, discussing and dissecting them as if they were part of the scheduled programming. *Mad Men* capitalizes on this familiarity—similar to the Super Bowl take on advertisements, in which the commercials become part of the spectacle—by using sponsorships and advertisements to add to the show's authority. For example, BMW served as the exclusive sponsor of the second-season premiere. The luxury brand created *Mad Men*–like commercials highlighting its heritage, thereby drawing a tight link between the show and brand name. In this way, one of the world's premier luxury brands tacitly elevates the show to its level and provides it with an additional stamp of validity.

Given the starring role of alcohol in the show, not surprisingly, Jack Daniel's also played a large role in *Mad Men's* early advertising, producing commercials and even having the whiskey appear on screen through product placement. As with BMW, Jack Daniel's has a unique image and meaning in the broader culture that melds into its role in the *Mad Men* universe. While not quite as upscale as BMW, Jack Daniel's has upgraded its brand recently, transforming from backwater moonshine into an alcohol for a wealthier—but not rich—urbane sophisticate. Ironically, the change in the whiskey's brand mirrors Don's as he moved from country Dick to dapper Don.

Television as History and Frame

Mad Men, set in a recognizable past that forces the audience to either rethink what it actually experienced or learned about the timeframe, raises questions about television's role in depicting history. According to historian Keith Jenkins, history at its essence is what remains, from documents and photographs to film and tapes, which lacks real meaning until the historian supplies a framework for interpretation. There may be a commitment to objectivity and diligent primary resource research employed, but historians certainly still bring pieces of themselves into the work either consciously or subconsciously.[8]

Given Jenkins's definition of historian as provider of interpretation, should viewers consider Weiner and his team of writers and directors historians? How about the actors, such as Jon Hamm or Elisabeth Moss, who portray the characters, thus providing human, personal depth and nuance as the written script becomes three-dimensional? In an interview with *Advertising Age* prior to the show's launch, Weiner outlined his preparation, despite having no actual advertising experience. Not surprisingly, his research mirrors that of a professional historian, including, "Months of compiling anecdotes from in-person interviews, combing through the books of David Ogilvy, and studying the films and TV series from the period." The interviewer concludes that Weiner "seemed to have a pretty firm grasp on his subject matter."[9] Another reporter visited Weiner on the set and discussed how he directs a team of researchers "who ensure period accuracy on all fronts" and the "stacks of Sears catalogs and *Better Homes and Gardens* issues from 1955 to 1962 to call on for inspiration." Although the show seems like an overnight sensation, Weiner actually began the pilot script in 1999, and the long gestation from idea to broadcast is similar to the path a historian might tread in creating a career-defining monograph.[10]

Historian Alun Munslow identifies the past as "what actually happened but which is now gone" and quite different from history, "only ever its narrative representation." The consequences are that the historian wields great power in determining "truth" or some version of it. In creating a narrative, Munslow sees the historian filtering through numerous personal and cultural lenses that then are reflected in the representation of the past.[11] In a case like *Mad Men*, although on the surface slavish to historical authenticity, the sexism, anti-Semitism, and cruelty within the confines of the narrative are presented in a manner that allows the audience to rebuke its characters in contrast to today's (supposedly) higher standards.

Given their important role in (re)creating *Mad Men*, the actors themselves perform a function similar to that of the audience. They craft an interpretation of the time period based on their personal and internal experiences (built through varying degrees of formal education, popular culture, and other stimuli) and the added guidance of the script and director. However, they also react, interpret, and read the lines that they may or may not find abhorrent. Elisabeth Moss addressed this point, saying, "We know it's a good script when we do our table read and the heads lower, like, five times. I definitely cringe at the sexist things the guys say. The guys cringe too."[12]

A television series like *Mad Men* that uses nostalgia and historical memory as a central feature necessarily sprints into unchartered territory. Just as the idea of nostalgia is contested on the show, the notion of history (and exactly who can be considered a historian) is as well. "History" has a general meaning in the broader culture, which orbits around foundational ideas such as truth, objectivity, chronology, and facts. However, history is also reworking the past. In that revision, one finds the historian slipping into the portrait. Munslow explains, "It is the historian's narrative acts—emplotment process, arguments, ideological and moral positions and all the other epistemic choices and preferences—that ultimately invest the past with meaning."[13] This decision-making process on Weiner's part accounts for why *Mad Men* is a drama versus a musical or a comedy, or even a film versus a television program. This discussion of history as a conscious, creative act on the part of the creator is fundamental to understanding *Mad Men* and what it asks of its viewers.

* * *

On one level, *Mad Men*'s attraction is simple: like its cousin *The Sopranos*, it is a show that thrives on strong writing and powerful acting, leading it to seem more like a film than a TV series. This aspect of the show—followed by years of critical accolades and positive press coverage—place it in the coveted "media darling" category. The benefit is that the small number of television series that attain this stature can use the label to draw in more upscale audiences and advertisers. In 2008, for example, *BusinessWeek* reported that 33 percent of the show's audience earns more than $100,000 annually.[14] *Mad Men*'s long list of awards insulates it somewhat from the financial and ratings demands placed on other shows.

The series did well enough in the ratings for AMC early in its run, averaging about a million households per episode, but that figure was dwarfed in comparison with the hit shows on the major networks. Subsequent years have served *Mad Men* better in the ratings, though the show has never generated the kind of viewership that would keep it afloat on a network. For example, in season four, U.S. viewers per episode ranged from 2.04 million to 2.92 million. After the delay in airing season five based on contract negotiations, *Mad Men* returned in 2012 to 3.54 million viewers, but it did not grow from there. The season ranged from 1.92 million to 2.94 after the kickoff episode.

An interesting question, given the show's focus on philandering, immoral behavior, and living life to excess, is what do contemporary viewers take from the show outside of its entertainment value? Here nostalgia plays a role in helping people frame current affairs within a historical context. Scholar Wu Jing says, "Nostalgia steps in to help us cope with the turbulence of time, to manage change and make sense of it, through a symbolic denigration of change and a wishful return to the stability of the past."[15] Perhaps here, the "stability of the past" also includes the "instability" *Mad Men* recreates, enabling the show's audience to make sense of the era's shortcomings as well. We recognize the reality in the fictional *Mad Men* world because good and bad coexist.

Writer Peter Suderman, however, criticizes *Mad Men* for serving up its characters for judgment by modern audiences. He calls the show "passionless," explaining, "*Mad Men*, though, is too timid to let its viewers in on the fun, choosing to judge its characters safely and subtly, through the lens of modernity."[16] Leboe and Ansons perhaps offer an explanation, revealing that something more may be at work regarding nostalgia's role on the show. "A sense of nostalgia may occur whenever a recollection is impressive enough in its detail that it provokes a positive response in the rememberer," they say. "Once achieved, the subjective experience of nostalgia simply awaits a misattribution that positive aspects of the past are the cause of this reaction."[17] In other words, viewers are more or less programmed to think of the past in a positive light, despite what may or may not have happened in the real past. As viewers, we draw out of *Mad Men* the glimpses of the past that we recognize or appeal to us, virtually discarding the rest.

One of the most interesting controversies surrounding *Mad Men* is whether its overt wickedness in some ways gives viewers a way to condone the very behavior that is meant to be repulsive. Journalist Susannah Breslin labeled the show "man porn," explaining that male viewers secretly watched the show to revel in Don's decadence. Writer Jaime J. Weinman supports the notion, saying, "Don Draper may live a lie, but if we didn't enjoy that lie, we wouldn't be watching."[18] For Weiner, showing Draper's dark side is part of being authentic and portraying the era realistically.

The interpretation that viewers actually (secretly) applaud Draper's naughtiness taps into the audiences' deepest—often conflicted and hidden—feelings about socioeconomic and cultural challenges. It might be impossible to ever prove, yet is intriguing—like the answers one would get conducting a survey on racism or sexism in which respondents give the answer they think the interviewer desires, rather than the truth that asks them to contemplate the complicated parts of themselves. There is an air of snickering, "Weren't we naughty boys" in the comments of advertising greats interviewed about the veracity of the show, as if they get a free pass because people "back then" did not know any better.

Weiner understands the slippery slope *Mad Men* travels. Asked whether he wants viewers to like Draper, he responded, "No one wants to look in the mirror and see the warts. I'd say just wait and stick with the story and see what happens, but I hope that the source of the entertainment is not judging these people. Everyone has a reason for what they're doing. It all comes from a human place . . . I'm trying to talk about what it is to be a person."[19] Being a "person," whether on television or in reality means that one's foibles are on display to some audience.

Returning to the carousel speech, one sees many divergent threads merge in a single two-minute span. Foremost, as a way to conclude the first season, the new business pitch solidifies Don's status as creative genius. Poor junior staffer Harry Crane is forced to flee the room after breaking into tears during the presentation, symbolizing Don's amazing powers and signaling for the audience that they should pay attention—nostalgia is a powerful topic.

In the climactic scene, Don also embodies the image of a dashing young executive, thus tapping directly into a nostalgic vision of 1960s America. For a certain segment of viewers who grew up in the era, Draper is the cool uncle they remember (or wanted) as children. For a younger audience, there are touches of Kennedyesque language and mannerisms that take them back to nostalgic visions of the decade. Also, the photos of Draper romping around with his young children and happy with his wife in their just-married years mirrored the kinds of publicity shoots that featured JFK with Jackie and their kids. Yet, in both cases, the viewer realizes that darker sides existed that flew in the face of the broad public smiles.

The speech is also a critical junction because in delivering it, Don experiences a moment of clarity, a brief flash of his life falling apart based on living in a web of lies. Again like JFK, who balanced an admired persona with unsavory private behavior, Don is masterful when tested. He represents the fulfillment of the American Dream, even though viewers understand that everything Draper projects on the screen is a lie.

The carousel scene encapsulates *Mad Men* by tugging on the viewer's nostalgic feelings, while at the same time showing nostalgia's power within the narrative. As a result, the show moves beyond the typical sappy use of the past to invoke romantic illusions, thereby illustrating its essential function for people as they make sense of the world around them.

Notes

1. William Bradley, "*Mad Men* Returns: The '60s Advertising Drama is a Time Tunnel," Huffington Post, August 14, 2009, http://www.huffingtonpost.com/william-bradley/mad-men-returns-the-60s-a_b_260076.html (accessed August 14, 2009).

2. Michael Janover, "Nostalgias," *Critical Horizons* 1, no. 1 (2000): 115.

3. Jason P. Leboe and Tamara L. Ansons, "On Misattributing Good Remembering to a Happy Past: An Investigation into the Cognitive Roots of Nostalgia," *Emotion* 6, no. 4 (2006): 596.

4. Quoted in Abbey Klaassen and Lisa Sanders. "AMC Show Puts 'Mad' Back in Mad Ave.," *Advertising Age* 77, no. 14 (2006), Academic Search Complete, EBSCOhost (accessed June 3, 2010).

5. Quoted in Brian Steinberg and Andrew Hampp, "Did the Admen Watch 'Mad Men'?" *Advertising Age* 78, no. 29 (2007): 4–28, Academic Search Complete, EBSCOhost (accessed March 30, 2010).

6. Leboe and Ansons, "On Misattributing Good," 607.

7. Barbara Lippert, "It's a Mad, Mad World," *Brandweek* 50, no. 6 (2009), Academic Search Complete, EBSCOhost (accessed May 5, 2010).

8. For a broader discussion of historical pedagogy, see Keith Jenkins, *Rethinking History* (New York: Routledge, 2003) and Alun Munslow, *Deconstructing History* (New York: Routledge, 1997).

9. Andrew Hampp, "The Three-Martini Lunch Is Alive and Well on AMC," *Advertising Age* 78, no. 25 (2007), Academic Search Complete, EBSCOhost (accessed April 1, 2010).

10. Missy Schwartz, " 'Mad Men': Inside Summer TV's No. 1 Hidden Gem," *Entertainment Weekly* 995/996 (2008): 26–33, Academic Search Complete, EBS-COhost (accessed May 4, 2010).

11. Alun Munslow, "Where Does History Come From?" *Today's History* 52, no. 3 (2002): 18–19.

12. Quoted in Schwartz, " 'Mad Men.' "

13. Munslow, "Where Does History Come From?" 20.

14. Tom Lowry, "How Mad Men Glammed Up AMC," *BusinessWeek* 4094, no. 34 (2008), Academic Search Complete, EBSCOhost (accessed May 20, 2010).

15. Wu Jing, "Nostalgia as Content Creativity: Cultural Industries and Popular Sentiment," *International Journal of Cultural Studies* 9, no. 3 (2006): 360.

16. Peter Suderman, "Boys Behaving Badly," *National Review*, December 3, 2007, 54.

17. Leboe and Ansons, "On Misattributing Good," 608.

18. Jaime J. Weinman, "Why We Can't Be Mad at 'Mad Men,' " *Maclean's* 121, no. 30–31 (2008): 78, Academic Search Complete, EBSCOhost (accessed March 30, 2010).

19. Matheson Whitney, "Peer into the Mind of the Man Who Made 'Mad Men,' " *USA Today*, October 26, 2009, 6D, Academic Search Complete, EBSCOhost (accessed June 5, 2010).

Bibliography

Bradley, William. "*Mad Men* Returns: The '60s Advertising Drama is a Time Tunnel." Huffington Post, August 14, 2009. http://www.huffingtonpost.com/william-bradley/mad-men-returns-the-60s-a_b_260076.html (accessed August 14, 2009).

Hampp, Andrew. "The Three-Martini Lunch Is Alive and Well On AMC." *Advertising Age* 78, no. 25 (2007). Academic Search Complete, EBSCOhost (accessed April 1, 2010).

Janover, Michael. "Nostalgias." *Critical Horizons* 1, no. 1 (2000): 113–33.

Jing, Wu. "Nostalgia as Content Creativity: Cultural Industries and Popular Sentiment." *International Journal of Cultural Studies* 9:3 (2006): 359–368.

Klaassen, Abbey., and Lisa Sanders. "AMC Show Puts 'Mad' Back in Mad Ave." *Advertising Age* 77, no. 14 (2006). Academic Search Complete, EBSCOhost (accessed June 3, 2010).

Leboe, Jason P., and Tamara L. Ansons. "On Misattributing Good Remembering to a Happy Past: An Investigation into the Cognitive Roots of Nostalgia." *Emotion* 6, no. 4 (2006): 596–610.

Lippert, Barbara. "It's a Mad, Mad World." *Brandweek* 50, no. 6 (2009). Academic Search Complete, EBSCOhost (accessed May 5, 2010).

Lowry, Tom. "How Mad Men Glammed Up AMC." *BusinessWeek* 4094, no. 34 (2008). *Academic Search Complete. EBSCOhost* (accessed May 20, 2010).

Munslow, Alun. "Where Does History Come From?" *Today's History* 52, no. 3 (2002): 18–20.

Schwartz, Missy. " 'Mad Men': Inside Summer TV's No. 1 Hidden Gem." *Entertainment Weekly* 995–996 (2008): 26–33. Academic Search Complete, EBSCOhost (accessed May 4, 2010).

Steinberg, Brian, and Andrew Hampp. "Did the Admen Watch 'Mad Men'?" *Advertising Age* 78, no. 29 (2007): 4–28. Academic Search Complete, EBSCOhost (accessed March 30, 2010).

Suderman, Peter. "Boys Behaving Badly." *National Review*, December 3, 2007.

Weinman, Jaime J. "Why We Can't Be Mad at 'Mad Men.' " *Maclean's* 121, no. 30–31 (2008): 78. Academic Search Complete, EBSCOhost (accessed March 30, 2010).

Whitney, Matheson. "Peer into the Mind of the Man Who Made 'Mad Men.' " *USA Today*, October 26, 2009, 6D. Academic Search Complete, EBSCOhost (accessed June 5, 2010).

CHAPTER TWO

David Ogilvy: Selling an Industry

Kristin Comeforo

I don't believe in tricky advertising. I don't believe in cute advertising. I don't believe in comic advertising.[1]

In the modern world of business, it is useless to be a creative, original thinker unless you can also sell what you create.[2]

Factual advertising ... always sells better than empty advertising.[3]

In *Ogilvy on Advertising*, David Ogilvy includes a chapter that pays tribute to "Six Giants Who Invented Modern Advertising"—Albert Lasker, Stanley Resor, Raymond Rubicam, Leo Burnett, Claude Hopkins, and Bill Bernbach. This chapter has a far humbler objective, as I am, after all, no David Ogilvy. It attempts to pay tribute to the one "giant" left off Ogilvy's list—Ogilvy himself. This is not to diminish the impact of the aforementioned giants on advertising as we know it today, but is rather a testament that Ogilvy was in many ways more of a student than a teacher. He encouraged young agency employees to "keep up your studies,"[4] and reveled in doing his own "homework" even though it was painstakingly tedious and sometimes took weeks to complete. He always tried to listen more than he talked.[5] Whether it was "picking [Rubicam's] brains"[6] or reading Hopkins's book, *Scientific Advertising*, "seven times,"[7] Ogilvy soaked in every lesson he could from the giants of his time.

If Ogilvy would consider himself a giant of his time also, it is hard to tell. At times he seemed to have an abundant ego, referring to his agency as "an *immediate and meteoric* success" (emphasis original)[8] while at other times he revealed a self-deprecating streak—saying once, in an interview with David Susskind, "if you had as little talent as I did, you'd have to work for it too."[9] He also liked to point out that his IQ score of 96 was "par for ditch diggers."[10] Others have described him as "British narcissism fused with hard-nosed American, self-serving salesmanship."[11] Narcissism and demanding nature aside, when asked if they "liked" David Ogilvy, his agency protégés, each in their own turn, responded unequivocally, "I loved him."[12] Ogilvy is a man who left an indelible mark on not only his employees, his clients, but also the advertising industry as a whole. Thus, in my book, he is indeed the seventh giant who invented modern advertising.

"I *Hate* Rules"[13]

While *Confessions of an Advertising Man* and *Ogilvy on Advertising* read more like instruction manuals—do this, don't do that—Ogilvy, in his real life, seemed to eschew rules in favor of pioneering his own path. Born in England in 1911 to a "Gaelic speaking Highlander" and a "beautiful and eccentric Irishwoman," David Mackenzie Ogilvy spent his younger years exhibiting an "original mind"[14] at aristocratic boarding schools in England and Scotland. His academic career, however, came to an abrupt end in 1931 when he was expelled from Oxford. He then spent the next 17 years "adventur[ing] around the world, uncertain of purpose."[15] In hindsight, this "adventuring" had an extraordinary purpose: it would lay the foundation upon which Ogilvy's advertising genius would be built.

Ogilvy's adventure began in Paris, where he worked as a chef at the Hotel Majestic. It was in the kitchen where he learned about management and developed an exacting perfectionism, especially in terms of service. Ogilvy once gave his entire commission ($6,000 a week) to Lorillard (the manufacturer of Old Gold and Kent cigarettes) to buy them out of an ad on *Play of the Week* that threatened the sponsorship of Jersey Standard, Ogilvy's client. Other than "appeasing clients on matters of grand strategy,"[16] Ogilvy would do just about anything to satisfy a client.

After valuable lessons learned in the kitchen, Ogilvy went to Scotland—at the height of an economic recession—to become a door-to-door stove salesman. It was here that Ogilvy developed his love, and respect, for selling. His penchant for "long copy" derives itself directly from this work, along with his aversion for jingles. According to Ogilvy, "if you have nothing to say, sing it;"[17] while long copy, on the other hand, "conveys the impression that you have *something important to say*" (emphasis original).[18] During his years selling those stoves to Scottish housewives, Ogilvy learned that all he needed to do to make a sale was to give his customers the facts. "It took [him]

40 minutes to make a sale; about 3,000 words."[19] Something very important to say, indeed. Throughout his career in advertising, Ogilvy would continually return to this personal selling experience, advising young creative upstarts to speak in their ads as if they were speaking to one consumer.

His next adventure brought him to the United States—New Jersey, more specifically, where he worked with Dr. George Gallup at his research organization. Ogilvy attributes much of his later success in advertising to "having had the great good fortune of working with Dr. Gallup in Princeton."[20] Ogilvy learned to become objective about people, a valuable skill when dealing with consumer motivations and their responses to messages. Leveraging this knowledge of human behavior, Ogilvy shifted his focus from consumerism to nationalism, doing a stint with the Intelligence Service at the British Embassy in Washington.[21] He then went on to become a farmer in Lancaster County, Pennsylvania, and lived among the Amish. In 1948, he started Hewitt, Ogilvy, Benson & Mather—"he had never written an advertisement in his life."[22]

"Our First Job [as an Agency] Was to Escape from Obscurity"[23]

Upon opening the agency in 1948, Ogilvy did two things. First, he issued an "Order of the Day," which concluded, "Agencies are as big as they deserve to be. We are starting this one on a shoestring, but we are going to make it a great agency before 1960."[24] Next, he wrote a list of the five clients he wanted most—General Foods, Bristol-Myers, Campbell Soup Company, Lever Brothers, and Shell. He may have been a little bit off, but by 1962, all five on his "most wanted" list had indeed become clients of Ogilvy, Benson & Mather.

Early clients such as Guinness, Hathaway Shirts, Schweppes, and Rolls-Royce were relatively small accounts, which appeared much bigger thanks to the strategy and craft of Ogilvy's work. This garnered more attention for the fledgling agency. The decision to throw entire media budgets into the *New Yorker*—a sophisticated magazine for a sophisticated audience— was an act of genius that paid dividends on many levels. It not only gave Ogilvy "a chance to produce the kind of sophisticated advertising which attracts attention,"[25] but also put these advertisements in front of people who hire advertising agencies.[26] The consistency and frequency generated by the concentrated media buy created impact for the client and gave the impression that the account was much larger, indicating the agency's ability to handle large, big-name clients. "The easiest way to get new clients," according to Ogilvy, "is to do good advertising."[27] And that they did.

Good work begat good work. Work for Rolls-Royce led to the winning of the Shell account, while work for Puerto Rico Tourism led to the winning of the Sears account.[28] It seemed, as Ogilvy remarked, that "getting clients was like shooting fish in a barrel."[29] Despite significant changes in the competitive nature and structure of the industry, Ogilvy & Mather continue to attract, and keep, clients who are among the most revered brands in the world. In 2012, American Express, BP, Coca-Cola, Ford, IBM, Johnson & Johnson, Kodak, Kraft, Lenovo, Mattel, Motorola, Nestlé, Unilever, and Yahoo! are just a few of the clients on Ogilvy & Mather's roster. The agency keeps these clients through the delivery of "big ideas."

"What Clients Want from Us Is Big Ideas"[30]

From the earliest days of Ogilvy & Mather, David Ogilvy realized that big ideas were his stock in trade. According to Ogilvy himself, he had about 10 great ideas in his life—advertising ideas—which is not many, but more than most people have had.[31] The art of generating a big idea starts where most of Ogilvy's advice does, with doing your homework, and ends with allowing your unconscious to mull over and pick apart what you have learned. Ogilvy was a big fan of "keeping the telephone line open to [his] unconscious" through listening to music, watching birds, gardening, taking hot baths, and vacationing frequently with "no golf, no cocktail parties, no tennis, no bridge, no concentration; only a bicycle."[32]

Ogilvy's first big idea came when he was the research director for the agency. Inspiration hit while he was on the train home from the office one night. He was so astounded that he would have an idea that he got out at the next stop and from the station called the office saying, "you won't believe it—I've had an idea." That idea would become the first ad Ogilvy ever wrote, "Guinness Guide to Oysters," which appeared in the *New Yorker* and inspired a long-running campaign that provided guides to a variety of other foods that one could enjoy better with Guinness.[33] Ogilvy's other big ideas included making Commander Whitehead, president of Schweppes USA, the hero in all the ads for his brand, and maximizing "story appeal" in Hathaway shirt advertisements by donning the "Hathaway Man" with a mysterious eye patch. Both campaigns piqued consumer curiosity, prompting them to read the copy, and were thus wildly successful. Each campaign, subsequently, ran for 18 and 19 years, respectively.

With a scarcity of big ideas in the marketplace, Ogilvy suggests asking the following five questions to help us avoid overlooking big ideas when they present themselves:

1. Did it make me gasp when I first saw it?
2. Do I wish I had thought of it myself?

3. Is it unique?
4. Does it fit the strategy to perfection?
5. Could it be used for 30 years?[34]

The big idea was so crucial to Ogilvy that, when asked about his regrets, or mistakes that he made during his career, he often remarked that his greatest lament was "failing to recognize a big idea someone else had."[35]

"If You Don't Have a Big Idea the Right Technique Won't Help You"[36]

While privileging the big idea as the crucial ingredient to good advertising, Ogilvy still provides some instruction in terms of what makes, or how to design, a "good" ad. In *Confessions of an Ad Man*, Ogilvy outlines three schools of thought on the subject. Cynics define a good advertisement as anything the client approves of, and signs off on. According to Rubicam, a good ad is one through which the public is strongly sold, and which is remembered for a long time as an "admirable piece of work." Ogilvy's own definition contends that "a good advertisement is one which sells the product *without drawing attention to itself*" (emphasis original).[37] The goal, according to Ogilvy, is not to have a reader say "what a clever advertisement," but rather, "I never knew *that* before. I must try this product."[38] Fundamental to a good ad, thus, is not only a big idea, but also the execution—copy and illustrations—which together form the selling power of the advertisement.

Throughout his writings, speeches, and career, Ogilvy continually returns to research, selling, long fact-based copy, and images with "story appeal" as working together to form good advertising. These areas, while already mentioned to some degree, represent the cornerstones of Ogilvy's legacy and thus demand fuller attention within the sections that follow.

"Advertising People Who Ignore Research Are as Dangerous as Generals Who Ignore Decodes of Enemy Signals"[39]

In the very first episode of the series *Mad Men*, Don Draper unceremoniously throws a research report on cigarettes in the trash, and instead chooses to power through his meeting with his client, Lucky Strike cigarettes, on the strength of bourbon and aspirin alone. This action, indicative of the broader, tumultuous relationship between research and creative, would have made David Ogilvy cringe. It is interesting to note that with the success of the show, commentators have been unable to resist christening Ogilvy as the "original mad man."[40] That moniker could not be further from the truth. Not only was Ogilvy the spitting image of the "gentlemen with brains" he tried to hire for his agency,[41] but he also introduced research into advertising decision-making as a means for adding credibility to, and solidifying ad work as, a profession.[42] He sought to refute the "lopsided reputation" that if an agency was strong in creative, it must be weak in research and marketing, and vice versa.[43] From his perspective, research plays a key role in creating good, creative, advertising.

Upon winning the Rolls-Royce account, Ogilvy set out to learn everything he could about cars. He did his *homework*—the very first step in his advice on "How to produce advertising that sells."[44] Buried in an article in a report he was reading was a comment—"at sixty miles an hour, the loudest noise comes from the electric clock." It became the headline for one of Ogilvy's most famous (and effective) advertisements for Rolls-Royce. Similarly, in doing his homework for the Shell account, Ogilvy discovered that gasoline was made up of several ingredients, including Platformate, which increases mileage.[45] Ogilvy produced a series of 800-word newspaper advertisements, which many people read, and learned a lot about gasoline. The campaign turned around Shell's decline in market share.[46]

Even with his research, Ogilvy was not infallible. "I once used the word OBSOLETE in a headline, only to discover that 43 percent of housewives had no idea what it meant. In another headline I used the word INEFFABLE, only to discover I didn't know what it meant."[47] Thus proving his own point, "advertising is still an inexact speculation."[48] Despite his love for research, Ogilvy was a realist, and diplomatic. He recognized that research could not predict which campaigns would, in the long run, do the most for the brand. As such, he valued judgment, which, he held, the more experienced, mature advertising managers would develop over time. This was, after all, as he proclaimed, "not a job for kids."[49] Combining research and judgment, Ogilvy gained a great understanding of people; and understanding people was fundamental to Ogilvy's first love, selling.

"Bad Advertising Can *Unsell* a Product"[50]

In addition to his commitment to research, perhaps what distinguishes Ogilvy most from his contemporary advertisers, was his unshakable belief that selling is at the heart and soul of the advertisement. This belief was planted during his years of selling door to door in Scotland and cultivated when he became acquainted with direct mail as a strategy for soliciting new clients during the early years of the agency. Ogilvy often referred to direct response as his "first love," which later became his "secret weapon."[51] In 1986, he was inducted into the Direct Marketing Hall of Fame. He was so taken by the knowledge and strategies of the direct response industry that he proclaimed "nobody should be allowed to write general advertisements until he has served his apprenticeship for direct response."[52] The trouble with copywriters, after all, is that they "don't think about selling."[53]

For Ogilvy, the correlation between copy and selling was positive. He viewed copy as information and resisted the temptation to see it as entertainment or an art form, a temptation to which many of his competitors succumbed.[54] He lived and died by direct response industry research, which ascertained that "long copy invariably outsells short copy."[55] Long copy, however, is useless if it is not read, and if it is to be read, it must be well written. Showing his narcissistic side, Ogilvy boasted, "I can make you read an ad with 5,000 words in it."[56] He had a penchant for burying interesting words, or intriguing tidbits toward the end of exceptionally long-copy ads. He used the extent to which these words or tidbits were "bandied" about in popular conversation as evidence that your everyday consumer would read upward of 719 words in a print advertisement.[57] Clearly, Ogilvy operated under the motto, "the more you tell the more you sell."[58]

In terms of layouts, Ogilvy engineered two "perfect" layouts to which he continually returned throughout his career. The first centered on a large photo, followed by a headline of up to nine words, and 240 words of copy. The second included a wide, shallow photograph, a slightly longer headline of up to 20 words, a sub-headline of up to 28 words, four or five cross-headlines, and 600 words of copy. The former is used when the illustration is to "carry the main load of selling," while the latter is used when the copy is more important than the illustration.[59] Both layouts were exceptional for selling, and that is why Ogilvy favored them in much of his creative work.

Combining these layouts with the fascinating copy that begged to be read, Ogilvy delivered on his mantra of "We Sell, or Else."[60] With Ogilvy and his agency at the helm, sales for Schweppes in the United States increased 517 percent,[61] a seven-year decline in Shell's share-of-market was reversed,[62] Mercedes sales in the United States increased by 300 percent,[63] and "scores" of industrialists built factories in Puerto Rico.[64]

"I'd Like to Be Remembered as . . . a Copywriter Who Had Some Big Ideas"[65]

As seen in the few examples provided here—Rolls-Royce, Hathaway Shirts, Schweppes, and Shell—Ogilvy can rest easy that he is remembered as he wanted to be. His big ideas solidified a legacy that continues today. Testament to the work done by Ogilvy to shape the culture and craft of his agency, are the accolades Ogilvy & Mather continually receives from industry award groups. In 2012, Ogilvy & Mather was not only awarded 18 Effie Awards and named "Most Effective Agency in North America,"[66] but was also named "Network of the Year" at the Annual Clio Awards.[67]

Whether Ogilvy would completely approve of such awards is open for debate. He abhorred where advertising was going in the 1980s and 1990s —taking too far a turn toward entertainment, and turning too far away from selling. Ogilvy was never one for the art school–trained creative types, saying that "their gods are not my gods. I have my own dogma, and it springs from observing the behavior of human beings, as recorded by Dr. Gallup, Dr. Starch, and the mail-order experts."[68] Always favoring research, and designing ads that sell, he admitted to having won an award at the Cannes Festival once, "but it wasn't a good commercial."[69] Instead Ogilvy preferred "campaigns that produce *results*," which, he lamented, would never win awards, "because they don't draw attention to themselves."[70] Part of Ogilvy's legacy stems from, perhaps, his ability to create campaigns that both produced results *and* drew attention to themselves because they were stunningly creative works of genius.

When asked why he started his agency, Ogilvy replied, "Well, I wanted to go into the agency business in New York and there was only one agency I wanted to work for and that was Young & Rubicam . . . but I didn't think I could ever get a job there. I had no qualifications, no credentials. I didn't even dare ask. So the only alternative was to start my own, which was what I did."[71] And we are so thankful that he did. Ogilvy's legacy is imprinted not only on Ogilvy & Mather, which continues to thrive today, but also on the advertising industry as a whole. Never before, and not since, has there been such a visionary leading the charge for the field. What was once simply advertising, in Ogilvy's day, is now more modernly "marketing communications" or MARCOM. Still, regardless of the progress in media technology and production techniques, most, if not all of Ogilvy's 11 Commandments, written in 1963, are still relevant and provide valuable guidance to marketing communicators of the twenty-first century:[72]

1. What you say is more important than how you say it.
2. Unless your campaign is based around a great idea, it will flop.
3. Give the facts.
4. You cannot bore people into buying.
5. Be well-mannered, but don't clown.
6. Make your advertising contemporary.
7. Committees can criticize advertisements, but they cannot write them.
8. If you are lucky enough to write a good advertisement, repeat it until it stops pulling.
9. Never write an advertisement you wouldn't want your own family to read.
10. [Focus on] The image and the brand.
11. Don't be a copycat.

Still, "the temptation to entertain instead of sell is contagious,"[73] and many advertisements and agencies violate Ogilvy's commandments. With clutter running rampant across all media platforms and an almost unfathomable level of competition for consumer attention, now more than ever, the advertising industry should be heeding Ogilvy's advice. Research builds understanding of the consumer; understanding of the consumer generates relevant messages; relevant messages engage the consumer; engaged consumers build relationships with brands; consumers with relationships with brands buy that brand's products. This is a somewhat obvious logic chain, whose reasoning can be found in marketing and advertising textbooks, and it all traces back to the one giant Ogilvy left off his list—David Ogilvy.

Notes

1. "David Ogilvy: Essentials," YouTube video, 4:04, uploaded by Adweek, June 14, 2011, http://youtu.be/yj9rokSeack.

2. David Ogilvy, *Confessions of an Advertising Man* (Herts: Southbank Publishing, 2011), 43.

3. David Ogilvy, *Ogilvy on Advertising* (New York: Vintage Books, 1985), 216.

4. Ibid., 159.

5. Ibid., 37.

6. Ogilvy, *Ogilvy on Advertising*, 193.

7. Ibid., 203.

8. Ogilvy, *Confessions*, 10.

9. "The Pope of Modern Advertising: David Ogilvy," *The David Susskind Show*, November 16, 1983, http://www.hulu.com/watch/46488.

10. "A Conversation about Advertising with David Ogilvy," interview by John Crichton (1977), YouTube video, 54:51, posted by "jpiedrahita," September 17, 2007, http://youtu.be/0kfsnjcUNiw.

11. Ogilvy, *Confessions*, 13.

12. Michael Wolff, "The First (and Last) Adman: Thoughts on the Writer, Rule-Maker, and Business Genius," *Adweek*, June 13, 2011, http://www.adweek.com/news/advertising-branding/first-and-last-adman-132449?page=1.

13. Ogilvy, *Ogilvy on Advertising*, 8.

14. Ogilvy, *Confessions*, 25.

15. Ibid., 26.

16. Ibid., 84.

17. "Conversation about Advertising."

18. Ogilvy, *Ogilvy on Advertising*, 88.

19. Ibid., 216.

20. "Pope of Modern Advertising."

21. Ogilvy & Mather, "David Ogilvy Biography," http://www.ogilvy.com/About/Our-History/David-Ogilvy-Bio.aspx.

22. Ibid.

23. Ogilvy, *Confessions*, 53.

24. Ibid., 47.

25. Ogilvy, *Ogilvy on Advertising*, 58.

26. Wolff, "First (and Last) Adman."

27. Ogilvy, *Ogilvy on Advertising*, 58.

28. "Conversation about Advertising."

29. Ogilvy & Mather, "Biography."

30. "The Life, Work and the Words of Wisdom of David Ogilvy," YouTube video, 4:02, Posted by "Ogilvy Sofia," June 22, 2011, http://youtu.be/pRYZslIdD-A.

31. "David Ogilvy: Essentials."

32. Ogilvy, *Confessions*, 42.

33. "Conversation about Advertising."

34. Ogilvy, *Ogilvy on Advertising*, 16.

35. "Pope of Advertising."

36. "Life, Work and the Words of Wisdom."

37. Ogilvy, *Confessions*, 108.

38. Ibid.

39. Ogilvy, *Ogilvy on Advertising*, 158.

40. Daniel Gross, "The Original Mad Man: How David Ogilvy Transformed Advertising and Americans' Shopping Habits," *Daily Beast*, February 11, 2009, http://www.thedailybeast.com/newsweek/2009/02/11/the-original-mad-man.html

41. Ogilvy, *Ogilvy on Advertising*, 48.

42. Gross, "Original Mad Man."

43. Ogilvy, *Confessions*, 68–69.

44. Ogilvy, *Ogilvy on Advertising*, 11.

45. Ibid.

46. Ibid., 87.

47. Ogilvy, *Confessions*, 128.

48. Ibid., 79.

49. "Conversation about Advertising."

50. Ogilvy, *Confessions*, 91.

51. "David Ogilvy: We Sell, or Else," YouTube video, 7:00, posted by "OgilvyGroup01," October 10, 2007, http://youtu.be/Br2KSsaTzUc.

52. Ibid.

53. Ibid.

54. Ogilvy, *Ogilvy on Advertising*, 7.

55. Ibid., 88.

56. "Conversation about Advertising."

57. Ogilvy, *Confessions*, 125.

58. Ibid., 124.

59. Ogilvy, *Ogilvy on Advertising*, 87.

60. "David Ogilvy: We Sell, or Else."

61. Ogilvy, *Ogilvy on Advertising*, 88.

62. Ogilvy, *Ogilvy on Advertising*, 12.

63. Ibid., 11.
64. Ibid., 87.
65. "Life, Work and the Words of Wisdom."
66. Ogilvy & Mather, "Ogilvy & Mather Wins 18 Effie Awards, Ranked Most Effective Agency in North America," *PR Newswire*, May 24, 2012, http://www .prnewswire.com/news-releases/ogilvy—mather-wins-18-effie-awards-ranked-most -effective-agency-in-north-america-153653315.html.
67. Ogilvy & Mather, "Ogilvy & Mather Cleans Up at Clios—Named Network of the Year," *PR Newswire*, May 16, 2012, http://www.prnewswire.com/news -releases/ogilvy—mather-cleans-up-at-clios—-named-network-of-the-year-15171 6835.html.
68. Ogilvy, *Confessions*, 137.
69. Ogilvy, *Ogilvy on Advertising*, 103.
70. Ogilvy, *Confessions*, 129.
71. "Conversation about Advertising."
72. Ogilvy, *Confessions*, 110–20.
73. Ibid., 22.

Bibliography

"A Conversation about Advertising, with David Ogilvy." Interview by John Crichton. Originally recorded 1977. YouTube, 54:51. Posted by "jpiedrahita," September 17, 2007. http://youtu.be/0kfsnjcUNiw.

"David Ogilvy: Essentials." YouTube video, 4:04. Posted by Adweek, June 14, 2011. http://youtu.be/yj9rokSeack.

"David Ogilvy: We Sell, or Else." YouTube video, 7:00. Posted by "OgilvyGroup01," October 10, 2007. http://youtu.be/Br2KSsaTzUc.

Gross, Daniel. "The Original Mad Man: How David Ogilvy Transformed Advertising and Americans' Shopping Habits." *Daily Beast*, February 11, 2009. http:// www.thedailybeast.com/newsweek/2009/02/11/the-original-mad-man.html.

"The Life, Work and the Words of Wisdom of David Ogilvy," YouTube video, 4:02. Posted by "Ogilvy Sofia," June 22, 2011. http://youtu.be/pRYZslIdD-A.

Ogilvy, David. *Confessions of an Advertising Man*. Herts: Southbank Publishing, 2011.

Ogilvy, David. *Ogilvy on Advertising*. New York: Vintage Books, 1985.

Ogilvy & Mather. "David Ogilvy Biography." Ogilvy.com. http://www.ogilvy.com/ About/Our-History/David-Ogilvy-Bio.aspx (accessed June 27, 2012).

Ogilvy & Mather. "Ogilvy & Mather Cleans Up at Clios—Named Network of the Year." *PR Newswire*, May 16, 2012. http://www.prnewswire.com/news-releases/ ogilvy—mather-cleans-up-at-clios—-named-network-of-the-year-151716835 .html.

Ogilvy & Mather. "Ogilvy & Mather Wins 18 Effie Awards, Ranked Most Effective Agency in North America." *PR Newswire*, May 24, 2012. http://www.pr

newswire.com/news-releases/ogilvy—mather-wins-18-effie-awards-ranked
-most-effective-agency-in-north-america-153653315.html.

"The Pope of Modern Advertising: David Ogilvy." *The David Susskind Show.* Originally recorded November 16, 1983. http://www.hulu.com/watch/46488.

Wolff, Michael. "The First (and Last) Adman: Thoughts on the Writer, Rule-Maker,
and Business Genius." *Adweek,* June 13, 2011. http://www.adweek.com/news/
advertising-branding/first-and-last-adman-132449?page=1.

CHAPTER THREE

Creating Celebrity through Advertising, and the Role of the Account Planner

Isaac I. Muñoz and Jason Flowers

Think of your favorite advertisement. Why do you like it? Is the advertisement funny, clever, or fanciful? Is your favorite "celebrity" the ad's spokesperson?

In an era when people hate to be interrupted by television advertising, DVRs and TiVos are no longer a nice addition to our entertainment systems, but a must. Consumers, in droves, have migrated to the Internet to watch their favorite shows hoping to reduce and ultimately escape the intrusive presence of advertising. Advertisers have had to think outside the "TV box" in order to grab the attention of their target markets and cause them to consider their products.

Historically, with the rise of mass production, consumer choice has increased. The numerous choices consumers must consider when making consumption decisions has led to "the paradox of choice."[1] With this ideology in mind, advertisers realized that a better way to position and sell their products was to leverage the power of association between celebrities and products. To date, the use of celebrities in advertisements continues to be a dominant practice among advertising strategists.

A plethora of papers have been published on the meaning of celebrity. These papers often highlight the influence celebrities exert on consumers as they decided what to purchase. An example of this is Paris Hilton in the 2005 Carl's Jr. car wash spot. This spot revolves around Hilton (the celebrity) and her interaction with the product. The Carl's Jr. spot references the 1967 *Cool Hand Luke*[2] car wash scene. The phallic references using the burger and the hose as objects of pleasure leverage Paris Hilton's sex appeal. This is one example, among many, of how advertisers use celebrities to accentuate certain brand and product attributes.

With the media and other external distractions constantly competing for the attention of consumers, advertisers must become more creative and find ways to cut through the clutter in order to be noticed. This chapter uses McCracken's "Meaning Movement and the Endorsement Process"[3] model as a base and proposes a new model of something not yet explored; how advertisers *create* celebrities through advertising. We argue that advertisers, account planners particularly, have the potential to transfer cultural meaning. By creating celebrity figures through advertising, account planners aid brand development by increasing brand awareness and consumption consideration.

We support our argument by examining three concepts regarding advertising in a consumer culture, which are: the purpose of "advertising" in a consumption society, the concept of "fantasy in advertising," and advertising as a "mimetic desire." Then, we will review McCracken's Celebrity Endorsement model and propose a new advertising celebrity model that addresses the role account planners have over message development. The chapter will conclude by applying this model to one of the best-known campaigns of the last decade, Dos Equis' "The Most Interesting Man in the World."

People have a love-hate relationship with advertisements. The advertisements we love can be watched repeatedly and become unconscious (and sometimes conscious) brand ambassadors for that product. By the same token, there are advertisements that consumers find irritating. Consumers often express disappointment, and resentment toward the brand for putting mediocre content in an already overcrowded media outlet. The purpose of mentioning the love-hate relationship we have with advertising is to show the influence this practice has had over consumers, particularly in the United States.

The Purpose of Advertising in a Consumer Culture

Advertising is also, in a sense, the official art of modern capitalist society: it is what "we" put up in "our" streets and use to fill up half of "our" newspapers and magazines: and it commands the services of perhaps the largest organized body of writers and artists, with their attendant managers and advisers, in the whole society.[4]

Advertising has evolved into a cultural phenomenon. The growth of advertising has mainly occurred due to the rise of choice and convenience. Pre–World War I, people bought products as needed, and choice was not usually a factor. But, with the birth of the industrialized era and mass production, product choice became a factor in consumer decision-making. Product choice benefited the consumer not only from a variety standpoint, but also from a price standpoint. Once different products of the same category began to bombard the marketplace, it became obvious that product differentiators would be the key to increase consumption. It was at this point that manufacturers realized the way to position their product in the marketplace had to be done by understanding what the product could potentially do for the end user. As manufacturers began to shift to a more consumer-centric business model, the strategic concept of *convenience* began to be incorporated into advertising strategy. According to Strasser, by focusing the marketing message on convenience, housewives felt the product could liberate them from their hard labor of creating soap or soup from scratch.[5] A great example referred to by Strasser is how the advertising of the 1920s suggested that by purchasing "rust-free aluminum pans or throwaway paper handkerchiefs consumers would have the leisured lifestyles once accessible only to wealthy people with servants."[6]

Therefore, with the selling of convenience, consumers became more and more divorced from the actual production of goods. By definition, the less they produced, the more they had to buy, and the more choices they would want to see in order to evaluate their purchase accordingly. Even though this ideology benefits the consumer from a wallet standpoint, the less involved consumers were in the production of products, the more they began to rely on the information given through advertising.

Critics of advertising argue that from the 1970s to the present, advertising has eclipsed solely selling goods and services. Advertisers have become meaning makers who teach social and personal values.[7] Though this may be true, it is important to understand that advertising, as a text, is not an all-powerful medium. Consumers are more than passive receivers of information.

The Concept of Fantasy within Advertising

The second concept that will bring greater understanding to advertising in a consumer society is this notion of fantasy. Advertisers have captured the interests of consumers by creating a fantasy that revolves around a life of ease. This fantasy is used to persuade consumers that the purchase of certain products will achieve a higher level of leisure and pleasure for the consumer. In 1994, Richard Overton sued Anheuser-Busch for allegedly creating beer advertisements that were untrue and deceptive. According to Parker's article, Overton claimed that the ads, which contained beer-related fantasies, persuaded him to overconsume the product, leading to self-inflicted mental injury, emotional distress, and financial loss.[8] The court wrote, "In support of his claims, [Overton] pointed to television ads featuring Bud Light as the source of fantasies coming to life, fantasies involving tropical settings and beautiful women and men engaged in unrestricted merriment."[9] Overton claimed it was advertising that caused him to alter his behavior. The pressures of a postmodern lifestyle may be used to substantiate his fantasy claims.

According to Williams, existing evidence suggests that consumers need to validate purchased objects, if not in real life, at least in fantasy. Consumers validate their purchased possessions by associating our products with social and personal meanings. Therefore:

> If consumers have made the right purchases within the system of meanings to which we are all trained, they will then be able to see a payoff. Thus the fantasy seems to be validated, at a personal level, but only at the cost of preserving the general unreality which it obscures: the real failures of the society which however are not easily traced to this pattern.[10]

Mimetic Desires and Advertising

The third concept to consider is the influence advertising has on a society's mimetic desires, which can also be called artful deceptions. In his book, *A Theater of Envy: William Shakespeare*, René Girard posed a very interesting theory on the envy of consumption. According to Girard, we desire what others desire, which he calls "the mimetic desire."[11] A mimetic desire is reflected in how we imitate those who have what we think we want. The interesting part of this theory is understanding that desire is not only bound to material possessions, but can extend to lifestyles and marriage partners.

> Individuals who desire the same thing are united by something so powerful that, as long as they can share whatever they desire, they remain the best of friends; as soon as they cannot, they become the worst enemies . . . the only reason the Greeks want her back is because the Trojans want to keep her. The only reason the Trojans want to keep her is because the Greeks want her back.[12]

Girard oversimplifies the Helen of Troy example, but what this example illustrates is the ability to show how we are, as people and consumers. To use Asa Berger's words, "it is mimetic desire that helps explain our consumer lust; we desire what others have desired and have purchased, especially those we look up to—such as celebrities, movie stars, and sport heroes."[13] Taking this into consideration, we begin to understand the importance "celebrity" has over the population.

Mimetic desires are why critics of advertising have claimed this practice to be unethical. A very good example of this is MacBride's take on the situation by claiming:

> [A]dvertising is essentially concerned with exalting the materialistic virtues of consumption by exploiting achievement drives and emulative anxieties, employing tactics of hidden manipulation, playing on emotions, maximizing appeal and minimizing information, trivializing, eliminating objective considerations, contriving illogical situation, and generally reducing men, women, and children to the role of irrational consumer.[14]

In other words, MacBride is arguing that advertising is encouraging people to replace certain goods before the old ones need to be replaced, introducing the idea of fashionable purchases. One can deduce that by encouraging fashionable purchases, advertisers and marketers are endeavoring to increase their market share via forced consumption. This forced consumption would then be driven by a product's efficiency, minimizing product usage to occasions versus needs.

McCracken's Celebrity Endorser Model

In 1989, McCracken published a model that has proven to be a key piece of literature for academics and practitioners trying to understand the meanings transferred from celebrities to products and brands. McCracken's article has been cited over 150 times, according to the web of knowledge database, and over two decades later, it continues to influence the way we see celebrity endorsements. For these reasons, this celebrity endorsement model was selected as the base for the proposed model. McCracken's model is divided into to three stages:

Stage 1: The first stage is to showcase how celebrities are able to influence their "brand" from the culture that surrounds them. Celebrities create meaning by the roles they are perceived to play in society. These meanings establish the denotation consumers associate with them. McCracken briefly points out that the difference between anonymous models and celebrities is not in their demographic information (i.e., gender, age, or status) or even beauty, but in the depth and range of personality meanings that celebrities carry with them. He goes on to explain in detail why celebrities are able to carry this meaning in the following quote:

> Celebrities "own" their meaning because they have created them on the public stage by dint of intense and repeated performance. Each new dramatic role brings the celebrity into contact with a range of objects, persons, and contexts. Out of these objects, persons, and contexts transferred meanings that then reside in the celebrity. The celebrity endorsement gives to the product was generated in distant movie performances, political campaigns, or athletic achievements.[15]

In other words, what celebrities are able to do is own and accumulate meanings by portraying similar roles over and over, giving depth not only to the character they play, but at the same time eliminating their real persona. Sylvester Stallone is a good example to display McCracken's three stages. Stallone has played the role of a hypermasculine male numerous times over his extensive acting career. Some of Stallone's most memorable roles are John Rambo in the *Rambo*[16] series, Rocky Balboa in the *Rocky*[17] series, Jack Carter in *Get Carter*,[18] and more recently, Barney Ross in *The Expendables*.[19] All of these roles have a few common themes that tie them together. Each role requires Stallone to be in extremely good shape, chauvinistic to a degree, and violent and aggressive to a fault.

Stage 2: It is during this stage when advertisers and marketers begin to search for celebrities that embody the values of the brand and have the potential to elevate the brand's values and meanings in the consumer's mind. This is a two-step process. The first step requires the advertising/marketing firm to understand how their product is perceived in the marketplace. The second step is to find a celebrity that exudes the personality traits deemed important in the first step. According to McCracken, the second stage of "meaning transfer" is of upmost importance because of the additional meanings celebrities carry over to the product advertised:

> It [the advertisement] must capture all the meanings it wished to obtain from the celebrity and leave no salient meanings untapped. All celebrities will encompass in their range of cultural significance some meanings that are not sought for the product. This will be accomplished by filling the advertisement with people, objects, contexts, and copy that have the same meanings as the celebrity.[20]

To make sure we are on the same page about meaning transfer, let us use Sylvester Stallone once more to further clarify this point. For this example, our product will be Vitamin X. Vitamin X is meant to help consumers exercise longer, cut fat faster, and build muscle. After considering a myriad of extremely fit celebrities, we decided Stallone is the best fit. Stallone is considered the best fit because he epitomizes extreme fitness and would provide legitimacy to the product claims.

Stage 3: The third stage of McCracken's model reveals how meaning transfers from product to consumer, which impacts consumption decisions. McCracken expresses what postmodern philosopher Jean Baudrillard referred to as "sign value." Sign value is the value of an object within a system of objects.[21] The third stage of McCracken's model helps researchers understand why consumers are constantly looking for meanings through celebrity-endorsed products.

> It is not enough for the consumer merely to own an object, to take possession of its meanings, or to incorporate these meanings into the self. The meanings of the object do not merely lift off the object and enter into the consumer's concept of self and world. The consumer must claim the meanings and the work with them. Celebrities are proof that the process works. Celebrities have been where the consumer is going. They have done in Stage 1 what the consumer is not laboring to do in Stage 3 of the meaning transfer process. Or, to put in another way, customers are laboring to perform their own Stage 1 construction of the self out of the meanings supplied by previous and present roles and the meanings accessible to them there.[22]

To conclude this third stage with our Stallone example, we would like to briefly refer to Freud's mirror stage. In our consumer society, people want to be "perfect." The following lyrics from the song "Creep" by Radiohead illustrate this point: "I want a perfect body, I want a perfect soul ... I wish I was special." These lyrics summarize what the majority of society feels. People are eager to better themself through products. Freud's concept of the "mirror stage" argues that people do not like the person they see in the mirror. People always believe they can be better than they currently are. Herein comes the celebrity. Stallone appears "perfect" to the average guy. The average guy has not achieved Stallone's level of "perfection" and never will. Who we see in the mirror is not who we are in our mind or the person to whom we compare ourselves on television. With all this in mind, the following meaning transaction happens:

A) Culture → Celebrity → Violent Movies → Stallone
    Stallone is perceived as a Hypermasculine persona

B) Celebrity → Product → Stallone → Vitamins
   Vitamins are now perceived as legitimate because of the endorsement
C) Product → Consumer → Stallone + Vitamins → Consumer
   Consumers will "think" he or she will close the perception gap by using the vitamins

Account Planning and the Creative Brief

Now that McCracken's celebrity endorsement model has been explained, the third portion of this chapter will focus on how advertising agencies play a key role in merging ideologies and cultural discourses when creating strategic messaging. These strategic messages have the potential to reach consumer targets, while having a spillover effect to the general population.

Advertisers tend to be looked at, by some, as puppeteers, because of the way they use art, psychology, and sociology (among other subjects) to infuse people with ideas of what to buy and why to buy it. Advertising agencies must create relevant content that attracts the correct target audience. To ensure that content produced by agencies is relevant to the consumer, key executives within the agency dedicate themselves to gaining a better understanding of the consumer by leveraging existing consumer research software as well as other types of research, i.e., focus groups, ethnographies, tracking studies, and attitude and usages studies, among others.

The role often tasked with this job is the account planner. Account planners go by numerous names: strategic planners, brand planners, marketplace planners, and/or consumer insight planners. In order to understand about this discipline, we have to look back to the advertising of the 1950s. During the mid-twentieth century, marketing and marketing research departments were part of advertising agencies. Advertising agencies were considered the sole owners of the communication message. In other words, manufacturers would focus on production and agencies on marketing the product. As companies began to grow their portfolio of products, there was a need to move the marketing research and marketing departments in house to better manage their product's information. As this trend began to change the way marketing departments operated, agencies began to adopt new ideologies that helped them remain relevant in the minds of their clients (product manufacturers). Two advertising executives, from different agencies, noticed this trend and decided to focus on something that marketing departments were not doing effectively: account planning. These two executives were Stephen King and Stanley Pollitt, who are regarded as the forefathers of account planning.

What Do Account Planners Do, and Why Are They So Important?

The role of the account planner has become an imperative one in advertising agencies. Account planners marry consumer understanding to the creation of strong, resonating creative concepts. It is important to note that the literature on the discipline is pretty stint. There are two key definitions that we would like to use to define account planning. The first definition is from Jon Steel, who says that "account planners, in addition to providing strategic insights for communication, should be telling the client how demographic, cultural, economic, competitive and attitudinal change is affecting their overall business, and how changes in fundamental business practices are required if they are to succeed."[23] The second definition, which is more of a list of roles, comes from London's APG (Account Planning Group). Account planners are:

> Strategic Thinker, Media Planner, Think Piece Polemicist, Social Anthropologist, Insight Miner, Knowledge Applicator, Market Researcher, Writer of Creative Brief, Brief Creatives, Data Analyst, Qualitative Focus Group Moderator, Information Center, Bad Cop to Account Management, NDP Consultant, Brainstorming Facilitator, Voice of Consumer and last, but not least, Futurologist.[24]

There is not an agreed-upon definition on account planning. But, it can be concluded that account planners, depending on the agency, are key to the creative development process because they are able to converge the three things that will create insightful communication. Account planners insightfully merge brand knowledge (product knowledge), the marketplace (business knowledge), and the consumer (buyer behavior insight) to create unique expressions of creativity.

Among the account planner's most important work output is the creative brief. The creative brief is a strategic document that serves two purposes: (1) to guide the creative team, and (2) to serve as the document against which all creative ideas will be evaluated. The brief itself should be creative. It should provide solutions rather than problems, it should be interesting, and it should motivate the agency team. Most importantly, the brief should be inspirational, but not viewed as a client checklist.[25]

The creative brief is meant to serve as a platform for all communication the advertising agency will employ on behalf of the brand. The brief is a document that merges the marketing brief (usually provided by the client), consumer behavior shifts (based on research), and how creative strategy should be executed.[26] A basic creative brief is composed of the following seven questions:

1. Why are we advertising? What are the objectives behind this advertisement?
2. Who are we talking to? Everything that is known about the consumer target; from demographics to specific psychographics.
3. What do they currently think? Once there is a good understanding of who they are, then one can understand how they feel about the product category and about the brand itself.
4. What would we like them to think? Knowing that they currently think about the brand and category, plus knowing what is currently going on in the marketplace, account planners can insert here what the advertising could trigger consumers to believe and/or feel after experiencing the advertisement.
5. What is the single most important idea? The single idea is usually based on a broader insight that will guide all of the strategic communications and/or campaign.
6. Why should they believe it? Here goes the "marketingspeak" explanation as to why consumers will believe that Stallone is really using the vitamins he is endorsing.
7. What are the creative guidelines? The creative guidelines usually have the project specifics (i.e., 30-second TV, legal taglines, special offers, etc.).

Proposed Model with Addition of Account Planning:

After that brief explanation about account planners and the creative brief, one can see the impact quality account planning has on the creation of relevant and resonating creative. Stage 1 of McCracken's model is all about the meaning transfer from culture to celebrity. But, this stage neglects to mention the power of the advertiser as a meaning creator. The latter portion of the proposed model, endorsement and consumption, remained as McCracken's. The initial two stages are where we propose a change: cultural research and communication strategy. This next section will then focus on the importance of meaning creation and transfer during the first two stages, since the latter two stages remain the same.

Stage 1: As stated above, the purpose of the account planner is to discover and merge brand, marketplace, and consumer insights. So, just like celebrities borrow from culture what they feel can make their brand have more circulation, account planners do the same. Account planners must be connoisseurs of cultural discourse. Cultural discourse often takes place within the context of movies, music, television, theater, news, or other types of advertising; anything that touches people. Knowing what is relevant to consumers is what keeps account planners ahead of the curve.

To this point, it is also important to note that account planners are not solely what Gladwell would call "cool hunters."[27] Account planners have to take into consideration what makes the most sense for the client's brand. Account planners ensure brands stay relevant through research. Account planners have access to consumer research software databases, secondary research data, and reports. Account planners also travel extensively to conduct qualitative exploratory research (ethnographies, in-home interviews, focus groups, etc.) and quantitative research (tracking studies, attitudes and usage studies, and consumer, product, and category segmentation studies). Because of the nature of the account planner's job, and the resources available to them, they are able to extract from culture not only what is "cool," but most important, what is relevant to the consumer.

Stage 2: This secondary stage is key to the meaning transfer process, because it is where account planners and creatives create and shape the communication message. At this stage, the account planner has written a creative brief that reflects all of their exploratory research, which is used to identify the target audience, understand consumer insights, and develop brand strategy. The brief will also reflect which trends (macro and micro) apply to the consumer and brand. In other words, the brief will reflect the key things that will make the consumer stop and notice the brand advertised. Once the creative team receives the brief, it is their job to write a breakthrough message. Like account planners, creatives will also use cultural discourses to find and give meaning to the advertising message.[28] Upon finding the appropriate meanings, a persona will be created, which will become the advertisement's "celebrity." The difference between McCracken's model and the proposed model is the former model emphasizes how celebrities borrow things from the culture that would go well with their persona. Our model expresses the idea that advertising agencies choose specific attributes that will resonate with the ad-created celebrity and the advertised brand. Advertising agencies create strategic communication plans that make the surreal persona have a planned circulation. An example of this process is that of "celebrity politicians":

> One way in which narratives come to constitute political reality is by giving an identity to "people." The suggestion is that who "we" are is created via, among other things, the rhetoric of those who seek political power. This is not marketing as selling to an established market or "demographic"; this is about creating an identity (that may subsequently be exploited by marketing strategies). Creating an identity depends on the use of the symbols and devices of poetry, song, processions and the like.[29]

So, just like politicians are given a certain identity in order to fit the party they represent, advertising agencies create a celebrity that sells the brand's fantasy. The brand will often mirror the consumer's mimetic desires.

The last portion of this chapter applies the proposed model to the 2009 Effie award winning advertising campaign, Dos Equis' "The Most Interesting Man in the World."[30] The purpose of this model is to explain how advertising account planners create celebrity. In order to increase the validity of our proposed model, we have used the published Effie case study and organized it into the appropriate stage of our four-stage model previously described.[31] The implications of the model will be written in the conclusion of the chapter.

Stage 1: Culture Research

A No-Name Brand from Mexico

At the beginning of 2007, Dos Equis' brand equity was going nowhere. Research showed that people had little association other than the fact that Dos Equis was from Mexico, which did not evoke quality or status cues, but rather the exact opposite. As a passably refreshing lager with little in the way of product differentiation, it was clear we would have to find something to say about the brand that did not rest on its flavor or its origins.

An Audience with a Short Attention Span and a Broad Repertoire

We were aiming to attract a twentysomething male audience who reportedly drank as many as 12 brands in a month. Gaining traction on any sort of lasting basis with this crowd would be a battle.

Consumer Insight

First, what these guys wanted more than anything, more than hot girls and designer toys, was to be seen as interesting. And conversely, they were terrified of being seen as boring. We sniffed an opportunity.

Stage 2: Communication Strategy

Inspired by this new insight, the Dos Equis team set out to turn the conventions of the category on their heads. In place of Joe Drinker in a polo shirt with an easily relatable lifestyle, we created the Most Interesting Man in the World, dashingly attired in Hemingway-style suits, and situated in highly exotic and intriguing locales. Instead of soothing the drinker with familiar and generic cues of masculinity, Dos Equis used the sophisticated figure of the Most Interesting Man (MIM) to imply that all their drinkers could and should be living a more interesting life.

Stage 3: Endorsement

Seeing how our drinkers wanted to believe in this character, we created a communications plan that presented the MIM as a bona fide celebrity. Using multiple touchpoints, we blurred the lines between fact and fantasy, allowing our audience to play along. "He would make the lovechild of James Bond and Hugh Hefner look like a complete douche"—Blogger, Badassasaurus Rex.

Bringing Celebrity to Life: Letting Fans Get Up Close and Personal with a "Real" Legend

Captivated by his fantastic lifestyle and magnetic presence, our target wanted to believe that the MIM really existed, so we treated him like a bona fide celebrity. Fifteen-second spots, set in a bar, functioned like snippets of behind-the-scenes interviews, as the MIM offered advice and opinions on various topics, such as careers or rollerblading. These pearls of wisdom are then memorialized in print ads, His website, http://staythirsty myfriends.com, provides more details of his fascinating past, colorful acquaintance, and a peek behind the scenes at his home, allowing people to get to know him better. We used social media such as Facebook to allow his "fans'" to interact with him online. Mini Web documentaries, "On Interestingness," broadcast on Break.com, are an homage to his charisma and show his influence on pop culture.

Stage 4: Consumption

We met and exceeded our goal of double-digit growth. Sales of Dos Equis increased 18 percent over the year, while growth in the import and specialty beer category remained flat to negative, and the Mexican segment posted an increase of only 6 percent.

Best of all, these clear signs of growing brand strength and campaign affinity translate into increased share of throat. Data shows that while Dos Equis drinkers' overall beer consumption declined in 2008 (from 17.5 to 15.6 units per week) they are drinking more Dos Equis (from 2.5 to 3 units per week). Maybe these drinkers are imitating the Most Interesting Man's motto: They don't always drink beer, but when they do, they prefer Dos Equis.

Conclusion

The purpose of this chapter was to show how advertising agencies create celebrities through relevant creative content. Advertising agencies have key people solely dedicated to understanding marketplace, brand, and consumer interactions for different products and product categories. As explained in the proposed model, the cultural knowledge available to account planners allows advertising agencies to create celebrities through advertisements.

EuroRSCG New York, Dos Equis' AOR (advertising agency of record) understood the power they had when creating a celebrity. EuroRSCG created a celebrity that not only resonated with potential consumers, but also could represent the brand. As seen in the case study, they used their account planners to deliver a strong creative brief through innovative insights that would inspire and cut through the clutter. What EuroRSCG New York's account planners, as well as creatives, knew, aside from the meaning transfer model, was how to leverage the advertising medium to create a celebrity. They operated with the following three principles in mind: (1) advertising in a consumer culture is a form of art that delivers meanings and values; (2) consumers in a consumer society want to buy products that help them be validated, even if it is through fantasy; (3) the creative team understood that celebrities, even when created, deliver mimetic desires for consumers. In addition to this third point, they also understood what went into the creation of the Most Interesting Man in the World's' cool personality. The MIM had to be narcissistic, detached, hegemonic, and chauvinistic, as per Pountain and Robins.[32]

We would like to leave you with the following closing remarks. If you heard the name Jonathan Goldsmith, who would come to mind? Jonathan Goldsmith has been an actor for over 20 years and has appeared in several films. Jonathan Goldsmith, in less than a year, went from a "guy who did a couple of movie appearances" to "the Most Interesting Man in the World"—with the help of EuroRSCG New York, of course.

Notes

1. Barry Schwartz, *The Paradox of Choice: Why Less Is More* (New York: HarperCollins, 2005). Schwartz's point is that given consumers have so many options for all the products they want to buy, it is hard to commit to one.

2. *Cool Hand Luke*, directed by Stuart Rosenberg, performers Paul Newman, George Kennedy, J. D. Cannon, Lou Antonio, Robert Drivas, and Jo Van Fleet (Warner Bros., 1967), DVD.

3. Grant McCracken, "Who Is the Celebrity Endorser? Cultural Foundations of the Endorsement Process," *Journal of Consumer Research* 16 (December 1989): 310.

4. Raymond Williams, "Advertising: The Magic System," in *The Advertising and Consumer Culture Reader*, ed. Joseph Turow and Matthew P. Mcallister (New York: Routledge, 2009), 20.

5. Susan Strasser, "The Alien Past. Consumer Culture in Historical Perspective," in *The Advertising and Consumer Culture Reader*, edited by Joseph Turow and Matthew P. Mcallister (New York: Routledge, 2009), 26.

6. Ibid., 29.

7. Williams, "Advertising," 24.

8. Betty J. Parker, "Exploring Life Themes and Myths in Alcohol Advertisements through Meaning-Based Model of Advertising Experiences," *Journal of Advertising* 27 (Spring 1998): 97.

9. Ibid., 98.

10. Williams, "Advertising," 23.

11. Rene Girard, *A Theater of Envy* (New York: McGraw Hill, 1991).

12. Arthur Asa Berger, ed., *Ads, Fads, and Consumer Culture* (Lanham, MD: Rowman & Littlefield, 2004), 36.

13. Ibid.

14. Sean MacBride, *Many Voices, One World: Communication and Society, Today and Tomorrow* (New York: Unipub [UNESCO], 1980).

15. McCracken, "Who Is the Celebrity Endorser?"

16. *First Blood*, directed by Ted Kotcheff, performers Sylvester Stallone, Brian Dennehy, and Richard Crenna (Orion, 1982), DVD.

17. *Rocky*, directed by John G. Avildesen, performers Sylvester Stallone, Talia Shire, and Burt Young (United Artists, 1976), DVD.

18. *Get Carter*, directed by Stephen Kay, performers Sylvester Stallone, Michael Caine, and Mickey Rourke (Warner Bros., 2000), DVD.

19. *Expendables*, directed by Sylvester Stallone, performers Sylvester Stallone, Jason Statham, Jet Li, Dolph Lundgren, and Eric Roberts (Lionsgate, 2010), DVD.

20. McCracken, "Who Is the Celebrity Endorser?" 316.

21. Jean Baudrillard, "The Ideological Genesis of Needs," in *The Consumer Society Reader*, ed. Juliet B. Schor and Douglas B. Holt (New York: New Press, 2011), 59.

22. McCracken, "Who Is the Celebrity Endorser?" 317.

23. Jon Steel, *Truth, Lies and Advertising: The Art of Account Planning* (New York: John Wiley & Sons, 1998), 37.

24. Account Planning Group (APG), 2008. http://www.apg.org.uk/wp-content/uploads/2011/01/WhatIsAccPlan2001.pdf.

25. Stanley Pollitt, "How I Started Account Planning in Agencies," *Campaign*, April 20, 1979.

26. Aidan Kelly, Kelly Lawlor, and Stephanie O'Donahoe, "Encoding Advertisements: The Creative Perspective," *Journal of Marketing Management* 21 (2005): 509.

27. Malcolm Gladwell, "The Coolhunt," in *The Consumer Society Reader*, ed. Juliet B. Schor and Douglas B. Holt (New York: New Press, 2011), 368.

28. Kelly, Lawlor, and O'Donahoe, "Encoding Advertisements."

29. John Street, "The Celebrity Politician: Political Style and Popular Culture," in *The Celebrity Culture Reader*, ed. P. David Marshall (New York: Routledge, 2006), 366.

30. Effie Worldwide 2009 Gold Winner—Beverages Alcohol. K. Tillman, L. Pfenning, E. Costa, M. Perhach, C. Kredlet, K. Milmoe, D. Weinstock, T. Woodley, M. Kutmanova, and D. Fried, "The Most Interesting Man in the World," case in PDF, http://s3.amazonaws.com/effie_assets/2009/3496/2009_3496_pdf_1.pdf.

31. For additional information, or to read the full case study, go to http://www.effie.org/winners/showcase/2009/3496. Here you will not only find the full case study, but also additional media submitted with the case study.

32. Dick Pountain, and David Robins, *Cool Rules. Anatomy of an Attitude* (London: Reaktion, 2000).

Bibliography

Berger, Arthur Asa, ed. *Ads, Fads, and Consumer Culture*. Lanham, MD: Rowman & Littlefield, 2004.

Buttle, Francis. "What Do People Do with Advertising?" *International Journal of Advertising* 10, no. 2 (1991): 95–110.

Cronin, Anne M. "Regimes of Mediation: Advertising Practitioners as Cultural Intermediaries?" *Consumption, Markets and Culture* 7, no. 4 (2004): 349–69.

Girard, Rene. *A Theater of Envy*. New York: McGraw Hill, 1991.

Gladwell, Malcolm. "The Coolhunt." In *The Consumer Society Reader*, edited by J. B. Schor and D. B. Holt, 360–74. New York: New Press, 2000.

Holt, Douglas B. *How Brands Become Icons: The Principles of Cultural Branding*, Boston: Harvard Business School Publishing Corporation, 2004.

Holt, Douglas B. "How Societies Desire Brands: Using Cultural Theory to Explain Brand Symbolism," Paper presented at the Dublin Institute of Technology Research Seminar Series, May 6, 2005.

Kelly, Aidan, Katrina Lawlor, and Stephanie O'Donahoe. "Encoding Advertisements: The Creative Perspective." *Journal of Marketing Management* 21 (2005): 505–28.

Levi-Strauss, Claude. *The Savage Mind*. London: Weidenfeld and Nicolson, 1966.

MacBride, Sean. *Many Voices, One World: Communication and Society, Today and Tomorrow*. New York: Unipub (UNESCO), 1980.

McCracken, Grant. "Culture and Consumption: A Theoretical Account of the Structure and Movement of the Cultural Meaning of Consumer Goods." *Journal of Consumer Research* 13 (June 1986): 71–84.

McCracken, Grant. "Who Is the Celebrity Endorser? Cultural Foundations of the Endorsement Process." *Journal of Consumer Research* 16 (December 1989): 310–21.

Parker, Betty J. "Exploring Life Themes and Myths in Alcohol Advertisements through Meaning-Based Model of Advertising Experiences." *Journal of Advertising* 27 (Spring 1998): 97–112.

Pollitt, Stanley. "How I Started Account Planning in Agencies." *Campaign*, April 20, 1979.

Pountain, Dick, and David Robins. *Cool Rules: Anatomy of an Attitude*. London: Reaktion, 2000.

Randazzo, Sal. *Mythmaking on Madison Avenue*. Chicago: Probus Publishing Company, 1993.

Russo, J. Edward, Barbara L. Metcalf, and Debra Stephens. "Identifying Misleading Advertising." *Journal of Consumer Research* 8 (September 1981): 119–31.

Scott, Linda M. "Understanding Jingles and Needledrop: A Rhetorical Approach to Music in Advertising." *Journal of Consumer Research* 17 (September 1990): 223–36.

Steel, Jon. *Truth, Lies and Advertising: The Art of Account Planning*. New York: John Wiley & Sons, 1998.

Stern, Barbara B. "Consumer Myths: Frye's Taxonomy and Structural Analysis of Consumption Texts," *Journal of Consumer Research* 22 (September 1995): 165–85.

Strasser, Susan. "The Alien Past: Consumer Culture in Historical Perspective." In *The Advertising and Consumer Culture Reader*, edited by Joseph Turow and Matthew P. Mcallister, 25–35. New York: Routledge, 2009.

Street, John. "The Celebrity Politician. Political Style and Popular Culture." In *The Celebrity Culture Reader*, edited by P. David Marshall, 359–70. New York: Routledge, 2006.

Thompson, Craig J. "Marketing Mythology and Discourse of Power." *Journal of Consumer Research* 31 (June 2004): 162–80.

Williams, Raymond. "Advertising: The Magic System." In *The Advertising and Consumer Culture Reader*, edited by Joseph Turow and Matthew P. Mcallister, 13–24. New York: Routledge, 2009.

CHAPTER FOUR

"I Hate the Way My Hair Looks": Controversies in Advertising to Women and Girls

Brian Cogan

While the study of advertising is nothing new, in the last few decades the prevalent idea in media studies is that advertising is something that works not to sell products, but to create environments. It is certainly worthwhile to examine individual advertisements to seek to decode the "messages" within, but perhaps a better question now is, what kind of an environment does advertising as a *whole* create? And, when examining an environment of any kind (air, water, temperature, etc.), one of the key factors to analyze is how *healthy* is the prevalent environment? Most scholars who have examined advertising have done so in the context of a capitalist system, and as Michael Schudson wrote, "the advertisement is just one small piece, even if the most visible piece of a major economic enterprise directed at getting consumers to buy (and getting people to think of themselves as consumers)."[1] The environment of advertising is just the most visible part of the enterprise of capitalism.

But if advertising is a part of capitalism as a whole, what kind of an environment do we see when we look at the mediated environment of television commercials, newspaper and magazine advertising, and even Internet banners? To many scholars who have examined contemporary advertising, the answer may well be that the environment created by advertising is largely unhealthy and in many ways, regarded as toxic. According to many scholars who have focused their work on advertising directed toward women and young girls (Goffman, Kilbourne, Wolf, etc.), advertising that is directly aimed at female consumers may be the most toxic advertising environment of all.

In this chapter I will argue that advertising to women is a specialized field that employs different techniques from most advertising aimed primarily toward men. While many advertising campaigns use themes such as shame, embarrassment, and perceived weakness in order to sell products, many gender studies and media scholars have argued that advertising toward women in particular utilizes imagery that infantilizes women and points out weaknesses both real and imagined. While much of the advertising aimed at men emphasizes power and masculinity, selling products such as beer and cars as well-deserved rewards for a tough day at the office, most advertising toward women tells them that there is inherently something wrong with them—something that can only be solved via passive consumption.

It might be helpful to start with a quick aside about the topic of advertising and media effects. While very early on as a discipline, media studies favored a strong effects model, one that imagined a "magic bullet" or "hypodermic needle" directly effecting the presumed media viewer; this view was quickly discarded in terms of a theoretical approach that emphasized limited effects and an active audience, one that makes their own choices. Modern media studies does not argue that consumers of an individual commercial watch it and decide that they must consume the product thanks to the one ad; but asks instead, what does it meant to live in an environment where advertising is a crucial part of the media landscape? No serious scholar really looks at advertising in terms of what it "makes" people do, but this does not mean that media has no influence at all, but rather that media helps create an environment where certain choices and ways of living are depicted as natural. As Neil Postman argued, the media creates an unreal world where choices such as consumerism are made natural and where the solution to the problems of life is not to looks inward or turn to religion or philosophy, but instead to engage in rituals of consumption in which "choice" is presented not as a way to live one's life, but of what products to buy. In particular, advertising to women also works to naturalize an environment where commercials point out weakness instead of strength, and to present a world where everything about the female body is flawed and in need of fixing.

There is now a movement among feminist scholars and others not only to point out how artificial and toxic the environment created by advertising is, but also to illustrate that vast numbers of consumers (both male and female) are opting out of the world of consumption by consciously objecting to the worldview promoted by most advertising and by choosing to concentrate not only on the globally marketed brands, but on the local and sustainable.

Modern Advertising

Advertising in one form or another has existed since human beings used recognizable symbols to communicate. The idea of the marketplace, a tradition that goes back to the dawn of civilization, recognized the need to promote one's shop or stall as superior to others, and in primarily oral cultures, the din and uproar of crowded markets must have been full of boasting, cajoling, and blandishments about the superiority of one's pottery or corn as opposed to other stalls. Human beings are natural advertisers, and there may be an inherent human desire to impress or even sell not only products, but also ourselves.

However, the idea of selling an idea as opposed to a product is a relatively new concept. At the start of the twentieth century, the advent of a world war on a scale never seen before led to increasing efforts to persuade people to participate in the war effort. Veterans of the campaigns to persuade people, such as Ivy Lee and Edward Bernays, realized that selling a product (even a war) did not involve a simple sales pitch, but involved the use of propaganda that emphasized a psychological appeal as opposed to one that asked reasonable questions. At the same time that many were bemoaning the lack of cohesion in a "mass society" and writers such as Walter Lippmann were asking if the general public needed firm leadership to aid in decision making, Bernays in particular started public relations campaigns that attempted to reach the id as opposed to the rational part of the consumers mind (this makes more sense when we recall that Bernays's uncle was none other than Sigmund Freud).[2]

Bernays realized that most people did not buy based on the wallet, but instead wanted products that appealed to core values and ideas about who they were and what their place was in the socioeconomic system. This led to changes in the fledgling advertising industry, where copywriters and illustrators tried to find the right combinations of words and images that would make a product more appealing, more "zesty" or "flavorful." Starting in the 1920s and 1930s, advertisers realized that women were the dominant class of consumers. As Roland Marchand noted, by the 1930s, scarcely anyone estimated women as comprising less than 80 percent of the consumer audience."[3] One of the key ways that advertisers approached this newly recognized demographic was through magazines aimed at women. Not that most ad men actually *read* those magazines, though. As Marchand wrote, "although the women's magazines regularly pictured their sophisticated readers as leading busy, diversified, action-packed lives, advertising agencies adopted a very different model of the typical woman consumer. This model owed more to the contemporary stereotypes of the movie-matinee fan and *True Story* reader than the bustling self-confident woman shown in ads by *McCall's* and *Ladies Home Journal*."[4] The trend from early in the twentieth century and culminating in the first few decades and onward was to concentrate more on women, and "the recognition of women as consumers legitimated an emotional rhetoric in advertising."[5] In order to appeal more to a presumed marketplace of female consumers, advertisers would have to use emotional, image-based approaches, instead of relying on the value of their product.

The rise of television commercials in particular completely married advertising with the image. As Postman wrote, "it was not until the 1950's that the television commercial made linguistic discourse obsolete as the basis for product decisions. By substituting images for claims, the pictorial commercial made emotional appeal, not tests of truth, the basis of consumer decisions."[6]

By the 1960s and 1970s, advertising had worked wonders with many useless products through the right combination of Psychology 101 and images of happy, smiling people. But, while there had been a successful market aimed at woman for many years, it was not until relatively recently that modern advertising, relying no longer on the old tropes and gender-based assumptions, began to target women in a different way, especially now that women were a key part of the workplace. If older advertisements were based on the idea that women could buy products based on an irrational and emotional basis, then maybe the best way to appeal to a female marketplace was to approach women the way in which advertisers approached children: to infantilize the consumer and make them buy not just to own something, but also to feel safe.

Modern Advertising and Women

From the 1960s to the 1980s, as demographic-based surveys became more clear-cut, the advertising industry began to reexamine how they marketed products to women. As Joseph Turow argued, in terms of advertising to women, "it was clear to all ad and media practitioners, [that women] were being buffeted by tides of change that that were making splintering them more useful than ever" and "that new emphasis was needed to address working women more aggressively."[7] A realization began to grow amongst agencies that the standard approach of advertising for men and women, simply to add a pretty girl next to a product, was no longer going to work in a world in which the women's movement had substantially changed the market for products aimed at women. As Gloria Steinem recalled about the founding of *Ms.* magazine, and about how the difficulties in getting companies to advertise in it, "car makers were still draping blondes in evening gowns over the hoods like ornaments. Authority figures were almost always male, even in ads for products that only women used."[8] The point was not who the product was geared to, but that the standard practice was that a beautiful woman was an essential element in advertising as a whole. Sut Jhally noted that the use of sexuality in advertising was useful to advertisers because "sexuality provides a resource that can be used to get attention and communicate instantly. Within this sexuality is also a powerful component of gender that again lends itself even easier to imagistic representation."[9]

In his seminal work on advertising that features women (whether for products geared toward women or men) sociologist Erving Goffman noted that similar themes, including placement, size, and power relations, are common to most advertising. As Goffman noted, common themes included women receiving "bodily-addressed help or service from another" women "are more commonly pictured receiving this type of help from men than giving it to them."[10]

Also, in what Goffman calls "The Ritualization of Subordination," women (as well as children) are often pictured literally below or smaller than the man around them, sometimes giving outright deference. In particular, Goffman also noted a series of advertisements with women lounging on beds or couches smiling at the presumably male viewer. Goffman noted that time and time again in advertisements, lying on a sofa or bed could be "a conventionalized expression of sexual availability" where the point of the advertisements is not to show deference in general, but sexual deference in particular.[11]

While Goffman's work was done in the 1970s, modern media critics have argued that not only has little changed, but that the sexualization and infantilization of women has increased. Jean Kilbourne, one of the most visible critics of modern advertising, has argued, "advertising encourages us not only to objectify ourselves, but to feel that our most significant relationships are with the products we buy. It turns lovers into things and things into lovers and encourages us to feel passion for our products rather than our partners."[12] To Kilbourne, advertising does not just use women's bodies as props to sell products; it also tries to create a sense of emotional resonance with products that seems strangely as fulfilling, if not more, than relationships with people. Kilbourne argues, "advertising corrupts relationships and then offers us products, both as solace and as substitutes for the intimate human connections we all want and need."[13]

Advertising, therefore, cannot be analyzed in terms of what it does directly, but in what kinds of truths it offers about our place in the world. Therefore, looking at the logic or consistency of modern advertising is a futile approach. Commercials, no matter how skillfully made, do not make us do anything unless we have some kind of emotional relationship with the product being advertised, and some perceived need that the product fulfills. This is particularly true with the many advertisements for products (shampoos, weight-loss products, makeup, etc.) that can be advertised as correctives to a perceived weakness. It is not that programs or advertisements geared toward women cause women to have negative body images and low self-esteem; just that they contribute to an environment where these ideas are rationalized and seen as normal. Also, it seems clear that women also have an interconnected role in that they use media for many purposes, and the danger is that they buy into one of the mythologies about body and help perpetuate these ideas.

In particular, it is the idea of feminine perfection and eternal youth that are codified through advertising and mediated images and perpetuated by women themselves. As Susan Douglas noted, "we have loved the media as much as we have hated them—and often at exactly the same time."[14] This reciprocal relationship, where programming and magazines are geared toward women, some essentially marketed as "guilty pleasures," serves to reinforce contradictory or unhealthy ideas about beauty and body images. As Douglas also noted, there is an internal ambivalence in many women about the many "roles" they are asked to play—"wife," mother," friend," boss," etc. Through socialization and media, women have "grown accustomed to compartmentalizing ourselves into a whole host of personas, which we occupy simultaneously."[15]

This coincides with a peak in advertising toward women in which, according to Douglas, "we were the first generation of preteen and teenage girls to be isolated as a distinct market segment. Advertisers and their clients wanted to convey a sense of entitlement, and a sense of generational power, because those attitudes on our part meant profits for them."[16] This led to an increasing focus on selling not just products, but images and a sense of self that could be achieved through buying the right products. Or, in the words of Douglas, women find that "our deepest aspirations and anxieties are carefully, relentlessly researched. Then they are repackaged and sold back to us as something we can get simply by watching or buying."[17]

While advertising changed decade by decade, from trivializing women or making them childlike, starting in the 1980s and continuing in many ways to the present day, was the idea that consumer goods were rewards for the schizophrenic work that women put into being productive providers of family life and at the workplace. As Douglas wrote, " 'I'm worth it' became the motto for the eighties women we saw in television and magazine ads. Endless images of women lounging on tiled verandas, or snuggling with their white angora cats while wearing white silk pajamas, exhorted us to be self-indulgent, self-centered, private, hedonistic."[18] As Michael Schudson noted, when advertising works, it "works *in concert* with other tools of marketing and it attacks the attentions of consumers who are simultaneously influenced by product information from a wide variety of other sources" (emphasis original).[19] The prevalent tendency in modern culture, not just modern marketing, helped create an environment where this logic of the advertising campaign could become naturalized. This even worked with the counterculture, as advertisers even saw that they could use a contemporary social movement such as women's liberation to sell products, as "women's liberation became equated with women's ability to do whatever they wanted for themselves, whenever they wanted, no matter what the expense. These ads were geared towards women who had made it in a man's world, or hoped that she would, and the message was, reward yourself, you deserve it."[20]

This was also tied into another factor, insecurity. In the dualistic messages of many advertisements geared toward women, they were assured over and over again that they deserved pampering, indulgence, and luxury. But this was countered by an ever-increasing emphasis on youth, or at least trying to hold onto youth as long as possible, most likely before you were supplanted by someone younger and prettier in their job or family. As Douglas noted, many new ads were "designed to convey one basic message: you get what you pay for, and if you scrimp on skin care products, you get what you deserve—crow's feet eye bags, turkey neck, the worst. Fail to spend $42.50 on one thirty-second of an ounce of skin cream and the next time you look in the mirror you'll see Lyndon Johnson in drag."[21] While the topical reference may have changed, the dichotomy in which women are told to pamper themselves but, as long as they buy these expensive products, they will look young and appeal to men has stayed relatively consistent.

This has led to a problem with body image in which even healthy women observe themselves in the mirror, all she can see staring back is a bundle of horrific imperfection and "all we can feel are disgust and shame."[22] Media critic Neil Postman, author of *Amusing Ourselves to Death*, argued that we risk falling for the idea that commercials present—that all problems, no matter how personal, moral, or spiritual, can be solved by buying into the idea that happiness is something that can—and should—be bought. As Postman wrote, "the commercial asks us to believe that all problems are solvable, that they are solvable fast, and that they are solvable fast though the interventions of technology, technique and chemistry"[23] and that "what the advertiser needs to know is not what is right with the product, but what is wrong with the buyer."[24]

To summarize, most media critics agree that what advertising does is twofold: it preys on perceived flaws in our bodies, and it presents a world of consumption for the answer to complex questions about who we are and what should matter in our lives. As Schudson noted, "Advertising picks up some of the things that people hold dear and re-presents them as *all* of what they value, assuring them that the sponsor is the patron of common ideals" (emphasis in original).[25] Sociologist Stuart Ewen agreed, writing that, "Without ever saying so explicitly, the media of style offer to lift the viewer out of his or her life and place him or her in a utopian netherworld where there are no conflicts, no needs unmet; where the ordinary is—by its very nature—extraordinary."[26]

In her book, *The Beauty Myth*, feminist critic Naomi Wolf critiques what she sees as how "[a]dvertising aimed at women works by lowering our self-esteem. If it flatters our self-esteem, it is not effective. Let's abandon this hope of looking to the index to include us. It won't, because if it does, it's lost its function. As long as the definition of 'beauty' comes from outside women, we will continue to be manipulated by it"[27] and that "as long as prime time TV and the mainstream press aimed at women are supported by beauty advertisers, the story line of how women are [depicted] in mass culture will be dictated by the beauty myth."[28] But the idea of the Beauty Myth, the ideal of perfection that can be achieved only through consumption cannot work unless it is supported by an overall environment that encourages consumption. Environments where changing the channel or watching a different commercial will not offer alternatives, but instead reaffirm an environment that is as consistent as it is toxic.

Advertising and Environments

In his seminal work on television, *Amusing Ourselves to Death*, Postman railed against an environment that trivialized the serious and lauded the silly that degraded the written word in favor of the inarguable image. While Postman's critique was about television in general, he took particular aim at television commercials and their contribution to a world closer to Huxley's

Brave New World than the Orwellian nightmare of *1984*. As Postman noted, "the television commercial has oriented business away from making products of value and toward making consumers feel valuable, which means the business of business has now become pseudo-therapy. The consumer is a patient assured by psycho-dramas."[29] Commercials do not just sell products, they help maintain an environment that is naturalized and that asks us not to consider how illogical and bizarre the narratives presented by commercials are in reality. As Postman also wrote, "It is a very bad commercial that engages the viewer in wondering about the validity of the point being made." Postman compared commercials to biblical "pseudo-parables," in the sense that they were not telling you much about a product (if at all), but were instead providing a moral lesson on how one should live their life via consumerism. As Postman further noted, "the television commercial is about products only in the sense that the story of Jonah is about the anatomy of a whale, which is to say, it isn't."[30]

Even if one rejects Postman's argument about how commercials help reinforce consumerism in terms of a moral judgment, cultural studies critics also argue that advertising has become a major factor in how we live our lives. As Sut Jhally wrote, "the marketplace (and its major ideological tool, advertising) is the major structuring institution of contemporary society,"[31] and as a result of this, "advertising is ubiquitous—it is the air that we breathe as we live our daily lives."[32]

To sum up the idea of advertising as an environment helps us to ask questions about what kind of an environment we live in, and how healthy is that environment. Yes, goods and services (especially food) can be the source of great happiness. But, to equate advertising not as satisfying a want, but instead as satisfying a need, is where that overall environment begins to look more like a poisonous cloud rather than a sunny vista—especially when the subject of the advertising is for women and girls. While preying on weaknesses already emphasized in other forms of society and mass media, advertising tells us how we should live our lives, and in the words of Jhally, "[f]fundamentally advertising talks to us as individuals and addresses us about how we can become happy. The answers it provides are all oriented to the marketplace, through the purchase of goods or services."[33] As previously mentioned, advertising critic Jean Kilbourne, in her many books and documentaries, specifically decries what she sees as the way in which commercialism and ubiquitous advertising, "creates a toxic society. Advertising corrupts us and … promotes a dissociative state that exploits trauma and leads to addiction."[34] In particular, advertising geared toward women leads to a world where "advertising promotes a corrupt and bankrupt idea concept of relationship" and "promises us things that will deliver when in fact they never can."[35] As the old cigarette ad boldly congratulated women, "You've come a long way, baby," but to *where* be the question.

Conclusion

Despite the negativity toward advertising expressed by many of its fiercest academic critics, most do not advocate a life of total abstinence from advertising, or even media; just more careful choices as well as a critical mindset in engaging with mass media and advertising. Jean Kilbourne argued that the only way to get away from the messages promoted by advertising is to "get past the cultural belief, promoted so heavily by advertising, that there is a quick fix, an instant solution to every problem."[36]

Anne Elizabeth Moore, the activist who wrote one of the quintessential books on the co-option of underground movements, *Unmarketable*, tried in her book to create strategies to fight the dominance of corporately created pseudo-environments. As she put it in summing up her work, she was trying to create an "effective language of dissent. Their language does not include brand names or corporate funding, and must take place in spaces that are already owned. Some things must remain unmarketable, and our ability to speak for ourselves, in the modes of communication that we have developed to register dissent, should be one of them."[37] For women and girls, this would work through realizing that specific products will only give momentary happiness, that some advertising can be toxic, and that we can only really find happiness through self-reflection and introspection. It would be healthier if the environments maintained by advertising can be ignored, or even become laughable. While there will always be ads geared at telling women and girls that there is something wrong with them that the product alone can cure, by developing ways to opt out of this environment, women need not live in a world in which people are told that the only source of happiness is at the store.

Notes

1. Michael Schudson, *Advertising, the Uneasy Persuasion: Its Dubious Impact on American Society* (New York: Basic Books, 1986), xx.

2. Bernays *literally* wrote the book on propaganda. Edward Bernays, *Propaganda* (New York: Ig Publishing, 2005), originally published in 1928 and finally reissued in 2005.

3. Roland Marchand, *Advertising the American Dream: Making Way for Modernity, 1920–1940* (Berkeley: University of California Press, 1985), 66.

4. Ibid., 67.

5. Schudson, *Advertising*, 61

6. Neil Postman, *Amusing Ourselves to Death: Public Discourse in the Age of Show Business* (New York: Penguin 1986), 128.

7. Joseph Turow, *Breaking Up America: Advertisers and the New Media World* (Chicago: University of Chicago Press, 1997), 63.

8. Gloria Steinem, "Sex, Lies and Advertising," in *Gender, Race and Class in Media: A Text-Reader*, ed. Gail Dines and Jean Lond Humez (Thousand Oaks, CA: Sage, 2003), 224.

9. Sut Jhally, "Image-Based Culture: Advertising and Popular Culture," in *Gender, Race and Class in Media: A Text-Reader*, ed. Gail Dines and Jean Lond Humez (Thousand Oaks, CA: Sage, 2003), 253.

10. Erving Goffman, *Gender Advertisements* (New York: Harper and Row, 1979), 34.

11. Ibid., 41.

12. Jean Kilbourne, *Can't Buy My Love: How Advertising Changes the Way We Think and Feel* (New York: Touchstone Books, 1999), 27.

13. Ibid., 26

14. Susan Douglas, *Where the Girls Are: Growing Up Female with the Mass Media* (New York: Times Books 1995),12.

15. Ibid., 13.

16. Ibid., 14.

17. Ibid., 15.

18. Ibid., 244.

19. Schudson, *Advertising*, 16.

20. Douglas, *Where the Girls Are*, 246.

21. Ibid., 252.

22. Ibid., 264.

23. Postman, *Amusing Ourselves to Death*, 130.

24. Ibid., 128.

25. Schudson, *Advertising*, 233.

26. Stuart Ewen, *All Consuming Images: The Politics of Style in Contemporary Culture* (New York: Basic Books, 1988), 14.

27. Naomi Wolf, *The Beauty Myth: How Images of Beauty Are Used against Women* (New York: Anchor Books, 1991), 276–77.

28. Ibid., 278.

29. Postman, *Amusing Ourselves to Death*, 128.

30. Ibid., 131.

31. Jhally, "Image-Based Culture," 250.

32. Ibid., 250–51.

33. Ibid., 251.

34. Kilbourne, *Can't Buy My Love*, 56.

35. Ibid., 77.

36. Ibid., 292–93.

37. Anne Elizabeth Moore, *Unmarketable: Brandalism, Copyfighting, Mocketing and the Erosion of Integrity* (New York: New Press, 2007), 215.

Bibliography

Douglas, Susan. *Where the Girls Are: Growing Up Female with the Mass Media.* New York: Times Books 1995.

Ewen, Stuart. *All Consuming Images: The Politics of Style in Contemporary Culture.* New York: Basic Books, 1988.

Goffman, Erving. *Gender Advertisements.* New York: Harper and Row, 1979.

Jhally, Sut. "Image-Based Culture: Advertising and Popular Culture." In *Gender, Race and Class in Media: A Text-Reader*, edited by Gail Dines and Jean Lond Humez, 249–57. Thousand Oaks, CA: Sage, 2003.

Kilbourne, Jean. *Can't Buy My Love: How Advertising Changes the Way We Think and Feel.* New York: Touchstone Books, 1999.

Marchand, Roland. *Advertising the American Dream: Making Way for Modernity, 1920–1940.* Berkeley: University of California Press, 1985.

Moore, Anne Elizabeth. *Unmarketable: Brandalism, Copyfighting, Mocketing and the Erosion of Integrity.* New York: New Press, 2007.

Postman, Neil. *Amusing Ourselves to Death: Public Discourse in the Age of Show Business.* New York: Penguin, 1986.

Schudson, Michael. *Advertising, the Uneasy Persuasion: Its Dubious Impact on American Society.* New York: Basic Books, 1986.

Steinem, Gloria. "Sex, Lies and Advertising." In *Gender, Race and Class in Media: A Text-Reader*, edited by Gail Dines and Jean Lond Humez, 223–29. Thousand Oaks, CA: Sage, 2003.

Wolf, Naomi. *The Beauty Myth: How Images of Beauty Are Used against Women.* New York: Anchor Books, 1991.

Turow, Joseph. *Breaking Up America: Advertisers and the New Media World.* Chicago: University of Chicago Press, 1997.

CHAPTER FIVE

Controversy in Advertising to Children

Jennifer L. McCullough

Advertising surrounds people in every aspect of their lives. Although there is some public concern about how media-saturated our lives have become, the public also worry about the ethics of advertising to children and the potential negative consequences of such advertising. A 2005 study found that children ages 8 to 18 spend over six hours a day using media and spend around three hours watching television each day.[1] Given this, they are exposed to an enormous amount of advertising on a daily basis from television alone.

In fact, in their 2007 study, Walter Gantz, Nancy Schwartz, James Angelini, and Victoria Rideout estimated that children between two and seven years of age see close to 14,000 television advertisements per year, while children ages 8 to 12 see more than 30,000 per year.[2] Even this number is on the conservative side, given the increase in technology and diversification of where advertising has begun to appear. Product placement, school promotions and sponsorship, in-store displays, and online advergames also expose children to a significant amount of advertising even if they are unable to recognize it as such. Although research looking into how frequently children are exposed to advertising in these other mediums is rare, a recent study found that during a 15-minute Internet searching session, children ages 9 to 15 had the potential to be exposed to 132 advertisements on average.[3] This count did not include any advertisements that might occur during online games. Children also are exposed to advertising in school through such places as school buses, books, and Channel One.[4]

Although the sheer amount of advertising directed at children is one of the more significant public concerns, there are other issues causing controversy that this chapter will explore in greater detail. Researchers have tried to address these issues, including how children process advertising and the possible unintended negative effects the ads can have on children. These findings reveal the major reasons behind the growing public concern in advertising to children and provide insight into what the people in a child's environment might do to help curb the impact of advertising.

Overview of Advertising Research on Children

As Bryant Jennings and Ellen Wartella note, a majority of the research on children and advertising was conducted in the 1970s and 1980s.[5] Below, the seminal pieces of this area, along with some of the more current studies, will be examined. First, the common features of advertising and the processing of advertising will be covered.

Common Features

One concern in advertising to children is the actual content of the advertising. Therefore, researchers have explored the common features children's advertising contains. One of these important features is the actual product being advertised. Earle Barcus found that more than 80 percent of all advertisements directed at children featured toys, cereal, candy, or fast food restaurants.[6] Toy advertisements are generally found to be seasonal; in other words, toys are advertised most heavily around Christmas. However, the rest of the year, cereal and candy commercials are the most frequent.[7] These findings were supported in a study conducted by the Federal Trade Commission in 2004, which found that 43 percent of all advertising directed at children were for sedentary products (e.g., toys, games, screen entertainment, and promos) and 21.6 percent were for food.[8]

Another common feature of children's advertising is the themes commercials tend to encompass. Researchers have found that most commercials emphasized the fun or happiness the product could provide (i.e., socially desirable attributes) and rarely emphasized the product features (i.e., how a product works).[9] A final common feature that many researchers have cited is the use of product disclosures and disclaimers such as "each part sold separately" or "part of a balanced diet." These are used to help curb the public concern of deceptive advertising. However, research has shown that these disclaimers are not understood by young children.[10]

Processing of Advertising

While some researchers have studied the common features of children's advertising, others have explored how much children comprehend those features. The vulnerability of children because of their lack of comprehension is a major controversy in advertising to this population. Many feel that because children are not able to fully comprehend advertising, they are more vulnerable to the persuasive appeals and need to be protected.

This area of study centers around two different cognitive skills needed to understand advertising messages fully. The first is the ability to distinguish between the commercial and the program. Researchers have found that around the ages of four or five, children are able to discern if they are watching a commercial or a program.[11] However, Dale Kunkel points out that distinguishing between a commercial and a program does not necessarily mean the child understands the commercial is not a part of the plot of the program.[12]

This understanding is not helped by bumpers. These devices, which say things like "We'll be right back after these messages," are designed to help children know when a program has stopped and a commercial is about to begin. However, research reveals that these do not help children because the bumpers do not seem to be different than the programming.[13] In fact, they sometimes use characters from the show to deliver the message.

The second ability needed to fully comprehend an advertisement is the ability to recognize the persuasive intent of advertisements. This capability requires the capacity to appreciate the advertiser's perspective. Several researchers have emphasized the fact that children under the age of seven have difficulty taking the perspective of another person because they are perceptually bound and egocentric.[14] Because children are perceptually bound, when they receive information, they focus on the visually salient images and concrete examples. This is why even very young children are able to recognize brands since they are visual cues that do not require interpretation.[15] Furthermore, since children of this age are egocentric, they process the information only in terms of how it is useful to them.

Therefore, if the children are unable to take the perspective of the advertiser, then they have difficulty recognizing what the goal of the advertiser is. Because of this cognitive limitation, much of the research indicates that children under the age of seven do not have the ability to ascertain the persuasive intent of advertisements.[16] What is more, when researchers measure persuasive intent, it is defined literally as the child knowing the advertiser was trying to sell them something.

This definition is conceptually different from recognizing that the messages in an advertisement might be biased.[17] It is not known when children are able to discern this information. Therefore, children may understand that advertisers want to sell them something but not understand that in order to do so, they may skew the presentation of products. In order to critically view commercials, children need to understand both the persuasive intent and inherent biases in advertising. If children understand these potential biases, then they may be more skeptical of advertising than if they only know that the advertiser is trying to get them to buy something.

These skills are even more difficult to master in today's media environment. The growing use of product placement and advergaming has created more complex media for children to process. Research on children's understanding of these areas still needs to be conducted. However, given the developmental issues discussed above, it can be predicted that young children (and perhaps older children as well) may find it difficult to understand that companies use product placement with the intent of persuading the audience to like or use their products. In addition, the websites and advergames children are exposed to online may make it more difficult to distinguish between new content and advertising, particularly when this media can be interactive.

Advertising is still a source of entertainment for younger children, largely because they still prefer fast-paced content.[18] In addition, although children between the ages of five and eight are able to distinguish between commercials and programming, they do not yet understand the persuasive intent of commercials. Combined, these perceptions could lead children to pay as much attention to the commercials as they do to an actual program.

As children get older, around the age of nine, their development allows them to consider multiple features of an item and multiple perspectives of the consumption of that item.[19] These developments allow children to recognize why commercials exist and why the messages presented in them are framed the way they are. Another major developmental milestone at this age is the child's ability to understand the social significance of material goods.[20] Not only can children recognize brands, but they also understand the status associated with these brands. At this stage, children are now able to form impressions of commercials and products based on social comparison and group norms.

Consumer Development

In addition to the work on the developmental differences of the processing of advertising, it is important to consider the development of children into consumers—especially since the commercialization of children is one of the larger public concerns. Patti Valkenburg and Joanne Cantor's descriptive model of this process allows researchers to begin to understand when children may be vulnerable to the negative effects of advertising.[21] The researchers explain that prior to age two, children merely are developing their own wants and preferences based on awareness. Therefore, this awareness could be created and/or exacerbated by advertising exposure.

In the toddler years, children begin to make requests for specific products.[22] As requests increase, there is an increase in parent-child conflict due to disappointments. What is more, at this age, children also have developed gender-typed schemas that guide their specific requests for and play with "sex-appropriate" toys.[23] These schemas can be reinforced and altered by television exposure.[24] Therefore, advertising exposure could be altering what children see as appropriate for themselves.

By the time children reach elementary school, their gender stereotypes already have been constructed.[25] These include what roles each gender should have and what types of things each gender is capable of doing. Also, children are becoming more independent consumers.[26] Combined, these studies could indicate that upon reaching elementary school, children already are prepared to begin purchasing items that they feel society has deemed appropriate for them. Plus, around age four is when children begin making independent purchases, and by age five, most have made such a purchase despite their inability to comprehend the advertisers' intent.[27]

This feeling of social pressure emerges on a more visible front by the time children reach late elementary school. According to Valkenburg and Cantor, this stage of consumer development emphasizes conformity.[28] This social conformity coincides with children's ability to role-take and decenter, two skills that help children take the perspective of other people and focus less on themselves. With these abilities, material goods now potentially have social value to children. In fact, at this age, children begin to prefer products that can lead to social interaction, like music.[29] Therefore, what children see on television at this stage could not only impact their preferences, but also how they feel other people think about the things being advertised.

Unintended Effects of Advertising

Even if children do not comprehend the purpose of advertising, the commercials still may have both intended and unintended effects. The obvious intended effects of most commercials are to establish brand preference, product desire, and eventually product purchase. However, the unintended effects could have a larger impact and are what cause more controversy. When a child is exposed to an enormous amount of advertising, the combined themes and images used could have a greater influence than just one advertisement trying to sell one product. Poor eating habits, more positive attitudes about alcohol, parent-child conflict, and materialistic attitudes are all unintended effects resulting from advertising exposure. Each of these will be reviewed in turn below.

Poor Eating Habits

It is not surprising that one of these unintended effects of advertising is the influence advertisements can have on a child's eating habits given the propensity of children's advertising to focus on food and candy. Public concern over this negative, unintended effect stems from research, which indicates eating habits started in childhood frequently are carried on through a person's adult life.[30] In addition, the percentage of children who are at risk of being overweight is increasing each year.[31] Other research has suggested that the increase in childhood obesity corresponds to the growing trend of advertising unhealthy foods to kids.[32]

To begin looking at the potential causes of children's poor eating habits, correlational research has found that those children who reported more frequent viewing also reported higher consumption of candy, sugared cereal, and advertised foods.[33] What is more, experimental research also has shown this relationship between commercial viewing and poor eating habits. Charles Atkin and Wendy Gibson exposed one group of children to a Pebbles cereal commercial while the control group was not exposed to the commercial.[34] Ninety percent of the experimental group wanted to eat the cereal, compared to 67 percent of the control group. In another experiment, Gerald Gorn and Marvin Goldberg exposed one group of children to commercials for candy and Kool-Aid, and another group to commercials for fruit and fruit juice.[35] They found that children's eating choices at camp were significantly influenced by the advertisements that they viewed.

Positive Attitudes about Alcohol

In 2009, the Centers for Disease Control and Prevention conducted their youth risk behavior surveillance and found that in the previous 30 days, 42 percent of high school students drank some alcohol and 24 percent binge-drank.[36] This is incredibly problematic for several reasons. Researchers have found that binge drinking correlates with poor school performance and participating in other risky behaviors such as smoking, using drugs, and attempting suicide.[37] What is more, self-reported alcohol advertising exposure has been positively related to alcohol use among youth.[38] Although these studies do not show causality, Leslie Snyder, Frances

Fleming Milici, Michael Slater, Helen Sun, and Yuliya Strizhakova sought to answer that question by comparing the alcohol advertising expenditures on television, radio, billboards, and newspapers in the top 75 media markets to the self-reported number of alcoholic drinks consumed in the previous month by youth in those markets.[39] The researchers found that increased advertising exposure was related to increased consumption of alcoholic drinks. For every additional advertisement, drinking increased by 1 percent per person, and drinking levels were higher for youth living in markets that spent the most on advertising per capita.[40]

Given this, what does alcohol advertising to children look like? Alcohol advertising has become more and more prominent on television. Victor Strasburger explains that although advertisers claim they do not specifically target an underage audience, there is a recent increase in alcoholic beverages that are more sugary and an increase in alcohol advertising during sports programming, which has a large youth audience.[41] According to a recent study from the Center on Alcohol Marketing and Youth, from 2001 to 2009, over $8 billion was spent in alcohol advertising on television alone.[42] In addition, 32 percent of alcohol advertisements on radio occurred on programs to which more children were listening than adults.[43] These are only some of the reasons why people have begun to question the impact advertising may be having on children's positive attitudes about alcohol and drinking.

The question then becomes whether this exposure really does impact children. Unfortunately, children's brand awareness does not stop with toys. In one study, 9- and 10-year-old children were able to recognize the Budweiser Frogs as much as Bugs Bunny.[44] Several studies have found that viewing of alcohol advertising correlates with favorable attitudes toward drinking.[45] What is even more alarming is that exposure to advertising has been shown to lead to drinking behavior in adolescence.[46]

Parent-Child Conflict

Parent-child conflict is defined as any disagreement or arguing that takes place between the parent and the child. One situation in which parent-child conflict often arises is when a child's purchase requests have been denied. Several cross-sectional studies have reported correlations between reported purchase request, denial of that toy or food request, and subsequent conflict.[47] In fact, Patti Valkenburg and Joanne Cantor reported that 70 percent of parents with five-year-old children have experienced a purchase-related conflict in a store with their child.[48] Furthermore, they found that 63 percent of parents of six-year-olds and 66 percent of parents with seven-year-olds experienced this situation.[49]

Due to the public's concern for these disagreements, researchers began looking at potential sources of influence that lead children to make the purchase requests in the first place. The media was one source that researchers investigated, and studies have reported positive correlations between reported exposure to advertising and purchase requests.[50] Additional survey research also found a direct link between exposure to advertising and parent-child conflict.[51] In an observational study, Charles Atkin found that children expressed high rates of disappointment and anger as a result of a parent's refusal to buy cereal at the grocery store.[52] Experimental research also found a positive relationship between exposure to commercials and increased purchase requests.[53] Taken together, these studies seem to indicate that exposure to advertising increases purchase requests. As a result of those purchase requests or as a direct result of exposure to advertising, there are increases in parent-child conflict.

Materialistic Attitudes

Materialism is another unintended effect of advertising exposure. Often, it is defined as the fixation on possessions. In other words, they are attitudes that place belongings and money at a central place in the person's life. Materialistic attitudes also have been said to lead to rising living standards, chaotic lifestyles, and little saving.[54] Moreover, research shows that materialism can lead to negative psychological outcomes such as lower self-esteem and lower life satisfaction.[55]

With all of these negative outcomes associated with materialism, researchers questioned whether advertising partially causes such beliefs. These questions in particular arise because television influences values and conceptions of reality by providing mediated images of rewards and consequences that can indicate social expectations and acceptance.[56] In support of this claim, experimental research has found that more materialistic attitudes are in part caused by exposure to television commercials.[57] Although these experiments may lack high levels of external validity, some surveys have shown that increased viewing of advertisements is correlated with higher levels of materialism.[58]

Curbing the Negative Effects of Advertising

Government Regulation

One of the possible ways to mitigate these negative effects is through the help of the government. Even though the government passed the Children's Television Act of 1990 to restrict the amount of advertising per hour during children's programming, little can be done to restrict advertising in general, although the Federal Communication Commission (FCC) and the Federal Trade Commission (FTC) have both considered it. This is not only in part because of the First Amendment, but also because corporations have such large economic resources. Still, the FCC has kept the time limit set at 10 minutes and 30 seconds of advertising per hour on weekends and 12 minutes per hour on weekdays. Putting this into perspective, Australia, Canada, and Great Britain have all banned television advertising directed at children.[59] That being said, any sort of government regulation in the private sector often causes controversy.

Industry Regulation

Given the lack of power organizations such as the FCC have over advertisers, it is important to note that the industry itself has set up guidelines for ethical advertising due to public concern. These guidelines are set up by the Children's Advertising Review Unit (CARU), which is a part of the National Council of Better Business Bureaus. These guidelines range from how the product is presented in the commercial to how much sales pressure is applied in the commercial. Overall, most of the guidelines are too general or vague to be tested empirically.[60] Therefore, although it is a step that the industry has decided they will at least formalize a self-regulating attempt, there is no economic or legal consequence to advertisers should they not conform to the regulations. Some parents believe that economic sanctions would be the only way advertisers would truly conform, but this proposal is controversial.

Media Literacy

In addition to the government and industry regulations, the education system also could be used to help socialize consumer behavior in children. Some schools have begun to encourage the integration of media literacy into their curriculums. Media literacy is defined as the critical viewing perspective through which one approaches the media.[61] Therefore, these programs usually involve a series of lessons that are designed to increase a child's understanding of the media. In addition, schools often have units that help children learn particular consumer skills such as the value of money, how to make purchases, or general economics. The combination of these trends creates an ideal environment to help children learn about the impact of the media on their consumer knowledge, attitudes, and behaviors.

In one such program, Thomas Robinson, Melissa Saphir, Helena Kraemer, Ann Varady, and Farish Haydel tested a media literacy curriculum that targeted third- and fourth-grade children in an effort to reduce their overall exposure to television.[62] The curriculum, consisting of 18 lessons over six months, encouraged children to reduce the time they spent with media and take part in other activities. In doing so, they found, as a result of viewing less television overall, those children who received the curriculum were less likely to make product requests than those children who did not receive the curriculum. Although this is encouraging, most media literacy curriculums have focused on critical viewing skills. In testing the effectiveness of these programs, most research measured and found that those children exposed to the curriculums were better able to recognize the persuasive intent of advertising.[63] However, it is important to note that these programs all used children eight years of age and older.

One media literacy curriculum went beyond instructing children to recognize persuasive intent and looked at how a media literacy curriculum could impact the desirability of the advertised products. Seymour Feshbach, Norma Feshbach, and Sarale Cohen tested a curriculum designed to increase children's understanding of the advertising process and techniques.[64] They found that second- and fourth-graders who had completed the curriculum desired the advertised products in commercials they were shown less than those children who had not been exposed to the curriculum. This indicates that with older children, the schools could have some power over influencing not only the understanding of persuasive intent but also the desirability of products. In spite of these findings on the effectiveness of media literacy programs, it is a controversial idea to incorporate this content into an already full school day because media literacy programs take extensive amounts of time and cooperation to fully enrich the children with the knowledge needed to critique television on their own.

Parental Interactions

In addition to possible laws and curriculum changes, the more realistic option may be for parents to discuss the advertisements their children are viewing. In fact, researchers have argued that the two greatest influences on consumer socialization are the media and the family.[65] There is some research that looks at how family consumer communication impacts how children interpret and react to advertising. This research indicates that there are two general dimensions of family consumer communication. The first is concept orientation, which emphasizes the expression of individual opinions and ideas. The other is socio-orientation, which emphasizes the obedience to authority and getting along with others.[66]

A series of studies found that those families that had a more concept-oriented communication style had children who were better able to understand the advertising techniques used in the commercials.[67] Additionally, these children also exhibited lower materialistic attitudes, fewer purchase requests, and fewer parent-child conflicts than children from socio-oriented families.[68] However, again, all of these studies were conducted with children over the age of eight. Therefore, researchers are still unsure as to what type of consumer communication might be more prevalent and effective in families with younger children.

Although this general consumer communication has an impact on how children interpret advertising, one type of parental communication might be even more direct when it comes to mitigating the effects of advertising. According to Patti Valkenburg, Marina Krcmar, Allerd Peeters, and Nies Marseille, adult mediation can be divided into three different types: restrictive mediation, coviewing, and active mediation.[69]

First, restrictive mediation is simply making rules as to what a child is allowed to watch. These rules could include the amount of time a child is allowed to watch television, when a child is able to watch, or the content or specific shows a child is not allowed to watch. The next possible solution is coviewing. In the literature, coviewing is defined as watching television with a child. Active mediation is the final strategy, and it is the discussion of the content that is being presented on television. Discussion can range from themes shown in programs to those presented in television advertisements.

In advertising mediation, restrictive mediation entails limiting the amount of commercial exposure. Although new technology is making this more possible, children are inundated with commercials even outside the home, so this might not be the most practical solution. The active mediation of advertising content involves comments made about the commercials or more specific explanations about the persuasive intent of the commercials.

Research on advertising mediation, particularly that which focuses on younger children, has been conducted only recently. Moneik Buijzen and Patti Valkenburg were interested in materialistic attitudes, purchase requests, and parent-child conflict.[70] In their survey of 360 parent-child dyads, they found that those parents who did not use active mediation of advertising were much more likely to have children that expressed materialistic attitudes and made more purchase requests than those children receiving active mediation.

In a study more theoretically grounded, Moneik Buijzen introduced a model of advertising mediation.[71] Results revealed that factual mediation (i.e., "These commercials are intended to sell.") reduced advertising persuasion by increasing skepticism and knowledge of persuasive intent. Furthermore, evaluative mediation (i.e., "These commercials are stupid.") reduced advertising persuasion by influencing the children's attitudes toward commercials. However, this model only worked for older children. More recently, Jennifer Chakroff found that when discussing advertising with younger children, focusing on the desirability (or lack thereof) of a character could mitigate the effects of advertising exposure on children's materialistic attitudes.[72]

Conclusion

Overall, the major controversies in advertising to children result from the frequency and content of the advertising, the developmental abilities or lack thereof of children to process advertising, and the research that indicates some negative unintended effects of advertising on children. Each of the potential solutions to the negative effects of advertising comes with their own controversies. As researchers, the industry, policy makers, educators, and parents attempt to grapple with these issues, it is important to keep in mind that the consumer socialization of children is important. Many factors contribute to a child's understanding of advertising and the subsequent impact it may have on the child. That being said, given the type of advertising directed at children and their limited cognitive abilities to process that advertising, children remain a vulnerable population.

Notes

1. Donald F. Roberts, Ulla G. Foehr, and Victoria Rideout, *Generation M: Media in the Lives of 8–18 Year-Olds* (Menlo Park, CA: Kaiser Family Foundation, 2005).

2. Walter Gantz et al., *Food for Thought: Television Food Advertising to Children in the United States* (Menlo Park, CA: Kaiser Family Foundation, 2007).

3. Helena Sandberg, Kerstin Gidlof, and Nils Holmberg, "Children's Exposure to and Perceptions of Online Advertising," *International Journal of Communication* 5 (2001): 21–50.

4. J. I. Richards et al., "The Growing Commercialization of Schools: Issues and Practices," *ANNALS of the American Academy of Political and Social Science* 557, no. 1 (May 1, 1998): 148–63.

5. Nancy A. Jennings and Ellen A. Wartella, "Advertising and Consumer Development," in *Children and Television: Fifty Years of Research*, ed. Nancy Pecora, John P. Murray, and Ellen A. Wartella (London: Routledge, 2006), 149–82.

6. F. Earle Barcus, "The Nature of Television Advertising to Children," in *Children and the Faces of Television: Teaching, Violence, Selling*, ed. Edward L. Palmer and Aimee Dorr (New York: Academic Press, 1980), 273–85.

7. Charles Atkin and Gary Heald, "The Content of Children's Toy and Food Commercials," *Journal of Communication* 27, no. 1 (March 1977): 107–14.

8. Debra Holt et al., *Children's Exposure to TV Advertising in 1977 and 2004: Information for the Obesity Debate* (Washington, DC: Federal Trade Commission, 2007).

9. Barcus, "Nature of Television Advertising to Children"; Dale Kunkel and Walter Gantz, "Children's Television Advertising in the Multichannel Environment," *Journal of Communication* 42, no. 3 (September 1992): 134–52.

10. Diane E. Liebert et al., "Effects of Television Commercial Disclaimers on the Product Expectations of Children," *Journal of Communication* 27, no. 1 (March 1977): 118–24; Edward L. Palmer and Cynthia N. McDowell, "Children's Understanding of Nutritional Information Presented in Breakfast Cereal Commercials," *Journal of Broadcasting* 25, no. 3 (June 1981): 295–301.

11. S. Ward, G. Reale, and D. Levinson, "Children's Perceptions, Explanations, and Judgments of Television Advertising; A Further Exploration," in *Television and Social Behavior*, ed. George Comstock and Eli A. Rubinstein, vol. 4 (Washington DC: US Government Printing Office, 1972).

12. D. Kunkel, "Children and Host-Selling Television Commercials," *Communication Research* 15, no. 1 (February 1, 1988): 71–92.

13. Edward L. Palmer and Cynthia N. McDowell, "Program/Commercial Separators in Children's Television Programming," *Journal of Communication* 29, no. 3 (September 1979): 197–201.

14. John Flavell, *The Development of Role-Taking and Communication Skills in Children* (New York: Wiley, 1968); John C. Gibbs, *Moral Development and Reality: Beyond the Theories of Kohlberg and Hoffman* (Thousand Oaks, CA: Sage, 2003); Jean Piaget, *The Construction of Reality in the Child* (New York: Basic Books, 1954); Janet Strayer, "Children's Concordant Emotions and Cognitions in Response to Observed Emotions," *Child Development* 64, no. 1 (February 1993): 188–201.

15. M. Carole Macklin, "Preschoolers' Learning of Brand Names from Visual Cues," *Journal of Consumer Research* 23, no. 3 (December 1996): 251–61.

16. Dale Kunkel, "Children and Television Advertising," in *Handbook of Children and the Media*, ed. Dorothy G. Singer and Jerome L. Singer (Thousand Oaks, CA: Sage Publications, 2001), 375–93.

17. Brian M. Young, *Television Advertising and Children* (Oxford and New York: Clarendon Press, (Oxford University Press, 1990).

18. Dan S. Acuff and Robert H. Reiher, *What Kids Buy and Why: The Psychology of Marketing to Kids* (New York: Free Press, 1997).

19. Ibid.

20. Patti M. Valkenburg and Joanne Cantor, "The Development of a Child into a Consumer," *Journal of Applied Developmental Psychology* 22, no. 1 (January 2001): 61–72.

21. Ibid.

22. Ibid.

23. Nancy J. Cobb, Judith Stevens-Long, and Steven Goldstein, "The Influence of Televised Models on Toy Preference in Children," *Sex Roles* 8, no. 10 (October 1982): 1075–80.

24. Sandra Calvert and Aletha Huston, "Television and Children's Gender Schemata," in *Television and Children's Gender Schemata*, ed. Sandra Calvert and Aletha Huston (San Francisco: Jossey-Bass Inc., 1987), 75–88.

25. Ronald S. Drabman et al., "Children's Perception of Media-Portrayed Sex Roles," *Sex Roles* 7, no. 4 (April 1981): 379–89.

26. Valkenburg and Cantor, "Development of a Child into a Consumer."

27. Ibid.

28. Ibid.

29. Moniek Buijzen and Patti M. Valkenburg, "The Impact of Television Advertising on Children's Christmas Wishes," *Journal of Broadcasting and Electronic Media* 44, no. 3 (September 2000): 456–70.

30. Michael F. Jacobson and Bruce Maxwell, *What Are We Feeding Our Kids?* (New York: Workman Pub., 1994).

31. Kaiser Family Foundation, *The Role of Media in Childhood Obesity* (Menlo Park, CA: Author, February 2004).

32. Katherine Horgen, Molly Choate, and Kelly Brownell, "Television Food Advertising: Targeting Children in a Toxic Environment," in *Handbook of Children and the Media*, ed. Dorothy G. Singer and Jerome L. Singer (Thousand Oaks, CA: Sage Publications, 2011), 447–61.

33. Charles K. Atkin, "Effects of Television Advertising on Children," in *Children and the Faces of Television: Teaching, Violence, Selling*, ed. Edward L. Palmer and Aimee Dorr (New York: Academic Press, 1980), 287–304.

34. Charles K. Atkin and Wendy Gibson, *Children's Nutrition Learning from Television Advertising* (East Lansing: Michigan State University, Department of Communication, 1978).

35. Gerald J. Gorn and Marvin E. Goldberg, "Behavioral Evidence of the Effects of Televised Food Messages on Children," *Journal of Consumer Research* 9, no. 2 (September 1982): 200.

36. Centers for Disease Control and Prevention, *Youth Risk Behavior Surveillance —United States, 2009*, Morbidity and Mortality Surveillance Summary 2010, http://www.cdc.gov/mmwr/PDF/ss/ss5905.pdf.

37. J. W. Miller et al., "Binge Drinking and Associated Health Risk Behaviors among High School Students," *Pediatrics* 119, no. 1 (January 1, 2007): 76–85.

38. Charles Atkin, John Hocking, and Martin Block, "Teenage Drinking: Does Advertising Make a Difference?" *Journal of Communication* 34, no. 2 (June 1984): 157–67.

39. Leslie B. Snyder, "Effects of Alcohol Advertising Exposure on Drinking among Youth," *Archives of Pediatrics and Adolescent Medicine* 160, no. 1 (January 1, 2006): 18–24.

40. Ibid.

41. Victor C. Strasburger, "Children, Adolescents, Drugs, and the Media," in *Handbook of Children and the Media*, ed. Dorothy G. Singer and Jerome L. Singer (Thousand Oaks, CA: Sage Publications, 2001), 415–46.

42. Center on Alcohol Marketing and Youth, *Youth Exposure to Alcohol Advertising on Television, 2001–2009*, December 15, 2010, http://www.camy.org/research/Youth_Exposure_to_Alcohol_Ads_on_TV_Growing_Faster_Than_Adults/_includes/CAMYReport2001_2009.pdf.

43. Center on Alcohol Marketing and Youth, *Youth Exposure to Alcohol Product Advertising on Local Radio in 75 U.S. Markets, 2009*, September 13, 2011, http://www.camy.org/research/Youth_Exposure_to_Alcohol_Advertising_on_Local_Radio_2009/_includes/report.pdf.

44. L. Lieber, *Commercial and Character Slogan Recall by Children Aged 9 to 11 Years: Budweiser Frogs versus Bugs Bunny* (Berkeley, CA: Center on Alcohol Advertising, 1996).

45. Charles K. Atkin and Martin Block, "Effectiveness of Celebrity Endorsers," *Journal of Advertising Research* 23, no. 1 (1983): 57–61; Joel W. Grube and Lawrence Wallack, "Television Beer Advertising and Drinking Knowledge, Beliefs, and Intentions among School Children," *American Journal of Public Health* 84 (1994): 254–59.

46. Atkin and Block, "Effectiveness of Celebrity Endorsers"; Erica Weintraub Austin and Christopher Knaus, "Predicting the Potential for Risky Behavior among Those 'Too Young' to Drink as the Result of Appealing Advertising," *Journal of Health Communication* 5, no. 1 (January 2000): 13–27.

47. Thomas S. Robertson et al., "Advertising and Children: A Cross-Cultural Study," *Communication Research* 16, no. 4 (August 1, 1989): 459–85.

48. Valkenburg and Cantor, "The Development of a Child into a Consumer."

49. Ibid.

50. Buijzen and Valkenburg, "The Impact of Television Advertising on Children's Christmas Wishes"; Thomas S. Robertson and John R. Rossiter, "Short-Run Advertising Effects on Children: A Field Study," *Journal of Marketing Research* 13, no. 1 (February 1976): 68–70; Thomas S. Robertson and John R. Rossiter, "Children's Responsiveness to Commercials," *Journal of Communication* 27, no. 1 (March 1977): 101–6.

51. Charles K. Atkin, *Effects of Television Advertising on Children: Survey of Children's and Mother's Responses to Television Commercials* (East Lansing: Michigan State University, 1975); Charles K. Atkin, *Survey of Pre-Adolescent's Responses to Television Commercials: The Effects of Television Advertising on Children* (East Lansing: Michigan State University, 1975).

52. Charles K. Atkin, "Observation of Parent-Child Interaction in Supermarket Decision-Making," *Journal of Marketing* 42, no. 4 (October 1978): 41.

53. Marvin E. Goldberg and Gerald J. Gorn, "Some Unintended Consequences of TV Advertising to Children," *Journal of Consumer Research* 5, no. 1 (June 1978): 22; Zolinda Stoneman and Gene H. Brody, "The Indirect Impact of Child-Oriented

Advertisements," *Journal of Applied Developmental Psychology* 2, no. 4 (January 1981): 369–76.

54. Juliet B. Schor, *The Overspent American : Upscaling, Downshifting, and the New Consumer* (New York: Basic Books, 1998).

55. Russell Belk, "Three Scales to Measure Constructs Related to Materialism: Reliability, Validity, and Relationships to Measures of Happiness," *Advances in Consumer Research* 11 (n.d.): 291–97; Marsha L. Richins and Scott Dawson, "A Consumer Values Orientation for Materialism and Its Measurement: Scale Development and Validation," *Journal of Consumer Research* 19, no. 3 (December 1992): 303–16.

56. Albert Bandura, *Social Foundations of Thought and Action: A Social Cognitive Theory* (Englewood Cliffs, NJ: Prentice-Hall, 1986).

57. Bradley S. Greenberg and Jeffrey E. Brand, "Television News and Advertising in Schools: The 'Channel One' Controversy," *Journal of Communication* 43, no. 1 (March 1993): 143–51; Goldberg and Gorn, "Some Unintended Consequences of TV Advertising to Children."

58. Gilbert A. Churchill Jr. and George P. Moschis, "Television and Interpersonal Influences on Adolescent Consumer Learning," *Journal of Consumer Research* 6, no. 1 (June 1979): 23; Marsha L. Richins, "Media, Materialism, and Human Happiness," *Advances in Consumer Research* 14 (1987): 352–56.

59. Kunkel, "Children and Television Advertising."

60. Dale Kunkel and Walter Gantz, "Assessing Compliance with Industry Self-Regulation of Television Advertising to Children," *Journal of Applied Communication Research* 21, no. 2 (May 1993): 148–62.

61. W. James Potter, *Media Literacy* (Thousand Oaks, CA: Sage Publications, 1998).

62. Thomas N. Robinson et al., "Effects of Reducing Television Viewing on Children's Requests for Toys: A Randomized Controlled Trial," *Journal of Developmental and Behavioral Pediatrics* 22, no. 3 (June 2001): 179–84.

63. Merrie Brucks, Gary M. Armstrong, and Marvin E. Goldberg, "Children's Use of Cognitive Defenses against Television Advertising: A Cognitive Response Approach," *Journal of Consumer Research* 14, no. 4 (March 1988): 471; Thomas R. Donohue, Lucy L. Henke, and Timothy P. Meyer, "Learning about Television Commercials: The Impact of Instructional Units on Children's Perceptions of Motive and Intent," *Journal of Broadcasting* 27, no. 3 (June 1983): 251–61; Lizette Peterson and Katberine E. Lewis, "Preventive Intervention to Improve Children's Discrimination of the Persuasive Tactics in Televised Advertising," *Journal of Pediatric Psychology* 13, no. 2 (1988): 163–70; Donald F. Roberts et al., "Developing Discriminating Consumers," *Journal of Communication* 30, no. 3 (September 1980): 94–105.

64. Seymour Feshbach, Norma Feshbach, and Sarale E. Cohen, "Enhancing Children's Discrimination in Response to Television Advertising: The Effects of Psycho-educational Training in Two Elementary School-Age Groups," *Developmental Review* 2 (1982): 385–403.

65. Thomas C. O'Guinn and Ronald J. Faber, "Mass Mediated Consumer Socialization: Non-Utilitarian and Dysfunctional Outcomes," *Advances in Consumer Research* 14 (1987): 473–77.

66. S. H. Chaffee, J. M. McLeod, and C. K. Atkin, "Parental Influences on Adolescent Media Use," *American Behavioral Scientist* 14, no. 3 (January 1, 1971): 323–40; George P. Moschis and Roy L. Moore, "Family Communication and Consumer Socialization," *Advances in Consumer Research* 6 (1979): 359–63.

67. George P. Moschis, "The Role of Family Communication in Consumer Socialization of Children and Adolescents," *Journal of Consumer Research* 11, no. 4 (March 1985): 898.

68. Moniek Buijzen and Patti M. Valkenburg, "Parental Mediation of Undesired Advertising Effects," *Journal of Broadcasting and Electronic Media* 49, no. 2 (June 2005): 153–65; Roy L. Moore and George P. Moschis, "The Role of Family Communication in Consumer Learning," *Journal of Communication* 31, no. 4 (December 1981): 42–51.

69. Patti M. Valkenburg et al., "Developing a Scale to Assess Three Styles of Television Mediation: 'Instructive Mediation,' 'Restrictive Mediation,' and 'Social Coviewing,' " *Journal of Broadcasting and Electronic Media* 43, no. 1 (January 1999): 52–66.

70. Buijzen and Valkenburg, "Parental Mediation of Undesired Advertising Effects."

71. Moniek Buijzen, "Reducing Children's Susceptibility to Commercials: Mechanisms of Factual and Evaluative Advertising Interventions," *Media Psychology* 9, no. 2 (April 13, 2007): 411–30.

72. Jennifer L. Chakroff, "Mitigating the Unintended Effects of Advertising on Young Children: The Effectiveness of Parent-administered Active Mediation" (paper presented at the annual conference of the International Communication Association, Montreal, Canada, 2008).

Bibliography

Acuff, Dan S., and Robert H. Reiher. *What Kids Buy and Why: The Psychology of Marketing to Kids*. New York: Free Press, 1997.

Atkin, Charles, and Gary Heald. "The Content of Children's Toy and Food Commercials." *Journal of Communication* 27, no. 1 (March 1977): 107–14. doi:10.1111/j.1460-2466.1977.tb01805.x.

Atkin, Charles, John Hocking, and Martin Block. "Teenage Drinking: Does Advertising Make a Difference?" *Journal of Communication* 34, no. 2 (June 1984): 157–67. doi:10.1111/j.1460-2466.1984.tb02167.x.

Atkin, Charles K. "Effects of Television Advertising on Children." In *Children and the Faces of Television: Teaching, Violence, Selling*, edited by Edward L. Palmer and Aimee Dorr, 287–304. New York: Academic Press, 1980.

Atkin, Charles K. *Effects of Television Advertising on Children: Survey of Children's and Mother's Responses to Television Commercials*. East Lansing, MI: Michigan State University, 1975.

Atkin, Charles K. "Observation of Parent-Child Interaction in Supermarket Decision-Making." _Journal of Marketing_ 42, no. 4 (October 1978): 41. doi:10.2307/1250084.

Atkin, Charles K. _Survey of Pre-Adolescent's Responses to Television Commercials: The Effects of Television Advertising on Children._ East Lansing: Michigan State University, 1975.

Atkin, Charles K., and Martin Block. "Effectiveness of Celebrity Endorsers." _Journal of Advertising Research_ 23, no. 1 (1983): 57–61.

Atkin, Charles K., and Wendy Gibson. _Children's Nutrition Learning from Television Advertising._ East Lansing: Michigan State University, Department of Communication, 1978.

Austin, Erica Weintraub, and Christopher Knaus. "Predicting the Potential for Risky Behavior among Those 'Too Young' to Drink as the Result of Appealing Advertising." _Journal of Health Communication_ 5, no. 1 (January 2000): 13–27.

Bandura, Albert. _Social Foundations of Thought and Action: A Social Cognitive Theory._ Englewood Cliffs, NJ: Prentice-Hall, 1986.

Barcus, F. Earle. "The Nature of Television Advertising to Children." In _Children and the Faces of Television: Teaching, Violence, Selling_, edited by Edward L. Palmer and Aimee Dorr, 273–85. New York: Academic Press, 1980.

Belk, Russell. "Three Scales to Measure Constructs Related to Materialism: Reliability, Validity, and Relationships to Measures of Happiness." _Advances in Consumer Research_ 11 (n.d.): 291–97.

Brucks, Merrie, Gary M. Armstrong, and Marvin E. Goldberg. "Children's Use of Cognitive Defenses against Television Advertising: A Cognitive Response Approach." _Journal of Consumer Research_ 14, no. 4 (March 1988): 471. doi:10.1086/209129.

Buijzen, Moniek. "Reducing Children's Susceptibility to Commercials: Mechanisms of Factual and Evaluative Advertising Interventions." _Media Psychology_ 9, no. 2 (April 13, 2007): 411–30. doi:10.1080/15213260701291361.

Buijzen, Moniek, and Patti M. Valkenburg. "The Impact of Television Advertising on Children's Christmas Wishes." _Journal of Broadcasting and Electronic Media_ 44, no. 3 (September 2000): 456–70. doi:10.1207/s15506878jobem4403_7.

Buijzen, Moniek, and Patti M. Valkenburg. "Parental Mediation of Undesired Advertising Effects." _Journal of Broadcasting & Electronic Media_ 49, no. 2 (June 2005): 153–165. doi:10.1207/s15506878jobem4902_1.

Calvert, Sandra, and Aletha Huston. "Television and Children's Gender Schemata." In _Television and Children's Gender Schemata_, edited by Sandra Calvert and Aletha Huston, 75–88. San Francisco: Jossey-Bass, 1987.

Center on Alcohol Marketing and Youth. _Youth Exposure to Alcohol Advertising on Television, 2001–2009_, December 15, 2010. http://www.camy.org/research/Youth_Exposure_to_Alcohol_Ads_on_TV_Growing_Faster_Than_Adults/_includes/CAMYReport2001_2009.pdf.

Center on Alcohol Marketing and Youth. _Youth Exposure to Alcohol Product Advertising on Local Radio in 75 U.S. Markets, 2009_, September 13, 2011. http://www

.camy.org/research/Youth_Exposure_to_Alcohol_Advertising_on_Local_Radio _2009/_includes/report.pdf.

Centers for Disease Control and Prevention. *Youth Risk Behavior Surveillance— United States, 2009.* Morbidity and Mortality Surveillance Summary, 2010. http://www.cdc.gov/mmwr/PDF/ss/ss5905.pdf.

Chaffee, S. H., J. M. McLeod, and C. K. Atkin. "Parental Influences on Adolescent Media Use." *American Behavioral Scientist* 14, no. 3 (January 1, 1971): 323–40. doi:10.1177/000276427101400304.

Chakroff, Jennifer L. "Mitigating the Unintended Effects of Advertising on Young Children: The Effectiveness of Parent-Administered Active Mediation." Paper presented at the annual conference of the International Communication Association, Montreal, Canada, 2008.

Churchill, Gilbert A., Jr., and George P. Moschis. "Television and Interpersonal Influences on Adolescent Consumer Learning." *Journal of Consumer Research* 6, no. 1 (June 1979): 23. doi:10.1086/208745.

Cobb, Nancy J., Judith Stevens-Long, and Steven Goldstein. "The Influence of Televised Models on Toy Preference in Children." *Sex Roles* 8, no. 10 (October 1982): 1075–80. doi:10.1007/BF00291001.

Donohue, Thomas R., Lucy L. Henke, and Timothy P. Meyer. "Learning about Television Commercials: The Impact of Instructional Units on Children's Perceptions of Motive and Intent." *Journal of Broadcasting* 27, no. 3 (June 1983): 251–61. doi:10.1080/08838158309386490.

Drabman, Ronald S., Stephen J. Robertson, Jana N. Patterson, Gregory J. Jarvie, David Hammer, and Glenn Cordua. "Children's Perception of Media-Portrayed Sex Roles." *Sex Roles* 7, no. 4 (April 1981): 379–89.

Feshbach, Seymour, Norma Feshbach, and Sarale E. Cohen. "Enhancing Children's Discrimination in Response to Television Advertising: The Effects of Psychoeducational Training in Two Elementary School-age Groups." *Developmental Review* 2 (1982): 385–403.

Flavell, John. *The Development of Role-Taking and Communication Skills in Children.* New York: Wiley, 1968.

Gantz, Walter, Nancy Schwartz, James R. Angelini, and Victoria Rideout. *Food for Thought: Television Food Advertising to Children in the United States.* Menlo Park, CA: Kaiser Family Foundation, 2007.

Gibbs, John C. *Moral Development and Reality: Beyond the Theories of Kohlberg and Hoffman.* Thousand Oaks, CA: Sage, 2003.

Goldberg, Marvin E., and Gerald J. Gorn. "Some Unintended Consequences of TV Advertising to Children." *Journal of Consumer Research* 5, no. 1 (June 1978): 22. doi:10.1086/208710.

Gorn, Gerald J., and Marvin E. Goldberg. "Behavioral Evidence of the Effects of Televised Food Messages on Children." *Journal of Consumer Research* 9, no. 2 (September 1982): 200. doi:10.1086/208913.

Greenberg, Bradley S., and Jeffrey E. Brand. "Television News and Advertising in Schools: The 'Channel One' Controversy." *Journal of Communication* 43, no. 1 (March 1993): 143–51. doi:10.1111/j.1460-2466.1993.tb01252.x.

Grube, Joel W., and Lawrence Wallack. "Television Beer Advertising and Drinking Knowledge, Beliefs, and Intentions among School Children." *American Journal of Public Health* 84 (1994): 254–59.

Holt, Debra, Pauline Ippolito, Debra Desrochers, and Christopher R. Kelly. *Children's Exposure to TV Advertising in 1977 and 2004: Information for the Obesity Debate.* Washington, DC: Federal Trade Commission, 2007.

Horgen, Katherine, Molly Choate, and Kelly Brownell. "Television Food Advertising: Targeting Children in a Toxic Environment." In *Handbook of Children and the Media*, edited by Dorothy G. Singer and Jerome L. Singer, 447–61. Thousand Oaks, CA: Sage Publications, 2011.

Jacobson, Michael F., and Bruce Maxwell. *What Are We Feeding Our Kids?* New York: Workman Pub., 1994.

Jennings, Nancy A., and Ellen A. Wartella. "Advertising and Consumer Development." In *Children and Television: Fifty Years of Research*, edited by Nancy Pecora, John P. Murray, and Ellen A. Wartella, 149–82. London: Routledge, 2006.

Kaiser Family Foundation. *The Role of Media in Childhood Obesity.* Menlo Park, CA: Author, February 2004.

Kunkel, Dale. "Children and Host-Selling Television Commercials." *Communication Research* 15, no. 1 (February 1, 1988): 71–92. doi:10.1177/0093650880 15001004.

Kunkel, Dale. "Children and Television Advertising." In *Handbook of Children and the Media*, edited by Dorothy G. Singer and Jerome L. Singer, 375–93. Thousand Oaks, CA: Sage Publications, 2001.

Kunkel, Dale, and Walter Gantz. "Assessing Compliance with Industry Self-Regulation of Television Advertising to Children." *Journal of Applied Communication Research* 21, no. 2 (May 1993): 148–62. doi:10.1080/009098893 09365363.

Kunkel, Dale, and Walter Gantz. "Children's Television Advertising in the Multi-channel Environment." *Journal of Communication* 42, no. 3 (September 1992): 134–52. doi:10.1111/j.1460-2466.1992.tb00803.x.

Lieber, L. *Commercial and Character Slogan Recall by Children Aged 9 to 11 Years: Budweiser Frogs versus Bugs Bunny.* Berkeley, CA: Center on Alcohol Advertising, 1996.

Liebert, Diane E., Joyce N. Sprafkin, Robert M. Liebert, and Eli A. Rubinstein. "Effects of Television Commercial Disclaimers on the Product Expectations of Children." *Journal of Communication* 27, no. 1 (March 1977): 118–24. doi:10.1111/j.1460-2466.1977.tb01807.x.

Macklin, M. Carole. "Preschoolers' Learning of Brand Names from Visual Cues." *Journal of Consumer Research* 23, no. 3 (December 1996): 251–61. doi:10.1086/209481.

Miller, J. W., T. S. Naimi, R. D. Brewer, and S. E. Jones. "Binge Drinking and Associated Health Risk Behaviors among High School Students." *Pediatrics* 119, no. 1 (January 1, 2007): 76–85. doi:10.1542/peds.2006-1517.

Moore, Roy L., and George P. Moschis. "The Role of Family Communication in Consumer Learning." *Journal of Communication* 31, no. 4 (December 1981): 42–51. doi:10.1111/j.1460-2466.1981.tb00449.x.

Moschis, George P. "The Role of Family Communication in Consumer Socialization of Children and Adolescents." *Journal of Consumer Research* 11, no. 4 (March 1985): 898. doi:10.1086/209025.

Moschis, George P., and Roy L. Moore. "Family Communication and Consumer Socialization." *Advances in Consumer Research* 6 (1979): 359–63.

O'Guinn, Thomas C., and Ronald J. Faber. "Mass Mediated Consumer Socialization: Non-utilitarian and Dysfunctional Outcomes." *Advances in Consumer Research* 14 (1987): 473–77.

Palmer, Edward L., and Cynthia N. McDowell. "Children's Understanding of Nutritional Information Presented in Breakfast Cereal Commercials." *Journal of Broadcasting* 25, no. 3 (June 1981): 295–301. doi:10.1080/08838158109386453

Palmer, Edward L., and Cynthia N. McDowell. "Program/Commercial Separators in Children's Television Programming." *Journal of Communication* 29, no. 3 (September 1979): 197–201. doi:10.1111/j.1460-2466.1979.tb01732.x.

Peterson, Lizette, and Katherine E. Lewis. "Preventive Intervention to Improve Children's Discrimination of the Persuasive Tactics in Televised Advertising." *Journal of Pediatric Psychology* 13, no. 2 (1988): 163–70. doi:10.1093/jpepsy/13.2.163.

Piaget, Jean. *The Construction of Reality in the Child.* New York: Basic Books, 1954.

Potter, W. James. *Media Literacy.* Thousand Oaks, CA: Sage Publications, 1998.

Richards, J. I., E. A. Wartella, C. Morton, and L. Thompson. "The Growing Commercialization of Schools: Issues and Practices." *ANNALS of the American Academy of Political and Social Science* 557, no. 1 (May 1, 1998): 148–63. doi:10.1177/0002716298557000012.

Richins, Marsha L., and Scott Dawson. "A Consumer Values Orientation for Materialism and Its Measurement: Scale Development and Validation." *Journal of Consumer Research* 19, no. 3 (December 1992): 303–16. doi:10.1086/209304.

Richins, Marsha L. "Media, Materialism, and Human Happiness." *Advances in Consumer Research* 14 (1987): 352–56.

Roberts, Donald F., Peter Christenson, Wendy A. Gibson, Linda Mooser, and Marvin E. Goldberg. "Developing Discriminating Consumers." *Journal of Communication* 30, no. 3 (September 1980): 94–105. doi:10.1111/j.1460-2466.1980.tb01996.x.

Roberts, Donald F., Ulla G. Foehr, and Victoria Rideout. *Generation M: Media in the Lives of 8–18 Year-Olds.* Menlo Park, CA: Kaiser Family Foundation, 2005.

Robertson, Thomas S., and John R. Rossiter. "Children's Responsiveness to Commercials." *Journal of Communication* 27, no. 1 (March 1977): 101–6. doi:10.1111/j.1460-2466.1977.tb01804.x.

Robertson, Thomas S., and John R. Rossiter. "Short-Run Advertising Effects on Children: A Field Study." *Journal of Marketing Research* 13, no. 1 (February 1976): 68–70. doi:10.2307/3150908.

Robertson, Thomas S., Scott Ward, Hubert Gatignon, and Donna M. Klees. "Advertising and Children: A Cross-Cultural Study." *Communication Research* 16, no. 4 (August 1, 1989): 459–85. doi:10.1177/009365089016004001.

Robinson, Thomas N., Melissa Nichols Saphir, Helena C. Kraemer, Ann Varady, and K. Farish Haydel. "Effects of Reducing Television Viewing on Children's Requests for Toys: A Randomized Controlled Trial." *Journal of Developmental and Behavioral Pediatrics* 22, no. 3 (June 2001): 179–84. doi:10.1097/00004703-200106000-00005.

Sandberg, Helena, Kerstin Gidlof, and Nils Holmberg. "Children's Exposure to and Perceptions of Online Advertising." *International Journal of Communication* 5 (2001): 21–50.

Schor, Juliet B. *The Overspent American: Upscaling, Downshifting, and the New Consumer.* New York: Basic Books, 1998.

Snyder, Leslie B. "Effects of Alcohol Advertising Exposure on Drinking Among Youth." *Archives of Pediatrics and Adolescent Medicine* 160, no. 1 (January 1, 2006): 18–24. doi:10.1001/archpedi.160.1.18.

Stoneman, Zolinda, and Gene H. Brody. "The Indirect Impact of Child-Oriented Advertisements." *Journal of Applied Developmental Psychology* 2, no. 4 (January 1981): 369–76. doi:10.1016/0193-3973(81)90021-6.

Strasburger, Victor C. "Children, Adolescents, Drugs, and the Media." In *Handbook of Children and the Media*, edited by Dorothy G. Singer and Jerome L. Singer, 415–46. Thousand Oaks, CA: Sage Publications, 2001.

Strayer, Janet. "Children's Concordant Emotions and Cognitions in Response to Observed Emotions." *Child Development* 64, no. 1 (February 1993): 188–201. doi:10.2307/1131445.

Valkenburg, Patti M., and Joanne Cantor. "The Development of a Child into a Consumer." *Journal of Applied Developmental Psychology* 22, no. 1 (January 2001): 61–72. doi:10.1016/S0193-3973(00)00066-6.

Valkenburg, Patti M., Marina Krcmar, Allerd L. Peeters, and Nies M. Marseille. "Developing a Scale to Assess Three Styles of Television Mediation: 'Instructive Mediation,' 'Restrictive Mediation,' and 'Social Coviewing.'" *Journal of Broadcasting and Electronic Media* 43, no. 1 (January 1999): 52–66. doi:10.1080/08838159909364474.

Ward, S., G. Reale, and D. Levinson. "Children's Perceptions, Explanations, and Judgments of Television Advertising; A Further Exploration." In *Television and Social Behavior*, edited by George Comstock and Eli A. Rubinstein, vol. 4. Washington, DC: U.S. Government Printing Office, 1972.

Young, Brian M. *Television Advertising and Children.* Oxford and New York: Clarendon Press, Oxford University Press, 1990.

CHAPTER SIX

Cigarettes and Feminism: You've Come a Long Way, Baby

Sarah LaCorte

It is no secret that smoking is bad for your health. Smoking contributes to 5 million deaths per year, and research suggests that the annual death toll could reach 80 million by the year 2030.[1] The health risks are staggering, and ever-increasing tobacco taxes have an equal effect on one's wallet. Why then, do so many Americans indulge in such a risky behavior? Advertising. Through aggressive and persistent marketing over the last century, the allure of smoking has woven itself into the fabric of American culture. From movies and cartoons to publicity stunts and spokespersons, cigarettes have carved out a choice spot in the marketplace. Through the various marketing tactics tobacco companies have employed, smoking a cigarette is considered a universal form of rebellion and style. Despite the millions of dollars that go toward antismoking campaigns, 3,800 people under the age of 18 smoke their first cigarette every day.[2]

Women have been an easy target for cigarette companies since the 1940s and the appeals used to market to them are a clear reflection of gender roles in the United States. Where marketing cigarettes to men was similar to other marketing strategies of the time, selling smokes to ladies was a different matter. Before heavy marketing efforts were put into place, no proper woman would be caught dead smoking a cigarette. This was an untapped market that needed to be assured that smoking was acceptable behavior. Tobacco ads geared expressly toward women soon emerged. Cigarettes became a part of the feminist movement through nothing more than clever marketing strategies. This chapter will examine this phenomenon and discuss how such a seemingly irrelevant act became iconic.

Late 1960s

In 1968, Philip Morris introduced Virginia Slims, the first cigarette designed specifically with a woman in mind. While the Marlboro Man looked tough, Virginia Slims told women how *glamorous* smoking was. Prior to Virginia Slims, women were targeted, but as housewives or girlfriends, and they smoked "gender-neutral" cigarette brands.

The original Virginia Slims ads featured the now infamous tagline "You've Come A Long Way, Baby," paired with images of confidently beautiful women. The copy painted them all as suffragettes. The cigarette itself was long and slender and came in colorful packaging. Women from coast to coast now had cigarettes just for them.

It was at this time that the second wave of feminism was in full force. With protests and bra-burning abounding, this was the perfect opportunity for Philip Morris to expand its product line to ladies. With femininity redefined, Virginia Slims was marketed as the cigarette these newly empowered women could identify with. Much like the Lucky Strike stunt orchestrated by Bernays, the Virginia Slims ads suggested that smoking claimed independence. Virginia Slims ads were not trying to convince women to smoke as much as they were convincing women to think for themselves. By pairing cigarettes with words and imagery, reminding women of the progress they had made since the 1920s, Virginia Slims directly associated itself with the celebration progress. This newfound female audience accepted this association, and female-specific brands continue today.

This brand positioning proved to be wildly effective. Only six years after Virginia Slims and other gender-specific cigarettes were introduced, the smoking initiation rate of 12-year-old girls increased by 110 percent.[3] The use of the women's liberation movement to sell cigarettes is a prime example of advertising reflecting the society to which it aims to convince. All over the country, women young and old were looking for ways to find an identity. Philip Morris recognized this as an opportunity to expand its customer base.

Independence was not the only way cigarette companies appealed to women. They also employed the need to feel desirable. The cigarette brand Eve was introduced with the tagline "Farewell to the ugly cigarette. Smoke pretty. Eve." Eves came in floral packaging and the cigarettes were long and slender, giving the smoker a more feminine appearance while puffing away. Select empty packs of Eves were redeemable for pairs of Silkies panty hose or discounted Anne Rothschild undergarments.

The 1970s

Although the first Surgeon General's warning about the risks of smoking was released in 1964, cigarette marketing to women did not drastically shift until the mid-1970s. As women's concern about personal health increased, tobacco companies needed to find a way to maintain their female audience.

Women were becoming more aware of the risks associated with smoking, and tobacco companies responded by introducing and heavily promoting "low-tar" and "tar-free" cigarettes. A Philip Morris document from 1976 stated that:

> Because of women's nurturing role in society, they are naturally more involved with low tar cigarettes than men (70% of low tar smokers are female). They do not want to stop smoking, yet they are guilt ridden with concerns for their families if smoking should badly damage their own health. Thus they compromise by smoking low tar cigarettes. . . . This new product can fit this positioning exactly.

These cigarettes were promoted under the assumption that less tar meant a healthier cigarette. Light cigarettes became a new alternative. In a 1976 ad for True cigarettes, a female tennis player said, "All the fuss about smoking got me thinking—I'd either quit or smoke True. I smoke True. The low tar low nicotine cigarette. Think about it."

While the risks and side effects of smoking cigarettes were being debated, there was still an audience that identified with smoking "healthier" cigarettes. Instead of quitting, many smokers switched over to these "healthier" options. This trend greatly affected female smokers, who made up the majority of the low-tar cigarette market. Major tobacco companies soon noticed this trend in female smokers and tailored promotional campaigns to hook them. Newport (a gender-neutral brand) offered free Aziza eye shadow with the purchase of two packs of Newport Slim Lights.[4] Virginia Slims began sponsoring professional women's tennis tournaments in an effort to increase a health-conscious image.

From the mid-1970s to the mid-1980s, low-tar cigarette sales were at their highest. In 1979, the height of the "healthy-cigarette trend," 82 percent of all cigarette ads promoted the safety of lighter alternatives. Those smokers who switched to low-tar alternatives were less likely to become former smokers. With the assumption that light and low-tar cigarettes were healthier, smokers lost motivation to quit.[5]

This may explain why cigarette companies disproportionately advertised their light alternatives over the others. Expenditures on promoting light and low-tar alternatives exceeded promotional expenditures of regular cigarettes and could have been a way cigarette companies attempted to discourage more health-conscious smokers from quitting. The aggressive promotion of low-tar alternatives directly preceded an increase of sales in this category.[6] Low-tar alternatives were not developed to be safer. They were developed as a reassuring, comforting alternative to the merely glamorous traditional cigarette.

The 1980s

The beginning of the 1980s showed just how far women had come with regard to smoking. The 1980 report from the surgeon general stated:

> This report points out that the first signs of an epidemic of smoking-related disease among women are now appearing. Because women's cigarette use did not become widespread until the onset of World War II, those women with the greatest intensity of smoking are now only in their thirties, forties, and fifties. As these women grow older, and continue to smoke, their burden of smoking-related disease will grow larger.[7]

Until the report, it was believed that women were not as susceptible to smoking-related diseases as their male counterparts. The surgeon general pointed out that this was only because women did not begin smoking in large amounts until the 1940s, and the long-term effects on women were just beginning to surface in the late 1970s. Women were every bit as vulnerable to the ravaging effect of smoking, if not more. The report also examined the harm smoking could cause to an unborn fetus or the lasting effects it could leave on a newborn.[8]

Incidentally, 1980 also brought the first smoking Lois Lane. During her first 50 years as Superman's main gal, Lane never smoked. For a reported $42,000, Philip Morris purchased over 20 appearances of the Marlboro logo for the movie *Superman II*. Lane's cigarette of choice was Marlboro Lights, which she chain-smoked throughout the film. The logo also appeared during climactic points in the film on the sides of vans, on billboards, and on taxis. Lois was considered a role model for young girls at the time, and the film was frequently rerun on television over the next decade.[9]

Also in 1980, the U.S. Supreme Court set the Central Hudson Test. The test was designed as a road map for advertisers to follow when designing commercial speech and consists of four basic parts:

1. For an ad to be protected by the First Amendment, the advertising must be lawful, and not misleading.

2. Given that, for an ad to be banned, the state's interest must be "substantial."
3. The ban must "directly advance" the state's interest.
4. The ban must be no more extensive than necessary to further the state's interest.[10]

The Central Hudson Test allowed both lawmakers and tobacco advertisers to understand where the line was between the First Amendment right to free speech and hazardous messages propagated by tobacco companies. Although cigarettes were a legal product and were protected under the First Amendment, the risks associated with smoking posed a substantial threat to the health of the general population. These guidelines altered the way cigarettes were advertised, but it was a gradual process, and it would be quite some time before cigarette ads were entirely removed from television and other major outlets.

With massive amounts of young women moving to crowded urban areas and entering the work force in the 1980s, tobacco companies began putting promotion to female smokers into overdrive. Out of these extreme limitations, advertising agency Saatchi & Saatchi created what is considered one of the most successful cigarette ad campaigns of all time for the tobacco company Silk Cut. The campaign, which began in 1982, never featured the product. Instead, each ad showed deep purple silk being literally cut. Sometimes the ads were funny or clever, sometimes they were topical, and others just used beautiful imagery of deep purple and white to sell cigarettes. Through this campaign, audiences anticipated how the company might next show the silk being cut. The ads were chic and mentioned only the low amount of tar in the cigarettes and a warning that they may damage your health.[11] These ads heavily targeted a female audience with their sleek designs and low-tar promotion. Silk Cut moved beyond the literal copy of companies like Virginia Slims that assured women smoking was chic and fashionable. Without saying anything about smoking, Silk Cut positioned itself as fashion-forward way to get a nicotine fix.

In a document from R. J. Reynolds, the company that manufactures Camel, More, and Salem, among others, stated that:

> RJR has a corporate gap in the younger adult female smoker market. While this in itself does not represent a market opportunity, penetration of this smoker group does pose a strategic corporate opportunity . . . younger adult smokers are strategically important to RJR's long-term growth . . . Specifically, these young adult females agree that smoking is: attractive to the opposite sex, sophisticated/stylish, less intelligent, more aggressive, more mature, less feminine, smoke because friends do, feel more comfortable around others, feel that I'm rebelling.[12]

The glamour of these ads was overshadowed by the fact that in 1987, lung cancer surpassed breast cancer as the leading cause of cancer deaths in women. As the 1980s drew to a close, people began to quit smoking. By 1988, 44 percent of smokers quit.[13]

The 1990s

The 1990s brought a rude awakening to smokers around the country as the health risks associated with smoking went from rumors to cold, hard facts. People knew smoking cigarettes was bad for their health and were slowly learning just how addictive they were. This decade was also particularly cruel to the tobacco industry, which, after nearly a century of marketing cigarettes, was finally being criticized.

The nicotine patch was introduced in 1992, the same year the Marlboro Man Wayne McLaren died from lung cancer at 51. The infamous 1994 congressional hearing brought seven executives from the major tobacco companies who testified that they did not believe nicotine was addictive.[14] ABC aired a two-part series called *DayOne* that discussed the manipulation of nicotine by the tobacco industry.[15] An ex-scientist for Philip Morris testified on his research of nicotine and stated that Philip Morris had prevented him from releasing his findings.[16] *Time* and *U.S. News and World Report* ran cover stories discussing the tobacco industry and nicotine.

In response, tobacco companies ramped up their marketing efforts to colossal proportions. A popular demonstration of how heavily tobacco companies were advertising is the Joe Camel versus Mickey Mouse example. Researchers in 1991 found that 91 percent of 6-year-olds could match Joe Camel to cigarettes. In four short years, Camel's share of the under-18 market had skyrocketed from 0.5 percent to 32.8 percent, leaving little doubt that Joe Camel was an alluring mascot to children.[17]

Tobacco companies knew they needed to revamp their brand images if they wanted to maintain their loyal consumers. Aside from children, women remained what tobacco companies considered easy targets for their ad messages. A 1992 Philip Morris document stated:

> In an effort to gain relevancy among young adult female smokers, Virginia Slims is exploring a new advertising direction ... its objective is to make Virginia Slims relevant to young adult female smokers through a proprietary attitude, in the context of female style ... To women smokers, Virginia Slims is the brand that best expresses their style and attitude about being a women today. The Virginia Slims Fashion program should dimensionalize the style and attitude of today's young women smoker.

Women in the 1990s experienced what many feminists consider the dawn of the "third wave of feminism," which changed the concept of femininity once more. The 1960s take on feminism emphasized female independence and sexual liberation, heavily focusing on upper middle-class white women. Third-wave feminism picked up where this theory left off and welcomed in women of diverse racial backgrounds, sexual orientations, and upbringings. In addition to this, third-wave feminism is also concerned with issues such as glass ceilings and equal pay within the workplace.[18]

With this new way of thinking spreading across the country, tobacco companies once again jumped at the chance to be a part of a cultural movement as a means of gaining identification with potential consumers. Virginia Slims introduced the "Find Your Voice" campaign, which encouraged women to speak up for themselves as independent women. The ads used a broad range of women, dominantly expressing themselves in various ways. The campaign was later pulled due to concern that it may offend smokers who had suffered from throat cancer.[19]

In 1990 a campaign from R. J. Reynolds was designed to reach blue-collar women who were less educated than the more affluent women targeted previously. RJR introduced Dakota cigarettes, which were designed to attract young and "virile females" who worked in the service industries. The advertisements were dusky, featuring attractive models in leather jackets. The Dakota brand attempted to identify with rebellious women from working-class families. However, the brand and campaign was short-lived and discontinued not long after its introduction.[20] Camel cigarettes attempted to compete for women's attention by featuring a female Joe Camel on select packaging and offering coupons for female-specific merchandise.[21]

In 1993, Philip Morris was the nation's number-two advertiser behind Procter & Gamble and Marlboro was ranked the world's most valuable brand by *Financial World* at $39.5 billion. Despite the mounting evidence against the tobacco industry, smokers continued to smoke.

Throughout the 1990s, attacks on the industry were endless. In 1999, Philip Morris first launched a website, stating: "There is an overwhelming medical and scientific consensus that cigarette smoking causes lung cancer, heart disease, emphysema and other serious diseases in smokers."[22]

The Millennium

In 2000, the American Legacy Foundation launched the Truth campaign to help educate teenagers on the dangers of smoking. Since the turn of the

century, great strides have been made to help educate the public and prevent young adults and teenagers from ever beginning the habit.

The tobacco industry soldiers on. Although advertising to women was
still existent, tobacco companies began taking a more subtle approach.
Rather than boldly proclaiming a cigarette was "a woman thing," tobacco
companies approached women more tactfully. In the early and mid-
2000s, Camel began the Pleasure to Burn campaign, featuring highly saturated illustrations of women smoking. The ads typically adopted a retro aesthetic with a modern twist. These ads promoted the sex appeal that had
become commonplace in cigarette ads but did not make use of heavy copy-
writing like the Silk Cut ads that had come before.

Today, the idea of women-specific cigarettes is still around. Having
shifted marketing efforts toward women in the early 2000s, Camel recognized an opportunity to make a female-exclusive brand. In 2007, Camel
introduced the ultra-chic Camel No. 9s. Intended to remind women of
the iconic Chanel No. 9 perfume, the packs were as fashion-forward as
can be, with shiny black packages accented with teal and hot pink. Advertisements for No. 9s can be found in magazines such as *Vogue*, *Glamour*,
and *Cosmopolitan* and feature taglines that emphasize fashion such as,
"now available in stiletto." Promotions of the product have included giveaways of feminine items such as hot pink lip gloss, cell phone charms,
and jewelry.[23]

Not to be outdone, in 2008, Philip Morris announced that it would
improve the Virginia Slims packaging into "purse packs." This new packaging was much smaller than the packs they typically came in and looks
extremely similar to cosmetic cases. Coming in mauve and teal, these new
boxes were promoted using direct-mail cards in the shape of clutch purses.
These purses contained coupons for the new packs as well as promotional
information that continued the positioning of independence, style and
beauty.

Conclusion

From a taboo that no women would consider to a mainstay in many
women's lives, cigarettes have become a huge part of American culture.
Cigarette marketing was center stage during the major social and political
movements over the past century. What started out as a "torch of freedom"
became an addiction that more than 140,000 liberated American women
die from each year. The history of cigarette advertising to women is a prime
example of the power of advertising.

Notes

1. World Health Organization. WHO Report on the Global Tobacco Epidemic. 2009.

2. "Smoking and Tobacco Use: Fast Facts," Centers for Disease Control and Prevention, http://www.cdc.gov/tobacco/data_statistics/fact_sheets/fast_facts/ (accessed June 20, 2012).

3. Robert Wood Johnson Foundation, "Deadly In Pink: Big Tobacco Steps Up Its Targeting of Women and Girls," Tobacco-Free Kids, February 18, 2009, http://www.lung.org/assets/documents/publications/other-reports/deadly-in-pink.pdf (accessed June 20, 2012).

4. "Themes and Targets of Tobacco Advertising and Promotion," http://cancercontrol.cancer.gov/tcrb/monographs/19/m19_5.pdf (accessed June 20, 2012).

5. Ibid.

6. U.S. National Library of Medicine, *The Temporal Relationship between Advertising and Sales of Low-Tar Cigarettes* (PubMed.gov, 2006).

7. U.S. Public Health Service, *The Health Consequences of Smoking for Women: A Report of the Surgeon General* (Washington, DC: Public Health Service, 1980).

8. Ibid.

9. Gene Borio, *The Tobacco Timeline*, chap. 7, "The Twentieth Century, 1950–1999: The Battle Is Joined," Illinois Smokers Rights, http://www.illinois smokersrights.com/tobacco_timeline_chap_7.html.20 (accessed June 20, 2012).

10. Center for Public Health and Tobacco Policy, "Commercial Speech Challenges to Tobacco Marketing Regulations," Tobacco Policy Center, New England Law Boston, May 2012.

11. Catherine R. Langan, "Intertextuality in Advertisements for Silk Cut Cigarettes," http://www.aber.ac.uk/media/Students/crl9502.html (accessed June 20, 2012).

12. "Tobacco Industry Targeting Women and Girls." Partnership for Smoking or Health, Missouri Association of Local Public Health Agencies, http://www.moalpha.org/docs/news/tob_partnership/women_target.html (accessed June 20, 2012).

13. Gene Borio, "Tobacco Timeline Notes," 2007, http://archive.tobacco.org/resources/history/Tobacco_Historynotes.html#aasg80 (accessed June 20, 2012).

14. *Frontline: Inside the Tobacco Deal 1994 Testimony*, Public Broadcasting Service, http://www.pbs.org/wgbh/pages/frontline/shows/settlement/timelines/april942.html.

15. *DayOne: Smoke Screen*, directed by Forrest Sawyer and Diane Sawyer, produced by ABC News.1994.

16. Peter Rowe, "Philip Morris Couldn't Snuff Out Victor DeNoble," *U-T San Diego*, January 25, 2012.

17. Borio, "Tobacco Timeline Notes."

18. "Third Wave: An Accurate and Succinct Rendering," *Rebecca Walker Blog*, http://www.rebeccawalker.com/blog/2009/09/04/third-wave (accessed June 20, 2012).

19. Robert Wood Johnson Foundation, "Deadly In Pink."

20. "Sizzling Hot Dakota Ethics," http://www.jimsburntofferings.com/packsdakota.html (accessed June 20, 2012).

21. Themes and Targets of Tobacco Advertising and Promotion.

22. "Smoking and Health Issues," Philip Morris USA, http://www.philip morrisusa.com/en/cms/Products/Cigarettes/Health_Issues/Cigarette.Smoking_and _Disease/default.aspx (accessed June 20, 2012).

23. Robert Wood Johnson Foundation, "Deadly In Pink."

Bibliography

Amos, Amanda, and Margaretha Haglund. "From Social Tobacco to 'Torch of Freedom': The Marketing of Cigarettes to Women." *Tobacco Control* 9 (2000): 3–8.

Borio, Gene. *The Tobacco Timeline*. Chap. 7, "The Twentieth Century, 1950–1999: The Battle Is Joined." Illinois Smokers Rights. http://www.illinoissmokers rights.com/tobacco_timeline_chap_7.html (accessed June 20, 2012).

Borio, Gene. "Tobacco Timeline Notes." Tobacco.org. 2007. http://archive.tobacco .org/resources/history/Tobacco_Historynotes.html#aasg80 (accessed June 20, 2012).

Center for Public Health and Tobacco Policy. "Commercial Speech Challenges to Tobacco Marketing Regulations." Tobacco Policy Center, New England Law Boston, May 2012. http://www.tobaccopolicycenter.org/documents/CPHTP _POS_First_Amendment_Fact_Sheet_20100524.pdf (accessed June 30, 2012).

Comforth, Tracee. "Smoking: Women's Health Perspective." About.com, June 20, 2012. http://womenshealth.about.com/cs/azhealthtopics/a/smokingeffects.htm (accessed June 30, 2012).

DayOne: Smoke Screen. Directed by Forrest Sawyer and Diane Sawyer. Produced by ABC News. 1994.

Department of Health and Human Services. *Women and Smoking: A Report of the Surgeon General*, 2001. Center for Disease Control and Prevention, 2001.

Frontline: Inside the Tobacco Deal 1994 Testimony. Public Broadcasting Service. http://www.pbs.org/wgbh/pages/frontline/shows/settlement/timelines/ april942.html.

Langan, Catherine R. "Intertextuality in Advertisements for Silk Cut Cigarettes." April 1998. http://www.aber.ac.uk/media/Students/crl9502.html (accessed June 20, 2012).

Riordan, Meg. "Tobacco Industry Targeting of Women and Girls." Tobacco-Free Kids, June 15, 2012. http://www.tobaccofreekids.org/research/factsheets/pdf/ 0138.pdf.

Robert Wood Johnson Foundation. "Deadly In Pink: Big Tobacco Steps Up Its Tar-
    geting of Women and Girls." Tobacco-Free Kids, February 18, 2009. http://
    www.lung.org/assets/documents/publications/other-reports/deadly-in-pink.pdf
    (accessed June 20, 2012).
Rowe, Peter. "Philip Morris Couldn't Snuff Out Victor DeNoble." *U-T San Diego*,
    January 25, 2012.
"Sizzling Hot Dakota Ethics." http://www.jimsburntofferings.com/packsdakota
    .html (accessed June 20, 2012).
"Smoking and Health Issues." Philip Morris USA. n.d. http://www.philip
    morrisusa.com/en/cms/Products/Cigarettes/Health_Issues/Cigarette_Smoking
    _and_Disease/default.aspx (accessed June 20, 2012).
"Smoking and Tobacco Use: Fast Facts." Centers for Disease Control and Preven-
    tion. n.d. http://www.cdc.gov/tobacco/data_statistics/fact_sheets/fast_facts/
    (accessed June 20, 2012).
"Third Wave: An Accurate and Succinct Rendering." *Rebecca Walker Blog*, Septem-
    ber 4, 2009. http://www.rebeccawalker.com/blog/2009/09/04/third-wave
    (accessed June 20, 2012).
"Tobacco Industry Marketing." American Lung Association. n.d. http://www
    .lung.org/stop-smoking/about-smoking/facts-figures/tobacco-industry-marketing
    .html (accessed June 20, 2012).
"Tobacco Industry Targeting Women and Girls." Partnership for Smoking or
    Health. Missouri Association of Local Public Health Agencies. n.d. http://www
    .moalpha.org/docs/news/tob_partnership/women_target.html (accessed
    June 20, 2012).
U.S. National Library of Medicine. *The Temporal Relationship between Advertising
    and Sales of Low-Tar Cigarettes.* PubMed.gov, 2006.
U.S. Public Health Service. *The Health Consequences of Smoking for Women: A Report
    of the Surgeon General.* Washington, DC: Public Health Service, 1980.
"*Vintage Ad Browser.*" n.d. http://www.vintageadbrowser.com/tobacco-ads-1960s/
    32 (accessed June 20, 2012).
World Health Organization. *WHO Report on the Global Tobacco Epidemic*, 2009.

CHAPTER SEVEN

Branding the Gender Binary: Stereotypical Representations of Men and Women in Ads

Heather Ann Roy

Companies target consumers by connecting with them through relatable storylines in commercials, but unfortunately, many of these advertisements use stereotypical messages to sell products and services. Stereotypes are generalizations about a group of people or things. When advertisers use stereotypes, the commercials reinforce negative perceptions about certain people. In particular, advertisements are notorious for gender stereotyping. The dominant stereotype in advertisements is the gender binary of man/ woman or masculine/feminine that shows women in conventional roles, such as a housewife, and men as breadwinners. These roles generalize society as whole and set social guidelines for how to be a man or a woman. Conventional representations of gender reinforce the gender binary and further exclude other types of self-identification. Advertisers are aware of the gender binary and market their brands to fit the stereotype. Each and every day, consumers are saturated by generalized understandings of gender in advertisements. According to Jean Kilbourne, people are exposed to 3,000 advertisements each day, which makes escaping advertisements unimaginable.[1] It is plausible to argue that in the United States this number rises each year with technology being more accessible.

A recent, more blatant example of marketing using gender stereotyping is from the commercials for Dr. Pepper 10, a beverage developed and marketed for men. On October 10, 2011, Mae Anderson from *USA Today* reported, "the soft drink was developed after the company's research found that men shy away from diet drinks that aren't perceived as 'manly' enough."[2] One of the lines from the Dr. Pepper 10 commercial says, "Hey ladies. Enjoying the film? Of course not. Because this is our movie and this is our soda. You can keep the romantic comedies and lady drinks. We're good."[3] Using hegemonic ideologies based on the gender binary, Dr. Pepper 10 markets their low-calorie beverage to men by making it appear masculine and too rugged for women. There is a clear us-versus-them dichotomy found in the plot of this commercial where the men are part of the conversation (us) and the women (them) are excluded. As the commercial says, Dr. Pepper 10 is not for women; therefore, only men should drink it. This is one brief example of gender stereotyping found in today's market, but the possibilities of further examples are limitless.

As consumers, it is important to be aware of how advertisers target their brands to consumers by using the gender binary. This chapter will examine how advertisers use gender stereotypes to market their products by examining the role of gender in advertising and consumers' self-identities with gendered brands. The gender binary of masculine men and feminine women has become so normalized that often people do not recognize its impact. Advertisers constantly bombard the public with gendered ads, but because the same types of messages about gender have been repeated throughout various discourses, the problems associated with marketing the gender binary typically goes unnoticed by consumers' eyes. Men are not inherently born masculine or wanting to use power tools and drink beer, and the same is true for women; they do not come out of the womb feminine or desiring the newest cleaning supplies and mascara. These understandings of gender have and continue to be reinforced by social constructions of what it means to be a man or a woman, which has normalized a stereotypical structure of gender as either being a masculine man or a feminine woman. This limited perception of gender has become expected and consumers need to recognize its power in the realm of advertising.

Understanding Gender and How It Is Branded

Gender is a concept that is commonly misunderstood. It is different from sex or sexuality, but is usually mistaken as a term that encompasses all three. Gender is a social construct and is not an innate quality. Gender is constantly read and negotiated in our society with binary relationships that are hegemonic in design. Judith Butler explains that gender should not be understood as a fixed identity: "Rather, gender is an identity tenuously constituted in time, instituted in an exterior space through a *stylized repetition of acts*" (emphasis in original).[4] The repetition of acts Butler is referring to is how people perform their gender identity. Susan Basow defines gender as "a psychological and cultural term, referring to one's subjective feelings of maleness or femaleness (gender identity)."[5] Basow furthers her definition by stating, "gender may also refer to society's evaluation of behavior as masculine or feminine."[6] The latter definition describes gender roles, which are also social constructs reinforced by society in order to conceptualize identities and positions in life. Being placed into a gender role begins before birth when the sex of the baby is requested and is further reinforced when the child is born; boys are wrapped in blue blankets and girls in pink blankets. Sandra Bem suggests that children are repeatedly "put into different 'learning environments' with different categories of 'social partners.'"[7] Before a child can make a conscious choice, parents have already assigned the children gender roles, which are fueled by society and carried on through adulthood.

Within the regulations of a binary gender system, men are expected to be masculine and women feminine. A binary gender consists of only two genders, one being an ultra-masculine male and the other an ultra-feminine female. Basow explains gender stereotypes as "oversimplified conceptions pertaining to our behavior as females or males . . . a cluster of socially or culturally defined expectations that individuals in a given situation are expected to fulfill."[8]

An example of such cultural expectations regarding gender can be viewed with young girls transitioning into their adolescent years. Young girls who prefer to be more masculine are usually labeled tomboys. Once these young girls reach adolescence, they are expected by others to transition from their childhood tomboyish ways and perform proper femininity. No longer is being a tomboy cute or acceptable for this young woman; it is unwanted and policed by others in order for her to fit the normalized understanding of her gender role, a feminine female. Elizabeth Payne explains how gender rules and conformity become more apparent during adolescence, which is connected to popularity. Payne contends: "Although popularity cannot be separated from heterosexuality, it cannot be separated from a feminine gender performance. Young women are bombarded with the guidelines for that gender performance through the media and widely read teen and women's magazines such as *YM, Seventeen*, and *Cosmopolitan.*"[9] Therefore, a young woman's parents, peers, and others will urge her to conform to what is expected of her at this time in her life; she will need to perform proper femininity. The cultural expectations of an adolescent girl include femininity, not masculinity. The gender binary categorizes and polices men and women into two understandable categories, which is why an adolescent girl, who is expected to be feminine, no longer fits into the tomboy role.

People work to police gender into two easily understood categories, masculine or feminine; however, this is not an accurate portrayal of civilization. Bem argues that the binary gender roles that society has created are, essentially, "gender polarization," which creates expected scripts individually for men and for women.[10] When a male's or female's script differs from the expected behavior, complications arise, and those individuals are depicted as abnormal, perverted, and controversial. People who break the dichotomous norms of gender could be classified as the Other, because they do not neatly categorize as male or female. The Other can be understood as anything not relating to or matching society's expected norms for gender. Simone de Beauvoir states, "Otherness is a fundamental category of human thought. Thus it is that no group ever sets itself up as the One without at once setting up the Other over against itself."[11] For example, some heterosexuals view heterosexuality as the One or normalized sexuality and believe gays, lesbians, transgendered, and bisexuals are the Others who deviate from the expected heteronormative male and female scripts. Also, the Other can be understood as being androgynous, or embodying both masculine and feminine personality traits. Mainstream media advertisements do not usually portray the other types of gender, or androgynous gender, because it is not the valued, normal gender role expected by society.

Individuals commonly misunderstand gender as an innate quality, but this is an incorrect view of gender. Gender is learned and socially reinforced, and it does not offer only two gender roles. Each and every one of us performs our gender identity whether we recognize it or not. The next section contains an analysis of how the gender binary is used in advertisements. One of the studies listed in the following section exemplifies how gender plays a dominant role in purchase decisions and requests from children. My aim is not to place blame on advertisers for creating the gender binary; rather, the goal here is to understand that the binary-gender structure society understands and reinforces can be found and is reproduced in advertisements. Stereotypical images and gendered branding utilized in advertisements supports the limited gender roles found in all discourses. Consumers should strive to have a keen awareness of the gendered messages all around them, and marketers should want to create less stereotypical messages so they can reach a larger consumer population.

Gender Stereotypes in Advertisements

Oversimplifying gender in advertisements is projected onto real-life agendas of children and adults. According to research done by Beth Hentges, Robert Bartsch, and Jo Meier, adults' attitudes, beliefs, and actions are impacted by stereotypical messages and images of gender.[12] More importantly, the authors specified the source of stereotypical gender learning that arises from television, which affects consumers' cognitive development. The mass portrayals of men and women on television fit into the binary gender system, which then sets the foundation for society's understanding of gender from lessons learned on television.

Hentges, Bartsch, and Meier studied the gender stereotypes found in commercials targeted at children, adolescents, and adults. With children, it was found that there are higher numbers of boys in ads versus girls, same-sex commercials are more common with boys than girls, and male voices are generally used for voice commentaries, and when higher numbers of girls are portrayed in ads, they are stereotypically shown in domestic settings.[13] Hentges, Bartsch, and Meier also found that there are more gender stereotypes in children's and adolescents' commercials than in those of adults, which is problematic considering "children are still actively in the process of figuring out what it means to be male and female."[14] Early cognitive development sets a foundation for understanding and formulating values and beliefs as an adult. Negative stereotypes of gender, learned at a young age, may be easily projected to adulthood. Hentges, Bartsch, and Meier coded 33 hours of television programs and 688 commercials to determine whether or not gender stereotypes in commercials varied depending on the age of the target audience. Findings show that school-aged targeted commercials portray "2.82 times as many male characters as female characters [and] each male character is 3.19 times likely as each female character of being an authority figure."[15]

Hentges, Bartsch, and Meier also found in this study that adolescent-targeted commercials focus solely on one gender to sell products.[16] For example, advertisements for adolescent girls show young females inside the home, normally alone putting on makeup and trying out new hair products, fashionable clothes, and shoes. Commercials with adolescent boys are commonly shot outside with other boys, selling active products like sports equipment or tennis shoes. The girls were shown indoors in solitude, while the boys were outside of the home and socializing. The individual difference in settings for the young boys and girls resemble the potential future roles of a housewife and breadwinner.

Susannah Stern and Dana Mastro acknowledged women are commonly paired with household items (e.g., vacuums, cleaners, fragrances) and men are associated with more public items (e.g., vehicles, sports equipment, alcohol).[17] Domestication has been assigned to females in advertisements, whereas men are illustrated as having no part of this idea. Furthermore, it is then socially understood "to position women firmly within the private realm, a realm commonly perceived as less valuable than the public realm."[18] Men are frequently shown outside the home, possessing a job, and women are shown at home, hidden from the public. Instead of showing ads with educated women with jobs and men at home raising children, the majority of ads reinforce expected gender roles. These depictions of men and women in commercials are problematic because it positions audience members to identify with the expected binary gender role, which deprives women from opportunities in the public sphere and assumes men only fill roles outside the home.

From a psychological perspective, Michael Kimmel explained how males and females are taught different gender characteristics in social learning environments filled with gendered messages and activities. Research has tested boys and girls together, with unidentified gender toys, and most children act out similar roles. Therefore, the child's gender is not innate, but is socially conditioned into a gender with markers in his or her environment.[19] Roles are set in place at an early age of development, and if a child chooses to break those roles, consequences must be faced.[20] One of the ways that adults reinforce children's roles is through the use of gendered toys and activities.

A study conducted by Cele Otnes, Young Chan Kim, and Kyungseung Kim examined brand requests listed on letters written by young children to Santa Claus. The research by Otnes, Kim, and Kim discovered that boys and girls wished for the same amount of toys; however, girls requested "domestic objects and dolls," while boys chose "military items and vehicles" when writing to Santa.[21] Furthermore, the authors reasoned that these findings illustrated that young girls are socially reinforced to stay out of the public sphere and young boys are socialized and made public.[22] Early on, gender roles are displayed in children's commercials by showing feminine gender roles associated with domestic items and activities like being a housewife and raising children, in contrast to masculine gender roles that are gender-neutral and a norm within society.[23] Boys are commonly depicted in commercials as rugged and dominant figures by playing in the dirt with combat toys or play guns. They are not afraid to get dirty, yell, or throw things. Masculinity is a desirable trait for boys to portray in commercials and is reinforced by masculine toys associated with the boys in the ads. The desired role for girls is to be feminine with product associations like baby dolls, playhouses, and dress-up clothes. Binary gender roles that are commonly understood in everyday life with adults, teenagers, and children are reinforced with commercials that display boys in masculine roles and girls in feminine roles. Even at a young age, children are able to decipher which role they fit in and which products they want to be associated with or not. Social norms and specially crafted advertisements target the gender binary, and in return, consumers connect with or deflect certain brands due to the lack of self-identification with the brand's personality. A consumer wants to connect with a brand to be encouraged to want it.

Brand Personality

Product association in accordance with one's gender identity can be understood with the use of brand personality. According to Jennifer Aaker, brand personality can be understood as "the set of human characteristics associated with a brand."[24] Brands take on personality traits like humans, which is done through a consumer's personal or unintentional exposure with a brand. Basically, the consumer's identity or human characteristics are immediately associated with the brand.[25] The association creates a sense of identification or loyalty to that brand. Lori Wolin argued that advertisers intend to increase positive brand image, understanding, and purchases by using spokespersons with their brands because research has shown they positively enhance consumers' attitudes of brands.[26] A consumer who is a fan of the celebrity might, then, want to reflect the celebrity's personality and try to do so by purchasing the brand endorsed by the celebrity.

A study done by Bianca Grohmann on spokespeople in advertisements and the direct correlation the spokesperson has on the consumers' perception of masculinity brand personality (MBP) traits and female brand personality (FBP) traits, showed "the most effective way to create or alter the gender image associated with a product is to vary the spokesperson."[27] This conclusion arose from 292 college students evaluating a print ad for a false brand that featured a feminine spokesperson, a masculine spokesperson, or no spokesperson. The findings show that when a masculine spokesperson was used, viewers' association to MBP increased. The same was true with female spokespersons; the FBP increased when placed with the brand.[28] This data shows that consumers are affected by the use of spokespersons in ads and specifically seek out products with high levels of masculinity or high levels of femininity to help reinforce one's gender identity. "Consumers prefer brands that are congruent with their self-concept because such brands allow them to reinforce their actual or desired view of themselves and thus help them achieve personal goals."[29] When a consumer can identify a brand's personality traits with his or her own personality traits, cognitive dissonance can be decreased, and self-assurance about one's identity is positively increased.

Gender has an effect on processing and brand consumption. Because gender has a direct effect on how ads are processed, advertisers have implemented strategies to appropriately reach target markets. Brian Till and Randi Priluck describe this strategy within product categories; "Virginia Slims and Marlboro use feminine and masculine imagery, respectively, to embody their brands with symbolic meaning, [similarly] cologne and perfume also associate with feminine (White Diamonds) or masculine (Stetson) images to give their product a distinctive personality."[30] Advertisers utilize strategies in ads to gender brands because they are helpful in reaching target audiences.

Brands are designed to fill consumers' needs, and sometimes those needs, whether consumers consciously are aware of it or not, is to enhance one's masculinity or femininity. Certain products are deliberately made for men or women and consumers choose brands that enhance their expected gender. Grohmann "suggests that the need to express masculinity and femininity through brand choice is based on the notion that gender is part of consumers' self-concept."[31] Consumers deliberately choose some products with the intention of enhancing one's gender. Consumers try to fit into the accepted gender roles that society reinforces. Using a product that will increase a man's masculinity or a woman's femininity is one goal behind the design of a brand's message, target audience, and package design.

It is important to understand how consumers engage with products and self-identify with specific brands. David Sprott, Sandor Czellar, and Eric Spangenberg have created the brand engagement in self-concept (BESC) scale to understand consumers' engagement with a particular brand and imply that buyers differ in engagement processes with brands.[32] BESC can be understood under the umbrella of brand personality because it focuses on personality traits of a brand and personality traits of consumers, and how these two variables form a relationship.[33]

BESC is a critical scale to use when studying brands and gender identity because of the abundance of advertisements that consumers are exposed to each day. Engagement with a brand that is harmonious to one's personal identity enhances a positive attitude and recall for a brand. "Increased levels of BESC should result in a greater propensity to include favorite brands as a part of the self-concept. Research has shown that the way people view themselves affects how they organize information in memory."[34] This is important for marketers to understand, considering that research has shown that consumers mentally remove themselves from brands that do not fit with their favored brands. Advertisers need to be aware that consumers shut out brands that are not congruent with their brand choice and identity. If there are no brands available that fit gender identities outside of the existing scripted gender binary, many markets are left out.

Product association and one's gender identity can be enhanced with brand personality. If there are not brands available to certain markets because the brand's frame is focused to only masculine men and feminine women, product association is faulted. For instance, a feminine male might not easily associate with a masculine-branded soap or clothing item, but instead desires to use a product originally targeted to women. The same scenario is true for a masculine woman who might not feel comfortable shopping in the women's department, but would prefer clothing from the men's department. Yes, these markets are available; however, a feminine man and a masculine woman are not scripted and represented in commercials, and therefore, connecting a brand personality with a gender identity is not always congruent.

Conclusion

The study of brands and gender stereotyping is a subject that will be discussed indefinitely. This chapter pointed out the presence of gender stereotyping with product brands. Advertisements are scripted to have a masculine male and a feminine female acting out stereotypical roles with expected products for each gender. These scripts reinforce the gender binary of what a woman or man should be. These commercials cannot be reduced to just advertisements that are selling a product without any other effect. Advertisements are much more powerful than tools to sell an item. Advertisements can tell a story, reinforce ideologies, and help shape our understandings of the world. Sometimes, this is a good thing, and in other cases, it can be problematic, as was examined in this chapter.

Overall, I hope this examination will provide new insights on gender stereotyping, not just in common discourse, but in the mass media. We are saturated by advertisements daily, and these ads are marginalizing and limiting large groups of people. Producers, consumers, and bystanders should consider the implications of stereotypical ads. A brand one commonly uses or consumes might be reinforcing hegemonic ideologies about gender, which should be unsettling for all.

As a case in point, the Dr. Pepper 10 ad that was mentioned at the beginning of this chapter is an ideal illustration of an advertisement reinforcing negative perceptions about men and women. There was a backlash from consumers who did not agree with Dr. Pepper 10's message, and they let the company know it. According to Anna North from *Jezebel*, consumers flooded the Dr. Pepper 10 Facebook page with their opinions regarding the new commercial: "Just heard about this Dr. Pepper Ten; must've been too busy being barefoot and pregnant in the kitchen." Another: "Rigid gender roles and rules are totally cool. Keep it classy, Dr. Pepper. It's a good thing you're here to tell us how to act and keep us all in our place."[35] More outcries and boycotts like these messages to Dr. Pepper 10 could make companies aware of what consumers really want in their ads. Consumers speaking out and requesting them to rethink their marketing strategies might help reduce the number of stereotypical advertisements in the future.

It is important to consider one's own beliefs and values and how they compare to a brand so that a consumer does not support a brand that stereotypes the consumer using it. Gender stereotyping is not something to take lightly. Misogynist taglines in commercials are not just jokes. Stereotypical images and messages negate and attack audience members, especially those who do not fit into the gender binary. I hope consumers and marketers become proactive about creating new messages that include a larger target audience instead of following on the track of marginalization that has been used for too long.

Notes

1. Jean Kilbourne, "What Are Advertisers Really Selling Us?" Jean Kilbourne.com, http://www.jeankilbourne.com/lectures/ (accessed June 18, 2012).

2. Mae Anderson, "Dr. Pepper Ten 'Not for Women,'" *USA Today*, October 10, 2011, http://www.usatoday.com/money/industries/food/story/2011-10-10/dr-pepper-for-men/50717788/1.

3. Ibid.

4. Judith Butler, *Gender Trouble* (New York: Routledge, 1990), 191.

5. Susan A. Basow, *Gender Stereotypes: Traditions and Alternatives* (Pacific Grove, CA: Cole Publishing Company, 1986), 23.

6. Ibid.

7. Sandra L. Bem, *The Lenses of Gender: Transforming the Debate on Sexuality Inequality* (New Haven, CT: Yale University Press, 1993), 134.

8. Basow, *Gender Stereotypes*, 3.

9. Elizabeth Payne, "Heterosexism, Perfection, and Popularity: Young Lesbians' Experiences of the High School Social Scene," *Educational Studies* 41, no. 1 (2007): 63.

10. Bem, *Lenses of Gender*, 134.

11. Simone de Beauvoir, *The Second Sex* (New York: Random House, 1989), xxiii.

12. Beth A. Hentges, Robert A. Bartsch, and Jo A. Meier, "Gender Representation in Commercials as a Function of Target Audience Age," *Communication Research Reports* 24, no. 1 (2007).

13. Ibid.

14. Ibid., 56.
15. Ibid., 60.
16. Ibid.
17. Susannah R. Stern and Dana E. Mastro, "Gender Portrayals across the Life Span: A Content Analytic Look at Broadcast Commercials," *Mass Communication and Society* 7, no. 2 (2004).
18. Ibid., 218.
19. Michael S. Kimmel, *The Gendered Society* (New York: Oxford University Press, 2000).
20. Bem, *Lenses of Gender*.
21. Cele Otnes, Young Chan Kim, and Kyungseung Kim, "All I Want for Christmas: An Analysis of Children's Brand Requests to Santa Claus," *Journal of Popular Culture* 9, no. 2 (2004).
22. Ibid.
23. Ibid.
24. Jennifer L. Aaker, "Dimensions of Brand Personality," *Journal of Marketing Research* 39, no. 3 (1997): 347.
25. Ibid.
26. Lori D. Wolin, "Gender Issues in Advertising—An Oversight Synthesis of Research," *Journal of Advertising Research* 43, no. 1 (2003).
27. Bianca Grohmann, "Gender Dimensions of Brand Personality," *Journal of Marketing Research* 46, no. 1 (2009): 111.
28. Ibid.
29. Ibid., 112.
30. Brian D. Till and Randi L. Priluck, "Conditioning of Meaning in Advertising: Brand Gender Perception Effects," *Journal of Current Issues and Research in Advertising* 23, no. 2 (2001): 2.
31. Grohmann, "Gender Dimensions of Brand Personality," 106.
32. David Sprott, Czellar Sandor, and Eric Spangenberg, "The Importance of a General Measure of Brand Engagement on Market Behavior: Development and Validation of a Scale," *Journal of Marketing Research* 46, no. 1 (2009).
33. Ibid.
34. Ibid., 94.
35. Anna North, "Dr. Pepper's Weird Anti-Woman Ads Backfire," *Jezebel*, October 12, 2011, http://jezebel.com/dr'-pepper-not-for-women/.

Bibliography

Aaker, Jennifer. L. "Dimensions of Brand Personality." *Journal of Marketing Research* 39, no. 3 (1997): 347–56.
Anderson, Mae. "Dr. Pepper Ten 'Not for Women.'" *USA Today*, October 10, 2011. http://www.usatoday.com/money/industries/food/story/2011-10-10/dr-pepper -for-men/50717788/1.

Basow, Susan A. *Gender Stereotypes: Traditions and Alternatives*. 2nd ed. Pacific Grove, CA: Brooks/Cole Publishing Company, 1986.

Beauvoir, Simone de. *The Second Sex*. New York: Random House, 1989.

Bem, Sandra L. *The Lenses of Gender: Transforming the Debate on Sexual Inequality*. New Haven, CT: Yale University Press, 1993.

Butler, Judith. *Gender Trouble*. New York: Routledge, 1990.

Grohmann, Bianca. "Gender Dimensions of Brand Personality." *Journal of Marketing Research*, 46, no. 1 (2009): 105–19.

Hentges, Beth A., Robert A. Bartsch, and Jo A. Meier. "Gender Representation in Commercials as a Function of Target Audience Age." *Communication Research Reports* 24, no. 1 (2007): 55–62.

Kilbourne, Jean. "What Are Advertisers Really Selling Us?" JeanKilbourne.com. http://www.jeankilbourne.com/ (accessed June 18, 2012).

Kimmel, Michael S. *The Gendered Society*. New York: Oxford University Press, 2000.

North, Anna. "Dr. Pepper's Weird Anti-Woman Ads Backfire." *Jezebel*, October 12, 2011. http://jezebel.com/dr-pepper-not-for-women/.

Otnes, Cele, Young Chan Kim, and Kyungseung Kim. "All I Want for Christmas: An Analysis of Children's Brand Requests to Santa Claus." *Journal of Popular Culture* 9, no. 2 (2004): 183–95.

Payne, Elizabeth. "Heterosexism, Perfection, and Popularity: Young Lesbians' Experiences of the High School Social Scene." *Educational Studies* 41, no. 1 (2007): 60–70.

Sprott, David, Sandor Czellar, and Eric Spangenberg. "The Importance of a General Measure of Brand Engagement on Market Behavior: Development and Validation of a Scale." *Journal of Marketing Research* 46, no. 1 (2009): 92–104.

Stern, Susannah R., and Dana E. Mastro. "Gender Portrayals across the Life Span: A Content Analytic Look at Broadcast Commercials." *Mass Communication and Society* 7, no. 2 (2004): 215–36.

Till, Brian D., and Randi L. Priluck. "Conditioning of Meaning in Advertising: Brand Gender Perception Effects." *Journal of Current Issues and Research in Advertising* 23, no. 2 (2001): 1–8.

Wolin, Lori D. "Gender Issues in Advertising—an Oversight Synthesis of Research: 1970–2002." *Journal of Advertising Research* 43, no. 1 (2003): 111–29.

CHAPTER EIGHT

Out of the Closet and Into Ads: Gays and Lesbians as a Target Market

Kristin Comeforo

On May 9, 2012, viewers of *Good Morning America* heard wedding bells striking a slightly different tune, when President Barack Obama proclaimed, "I think same-sex couples should be able to get married."[1] Almost exactly one month later, ABC News reported that the Boy Scouts of America was opening a review of its longstanding policy prohibiting openly gay men and lesbians from serving in the organization.[2] The Girl Scouts supported a transgendered girl refused by a local troop, stating, "If a child identifies as a girl and the child's family presents her as a girl, Girl Scouts of Colorado welcomes her as a Girl Scout."[3] Similarly, transgender contestants have been permitted to compete in the Miss Universe Canada[4] and Miss England[5] beauty pageants. Retailer J. C. Penney recruited out talk show host Ellen DeGeneres to be the new face of its brand, while the Gap launched its "Be Bright, Be One" campaign, hinging on the visual of two gay boys embracing sweetly, dressed together in one, single Gap T-shirt.[6]

It seems as if 2012 stood as a banner year for LGBT visibility. Still, critics have been vocal and have rallied against LGBT inclusion. One Million Moms (OMM), an offshoot of the American Family Association, suggested not one, not two, but three boycotts of J. C. Penney—one for the use of DeGeneres as spokesperson, a second for depicting gay moms in its Mother's Day campaign, and a third for depicting gay dads in its Father's Day campaign. OMM also suggested action against the Gap for its "Be One" campaign, and Macy's for running a "two groom" advertisement.[7] What makes

2012 different is the response of marketers to this vocal antigay segment. All the brands mentioned here—the Girl Scouts, J. C. Penney, the Gap, and Macy's—chose to stand by their marketing communications decisions. "Corporate America has found that it's a smart business decision to stand with the majority of Americans who support gay and lesbian couples," said Rich Ferraro, vice president of communications at the Gay & Lesbian Alliance Against Defamation (GLAAD).[8] In the past, brands were not as bold, crumbling under the fear of alienating their customers and subsequently caving in to antigay sentiment. Today, brands recognize that LGBT folk *are* their customers, and that they must take great pains to include them within their marketing communications. This chapter endeavors to trace the history of the LGBT market, along with the advertising efforts made to communicate with this segment. The importance of LGBT visibility as both an economic and social imperative of advertising will be discussed, and past and present strategies will be evaluated on their ability to deliver on these imperatives.

LGBT Visibility: The Social Imperative of LGBT Advertising

At the 2005 "Reaching Out" conference, Michael Wilke, founder and executive director of the Commercial Closet Association cited the success of shows such as *Queer as Folk, The L Word*, and *Queer Eye for the Straight Guy*, plus the launch of LOGO (the "gay network") as evidence that gays and lesbians have "gone from being invisible to inescapable" on television.[9]

By 2012, these shows had long left the airwaves, but new gay and lesbian characters and storylines had popped up in shows such as *Glee, True Blood, The Good Wife, Modern Family*, and *Grey's Anatomy*. "Visibility," according to Matt Farber, founder of LGBT cable network LOGO, "is leading to more acceptance in the mainstream."[10] Still, GLAAD's "Where We Are On TV" reports that LGBT characters accounted for only 2.9 percent of scripted series regulars in the 2011–2012 season, down from 3.9 percent in the previous year.[11]

Visibility, thus, comes in fits and starts, and is never a completed process. Similarly, while the blanket term "visibility" is favored in discourse, it is important to distinguish between political/social visibility and consumer visibility. Social critics would value the former, while condemning the latter; marketers, generally, attempt to conflate the two. The term becomes even more complicated when we distinguish it in another way—between the visibility of LGBT folk, and the visibility of the brands that court them. The former may seek visibility, while the latter may not.

Generally speaking, targeted minority groups, and the general market audiences that are exposed to minority targeted ads, see the ads as an indication that the minority is a viable segment of society. In their ubiquity, ads can provide social capital to minority groups in new and unique ways. "TV commercials are a culturally powerful force, shaping society and giving voice to those outside the mainstream . . . product advertising can move public opinion faster, and farther, than any other influencing factor."[12] This places a twofold pressure on advertisers, who must carry the "political weight" of LGBT visibility.[13] First, LGBT individuals must be represented in such a way as to provide *favorable* visibility. Second, the brand must balance its own visibility, as a LGBT marketer, in order to preserve its brand image and bottom line. In many cases, the fear of "unwanted visibility" for the marketer leads to "conditional" or "contained" visibility for the LGBT community,[14] which does little to move LGBT people forward politically and socially. Brands must also be weary not to be found to be "exploiting" visibility, or simply chasing the dollars of LGBT consumers, with no care for nurturing the LGBT community.

As LGBT visibility grows, not only does social acceptance of LGBT folk grow in the broader, mainstream society, but also the attractiveness of the LGBT community grows as a target market. Now that marketers can better see LGBT folk, they get a better sense of how targeting them makes economic sense for their brands.

The LGBT Market: Delineating the Economic Imperative of LGBT Advertising

Despite increases in visibility, researching the demographic and projecting market potential has still been a difficult task. Researchers must not only find openly LGBT individuals who feel comfortable enough to provide data, but they must also find the right media through which to reach them. Even when these difficulties are overcome, researchers must then consider whether self-selected, "openly" LGBT individuals are representative of the LGBT population as a whole.

Even simple population estimates have been challenging. Findings appear to be all over the map—ranging from estimates of 2 percent of the overall population, to the 10 percent estimated by Kinsey in his seminal work in the 1940s. More recently, research from Packaged Facts found the LGBT population to be 16 million in size, and with $743 billion in buying power.[15] The Williams Institute on Sexual Orientation Law and Public Policy found a significantly lower number—9 million LGBT population, or, approximately 3.8 percent of the overall population.[16] Despite the disparities in population estimates, marketers still have strong reasons to believe that LGBT consumers form an attractive target market.

Even though the widely held belief in "gay affluence" has been proven myth, Shullman and Kraus find that there are indeed affluent LGBT folk who are, when compared to their non-LGBT counterparts, a unique and attractive market.[17] LGBT affluents were not only "more affluent" but also younger, and more likely to be social and cultural leaders (i.e., active voters, theater/museum/concert goers) than hetero-identified affluents. LGBT affluents were also more likely to use new media platforms such as smartphones and tablets, be interested in new and luxury products and brands, and be willing to pay more for brands that fit their values and beliefs (i.e., organic or environmentally friendly) and deliver higher quality. Further, LGBT consumers have been found to be more brand loyal[18] and more likely to actively advocate for or against brands that they feel address, or do not address, issues that are important to them.[19]

Recognizing, and Attending to, the LGBT Market: A Brief History

Much of the literature surrounding marketing to LGBT consumers notes how far brands have come since the beginnings of "gay" advertising in the 1970s.[20] Attention paid to this segment—in ways that can be measured and recognized—has come in fits and starts, with steps forward often followed by a few steps back. Still, several key moments, and examples, illustrate how the practice of strategic marketing communications with LGBT audiences has moved from low profile/least involvement to a more prominent role in the strategies enacted by a wide variety of brands.

Peering through the Gay Window

Even before it had a name—"gay vague," "gay window," or "purposive polysemy"—the strategy of embedding implicit or ambiguous homosexual cues in mainstream communications[21] brought homosexual images onto the pages of some of the most broadly circulated magazines in the United States. J. C. Leyendecker's 1917 advertisement for Ivory Soap is often noted as the earliest example, which features an athlete peering in on the half-naked bodies of his teammates as they shower. The copy suggests, "Not the least of the pleasures of a hard game is the bath that follows it."[22]

For much of the early history of gay advertising, gay vague was less a strategic decision, and more of an imperative. With publications such as the *New York Times*, the *New York Daily News*, and *Esquire* magazine refusing ads that used the words "gay" or "homosexual," and a national gay press still in its nascent stages into the mid-to-late 1970s, advertisers had no other option than to address the LGBT audience (really, gay men) with a wink and a nudge.[23]

Bold, Yet Cautious

Management change at the *Advocate* not only transformed the publication into a vehicle in which national brands could feel comfortable buying ad space (by removing most, if not all, sexual and political content), but also transformed the way brands perceived gay men, and the way gay men perceived themselves. The gay male specimen was placed under the microscope and proclaimed to be "stylish, trendsetting, and affluent," with "A convertible . . . Some fabulous wardrobe . . . vacations . . . a second home" on its list of "must-haves"[24]

By the 1980s, brands were becoming more comfortable with the gay press. Alcohol brands were early suitors of the market, with Absolut vodka emerging as the most attentive. Even when other brands known for courting LGBT consumers turned their backs as the AIDS crisis became more and more devastating in the mid-to-late 1980s, Absolut maintained its voice in the gay press and its support of the LGBT community.

Absolut's first forays into the pages of the gay press hint at the underlying contradictions of LGBT marketing. The ads were, at once, bold *and* cautious. As the first cases of AIDS were emerging and almost exclusively linked to gay men, it was quite bold for a brand to openly affiliate with the community. The choice of execution, however, was cautious. The brand chose to run its mainstream "Absolut Perfection" ad featuring the infamous Absolut bottle, capped with an angelic halo, rather than develop a gay-specific ad for the back cover of the *Advocate*.[25]

Moving into the mid-to-late 1990s, Absolut strengthened its commitment to the LGBT market by coming "out" to mainstream audiences, even if it still leaned more toward the "cautious" rather than the "bold." Ads such as Absolut Au Kurant, and Absolut Haring, supposedly embedded with gay cues, ran in both mainstream and gay media. This "gay vague" strategy allowed for LGBT audiences to read "gay pride" in the purple laces and leather of the corset in the Au Kurant ad. Similarly, what hetero-audiences saw as cool pop art in the Haring ad, LGBT folks saw as the credentials of a famed out artist and AIDS activist.

Absolut's commitment to the LGBT market has been solidified into the twenty-first century, as the brand came "out" in bold ways. It developed gay-specific ads for gay-specific media, and gay-themed packaging for retailers in key "gay" cities. In 2001, the brand customized an ad for the gay press that transformed the iconic bottle into a lava lamp, with the GLAAD logo rising in blobs. It was the first time Absolut had done so for any of its not-for-profit partners.[26] In 2008, gay-specific executions were created as part of the broader "In an Absolut World" campaign,[27] and in 2009, they brought a rainbow bottle to market, in celebration of gay pride.[28] In 2011, Absolut celebrated its 30-year anniversary with the LGBT market, highlighted by its Absolut Outrageous execution, which ran in gay publications—*Out*, the *Advocate*, and *Instinct*—along with mainstream titles *Vanity Fair* and *Vogue*. The creative included "fantastic images— featuring closets, divas, disco turntables, the performance artist Amanda Lepore and unicorns."[29]

Trading Closets for Living Rooms

Unlike print media, which tended to include some LGBT representation early on, representation on network television took longer to emerge. When it did, it did so in a big way, bypassing the ambiguity of gay vague/gay window and moving directly to an overt, openly gay-themed ad.

In 1994, Swedish furniture marketer IKEA presented an ad that documented a gay male couple's quest for a dining room table. The execution itself was somewhat mundane—the men were positioned a safe distance away from one another at all times, and nothing more than a pat on the back was included by way of physical contact. Despite the nonthreatening, nonsexual images of gay men engaged in a very heteronormative activity, angry protests and bomb threats led the retailer to pull the ad,[30] even though they vowed it would "continue to air over the next year."[31]

Whether a direct consequence of IKEA's experience or not, the next example of LGBT imagery in mainstream advertising was far less explicit, and led to the formal coining of the term "gay vague." Volkswagen's infamous "Da, Da, Da" ad followed two nondescript men as they drove around a city aimlessly one afternoon. The men find, and take, an armchair discarded at the curb. Their precipitous find is soon found to be aromatically unpleasant, and the chair is promptly discarded on some other curb. With no physical contact, no longing glances, or sly smiles, it is hard to imagine how or why this execution would be read as "gay" by so many, but it was, and it touched off the "gay vague" trend in mainstream advertising that remains today. An interesting wrinkle that impacts how an ad is read, however, is the media placement, and in this case it is telling—the ad debuted at the same time the "real" Ellen did, during her coming-out episode.[32]

It is hard to tell whether the success of gay vague executions in the late 1990s gave advertisers extra courage to push the envelope of LGBT messaging in mainstream media. Regardless, in 2000, financial services firm John Hancock ran an ad during the U.S. gymnastics championship that featured two women and a baby passing through immigration. Their conversation, an exchange almost whispered against the loud airport setting:

"Do you have her papers?"
"They're in the diaper bag."
"Can you believe this?"
"We're a family."
"You're going to make a great mom."
"So are you."

After airing once, John Hancock quickly edited the spot, removing the last lines that make explicit the relationship of the women as both mothers to the child. Once again, the step forward, taken by a brand trying to bring LGBT depictions into the mainstream, resulted in two steps back into the closet.

Trading the Closet for the Gridiron

Who better to bust LGBT depictions out of the commercial closet than "Fab Five" (*Queer Eye for the Straight Guy*) cast member Carson Kressley, and what better stage for him to do it on than the 2005 Super Bowl? Kressley's role in Diet Pepsi's "Lady's Man" spot is brief, but hard hitting when it comes to a global brand's willingness to recognize same-sex attraction in an ad that will reach hundreds of millions of people. The ad follows a "hot guy" walking down the street to the tune of "Stayin' Alive" and drinking a Diet Pepsi. He captures the gaze of women, who begin to follow him, as if he were the Pied Piper. He passes "hot chick" Cindy Crawford, who lowers her sunglasses seductively to get a better look. As the action reaches its climax, he passes Carson Kressley, who stops in his tracks, lowers his own shades, and uncontrollably drops his jaw in awe and admiration. He promptly turns and begins following the "hot guy" as the Bee Gees carry us out of the spot, and carry LGBT imagery in advertising out of the closet on TV.

Or did it? As with John Hancock, Pepsi subsequently ran a different edited version as part of its regular TV buys. That edited version minimized the role of Mr. Kressley to a passing shot of his back, and focused more heavily on Cindy Crawford and her heterosexual, heteronormative, attraction to the "hot guy."

Out Online

The Internet has created a plethora of opportunity for marketers to reach LGBT audiences in spaces that feel "safer" and more "private" than main-stream media or overtly gay media like *Out*, the *Advocate*, or LOGO. Early online communications with LGBT folk emphasized gay websites, newsletters, and other gay-specific online vehicles. As social media exploded in the years leading up to 2012, brands have tested the waters with being more "out" on their own social media sites. On June 26, 2012, for instance, Oreo posted a photo on its Facebook Wall of an Oreo filled with seven layers of cream, corresponding to the colors of the rainbow. The photo included simple copy—June 25 | Pride—and the status comment, "Proudly support love!" Within 12 hours, the posting received 142,414 "Likes," 32,625 "Shares," and 17,730 "Comments." A nonscientific review of the comments left the general impression that positive feedback was more prevalent, although there was quite a spirited debate and exchange of "I will eat more Oreos because of this" versus, "I have eaten my last Oreo because of this."

Constructing a New Closet

The rise in gay-specific media opportunities—crowned by the launch of the gay cable TV network LOGO in 2005—is indicative of the boom and bust of more pointed attention from marketers. Gay-specific media, while allowing advertisers to speak directly to LGBT consumers with messages that are "in culture," also allows advertisers to leverage a "commercial closet" and avoid making tough decisions about including LGBT cues and sources in more mainstream vehicles. By relegating messages and attention to gay media alone, the possibility of social progress through economic validation is minimized. It has been recognized that inclusion in advertising—which is a pervasive persuasive, and consciousness tool—may be a path to social, political, and cultural empowerment for LGBT folk.

In modern advertising history, brands have proven quite comfortable with communicating directly with LGBT consumers through gay-specific messages in gay-specific media. The 2009 Gay Press Report found that ad revenue in the gay and lesbian press grew more than 10 times faster than that in the mainstream press.[33] Similarly, almost 90 percent of the ads in national LGBT magazines were gay-specific, indicating that national brands are tailoring their messages, and committing to, the market. When it comes to including LGBT imagery in mainstream vehicles, however, brands have proven far less comfortable. In fact, they have proven to be downright uncomfortable, preferring to closet LGBT imagery and appeals in the subtext, via a "gay vague" strategy; or, worse, to draw on stereotypes that present the LGBT individual, or their "gayness," as a foil or comic relief. These forms of representation fail in delivering either the social or economic imperative required from advertising.

For social good or not, brands must rethink the commercial closet they have created. Even though gay publications and other gay media deliver respectable audience sizes, these media are still thought to deliver less than 50 percent of the overall LGBT population.[34] Most LGBT folk, it seems, consume mainstream media, just like their heterosexual counterparts. The challenge becomes, how do advertisers represent the LGBT community in mainstream advertising? Recent examples from 2011 and 2012 provide a mixed-bag in terms of representation.

J. C. Penney's Father's Day print ad showcasing two dads with their kids offers a heartfelt look at gay parenting—"What makes Dad so cool? He's the swim coach, tent maker, best friend, bike fixer and hug giver—all rolled into one. Or two."[35] Despite, or perhaps as a result of, complaints by One Million Moms, feedback on the ad gleaned from Web comments was mostly positive. In May 2012, J. C. Penney also included lesbian moms in its Mother's Day weekly mailing, a move that raised J. C. Penney's BrandIndex, determined by online market research group YouGov, by eight points, surpassing industry rival Kohl's.[36] The Gap's "Be Bright, Be One" execution is the second exemplary ad on a very short list of exemplars. The placement of a gay-themed ad via outdoor vehicles (billboards, buses) brings LGBT imagery and relationships out of the closet and onto Main Street.

Other advertisers have struggled to find the right imagery to connect with the LGBT market. The problem of misrepresentation is rampant, but perhaps more chilling are situations in which a brand could have included or represented, but chose not to. Consider, for example, a recent "Got Milk" ad starring "the Dunphys" from the hit ABC sitcom *Modern Family*. The show features several "families," however, which *could have* been used in the ad. In addition to the Dunphys (hetero married couple with three kids), there is also Jay and Gloria, a May-December interracial couple who are raising Gloria's son, Manny; and Mitchell and Cameron, same-sex partners raising Lily, an adopted daughter. The "Why Milk?" website describes the Dunphys as "a typical modern family."[37] Eschewing the diversity embraced by the show itself, the Milk group puts clear-cut bounds on what family is and how one should look.

A similar exclusion occurs in Sealy Mattress' Super Bowl ad, which features a diverse array of hetero couples falling back in bed in ecstasy to the tune of Dusty Springfield's *Just a Little Lovin'*. The ad carries Sealy's familiar slogan, "Whatever you do in bed, Sealy supports it." Consider how much more powerful the slogan would be if Sealy actually *did* support whatever *you* do in bed. Another missed opportunity for representation, which not only would have appealed to the LGBT community but would have also strengthened the resonance of the message with mainstream consumers. Despite advertisers' fears, research has shown that gays and lesbians respond positively to gay brand positioning, while heterosexuals respond neutrally at worst, but even showed somewhat positive responses.[38]

Conclusion

As more becomes known about the gay market, and its potential becomes better understood, directly appealing to the LGBT consumers via marketing communications becomes not only a necessity for brands, but also a challenge. Unlike general market consumers, who are more likely to interpret and evaluate messages based on the product itself,[39] LGBT consumers are more holistic and include consideration of whether a brand is "gay friendly"—that is, "proactive in respecting and addressing the needs of gays"[40] through advertising, employment practices, and event sponsorships.[41] Whether brands like it or not, LGBT consumers, and advocacy groups like the Human Rights Campaign (HRC), are "watching to see if the businesses they patronize understand and honor issues important to them, giving buying power to issues [like] LGBT inclusiveness."[42] Each year, HRC rates businesses on their workplace policies, and publishes its findings in a Buyer's Guide distributed on its website, and as a smartphone application. These ratings have real ramifications for brands, as LGBT consumers not only prefer gay-friendly brands, but also actively avoid brands perceived to be anti-gay-friendly. Perhaps more importantly, however, heterosexuals also seem to have favorable feelings, responding neutrally at worst, somewhat positively at best, to gay-friendly positioning. This opens up a space for brands to be more visible in their approaches to, and representations of, the LGBT market.

Notes

1. Rick Klein, "President Obama Affirms His Support for Same Sex Marriage," *ABC News Blogs*, May 9, 2012, http://gma.yahoo.com/blogs/abc-blogs/president -obama-affirms-his-support-for-same-sex-marriage.html.

2. Susan Donaldson James, "Boy Scouts Consider Opening Organization to Gays," ABC News, June 7, 2012, http://abcnews.go.com/Health/boy-scouts -allowing-gays-join-local-troops/story?id=16513417.

3. Katia Hetter, "Girl Scouts Accepts Transgender Kid, Provokes Cookie Boycott," CNN, January 13, 2012, http://articles.cnn.com/2012-01-13/living/living_girl-scout-boycott_1_gsusa-cookie-boycott-troop-leader?_s=PM:LIVING.

4. Paula Newton, "Transgender Miss Universe Canada Contestant Falls Short of Title," CNN, May 21, 2012, http://www.cnn.com/2012/05/19/showbiz/canada-miss-universe-transgender/index.html.

5. "Jackie Green, Transgendered Beauty Queen, to Enter Miss England Semi-Final," Huffington Post, May 10, 2012, http://www.huffingtonpost.com/2012/05/10/jackie-green-transgender-beauty-queen-miss-england_n_1506562.html.

6. Edmund Broch, "Gap Releases Pro-Gay Ad, under Fire from One Million Moms," PinkNews, May 20, 2012, http://www.pinknews.co.uk/2012/05/20/gap-releases-pro-gay-ad-under-fire-from-one-million-moms/.

7. One Million Moms, http://www.onemillionmoms.com/.

8. Ryan Ruggiero, "Boardrooms Are the New Battlefield for Gay Rights," The Bottom Line, http://bottomline.msnbc.msn.com/_news/2012/06/19/12286562-boardrooms-are-the-new-battlefield-for-gay-rights?lite.

9. Julia Hanna, "How Advertising Depicts Gays and Lesbians," *Harvard Business School Working Knowledge*, February 21, 2005, http://hbswk.hbs.edu/archive/4649.html.

10. Michael Paoletta, "Gay Oriented Entertainment Emerges as Powerful Entertainment," *Billboard*, July 7, 2007, http://www.keonozari.com/press/press-clips/gay-billboard.html.

11. GLAAD, "Fox Becomes Most LGBT Inclusive Broadcast TV Network, HBO Tops List of Cable Networks," September 27, 2011, http://www.glaad.org/releases/fox-becomes-most-lgbt-inclusive-broadcast-tv-network-hbo-tops-list-cable-networks.

12. Avi Dan, "Advertising Helped Bring Gay Rights into the Mainstream," *Forbes*, June 27, 2011, http://www.forbes.com/sites/avidan/2011/06/27/advertising-helped-bring-gay-rights-into-the-mainstream/.

13. Katherine Sender, *Business, Not Politics: The Making of the Gay Market* (New York: Columbia University Press, 2004).

14. Ibid.

15. Fred Lameck and Bob Witeck, "The Growing Gay Market," *Public Relations Tactics*, January 2011, 6.

16. Lisa Leff, "Gay Population in US Estimated at 4 Million, Gary Gates Says," Huffington Post, April 7, 2011, http://www.huffingtonpost.com/2011/04/07/gay-population-us-estimate_n_846348.html.

17. Bob Shullman and Stephen Kraus, "Stat of the Day: The Unique Profile of LGBT Affluents," *Advertising Age*, September 14, 2011, http://adage.com/article/adagestat/unique-profile-lgbt-affluents/229777/.

18. Tracey L. Tuten, "The Effect of Gay-Friendly and Non-Gay-Friendly Cues on Brand Attitudes: A Comparison of Heterosexual and Gay/Lesbian Reactions," *Journal of Marketing Management* 21 (2005): 441–61.

19. Robert Witeck and William Combs, *Business Inside Out* (Chicago: Kaplan Publishing, 2006).

20. Sender, *Business, Not Politics*.

21. Stefano Puntoni, Joelle Vanhamme, and Ruben Visscher, "Two Birds and One Stone: Purposeful Polysemy in Minority Targeting and Advertising Evaluations," *Journal of Advertising 40*, no. 1 (2011): 25–41.

22. Blaine Branchik, "Pansies to Parents: Gay Male Imagery in American Print Advertising," paper presented at the 12th Conference on Historical Analysis and Research in Marketing, 2005, http://faculty.quinnipiac.edu/charm/CHARM %20proceedings/CHARM%20article%20archive%20pdf%20format/Volume %2012%202005/25%20branchik.pdf.

23. Sender, *Business, Not Politics*.

24. Ibid., 35.

25. Stuart Elliott, "Absolut Celebrates 30 Years of Marketing to Gay Consumers," *New York Times*, October 27, 2011.

26. Sender, *Business Not Politics*, 115.

27. Absolut, "In an Absolut World All Men Are Created Equal and Gay Marriage Is a Celebrated Reality," *PR Newswire*, April 7, 2008, http://www.prnewswire .com/news-releases/in-an-absolut-world-all-men-are-created-equal-and-gay-marriage -is-a-celebrated-reality-57120347.html.

28. Jim Edwards, "30 Years of Absolut Ads Targeting the Gay Community," *CBS Money Watch*, October 31, 2011, http://www.cbsnews.com/8301-505123 _162-42750925/30-years-of-absolut-ads-targeting-the-gay-community/?tag =contentMain;contentBody.

29. Elliott, "Absolut Celebrates," para. 9.

30. Peter Graff, "Advertisers Out of the Closet with Gay Themed Ads," *Reuters*, August 24, 2006, http://www.aef.com/industry/news/data/2006/6076.

31. Bruce Horovitz, "TV Commercial Featuring Gay Couple Creates Madison Avenue Uproar," *Los Angeles Times*, April 5, 1994, http://articles.latimes.com/ print/1994-04-05/business/fi-42403_1_madison-avenue.

32. Michael Wilke, "Saturn and VW Take Different Roads," *Gully*, November 11, 2002, http://www.thegully.com/essays/gay_mundo2/wilke/021111 _commercial_closet.html.

33. Prime Access, Inc. and Rivendell Media Company, "2009 Gay Press Report," 7.

34. Gillian Oakenfull and Timothy Greenlee, "Queer Eye for a Gay Guy: Using Market Specific Symbols in Advertising to Attract Gay Consumers without Alienating the Mainstream," *Psychology and Marketing 22*, no. 5 (2005): 421–35.

35. Michael Krumboltz, "J. C. Penney Releases Father's Day Ad Featuring Two Gay Dads," *Yahoo Finance*, May 31, 2012, http://finance.yahoo.com/news/ j-c—penney-releases-father-s-day-ad-featuring-two-gay-dads.html.

36. Ted Marzilli, "J. C. Penney Index Score Rises with Mothers," *YouGov*, (May 10, 2012), http://www.brandindex.com/article/jc-penney-index-score-rises -mothers.

37. http://bodybymilkmail.bodybymilk.com/celebrity/modern_family.

38. Tuten, "Effect of Gay-Friendly and Non-Gay-Friendly Cues."

39. Sonya A. Grier and Anne M. Brumbaugh, "Noticing Cultural Differences: Ad Meanings Created by Target and Non-Target Markets," *Journal of Advertising* 28, no. 1 (1999): 79–93.

40. Tuten, "Effect of Gay-Friendly and Non-Gay-Friendly Cues," 442.

41. David Gudelunas, "Consumer Myths and the Gay Men and Women Who Believe Them: A Qualitative Look at Movements and Markets," *Psychology and Marketing* 28, no. 1 (2011): 53–68.

42. HRC, "Buyers Guide," 2011, http://www.hrc.org/apps/buyersguide/index.php#.TxguFRyROls.

Bibliography

Absolut. "In an Absolut World All Men Are Created 'Equal' and Gay Marriage Is a Celebrated Reality." *PR Newswire*, April 7, 2008. http://www.prnewswire.com/news-releases/in-an-absolut-world-all-men-are-created-equal-and-gay-marriage-is-a-celebrated-reality-57120347.html.

Branchik, Blaine. "Pansies to Parents: Gay Male Imagery in American Print Advertising." Paper presented at the 12th Conference on Historical Analysis and Research in Marketing, 2005. http://faculty.quinnipiac.edu/charm/CHARM%20proceedings/CHARM%20article%20archive%20pdf%20format/Volume%2012%202005/25%20branchik.pdf.

Broch, Edmund. "Gap Releases Pro-Gay Ad, under Fire from One Million Moms." *PinkNews*, May 20, 2012. http://www.pinknews.co.uk/2012/05/20/gap-releases-pro-gay-ad-under-fire-from-one-million-moms/.

Dan, Avi. "Advertising Helped Bring Gay Rights into the Mainstream." *Forbes*, June 27, 2011. http://www.forbes.com/sites/avidan/2011/06/27/advertising-helped-bring-gay-rights-into-the-mainstream/.

Edwards, Jim. "30 Years of Absolut Ads Targeting the Gay Community." CBS MoneyWatch, October 31, 2011. http://www.cbsnews.com/8301-505123_162-42750925/30-years-of-absolut-ads-targeting-the-gay-community/?tag=contentMain;contentBody.

Elliott, Stuart. "Absolut Celebrates 30 Years of Marketing to Gay Consumers." *New York Times*, October 27, 2011.

GLAAD. "Fox Becomes Most LGBT Inclusive Broadcast TV Network, HBO Tops List of Cable Networks." September 27, 2011. http://www.glaad.org/releases/fox-becomes-most-lgbt-inclusive-broadcast-tv-network-hbo-tops-list-cable-networks.

Grier, Sonya A., and Anne M. Brumbaugh. "Noticing Cultural Differences: Ad Meanings Created by Target and Non-Target Markets." *Journal of Advertising* 28, no. 1 (1999): 80–93.

Gudelunas, David. "Consumer Myths and the Gay Men and Women Who Believe Them: A Qualitative Look at Movements and Markets." *Psychology and Marketing* 28, no. 1 (2011): 53–68.

Hanna, Julia. "How Advertising Depicts Gays and Lesbians." *Harvard Business School Working Knowledge*, February 21, 2005. http://hbswk.hbs.edu/archive/4649.html.

Hetter, Katia. "Girl Scouts Accepts Transgender Kid, Provokes Cookie Boycott." CNN, January 13, 2012. http://articles.cnn.com/2012-01-13/living/living_girl-scout-boycott_1_gsusa-cookie-boycott-troop-leader?_s=PM:LIVING.

Horovitz, Bruce. "TV Commercial Featuring Gay Couple Creates a Madison Avenue Uproar." *Los Angeles Times*, April 5, 1994. http://articles.latimes.com/print/1994-04-05/business/fi-42403_1_madison-avenue.

HRC. *Buyer's Guide*. 2011. http://www.hrc.org/apps/buyersguide/index.php#.TxguFRyROls.

James, Susan Donaldson. "Boy Scouts Consider Opening Organization to Gays." ABC News, June 7, 2012. http://abcnews.go.com/Health/boy-scouts-allowing-gays-join-local-troops/story?id=16513417.

"Jackie Green, Transgendered Beauty Queen, to Enter Miss England Semi-Final." Huffington Post, May 10, 2012. http://www.huffingtonpost.com/2012/05/10/jackie-green-transgender-beauty-queen-miss-england_n_1506562.html.

Klein, Rick. "President Obama Affirms His Support for Same Sex Marriage." *ABC News Blogs*. May 2, 2012. http://gma.yahoo.com/blogs/abc-blogs/president-obama-affirms-his-support-for-same-sex-marriage.html.

Lameck, Fred, and Bob Witeck. "The Growing Gay Market." *Public Relations Tactics*, January 2011.

Leff, Lisa. "Gay Population in US Estimated at 4 Million, Gary Gates Says." Huffington Post, April 7, 2011. http://www.huffingtonpost.com/2011/04/07/gay-population-us-estimate_n_846348.html.

Newton, Paula. "Transgender Miss Universe Canada Contestant Falls Short of Title." CNN, May 21, 2012. http://www.cnn.com/2012/05/19/showbiz/canada-miss-universe-transgender/index.html.

Oakenfull, Gillian, and Timothy Greenlee. "Queer Eye for a Gay Guy: Using Market Specific Symbols in Advertising to Attract Gay Consumers without Alienating the Mainstream." *Psychology and Marketing* 22, no. 5 (2005): 421–35.

One Million Moms. http://www.onemillionmoms.com/ (accessed June 27, 2012).

Paoletta, Michael. "Gay Oriented Entertainment Emerges as Powerful Entertainment." *Billboard*. July 7, 2007. http://www.keonozari.com/press/press-clips/gay-billboard.html.

Prime Access, Inc. and Rivendell Media Company. "2009 Gay Press Report."

Puntoni, Stefano, Joelle Vanhamme, and Ruben Visscher. "Two Birds and One Stone: Purposeful Polysemy in Minority Targeting and Advertising Evaluations." *Journal of Advertising* 40, no. 1 (2011): 25–41.

Ruggiero, Ryan. "Boardrooms Are the New Battlefield for Gay Rights." *The Bottom Line*, June 19, 2012. http://bottomline.msnbc.msn.com/_news/2012/06/19/12286562-boardrooms-are-the-new-battlefield-for-gay-rights?lite.

Sender, Katherine. *Business, Not Politics: The Making of the Gay Market*. New York: Columbia University Press, 2004.

Shullman, Bob, and Stephen Kraus. "Stat of the Day: The Unique Profile of LGBT Affluents." *Advertising Age*, September 14, 2011. http://adage.com/article/adagestat/unique-profile-lgbt-affluents/229777/.

Tuten, Tracey L. "The Effect of Gay-Friendly and Non-Gay-Friendly Cues on Brand Attitudes: A Comparison of Heterosexual and Gay/Lesbian Reactions." *Journal of Marketing Management* 21 (2005): 441–61.

Wilke, Michael. "Saturn and VW Take Different Roads." *Gully*, November 11, 2002. http://www.thegully.com/essays/gay_mundo2/wilke/021111_commercial_closet.html.

Witeck, Robert, and William Combs. *Business Inside Out*. Chicago: Kaplan Publishing, 2006.

CHAPTER NINE

Fast Food Advertising

Jennifer L. McCullough and Catherine E. Goodall

More and more Americans are eating fast food on a regular basis. In fact, in 2003 and 2004, researchers found that fast food contributed to around 17 percent of the caloric intake of adolescents.[1] Not surprisingly, food and beverage advertising has become a thriving industry. In 2006, the industry spent nearly $10 billion on marketing.[2] This made it an industry second only to the automotive industry in advertising expenditures.[3] What is more concerning is of the $10 billion spent, 16 percent was spent directly targeting youth.[4]

In 2006, the Federal Trade Commission (FTC) analyzed confidential advertising expenditures of 44 food and beverage companies promoting their products to youth. Of the approximately $2 billion that fast food companies spent on advertising altogether, the FTC found that $161 million was spent marketing to children under 12 years old, and $145 million on children 12 to 17 years old. When accounting for the small amount of overlap in advertising to both segments of the population, this calculates to nearly 14 percent of the overall fast food advertising budget being devoted to marketing to youth. This percentage does not include the additional $360 million fast food companies spent on promotional toys obviously targeting youth. Adding this figure raises the percentage of fast food advertising budgets devoted to targeting youth up to 37 percent.[5]

This chapter investigates the fast food industry's targeting of children in advertising. We emphasize this particular demographic, as the practice of marketing fast food to children has fueled great public and media attention, raising questions about ethics, and heightening concerns about detrimental impact on American youth. Concerns predominantly arise due to the vulnerable nature of children, notably their limited cognitive development (see Chapter 5 in this volume for further discussion). Of all food advertising, fast food is one of the more heavily advertised categories, making it a prime topic of research and debate. This chapter examines trends and content of fast food advertising, effects of fast food advertising, and legal issues and regulation of such advertising.

Trends and Content

Fast food restaurants use a variety of media to target children and teens. Doing so makes for a complicated media landscape for youth to navigate. In fact, advertising surrounds almost every aspect of a child's life. This section will review the various mechanisms fast food restaurants use to reach children.

Traditional Television Advertising

In 2006, food and beverage companies spent $853 million on youth-oriented television advertising.[6] Of those expenditures, fast food companies contributed $91 million to target children, and another $105 million to target teens. The FTC found some overlap in the child- and teen-directed television advertising, so all together, fast food companies spent $187 million on youth-oriented television advertising. However, the FTC used the strict guideline that ads must be placed in television shows that garnered at least 20 percent youth audience share in order to be added to the calculations. Therefore, these numbers are conservative on their own. Since children and teens are often exposed to advertising in general audience programming (e.g., primetime broadcast shows), the FTC also analyzed the top five teen broadcast shows and found that fast food restaurants spent an additional $60 million on advertising on these five shows alone.

With the enormous amount of money companies spend on television advertising, it is critical to look at the amount of fast food advertising children and teenagers are exposed to as a result. From 2003 to 2009, fast food advertising exposure increased for children under five years old by 21 percent; for children between the ages of 5 and 12, exposure increased by 34 percent; and for teenagers, exposure increased by 39 percent.[7] On average, this equates to be 2.8 fast food television ads per day for the youngest children, 3.5 per day for elementary school–aged children, and 4.5 per day for teenagers.[8] What is more though, black youth saw 50 percent more fast food advertisements than white children, and black teens were exposed to 75 percent more advertisements for KFC and McDonald's than white teens.[9]

Given these staggering numbers from television advertisements alone, it is important to look at what messages these ads have been sending. In a study of the top 12 fast food restaurants in 2009, researchers first looked at which products were being promoted in television advertisements.[10] Three main categories emerged: kids' meals, lunch/dinner items, and value/combo meals. Thirty-seven percent of fast food ads preschoolers saw were for kids' meals, while 26 percent were for lunch/dinner items, and 15 percent were for value/combo meals. Elementary school–aged children saw a similar pattern of advertisements: 35 percent for kids' meals, 30 percent for lunch/dinner items, and 15 percent for value/combo meals. Since, as will be discussed later, fast food kids' meals do not meet the FTC guidelines for nutritional foods advertised to children, these exposure levels are concerning.

The pattern for teenagers, however, more closely resembled the one that emerged for adults. Of advertising directed at teenagers, 12 percent was for kids' meals, 44 percent for lunch/dinner items, and 23 percent for value/combo meals. Although the researchers also investigated the fast food industry's advertising of healthy options, these ads accounted for only 5 percent or less of the total advertisements seen by each age group. This means a child under the age of 12 saw a healthy-options advertisement about once every two weeks.[11]

Although these initial findings explain what products are being advertised, it also is helpful to understand the persuasive appeals being used in advertising to youth. In order to assess content of child-directed advertising, researchers defined child-targeted ads to be advertising that contained at least one of the following: only kids eating the food, only kids as the main roles, a narrator speaking directly to kids, or a toy or other product for kids being featured with the food.[12] As previous research has found, child-targeted ads used persuasive appeals like humor and fun in a majority of ads.[13] Interestingly though, this study also found that close to 30 percent of child-targeted ads depicted adults as either negative or incompetent, which could have implications on family dynamics as well. Finally, more than 35 percent of ads contained tie-ins to movies, television shows, or video games, and more than 30 percent contained licensed characters popular among children.[14] A more in-depth discussion of cross-promotion and licensed characters will be reviewed later.

These depictions can be compared with the persuasive appeals used most frequently with adults: value of food, new or improved items, and food quality.[15] When comparing the types of appeals used for youth and adults, it is interesting to note that adult appeals are more factual and provide more information, while child appeals are more emotional and serve to create positive associations. This has the potential to be more problematic for children because those appeals are not as straightforward for children, particularly those who have yet to understand that advertising is trying to persuade them. In addition, since research has linked emotional food choices with obesity, the dominance of emotional appeals is even more concerning.[16]

Finally, when looking at the content of youth-directed advertising and making claims about the impact this advertising could have on eating habits, it is important to consider the context in which eating occurs during commercials and what exactly is being consumed. Researchers found that less than 10 percent of child-targeted ads depicted eating the food at a family meal.[17] In fact, in close to 60 percent of these ads, it was unclear when consumption was taking place. This could have important health considerations, given that it is recommended that families eat at least two or three meals together each week. What is more, when calculating the nutritional content of fast food advertising, researchers found that each day children younger than five years old are exposed to over 1,100 calories in fast food advertising, children 6 to 11 years old are exposed to over 1,400 calories, and teenagers are exposed to over 2,100 calories.[18] This contributes to concerns about the type of food children are seeing in television advertisements.

Online Advertising

Even though television is a main source of fast food advertising exposure, young consumers use a variety of media on a daily basis, and fast food companies use this to their advantage. Most 8- to 18-year-olds spend roughly an hour per day on the computer, and 26 percent of children ages four to six typically spend 50 minutes on the computer. Thus, it is important to consider the fast food advertising they may encounter online.[19] Even though children and teens use computers for a variety of activities, researchers have found that children tend to spend over 30 minutes on average per day playing games and visiting websites.[20] These websites and games are often loaded with fast food advertising, from banner ads to company websites.

In the interest of determining exposure to messages, researchers used comScore data to determine the website traffic to main restaurant websites and child-targeted restaurant websites.[21] They found that the 13 McDonald's websites drew around 365,000 unique child visitors and about 294,000 unique teen visitors each month while PizzaHut.com and

Dominos.com had a combined total of over 430,000 unique youth visitors. ClubBK.com, which was sixth in the rankings, had 49,900 unique youth visitors. On average, child and teen visitors spent between five and seven minutes on any one of these websites.[22]

Because of the levels of exposure to these websites, it is useful to have a more clear understanding of what youth are seeing when they visit. Close to 80 percent of the websites youth were visiting contained branding messages, and only the Subway and Sonic child-directed sites contained any health or nutrition messages.[23] Instead, like television advertising, the main persuasive appeal used was fun and happiness.[24] These figures are very similar to other studies that have found 79 percent of all food websites contain mention of product benefits.[25] In addition to the overall message of the brand being fun, this medium provides unique opportunities for engaging the audience. To do so, 74 percent of pages had flash animation, 45 percent had music, and almost 30 percent had advergames.

Advergames are branded computer games.[26] These games encourage interactivity with advertising and are generally designed for children. Although a specific analysis of fast food advergames has not been conducted, researchers found in an analysis of all food websites that food websites with advergames had 1.2 million unique child visitors and 900,000 unique teen visitors each month in 2009.[27] Plus, children have been found to be more likely to visit websites with games and spend more time on those sites than sites that do not have games.[28]

The question then remains as to what types of messages youth may be receiving in these games. It was found in a recent study that 80 percent of food advergames had two or more brand images in the game. What is more, 64 percent of games featured the brand as a main attraction, like a game piece or a prize. Finally, an additional concern researchers, policy makers, and parents may have is that 71 percent of the games deliberately encourage children to play again, which would multiply the exposure to and subsequent effect of the game.[29] Since younger and older children appear to be impacted in the same way by these games, it is important for researchers to continue exploring the potential negative effects.[30]

Other Forms of Advertising

Although fast food companies spend money targeting youth through radio, print, and in-store advertising, one of the methods of targeting youth that fast food companies spend a significant amount of money on is cross-promotion. Cross-promotion often involves the use of licensed characters from television shows and movies that appeal to youth. As mentioned earlier, fast food restaurants spent $360 million on the toys sold with kids' meals in 2006. These meals make up 38 percent of the meals sold to children.[31] Not including the $360 million spent on the toys, fast food restaurants spent 46 percent of their child-directed expenditures on cross-promotion advertising.[32] This $74 million includes the use of licensed characters. What is more, over 30 movies and television shows were cross-promoted with fast food restaurant kids' meals in 2006 alone.[33] Because children as young as two years of age recognize branding, the use of cross-promotion has a high appeal for companies.[34]

Effects of Food Advertising on Children

Aggressive tactics used by the fast food industry to target young consumers have generated much discussion and criticism. This criticism is warranted in light of the reality that food advertising to children has been demonstrated to be highly effective. Specifically, a large body of research has led to the following conclusions: food advertising to children (1) results in more positive attitudes toward unhealthy foods, (2) influences food choices, preferences, and consumption patterns, and (3) influences perceived enjoyment of unhealthy foods.

Attitudes toward Food

Research indicates that heavier television use among children (and subsequently higher food advertising exposure) leads to more favorable attitudes toward high-fat, high-sodium, and high-sugar junk and fast food products.[35] Although this is a concerning effect given the prevalence of fast food advertising, research also has indicated that this effect can apply to advertising of nutrient-rich healthy products.[36] Thus, health food advertising, if done as skillfully as junk and fast food advertising, has the potential to shift attitudes in favor of healthier products. Unfortunately, the present dominance of junk and fast food advertising outweighs health food advertising to children. This sort of marketing could potentially make it more difficult for parents to shape healthy attitudes toward food in their children.

Impact on Choices, Preferences, and Consumption

Attitudes are important determinants of behavior. Thus, when fast food advertising leads individuals to view advertised items more favorably, they are also more likely to request, select, and consume those items.[37] This effect has been observed in children as young as preschool.[38] Research indicates that food advertising impacts kids' brand choices (e.g., McDonald's, Wendy's, Coca-Cola), as well as their preferences and consumption of advertised high-calorie foods. This is especially the case among lower-income children.[39] Thus, there is evidence that food consumption patterns of low-income children are more strongly influenced by food advertising than higher-income children. This may contribute in part to the trend for low-income children to be at a heightened risk of becoming obese than higher-income children.[40]

Children who are exposed to food advertising while watching cartoons tend to consume more snack foods. In one study, kids who ate snacks while watching cartoons embedded with food advertisements ate 45 percent more than kids who watched the same shows containing nonfood advertisements. It is proposed that this effect occurs because the cues in the food ads automatically prompt food-related thoughts and behaviors.[41] Generally, people are not consciously aware of this effect. Interestingly, the effect can occur even when the advertised products are unrelated to the snack being consumed. For example, a child who sees a McDonald's advertisement while eating potato chips likely will consume more chips than a child who sees a toy advertisement or other nonfood advertisement. This occurs simply as a result of the McDonald's advertisement activating food-related thoughts and desires.

Impact on Perceived Enjoyment

Effective advertising can create wide-scale brand recognition and preference among children. When a brand is well liked and recognized by children, it actually can skew their perceptions of how enjoyable the food is. For example, in one study, researchers had preschool-aged children eat McDonald's food. Some of the children were presented the meal in McDonald's packaging—in which the brand is clearly present and recognizable. On the other hand, some of the children were given the exact same McDonald's meal in generic, unbranded packaging. They then asked all the children to rate how enjoyable the food was. Although the food was exactly the same, the children who knew they were eating McDonald's rated the food as more enjoyable than those who thought they were eating a non-McDonald's, generic-brand meal.[42]

This finding suggests that McDonald's has created a strong and effective brand among child consumers. Positive associations toward the brand established via advertising shape how children feel about the food when that brand is made salient. The researchers who conducted this study found that effects of brand salience on enjoyment of the food were heightened among children who watched more television and subsequently were exposed to a greater amount of McDonald's advertising.[43] Thus, among this consumer segment, brand associations were more strongly developed. As a result, exposure to the brand more greatly influenced their perception of the food than children with weaker brand associations. This study illustrates powerful effects of branding on children, notably in the fast food industry.

Regulation, Legal Issues, and Public Relations

The growing body of evidence suggesting that food advertising to children can contribute to unhealthy food preferences and choices has resulted in increased public concern about the common practice of marketing to children. As such, the fast food industry has seen increased threat of legal and regulatory action, though the industry at present remains self-regulated.

Pelman v. McDonald's Corporation

The historic court case that brought the issue of fast food marketing and children to the height of American public and media attention was *Pelman v. McDonald's Corp.* in 2003. It was the first legal action of its kind against a fast food restaurant to make it into a U.S. court. The suit was filed in 2002 by parents of two girls who allegedly had become overweight by consuming McDonald's food. The parents claimed that they believed McDonald's was healthy because the company did not provide sufficient nutrition information in its stores or advertisements. The Pelmans' lawyer claimed that McDonald's excessive use of marketing to children made it impossible for children to make proper nutritional judgments, contributing to the development of a variety of health problems including obesity. In this case, the judge ruled that McDonald's was not responsible for an individual's obesity. Although the fast food giant was found not guilty, the case opened the door for much discussion about corporate responsibility of the fast food industry, specifically in light of the reality that it engages in aggressive marketing to children who may lack the ability to make sound nutritional judgments.[44]

San Francisco Ban on Happy Meal Toys

Since *Pelman v. McDonald's*, there have been a number of similar cases to rule that the fast food industry is not responsible for an individual's health problems. There also have been proposals at the local level to deal with food marketing toward children. An example that gained national attention occurred in 2011 in San Francisco. It involved passage and implementation of a law banning restaurants from including free toys with children's meals when those meals fail to meet the city's nutritional standards. The standards require that meals contain fewer than 600 calories, include fruits and vegetables, and have less than 35 percent of calories coming from fat, fewer than 640 milligrams of sodium, and fewer than 0.5 milligrams of trans fat. McDonald's Happy Meal failed the nutritional standard's fruit and vegetable quota.[45]

Thus, in accordance with this law, toys cannot be given with Happy Meals sold in San Francisco. However, in an effort to overcome the legislation, McDonald's elected to instead sell Happy Meal toys for 10 cents each with a meal purchase, donating the money collected to charity.[46] The move raised critiques about the corporation and its decision to use charity donations to defend its practice of aggressively marketing to children. This case has helped continue the debate about whether the food industry should be able to market directly to children—an issue that remains heated and unresolved to date.

Federal Trade Commission Response

The U.S. government has responded to heightened concern about food advertising to children by providing industry guidelines, which, if enforced, would greatly change the landscape of food advertising to children. However, the guidelines released by the Federal Trade Commission (FTC) in 2011 are merely voluntary guidelines and are not required by law. As such, fast food marketers may choose freely to adhere or ignore the recommendation that advertisements targeting children (1) contain some kind of healthful ingredient (whole grains, fruits and vegetables, low-fat milk), and (2) not contain unhealthy amounts of sodium, sugar, and/or saturated and trans fats. Specifically, the guidelines suggest that an advertised meal contain no more than 8 grams of sugar per serving, and no more than 210 grams of sodium per serving.[47]

To illustrate what this might mean for fast food advertisers, consider the following examples. A McDonald's Happy Meal contains kid's-sized french fries, apple slices, low-fat milk or juice, and a choice of chicken nuggets, a hamburger, or cheeseburger. According to McDonald's nutrition information, the sodium and sugar counts on these meal options would range from 690 milligrams of sodium and 22 grams of sugar to 932 milligrams of sodium and 32 grams of sugar, grossly surpassing FTC guidelines.[48] The kid's menu for competitor Wendy's also would fail to meet FTC marketing standards. Specifically, Wendy's offers a selection of (1) hamburger, cheeseburger, chicken sandwich, or chicken nuggets, (2) fries or apple slices, and (3) milk, juice, or soda. The sandwiches and nuggets alone have sodium counts that range from 370 to 750 milligrams, well surpassing FTC guidelines.[49]

The FTC guidelines represent the government's increasing concern about food advertising to children. However, it is a modest step compared to regulatory action taken internationally. For example, in 2007, the United Kingdom's Food Standards Agency implemented a system to determine whether products marketed to children meet required nutritional standards.[50] Products not meeting these standards are subject to marketing bans and restrictions.[51] Thus, the UK government has moved beyond providing mere guidelines to enforced regulation.

An Era of "Corporate Responsibility"?

The threat of regulation and the public and media's increasing discussion of appropriateness of food advertising to children seems to be pressuring the food industry to demonstrate corporate responsibility. For example, many fast food kid's menus have changed in recent years, accommodating a wider variety of options for parents. Additionally, a children's entertainment giant, the Walt Disney Corporation, recently illustrated what seems to be an emerging trend by announcing that it would restrict food advertisements on its children's programming for products not meeting the company's nutrition standards by 2015. These standards include banning products with more than 10 grams of sugar per serving, and whole meal products in excess of 600 calories. It also has guidelines limiting fat and sodium content.[52]

However, these guidelines may not be the game changer they have been proclaimed to be by policy makers and the news media. Consider that Disney states that it will ban breakfast cereals in excess of 10 grams of sugar per serving. This presumably would restrict a number of high-sugar products. However, making the cut does not necessarily mean the product is healthy. Ten grams of sugar equates to 2.5 teaspoons of sugar. The American Heart Association recommends that children between the ages of four and eight consume no more than 3 teaspoons of sugar in an entire day[53] (their standards are consistent with calorie recommendations for children provided by the Mayo Clinic[54] and the American Academy of Pediatrics[55]). This means that a child consuming only 1 serving of a cereal (assuming he only eats one serving) deemed acceptable by Disney's nutrition guidelines would be consuming *nearly* his entire recommended allotment of sugar for that day in that single food item.

The problem with this approach is that government nutrition guidelines are holistic and require that individuals consider everything they consume in a given day.[56] The guidelines do not treat items individually, nor do they indicate whether a single food item exceeds recommended fat, sodium, and sugar allotments. If parents come to rely on Disney's advertising standards and deem advertised products as "nutritious," or "smart choices," they may risk feeding their children a combination of products that together may not only fail to meet federal nutrition guidelines, but may adversely affect a child's health. Thus, the concern is that this sort of approach—although perhaps a step forward—may fail to produce the positive "game-changing" effect being proclaimed in the media.[57] As such, one may reasonably question whether the movement we are observing is just an illusion of corporate responsibility, rather than a genuine effort to aggressively transform America's poor nutrition landscape.

Conclusion

As has been demonstrated in this chapter, the fast food industry has not only been rapidly increasing its advertising expenditures over time, but has been aggressively expanding marketing efforts to children. We argue that members of the public should be concerned about this trend for the following reasons. As noted in this chapter, the increase in children's exposure to fast food advertising over the past decade is alarming. Because fast food advertising dominates so many different forms of media, it is nearly impossible for parents to prevent children's exposure to these messages. We question the ethics of these advertising efforts, as fast food marketers use persuasive tactics that effectively appeal to children, yet young children lack the cognitive capacity to even recognize persuasive appeals. As we have illustrated, fast food marketing to children can be extremely effective, particularly when the ads successfully develop positive brand associations in young consumers. Given the increasing problem of childhood obesity and the rise of associated illnesses, the debate over whether the fast food and junk food industries should be allowed to market directly to children is likely to remain a lively one.

Notes

1. Rhonda S. Sebastian, Cecilia Wilkinson Enns, and Joseph D. Goldman, "US Adolescents and MyPyramid: Associations Between Fast-Food Consumption and

Lower Likelihood of Meeting Recommendations," *Journal of the American Dietetic Association* 109, no. 2 (February 2009): 226–35.

2. Federal Trade Commission, *Marketing Food to Children and Adolescents: A Review of Industry Expenditures, Activities, and Self-Regulation*, A Report to Congress, July 2008, http://www.ftc.gov/os/2008/07/P064504foodmktingreport.pdf.

3. Nielsen Media Research, "Automotive Ad Spending Down; Spot Radio and TV Up," n.d., http://www.marketingcharts.com/television/automotive-ad -spending-down-spot-radio-and-tv-up-295/.

4. Federal Trade Commission, *Marketing Food to Children and Adolescents*.

5. Ibid.

6. Ibid.

7. Jennifer L. Harris et al., *Fast Food FACTS: Evaluating Fast Food Nutrition and Marketing to Youth* (Rudd Center for Food Policy & Obesity, November 2010).

8. Ibid.

9. Ibid.

10. Ibid.

11. Ibid.

12. Ibid.

13. F. Earle Barcus, "The Nature of Television Advertising to Children," in *Children and the Faces of Television: Teaching, Violence, Selling*, ed. Edward L. Palmer and Aimee Dorr (New York: Academic Press, 1980), 273–85; S. M. Connor, "Food-Related Advertising on Preschool Television: Building Brand Recognition in Young Viewers," *Pediatrics* 118, no. 4 (October 1, 2006): 1478–85; Sara C. Folta et al., "Food Advertising Targeted at School-Age Children: A Content Analysis," *Journal of Nutrition Education and Behavior* 38, no. 4 (July 2006): 244–48; Harris et al., *Fast Food FACTS*.

14. Harris et al., *Fast Food FACTS*.

15. Ibid.

16. Caroline Davis et al., "Decision-Making Deficits and Overeating: A Risk Model for Obesity," *Obesity* 12, no. 6 (June 2004): 929–35.

17. Harris et al., *Fast Food FACTS*.

18. Ibid.

19. Victoria J. Rideout and Elizabeth Hamel, *The Media and the Family: Electronic Media in the Lives of Infants, Toddlers, and Preschoolers and Their Parents* (Menlo Park, CA: Kaiser Family Foundation, May 2006); Donald F. Roberts, Ulla G. Foehr, and Victoria Rideout, *Generation M: Media in the Lives of 8–18 Year-Olds* (Menlo Park, CA: Kaiser Family Foundation, 2005).

20. Roberts, Foehr, and Rideout, *Generation M*.

21. Harris et al., *Fast Food FACTS*.

22. Ibid.

23. Ibid.

24. Ibid.

25. Elizabeth S. Moore, *It's Child's Play: Advergaming and the Online Marketing of Food to Children* (Menlo Park, CA: Kaiser Family Foundation, July 2006).

26. Jennifer L. Harris et al., "US Food Company Branded Advergames on the Internet: Children's Exposure and Effects on Snack Consumption," *Journal of Children and Media* 6, no. 1 (February 2012): 51–68; Elizabeth S. Moore and Victoria J Rideout, "The Online Marketing of Food to Children: Is It Just Fun and Games?" *Journal of Public Policy & Marketing* 26, no. 2 (November 2007): 202–20.

27. Harris et al., "US Food Company Branded Advergames on the Internet."

28. Harris et al., "US Food Company Branded Advergames on the Internet"; Moore and Rideout, "The Online Marketing of Food to Children."

29. Moore, *It's Child's Play*.

30. Harris et al., "US Food Company Branded Advergames on the Internet."

31. Harris et al., *Fast Food FACTS*.

32. Federal Trade Commission, *Marketing Food to Children and Adolescents*.

33. Ibid.

34. Mary Story and Simone French, "Food Advertising and Marketing Directed at Children and Adolescents in the US," *International Journal of Behavioral Nutrition and Physical Activity* 1, no. 3 (2004), http://www.ijbnpa.org/content/1/1/3.

35. Helen G. Dixon et al., "The Effects of Television Advertisements for Junk Food versus Nutritious Food on Children's Food Attitudes and Preferences," *Social Science and Medicine* 65, no. 7 (October 2007): 1311–23.

36. Ibid.

37. Moniek Buijzen, Joris Schuurman, and Elise Bomhof, "Associations between Children's Television Advertising Exposure and Their Food Consumption Patterns: A Household Diary–Survey Study," *Appetite* 50, no. 2–3 (March 2008): 231–39.

38. Dina Borzekowski and Thomas N. Robinson, "The 30-Second Effect: An Experiment Revealing the Impact of Television Commercials on Food Preferences of Preschoolers," *Journal of the American Diabetic Association* 101 (2001): 42–46.

39. Buijzen, Schuurman, and Bomhof, "Associations between Children's Television Advertising Exposure and Their Food Consumption Patterns."

40. Centers for Disease Control and Prevention, *Obesity among Low-Income Preschool Children*, n.d., http://www.cdc.gov/obesity/downloads/PedNSSFact Sheet.pdf.

41. Jennifer L. Harris, John A. Bargh, and Kelly D. Brownell, "Priming Effects of Television Food Advertising on Eating Behavior," *Health Psychology* 28, no. 4 (2009): 404–13.

42. Thomas N. Robinson et al., "Effects of Fast Food Branding on Young Children's Taste Preferences," *Archives of Pediatrics and Adolescent Medicine* 161, no. 8 (August 1, 2007): 792.

43. Ibid.

44. Jonathan Wald, "McDonald's Obesity Suit Tossed: U.S. Judge Dismisses Obesity Suit vs. McDonald's," CNN Money, February 17, 2003, http://money.cnn.com/2003/01/22/news/companies/mcdonalds/index.htm.

45. Michael Martinez, "San Francisco Bans Happy Meals with Toys," CNN, November 9, 2010, http://articles.cnn.com/2010-11-09/us/california.fast.food.ban_1_meal-combinations-apple-dippers-yale-university-s-rudd-center?_s=PM:US.

46. Ibid.

47. William Neuman, "U.S. Seeks New Limits on Food Ads for Children," *New York Times*, April 28, 2011, http://www.nytimes.com/2011/04/29/business/29 label.html?_r=1.

48. McDonald's, "Nutrition Choices," n.d., http://www.mcdonalds.com/us/en/ food/food_quality/nutrition_choices.html.

49. Wendy's, "Wendy's Nutrition," n.d., http://www.wendys.com/food/ NutritionLanding.jsp.

50. Food Standards Agency, "Enforcement and Regulation," n.d., http:// www.food.gov.uk/enforcement/.

51. "Ban on Junk Food Ads Introduced," BBC News, January 1, 2008, http:// news.bbc.co.uk/2/hi/health/7166510.stm.

52. Public Radio International, "Disney Sets New Nutritional Standards for Advertisers," *Takeaway*, June 7, 2012, http://www.pri.org/stories/business/disney -sets-new-nutritional-standards-for-advertisers-10161.html.

53. R. K. Johnson et al., "Dietary Sugars Intake and Cardiovascular Health: A Scientific Statement from the American Heart Association," *Circulation* 120, no. 11 (August 24, 2009): 1011–20.

54. Mayo Clinic, "Nutrition for Kids: Guidelines for a Healthy Diet," n.d., http://www.mayoclinic.com/health/nutrition-for-kids/NU00606.

55. Tamekia Reese, "Childhood Nutrition," *Healthy Children Magazine*, 2008, http://www.healthychildren.org/English/healthy-living/nutrition/Pages/Childhood -Nutrition.aspx.

56. U.S. Department of Agriculture, "Choose My Plate," n.d., http://www .choosemyplate.gov/.

57. Travis Butterworth, "Disney's Junk Food Crackdown: Can Cutting Junk-Food Ads Make Kids Healthier?" *Newsweek*, June 11, 2012.

Bibliography

Acuff, Dan S., and Robert H. Reiher. *What Kids Buy and Why: The Psychology of Marketing to Kids*. New York: Free Press, 1997.

"Ban on Junk Food Ads Introduced." BBC News. January 1, 2008. http://news .bbc.co.uk/2/hi/health/7166510.stm.

Barcus, F. Earle. "The Nature of Television Advertising to Children." In *Children and the Faces of Television: Teaching, Violence, Selling*, edited by Edward L. Palmer and Aimee Dorr, 273–85. New York: Academic Press, 1980.

Borzekowski, Dina, and Thomas N. Robinson. "The 30-Second Effect: An Experiment Revealing the Impact of Television Commercials on Food Preferences of Preschoolers." *Journal of the American Diabetic Association* 101 (2001): 42–46.

Buijzen, Moniek, Joris Schuurman, and Elise Bomhof. "Associations between Children's Television Advertising Exposure and Their Food Consumption Patterns: A Household Diary–Survey Study." *Appetite* 50, no. 2–3 (March 2008): 231–39.

Butterworth, Travis. "Disney's Junk Food Crackdown: Can Cutting Junk-Food Ads Make Kids Healthier?" *Newsweek*, June 11, 2012.

Centers for Disease Control and Prevention. *Obesity among Low-Income Preschool Children*. N.d. http://www.cdc.gov/obesity/downloads/PedNSSFactSheet.pdf.

Connor, S. M. "Food-Related Advertising on Preschool Television: Building Brand Recognition in Young Viewers." *Pediatrics* 118, no. 4 (October 1, 2006): 1478–85.

Davis, Caroline, Robert D. Levitan, Pierandrea Muglia, Carmen Bewell, and James L. Kennedy. "Decision-Making Deficits and Overeating: A Risk Model for Obesity." *Obesity* 12, no. 6 (June 2004): 929–35.

Dixon, Helen G., Maree L. Scully, Melanie A. Wakefield, Victoria M. White, and David A. Crawford. "The Effects of Television Advertisements for Junk Food versus Nutritious Food on Children's Food Attitudes and Preferences." *Social Science and Medicine* 65, no. 7 (October 2007): 1311–23.

Federal Trade Commission. *Marketing Food to Children and Adolescents: A Review of Industry Expenditures, Activities, and Self-Regulation*. A Report to Congress, July 2008. www.ftc.gov/os/2008/07/P064504foodmktingreport.pdf.

Folta, Sara C., Jeanne P. Goldberg, Christina Economos, Rick Bell, and Rachel Meltzer. "Food Advertising Targeted at School-Age Children: A Content Analysis." *Journal of Nutrition Education and Behavior* 38, no. 4 (July 2006): 244–48.

Food Standards Agency. "Enforcement and Regulation." N.d. http://www.food.gov.uk/enforcement/.

Harris, Jennifer L., John A. Bargh, and Kelly D. Brownell. "Priming Effects of Television Food Advertising on Eating Behavior." *Health Psychology* 28, no. 4 (2009): 404–13.

Harris, Jennifer L., Marlene B. Schwartz, Kelly D. Brownell, Vishnudas Sarda, Amy Ustjanauskas, Johanna Javadizadeh, Megan Weinberg, et al. *Fast Food FACTS: Evaluating Fast Food Nutrition and Marketing to Youth*. Rudd Center for Food Policy & Obesity, November 2010.

Harris, Jennifer L., Sarah E. Speers, Marlene B. Schwartz, and Kelly D. Brownell. "US Food Company Branded Advergames on the Internet: Children's Exposure and Effects on Snack Consumption." *Journal of Children and Media* 6, no. 1 (February 2012): 51–68.

Johnson, R. K., L. J. Appel, M. Brands, B. V. Howard, M. Lefevre, R. H. Lustig, F. Sacks, L. M. Steffen, J. Wylie-Rosett, and on behalf of the American Heart Association Nutrition Committee of the Council on Nutrition, Physical Activity, and Metabolism and the Council on Epidemiology and Prevention. "Dietary Sugars Intake and Cardiovascular Health: A Scientific Statement From the American Heart Association." *Circulation* 120, no. 11 (August 24, 2009): 1011–20.

Martinez, Michael. "San Francisco Bans Happy Meals with Toys." CNN, November 9, 2010. http://articles.cnn.com/2010-11-09/us/california.fast.food.ban_1_meal-combinations-apple-dippers-yale-university-s-rudd-center?_s=PM:US.

Mayo Clinic. "Nutrition for Kids: Guidelines for a Healthy Diet." N.d. http://www.mayoclinic.com/health/nutrition-for-kids/NU00606.

McDonald's. "Nutrition Choices." N.d. http://www.mcdonalds.com/us/en/food/
    food_quality/nutrition_choices.html.
Moore, Elizabeth S. *It's Child's Play: Advergaming and the Online Marketing of Food to
    Children.* Menlo Park, CA: Kaiser Family Foundation, July 2006.
Moore, Elizabeth S., and Victoria J. Rideout. "The Online Marketing of Food to
    Children: Is It Just Fun and Games?" *Journal of Public Policy and Marketing* 26,
    no. 2 (November 2007): 202–20.
Neuman, William. "U.S. Seeks New Limits on Food Ads for Children." *New York
    Times*, April 28, 2011. http://www.nytimes.com/2011/04/29/business/29
    label.html?_r=1.
Nielsen Media Research. "Automotive Ad Spending Down; Spot Radio and TV Up."
    N.d. http://www.marketingcharts.com/television/automotive-ad-spending
    -down-spot-radio-and-tv-up-295/.
Public Radio International. "Disney Sets New Nutritional Standards for Advertis-
    ers." *Takeaway*, June 7, 2012. http://www.pri.org/stories/business/disney-sets
    -new-nutritional-standards-for-advertisers-10161.html.
Reese, Tamekia. "Childhood Nutrition." *Healthy Children Magazine*, 2008. http://
    www.healthychildren.org/English/healthy-living/nutrition/Pages/Childhood
    -Nutrition.aspx.
Rideout, Victoria J., and Elizabeth Hamel. *The Media and the Family: Electronic
    Media in the Lives of Infants, Toddlers, and Preschoolers and Their Parents.* Menlo
    Park, CA: Kaiser Family Foundation, May 2006.
Roberto, C. A., J. Baik, J. L. Harris, and K. D. Brownell. "Influence of Licensed
    Characters on Children's Taste and Snack Preferences." *Pediatrics* 126, no. 1
    (June 21, 2010): 88–93.
Roberts, Donald F., Ulla G. Foehr, and Victoria Rideout. *Generation M: Media in the
    Lives of 8–18 Year-Olds.* Menlo Park, CA: Kaiser Family Foundation, 2005.
Robinson, Thomas N., Dina Borzekowski, Donna Matheson, and Helena C.
    Kraemer. "Effects of Fast Food Branding on Young Children's Taste Preferences."
    Archives of Pediatrics and Adolescent Medicine 161, no. 8 (August 1, 2007): 792.
Sebastian, Rhonda S., Cecilia Wilkinson Enns, and Joseph D. Goldman. "US Ado-
    lescents and MyPyramid: Associations between Fast-Food Consumption and
    Lower Likelihood of Meeting Recommendations." *Journal of the American
    Dietetic Association* 109, no. 2 (February 2009): 226–35.
Story, Mary, and Simone French. "Food Advertising and Marketing Directed at
    Children and Adolescents in the US." *International Journal of Behavioral Nutrition
    and Physical Activity* 1, no. 3 (2004). http://www.ijbnpa.org/content/1/1/3.
United States. U.S. Department of Agriculture. "Choose My Plate," n.d. http://www
    .choosemyplate.gov/.
Wald, Jonathan. "McDonald's Obesity Suit Tossed: U.S. Judge Dismisses Obesity
    Suit vs. McDonald's." CNN Money, February 17, 2003. http://money.cnn.com/
    2003/01/22/news/companies/mcdonalds/index.htm.
Wendy's. "Wendy's Nutrition." n.d. http://www.wendys.com/food/Nutrition
    Landing.jsp.

CHAPTER TEN

Selling Vice: Cigarettes and Alcohol

Mitch McKenney

You could see him up there, surveying the crowds at Cleveland Municipal Stadium, the Marlboro Man adorning the largest cigarette-themed stadium billboard in all the land.[1] It stood a proud 20 feet high and stretched 134 feet above the bleachers, its "Marlboro Country" declaration in big, black letters next to the Man in chaps and a cowboy hat.[2] Two oversized packs of Marlboro filled out the ample sign, which ceded space below it for the scoreboard and some smaller ads for beer and banks.

This was the 1970s, long before changeable video screens could switch between scores, replays, and ads, so Marlboro had the crowd all to itself. By 1980, its maker Philip Morris had long-term contracts for signs like this in 35 U.S. sports facilities including Yankee Stadium in New York and Anaheim Stadium in California—though none were as big as Cleveland's. As part of the deal, only Philip Morris products could be sold or offered as free samples in the stadiums. According to a company newsletter, no tobacco company came close to Philip Morris in stadium visibility.[3]

"The benefits of this program are numerous," the promotions manager boasted in the company newsletter. "Obviously, the signs present the Marlboro message to many thousands of consumers each year. In addition, as soon as we sign, we notify local field sales personnel of the particulars so that they can begin their part of this program: insuring that Marlboro and other PM brands are available and visible throughout the facility."[4]

For two decades, Cleveland's Marlboro Man presided over Browns games, Indians games, Rolling Stones concerts and even a Billy Graham evangelism crusade. But like the Browns, he left the stadium after the 1995 season. When a new Cleveland Browns team debuted in 1999—replacing the one that owner Art Modell took to Baltimore, and in a new stadium—there was no big Marlboro clock. Former Browns kicker Matt Stover even noted on its absence the first time he played in the new stadium as a Baltimore Raven.[5]

Much had changed in the world of tobacco advertising in the late 1990s. Lawmakers were pursuing rules to extend their ban on cigarette advertising beyond television, which had not carried a cigarette ad since 1971. R. J. Reynolds faced full-throated attacks from antismoking advocates and federal officials for its venerable Joe Camel cartoon character, who many believed existed solely to get children smoking. Sick former smokers and states who paid to treat them won settlements against tobacco companies. Tobacco companies agreed to take down their billboards by early 1999, in some cases paying for the antismoking ads that replaced them.

Fast forward another 10 years to 2009, and U.S. lawmakers, regulators, and activists were agreeing to stronger regulations on tobacco marketing, including stricter limits on printed tobacco advertisements as well as requirements that cigarette and smokeless tobacco put big graphics on their packs showing in horrifying visuals what the products can do to the body. By late 2012, as Europe and Australia were adopting ever-stronger prohibitions on cigarette advertising, the U.S. version was on hold while federal courts sorted out the free-speech implications of such restrictions.

Perhaps not surprisingly, the Marlboro Man stood near ads for Miller High Life and other alcoholic products during his stadium reign. But in sharp contrast to tobacco advertising, beer advertising lives on in professional sports stadiums across the country, as well as in print, on billboards, and on television—with the Super Bowl serving as a showpiece of creative pitches for beer. Even the once-taboo ads for hard liquor are becoming more visible.

How to explain the increasingly strict regulatory limits placed on advertising of one vice, tobacco, while another that also has an effect on the health of consumers, alcohol, has avoided most of those barriers? The disparity raises questions about the First Amendment rights of those who make legal products, the government's interest in changing consumer behaviors, and the role our cultural values play in shaping product marketing in media.

Tobacco Executive Defects

I got to know about the tobacco industry's 1990s tangles with regulators because of a story that was one of my most difficult assignments as a newspaper reporter. It was 1996, and my editor at the *Palm Beach Post* wanted me to write a profile of Bennett LeBow, a Liggett tobacco executive who had just broken ranks with leaders of other firms by settling government claims that smoking makes people sick.

As I wrote at the time, even as the industry denounced him as a traitor, LeBow argued his company would not have been able to pay for an appeal if it lost the suit. "What am I supposed to do, be a nice guy and go bankrupt possibly for the purposes of solidarity?" he asked the *New York Times*. "I did what was best for my shareholders and me."[6] Then he stopped talking—which does not give a reporter much to go on for a Sunday-length personality profile. LeBow's personal publicists were turning down interview requests from ABC's *Nightline* and CNN's *Larry King Live*, as one of them told me, "just because he's under a microscope right now." Plus, he lived on the private Fisher Island near Miami Beach, which meant I could not talk to his neighbors.

Somehow I strung together 1,300 words from analysts, experts, and people who used to work with him. One quote I had from an American Medical Association doctor was prescient. LeBow in the settlement had agreed not to market tobacco to youths, and later said he would abide by the same terms if he was successful in his bid to take over R. J. Reynolds. Referring to RJR's ad campaign with a cartoon character, the doctor took delight in predicting, "That means no more Joe Camel."[7] Sure enough, within a year, the face of that hip camel bearing a startling (though unintentional, we were told) resemblance to male genitalia no longer graced billboards or magazine pages.[8]

As my story put it in 1996, President Clinton, tobacco plaintiffs, and antismoking groups cheered LeBow's defection: "It appears to be the first of the rats to leave the sinking ship," said Dr. Tom Houston, preventive medicine director for the American Medical Association.[9] Over the next two years, more challenges would limit the industry's efforts to acquire customers, but at this point it would be valuable to back up to see how cigarette advertising came to face government scrutiny in the first place.

Tobacco's Early Ad Limits

The late 1990s movement in tobacco marketing regulation was preceded by events a quarter-century before, starting with the U.S. surgeon general's 1964 release of his Advisory Committee Report that linked smoking with diseases such as lung cancer, emphysema, and other diseases, and that called for warning labels on packs and bans on radio and TV advertising. By 1966, cigarette packs for the first time carried government-mandated warnings on the side, initially offering a simple caution that "cigarettes may be hazardous to your health."[10]

Because my media-literacy classes necessarily focus on the government intersection with the work of publishers and broadcasters, students become acquainted with how regulatory agencies with acronyms such as FTC, FDA, FCC, and FEC have sought to control ads. Each semester, the student who presents on "tobacco ads through the years" would say the last cigarette commercial to appear on TV was during Johnny Carson's *Tonight Show* at 11:59 p.m. on New Year's Day 1971. (It was young actress Veronica Hamel, who later would play Joyce Davenport on the 1980s drama *Hill Street Blues*, appearing in a commercial for Virginia Slims.) Note that this was not New Year's Eve—the ads were permitted through the end of January 1. As Ohio University telecommunications professor Charles Clift explained, "The Federal Communications Commission held off on the ban until January 2, which gave the tobacco companies a chance to advertise on the bowl games," noting that "beer companies quickly filled the sports broadcast ad gap created by the exodus of cigarette ads."[11]

Students taking up this topic also delight in finding on YouTube a clip from the early 1960s that ran during the Winston-sponsored Flintstones cartoon. In it, Fred and Barney are having a smoke while their wives do chores. (It ends with Wilma joining Fred for a cigarette.) Fred even declares the brand's ungrammatical slogan: "Winston tastes good like a cigarette should."[12] It has been so long since cigarette ads aired on TV that almost no one under age 50 has a memory of them.

Joe Camel and the Children

It was children's television icon Bob Keeshan who sounded one the latter-day alarms that the TV commercial ban was not enough to keep kids away from cigarettes. In 1986, the man known to generations of grownups as Captain Kangaroo appeared before a U.S. House subcommittee as an ex-smoker warning that too many teens were taking up a habit with grave consequences.[13] Congress two years before had strengthened the warnings on packages to a rotating set of stern warnings, but the bill before Congress now would, if passed, go much further. Sponsored by Democrat Mike Synar of Oklahoma, it would have banned all tobacco advertising and promotion—which then amount to about $2 billion, with the most ad revenues going to (in order) magazines, billboards, and newspapers.[14]

At the same hearings, an R. J. Reynolds tobacco company heir told lawmakers that he endorsed the idea of banning all such ads: "I believe that cigarette advertising is promotion of a poisonous product and that it is moral, right and good to eliminate all advertising of cigarettes," Patrick Reynolds told the subcommittee. Still, news coverage of the 1986 hearing suggested it could be years before any such limits would have any chance of passing.[15]

The following year, R. J. Reynolds introduced one of its most successful and controversial ad campaigns: Joe Camel. Also called "Old Joe," and "Smooth Character," the campaign featured a shades-wearing cartoon playboy, confident and popular, enjoying a Camel cigarette. Everyone around him seems to be having a good time, too. Opponents immediately complained that the cartoon appealed most to minors and accused the tobacco company with seeking to introduce children to its product.

By 1991, researchers at the Medical College of Georgia determined that preschoolers were just as good at identifying Joe Camel with cigarettes as the Mickey Mouse logo with the Disney Channel.[16] They asked 229 children in Atlanta and Augusta, Georgia, preschools to identify 12 logos, and found that 91.3 percent of six-year-olds could correctly match "Old Joe" with a picture of a cigarette. Even 30 percent of three-year-olds got it right.[17] The authors concluded that curbs on tobacco advertising may be in order: "Very young children see, understand, and remember advertising. Given the serious health consequences of smoking, the exposure of children to environmental tobacco advertising may represent an important health risk and should be studied further."[18]

From then forward, antismoking arguments against the character's continued use routinely include a Mickey Mouse reference. The Federal Trade Commission in 1994 declined to pursue a case against R. J. Reynolds, but in 1997, it filed a complaint alleging that the company's ads put the health of minors at risk.[19] The charge said as early as 1984, R. J. Reynolds sought to make Camel the "first usual brand" of young smokers, and that executives had deviously settled on Joe Camel as a way to get their attention early:

> The purpose of the Joe Camel campaign . . . was to reposition the Camel brand to make it attractive to younger smokers. In fact, according to the complaint, the Joe Camel campaign was successful in appealing to many children and adolescents under the age of 18 and induced many of these underage consumers to smoke Camel cigarettes or increased the risk that they would do so. For many of these children and adolescents, the decision to smoke Camel cigarettes was a decision to begin smoking; for others, it was a decision to continue smoking.

But two of the five FTC commissioners dissented, saying nothing had changed since the agency's 1994 decision not to bring action. Commissioner Roscoe B. Starek III said the intuition that more kids were smoking because of the Camel ads was not enough evidence:

I am very concerned about the harm that cigarette smoking poses to children, but I also take seriously the statutory limits on the Commission's authority to pursue enforcement actions against allegedly unfair practices. The evidence before us now, including the evidence obtained since the Commission considered this matter in 1994, does not convince me that there is reason to believe that the law has been violated.

Forty-three days later, in July 1997, R. J. Reynolds announced it was retiring Joe Camel after a decade of service to the brand, describing it as unrelated to the FTC complaint or the current status of lawsuits by state attorneys general against the industry.[20] ABC's Peter Jennings, in introducing the story, called Joe Camel "one of the most successful cigarette ad campaigns ever devised, so successful in fact that it infuriated many anti-smoking advocates."[21] (Jennings, a former smoker, died of lung cancer in 2005.)

States Band Together

Around that same time, attorneys general from numerous states were getting traction in their lawsuits against tobacco companies to recover their Medicaid costs from treating sick smokers. Mississippi brought the first such case 1994 and was first to settle, but by late 2008, 46 states agreed to share a $206 billion settlement with the industry.[22] The conditions of the settlement included the end of ads on billboards, buses, and taxis; the elimination of cartoon characters; and no placement of brand logos on shirts or other products.

Some of the billboards were already down. 3M Media, the third-largest billboard company, stopped displaying tobacco ads in 1997, having made a joint announcement of its decision with the Interfaith Center on Corporate Responsibility.[23] Joe Camel was now retired, and the spoof site "Joe Chemo" had emerged (courtesy of Adbusters) with images of an emaciated, beaten-down camel undergoing cancer treatments.[24] The actors who portrayed the Marlboro Man could continue in magazines and newspapers—though one of their number had died of lung cancer two years earlier, at age 73.[25]

The settlement with the states included $1.7 billion be set aside for anti-smoking ad campaigns aimed at commercials and other promotions to discourage youths from smoking.[26] It left magazines, newspapers, and event sponsorships as the most visible places to advertise cigarettes—though as smoking increasingly fell into disfavor in the early 2000s, it would not be long before opponents turned their attention to the ads that remained.

Renewed Legislative Attention

U.S. regulation on tobacco ads hit a new gear in 2009, with a law that gave the Food and Drug Administration unprecedented power to dictate package design, limit printed and billboard advertising, and other measures to discourage smoking and smokeless tobacco use. The Family Smoking Prevention and Tobacco Control Act was sponsored by U.S. representative Henry Waxman of California and enthusiastically signed by President Barack Obama—himself a smoker—in his first year in office.[27] At the bill signing, he complained that teens were "aggressively targeted as customers by the tobacco industry. They're exposed to a constant and insidious barrage of advertising where they live, where they learn, and where they play."[28]

The new law banned billboards within 1,000 feet of schools and playgrounds, prohibited tobacco-brand sponsorships of athletic, social, and cultural events, and ended the practice of giving away free samples or free items (sunglasses, T-shirts, etc.) with tobacco purchases.[29] The FDA's goal was explicitly to reduce the U.S. smoking rate from one person in five to one person in eight.[30]

But perhaps the most dramatic feature was the new requirement that packs display large, hideous color images of what cigarettes can do to the lungs. As the *Washington Post* explained, the FDA's plan was "to shock customers with nine graphic images of tobacco's effects, including smokers exhaling through a tracheotomy hole, struggling for breath in an oxygen mask and lying dead on a table with a long chest scar."[31] Cigarette packs would need to include the 1-800-QUIT-NOW hotline, and carry one of nine revised warnings:

WARNING: Cigarettes are addictive.
WARNING: Tobacco smoke can harm your children.
WARNING: Cigarettes cause fatal lung disease.
WARNING: Cigarettes cause cancer.
WARNING: Cigarettes cause strokes and heart disease.
WARNING: Smoking during pregnancy can harm your baby.
WARNING: Smoking can kill you.
WARNING: Tobacco smoke causes fatal lung disease in nonsmokers.
WARNING: Quitting smoking now greatly reduces serious risks to your
   health.[32]

Full-page newspaper ads would have to include the warning in 45-point type. Tobacco ads running in magazines with "a significant readership of people" under 18 would have to be a "tombstone" ad, limiting the design to black-and-white text.[33] Male-oriented magazines with the most income from cigarette ads—*Maxim*, *Playboy*, *Men's Journal*, *Field and Stream*, and *Sports Illustrated*—stood to lose the most, as they commanded between $3 million and $6 million each in tobacco advertising in 2008.[34]

Tobacco companies immediately saw the rules as an impingement on their free speech, noting that the law's main purpose seemed to be to make it harder for them to get their own message out about their product.[35] Publications that depend on advertising complained, as well. The Association of National Advertisers called the law "the most restrictive advertising bill ever passed in the U.S. for a legal product."[36]

For two years, the industry lost free-speech challenges to the law, but in November 2011 a judge agreed that the law's provisions were at least worthy of review and delayed their implementation.[37] In his decision, U.S. District Judge Richard J. Leon said the federal requirements went far beyond a simple requirement for disclosure: "It is abundantly clear from viewing these images that the emotional response they were crafted to induce is calculated to provoke the viewer to quit, or never to start, smoking: an objective wholly apart from disseminating purely factual and uncontroversial information."[38]

Leon paused the law's earliest enforcement until 2013, but he said in his opinion that the companies "have demonstrated a substantial likelihood" of winning on constitutional grounds.[39] President Obama responded in a statement that tobacco makers "shouldn't be standing in the way of common-sense measures that will help prevent children from smoking."[40] Some predict the U.S. Supreme Court will ultimately settle the matter.

Meanwhile, on the world stage, Australia's highest court in summer 2012 upheld its government's new rules for plain packaging, turning aside tobacco company arguments that requiring alterations to package designs violated intellectual property rights. The *Sydney Morning Herald* noted at the time that Britain, Canada, India, New Zealand, and Norway were considering similar rules.[41] Cigarette packs in Australia now must have a plain type font on dark olive-brown packets, with health warnings and graphic images taking up 75 percent of the front and 90 percent of the back.[42]

Contrast with Alcohol

If 1996 was a key year in the restrictions on tobacco advertising, it also was the year when alcohol advertising began to push the limits, as it marked the first time hard-liquor ads found their way to television. The airing of a Crown Royal spot on a local station in Corpus Christi, Texas, broke the ice in June.[43] Five months later, the Distilled Spirits Council of the United

States—a trade group made up of the industry's leading companies—reversed its nearly half-century-old voluntary ban on television ads for such alcohols as whiskey, vodka, and rum. As one story put it at the time, the council announced "in a dramatic about-face that it had changed its 48-year-old code against advertising hard liquor on television (as well as its 60-year radio ban), once lauded by federal policymakers as a model of responsible corporate behavior."[44]

Then FCC chairman Reed Hundt issued a not-so-subtle threat that he would take action against station owners who dared to air such commercials: "The choice right now is up to broadcasters," he said. "Broadcasters have the constitutional right not to carry this advertising." But while the networks resisted the ads at first, local affiliates and cable outlets were happy to get the income.[45]

Regulatory Attempts

The strategy of alcohol makers to avoid regulation dates to the first days after Prohibition. The Distilled Spirits Council points to its voluntary ban from radio and television as evidence of its social responsibility, and it keeps a timeline on its website showing messages beginning in the 1930s saying "drinking and driving do not mix" and "some men should not drink."[46]

While alcohol advertising bans were proposed at congressional hearings in 1976, it was 1988 when Republican senator Strom Thurmond delighted public health advocates by proposing five rotating warning labels for alcohol containers.[47] Ultimately, Congress passed this simpler government warning that has been required since 1989 and still appears on bottles today:

> (1) According to the Surgeon General, women should not drink alcoholic beverages during pregnancy because of the risk of birth defects. (2) Consumption of alcoholic beverages impairs your ability to drive a car or operate machinery, and may cause health problems.

Sensing momentum from this and a 1990 amendment to make the warning prominent, opponents of alcohol advertising were further bolstered by a Center for Science in the Public Interest study that found two-thirds of the public wanted a ban on televised beer commercials.[48] In 1993, another Thurmond-sponsored bill that would require warnings on broadcast alcohol advertisements, the Sensible Advertising and Family Education Act (SAFE), was working its way through Congress when the senator's daughter was killed by a drunken driver.[49] Thurmond's bill now faced even easier passage, but broadcasters and the industry persuaded him to accept a voluntary publicity campaign rather than pursue government scrutiny of TV ads.[50] A 1996 attempt by Democratic representative Joe Kennedy to reintroduce the SAFE bill as part of the Comprehensive Alcohol Abuse Prevention Act never came up for a vote.[51]

Alcohol Ads in High Gear

Even while distillers refrained from advertising on TV, the proliferation of beer advertising there rankled some. A 1992 position paper by the American Public Health Association complained that Anheuser-Busch helped finance "all 26 major league baseball teams, 20 of the 28 NFL teams, more than 300 college teams, and about 1,000 other sporting events."[52] (Twenty years later, the company would lead all Super Bowl advertisers with 4.5 minutes of commercials, when ads were running $3.5 million per 30-second spot.[53])

In 2000, the industry was spending just $4.3 million a year on television advertising—a fraction of the more than $600 million spent annually on beer and wine ads—but the liquor-ad business on local stations and cable grew $100 million by 2006.[54] Along the way, NBC tried airing a Smirnoff vodka ad on *Saturday Night Live* in 2001, but did not continue with the ads following public outcry.[55] For the next 10 years, even without network acceptance of liquor ads, local station and cable network advertising topped $140 million.[56] Then in November 2011, CBS started airing Grey Goose vodka ads during *Late Show with David Letterman*, and the industry saw little pushback.[57] By March 2012, *Advertising Age* reported that the other major networks had warmed to carrying them:

> ABC has been taking hard-booze during *Jimmy Kimmel Live* for several months. And this spring, NBC began accepting spirits shows airing after 11 p.m. Eastern as long as 90 percent of the audience is of legal drinking age. (Industry self-regulations allow beer, wine or liquor ads only on programs where at least 71.6 percent of the audience is 21 or older.) More broadcast deals are "in the works," one industry insider told *Ad Age*.[58]

By August 2012, a nearly doubled budget for Southern Comfort ads meant SNL, Letterman, and Kimmel were giving wide play to its "Whatever's Comfortable" campaign, which shows a pot-bellied man roaming the beach in a too-small bathing suit.[59]

Like Repeating Prohibition?

Charles K. Atkin, a University of Wisconsin telecommunications professor, in 1993 argued against a government prohibition of beer commercials from the airwaves. Even an outright ban on alcohol advertising by the Federal Communications Commission, he said, may not dissuade consumers from drinking, plus the messages might still air on cable:

> In addressing these concerns, a complete ban on broadcast commercials is an enticing policy option for many public health activists and a majority of the public. However, behavioral science theory and research indicates that prohibiting ads would be relatively ineffectual in reducing drinking problems and might produce counterproductive outcomes such as fewer responsible drinking messages and more influential advertising via non-broadcast channels.[60]

Atkin instead proposed stricter controls with "pro-health" public service announcements, something that he said stopped in the case of tobacco once the 1971 ban took effect.[61] "With a ban, networks and local stations would no longer feel any obligation to provide free time to tell the 'other side' on alcohol-related issues," he wrote. "Public health and safety organizations would no longer be able to claim the need to balance pro-alcohol messages from advertisers with their PSAs."

Discussion

So why are cigarette advertisements and alcohol advertisements treated differently? Why has the bulk of legislative and cultural attention been directed at restricting tobacco advertisements in the past half-century? Perhaps it is because of timing that the harmful health effects of cigarettes came to light first, and in a different era. Perhaps it is how the culture still accepts social drinking but banishes smokers outside (including at bars).

It could be argued that the difference has its antecedent in media history, similar to how the sound recording and movie industries chose to self-regulate for offensive content. Just as when the recording industry added labels and movie producers imposed the Hayes codes, alcohol marketers prevented the government's intrusion into their work and avoided the conditions that radio and television faced for their use of the public airwaves. By imposing a voluntary ban on liquor ads, alcohol makers may have prevented—or at least delayed—receiving the sort of regulatory scrutiny on advertising that cigarette makers have faced.

Still, it may be too early to consign tobacco advertising to the ashtray of history. The Marlboro Man continues, just without the prominence he had when he appeared on television, in stadiums and along the highways. Baylor physician Alan Blum, commenting in 1998 on the antismoking ads, predicted that tobacco companies, "the most versatile force in advertising history, will prevail." Even well-crafted antismoking ads will not put an end to it, said Blum, an expert on tobacco marketing. "There has never been a product that has been unsold through advertising."[62]

Notes

1. "Marlboro Goes to the Ballgame," *Force* (company newsletter), October 1980, 14, http://tobaccodocuments.org/pollay_ads/Marl06.01.html (accessed August 15, 2012).

2. Ibid.

3. Ibid.

4. Ibid.

5. Jamison Hensley, "Stover: Return to Cleveland Different," *Baltimore Sun*, October 2, 2000, http://articles.baltimoresun.com/2000-10-02/sports/0010020047_1_browns-stadium-ravens-starks (accessed July 19, 2012). Stover's actual quote was: "It would be one thing if I was kicking into the old Marlboro sign or if the Dawg Pound was throwing beer at me or batteries barely missing me. But because of the new stadium, it's changed a whole lot for me."

6. Mitch McKenney, "Florida's LeBow Has Tobacco in a Huff," *Palm Beach Post*, April 14, 1996.

7. Ibid.

8. Aaron Brown, "R. J. Reynolds Tobacco Company Retires Joe Camel from Advertisements," ABC News, July 10, 1997, http://abcnews.go.com/Archives/video/july-10-1997-end-joe-camel-ads-10616510 (accessed July 15, 2012).

9. McKenney, "Florida's LeBow Has Tobacco in a Huff."

10. Rob Stein, "Graphic Cigarette Warning Labels Blocked by Judge," *Washington Post*, November 7, 2011, http://www.washingtonpost.com/national/health-science/graphic-cigarette-warning-labels-blocked-by-judge/2011/11/07/gIQAglidvM_story.html (accessed June 18, 2012).

11. Charles Clift, quoted in Peggy Peck and Edward Susman, "40 Years of Fighting Tobacco," *Oncology Times*, March 10, 2004, 30.

12. "Flintstones Cigarette Commercial" (circa 1960), YouTube video, 1:20, posted by "Psychotronic42," January 18, 2007, http://www.youtube.com/watch?v=NAExoSozc2c (accessed August 17, 2012).

13. Richard Stevenson, "Congress Urged to Ban Cigarette Advertising," *New York Times*, July 19, 1986.

14. Ibid.

15. Ibid.

16. Paul M. Fischer et al., "Brand Logo Recognition by Children Aged 3 to 6 Years: Mickey Mouse and Old Joe the Camel," *Journal of the American Medical Association*, December 11, 1991.

17. Ibid.

18. Ibid.

19. "Joe Camel Advertising Campaign Violates Federal Law, FTC Says," news release by the Federal Trade Commission, May 28, 1997, http://www.ftc.gov/opa/1997/05/joecamel.shtm (accessed August 14, 2012).

20. Brown, "R. J. Reynolds Tobacco Company Retires Joe Camel."

21. Ibid.

22. Richard Wolf, "Tobacco's Last Stands," *USA Today*, December 28, 1998.

23. Glenn Collins, "Major Advertising Company to Bar Billboard Ads for Tobacco," *New York Times*, May 3, 1996.

24. "Joe Chemo" website, http://www.joechemo.org/about.htm.

25. "Obituaries: David McLean," *Washington Post*, October 21, 1995, 6C.

26. Wolf, "Tobacco's Last Stands."

27. Family Smoking Prevention and Tobacco Control Act, introduced by U.S. Representative Henry Waxman (D-California), GovTrack.us, March 3, 2009, http://www.govtrack.us/congress/bills/111/hr1256 (accessed July 15, 2012).

28. Ibid.

29. Suzanne Vranica and Russell Adams, "Ad Industry Fights Tobacco Bill; Further Loss of Revenue Would Hurt Magazines," *Wall Street Journal*, June 18, 2009, http://online.wsj.com/article/SB124528568710625775.html (accessed June 19, 2012).

30. Mike Esterl and Jennifer Corbett Dooren, "Judge Blocks Graphic Labels," *Wall Street Journal*, November 8, 2011.

31. Stein, "Graphic Cigarette Warning Labels Blocked by Judge."

32. Family Smoking Prevention and Tobacco Control Act.

33. Vranica and Adams, "Ad Industry Fights Tobacco Bill."

34. Ibid.

35. Nathan Koppel, "Do Smoking Regs Violate Tobacco Companies' Free-Speech Rights?" *Wall Street Journal Law Blog*, July 21, 2011, http://blogs.wsj.com/law/2011/07/27/do-federal-smoking-regs-violate-tobacco-companies-free-speech-rights (accessed June 19, 2012).

36. Ibid.

37. Stein, "Graphic Cigarette Warning Labels Blocked by Judge."

38. Ibid.

39. Esterl and Dooren, "Judge Blocks Graphic Labels."

40. Ibid.

41. Chris Zappone, "Tobacco Fight Not Over, Philip Morris Says," *Sydney Daily Herald*, August 15, 2012, http://www.smh.com.au/business/tobacco-fight-not-over-phillip-morris-says-20120815-2488s.html (accessed August 16, 2012).

42. Ross Kelly, "Cigarette Maker Sues over Marketing Curbs," *Wall Street Journal*, December 2, 2011.

43. E. J. Schultz, "Hard Time: Liquor Advertising Pours into TV," *Advertising Age*, March 14, 2012, http://adage.com/article/news/hard-time-liquor-advertising -pours-tv/234733 (accessed August 11, 2012).

44. Doug Halonen, "Ad Ruckus May Trigger Backlash; Liquor Industry Reverses Ban," *Electronic Media*, November 11, 1996.

45. Ibid.

46. "History of Social Responsibility," Distilled Spirits Council of America, http://www.discus.org/responsibility/history (accessed August 15, 2012).

47. Norman Giesbrecht et al., "Alcohol Advertising Policies in the United States: National Promotion and Control Initiatives," *Contemporary Drug Problems*, Winter 2004, 683.

48. Charles K. Atkin, "On Regulating Broadcast Alcohol Advertising," *Journal of Broadcasting and Electronic Media*, Winter 1993.

49. Giesbrecht et al., "Alcohol Advertising Policies in the United States," 684.

50. Ibid.

51. Ibid.

52. "Alcohol and Tobacco Products," position paper from the American Public Health Association, *Nation's Health*, September 1992.

53. Suzanne Vranica, "Higher Prices Don't Keep Marketers Away from Ad Time for Super Bowl," *Wall Street Journal*, January 3, 2012.

54. Phil Trexler, "Ohioans Loading Up on More Liquor," *Akron Beacon Journal*, December 9, 2006.

55. Mike Esterl, "Liquor Ads Win Airtime," *Wall Street Journal*, August 24, 2012.

56. Schultz, "Hard Time."

57. Esterl, "Liquor Ads Win Airtime."

58. Schultz, "Hard Time."

59. Esterl, "Liquor Ads Win Airtime."

60. Atkin, "On Regulating Broadcast Alcohol Advertising."

61. Ibid.

62. Wolf, "Tobacco's Last Stands."

Bibliography

"Alcohol and Tobacco Products." Position paper from the American Public Health Association. *Nation's Health*, September 1992, 18.

Atkin, Charles K. "On Regulating Broadcast Alcohol Advertising." *Journal of Broadcasting and Electronic Media*, Winter 1993, 107.

Brown, Aaron. "R. J. Reynolds Tobacco Company Retires Joe Camel from Advertisements." ABC News, July 10, 1997. http://abcnews.go.com/Archives/video/july-10-1997-end-joe-camel-ads-10616510 (accessed July 15, 2012).

Collins, Glenn. "Major Advertising Company to Bar Billboard Ads for Tobacco." *New York Times*, May 3, 1996, 15A.

Esterl, Mike. "Liquor Ads Win Airtime." *Wall Street Journal*, August 24, 2012, 6B.

Esterl, Mike, and Jennifer Corbett Dooren. "Judge Blocks Graphic Labels." *Wall Street Journal*, November 8, 2011, 5B.

Family Smoking Prevention and Tobacco Control Act. Introduced by U.S. Representative Henry Waxman (D-California), March 3, 2009. GovTrack.us, March 3, 2009. http://www.govtrack.us/congress/bills/111/hr1256 (accessed July 15, 2012).

Fischer, Paul M., Meyer P. Schwartz, John W. Richards Jr., Adam O. Goldstein, and Tina H. Rojas. "Brand Logo Recognition by Children Aged 3 to 6 Years: Mickey Mouse and Old Joe the Camel." *Journal of the American Medical Association*, December 11, 1991, 3145–48.

"Flintstones Cigarette Commercial" (circa 1960). YouTube video, 1:20. Posted by "Psychotronic42," January 18, 2007. http://www.youtube.com/watch?v=NAExo Sozc2c (accessed August 17, 2012).

Giesbrecht, Norman, Suzanne Johnson, Lise Anglin, Thomas Greenfield, and Lynn Kavanagh, "Alcohol Advertising Policies in the United States: National Promotion and Control Initiatives," *Contemporary Drug Problems*, Winter 2004, 673–710.

Halonen, Doug. "Ad Ruckus May Trigger Backlash; Liquor Industry Reverses Ban." *Electronic Media*, November 11, 1996, 1.

Hensley, Jamison. "Stover: Return to Cleveland Different." *Baltimore Sun*, October 2, 2000. http://articles.baltimoresun.com/2000-10-02/sports/0010 020047_1_browns-stadium-ravens-starks (accessed July 19, 2012).

"History of Social Responsibility." Distilled Spirits Council of America. http://www.discus.org/responsibility/history (accessed August 15, 2012).

"Joe Camel Advertising Campaign Violates Federal Law, FTC Says." News release by the Federal Trade Commission, May 28, 1997. http://www.ftc.gov/opa/1997/05/joecamel.shtm (accessed August 14, 2012).

Kelly, Ross. "Cigarette Maker Sues over Marketing Curbs." *Wall Street Journal*, December 2, 2011, 3B.

Koppel, Nathan. "Do Smoking Regs Violate Tobacco Companies' Free-Speech Rights?" *Wall Street Journal Law Blog*, July 21, 2011, http://blogs.wsj.com/law/2011/07/27/do-federal-smoking-regs-violate-tobacco-companies-free-speech-rights (accessed June 19, 2012).

"Marlboro Goes to the Ballgame." *Force* (company newsletter), October 1980, 14. http://tobaccodocuments.org/pollay_ads/Marl06.01.html (accessed August 15, 2012).

McKenney, Mitch. "Florida's LeBow Has Tobacco In a Huff." *Palm Beach Post*, April 14, 1996, 1E.

"More about Joe Chemo." "Joe Chemo" website, first appearing in Adbusters. http://www.joechemo.org/about.htm (accessed August 14, 2012).

"Obituaries: David McLean." *Washington Post*, October 21, 1995, 6C.

Peck, Peggy, and Edward Susman. "40 Years of Fighting Tobacco." *Oncology Times*, March 10, 2004, 30.

Schultz, E. J. "Hard Time: Liquor Advertising Pours Into TV." *Advertising Age*, March 14, 2012. http://adage.com/article/news/hard-time-liquor-advertising-pours-tv/234733 (accessed August 11, 2012).

Stein, Rob. "Graphic Cigarette Warning Labels Blocked by Judge," *Washington Post*, November 7, 2011. http://www.washingtonpost.com/national/health-science/graphic-cigarette-warning-labels-blocked-by-judge/2011/11/07/gIQAglidvM_story.html (accessed June 18, 2012).

Stevenson, Richard. "Congress Urged to Ban Cigarette Advertising." *New York Times*, July 19, 1986, 43.

Trexler, Phil. "Ohioans Loading Up on More Liquor." *Akron Beacon Journal*, December 9, 2006, 1A.

Vranica, Suzanne. "Higher Prices Don't Keep Marketers Away from Ad Time for Super Bowl," *Wall Street Journal*, January 3, 2012, 1B.

Vranica, Suzanne, and Russell Adams. "Ad Industry Fights Tobacco Bill; Further Loss of Revenue Would Hurt Magazines." *Wall Street Journal*, June 18, 2009. http://online.wsj.com/article/SB124528568710625775.html (accessed June 19, 2012).

Wolf, Richard. "Tobacco's Last Stands." *USA Today*, December 28, 1998, 1A.

Zappone, Chris, "Tobacco Fight Not Over, Philip Morris Says," *Sydney Daily Herald*, August 15, 2012, http://www.smh.com.au/business/tobacco-fight-not-over-phillip-morris-says-20120815-2488s.html (accessed August 16, 2012).

CHAPTER ELEVEN

Party Down: Drinking Culture and TV Advertising

Huston Ladner

Nestled in the rolling hills of northern Mississippi sits the town of Oxford, a quiet kind of college town not unlike many strewn across the United States. The setting in Oxford is similar to that in any American college town. There is the University of Mississippi campus and the students, and there are the locals that are often left sitting in the role of steward for both the college and the town. It is here that the strange specter of alcohol casts a lingering presence. The laws of the town with regard to alcohol bring their own confusion, depending on what day it is and what time it is and where you are. There is a reason why many people in the area make runs to the neighboring county for beer on Sundays—but that is just how it is. Except for game days.

On game days, a whole different set of rules is in play. For a town that affects an air of provinciality, the days when the Ole Miss football team is playing at home offer a different environment. For starters, game day is as much about the social event as it is the contest, notably by hanging out at the Grove. Included in that aspect is the notion that attendees should dress in what is kind of like their Sunday best. But the subtext of the day is one that is also soaked in booze—and the preferred type is hard alcohol, usually bourbon or another whiskey. Not just the students are often spotted in an alcoholic haze, but alums and older fans are as well.

It is under this auspice that Ole Miss has created what the *Oxford Eagle* and the student paper, the *Daily Mississippian*, term the "culture of alcohol." This notion is a conflicted one. The Grove is sold as a must-do. Billboards in town and ads in the papers encourage people to buy the right clothes for the six or seven party dates each year, while others tout where to get the booze needed to enjoy oneself in the manner that is expected. All of this is done in a town that is decidedly Christian and with it an attitude that seems to be one of looking down its nose toward the familiar drunkenness. Then again, this is the same town that harbored a Nobel Prize–winning writer and known alcoholic, William Faulkner.

What makes all of this interesting is not the specificity of Oxford, Mississippi, though it can be stated with certainty that the town has its own idiosyncrasies. But every town does. No, the interesting feature of Oxford is that much of the behavior can be found anywhere. To compare it to a place like Madison, Wisconsin, or Tucson, Arizona, is a task fraught with complications; but the concept that can be found in these places is that same one already noted, the culture of alcohol.

The culture of alcohol is right now left undefined, lending itself to a murky kind of understanding, similar to the idea of knowing it when someone sees it. As yet, no scholarly articles exist detailing the idea, and even those from the Mississippi papers fail to explicate what their true intention is by using the term. Hence, the first task here is to attempt to clarify that. As such, what a culture of alcohol seems to imply is not particular cultural practices, but instead being immersed in a culture where drinking is a key aspect. Whether this drinking happens at a bar, a party, or a snazzy exclusive event is not important, as instead it is the recognizable tie to having a drink in hand that marks one's having joined the culture. It should also be stated that sobriety should be a questionable element of said situation, believing that some form of intoxication is expected.

To ensure that there is a sense of understanding here, the culture of alcohol is not the same concept espoused by Malcolm Gladwell in his essay on how culture and environment can change the expected effects of alcohol.[1] Nor is it one that looks at how different cultures around the world have different drinking tendencies. What is being addressed here is that culture that is shown on a regular basis, and there is no better place to look at this culture than through advertisements. While television and film might provide an elongated if not well-rounded depiction of the culture of alcohol, they also create different messages and are not establishing the explicit suggestion of inclusion. Advertisers, in comparison, are aggressively trying to sell this inclusion, encouraging the consumers to, in essence, join the party.

Alcohol advertising is nothing new, but the tactics and the themes have evolved. As such, there seem to be four motifs being used to invigorate purchasers to join the culture of alcohol. The first is possibly the most common, that being the typical party culture. The second uses an air of sophistication to sell its product. A relatively new way of selling alcohol has been the advent of combining fitness with a product. The less pervasive but still distinct theme that has emerged is that of the alcopops.

The Big Party

It is important to discern the difference between the Big Party and the parties that are all part of the other categories being examined. The Big Party is just what it means, but it is also something that comes across as an event. Included in this concept is the fact that those being represented in the commercials and ads are all part of something that seems akin to a grown-up fraternity party.

When looking at the Big Party, a few products are prevalent, and they are all light beers—Coors Light, Miller Lite, Bud Light. These beers should be thought of as the industry standards, and that is not surprising as these three are all represented in the top four of American beer sales as of 2011.[2] The important factor with regard to these beers is that they are all light, meaning less of a full body and easier to drink.

Much of the research that has been done on alcohol and advertising has focused on the relationship between the product and the target audience, with researchers establishing the link between these companies and the youth market. What better product to sell to a demographic with undiscerning palettes than light beer to adolescents and twentysomethings. The fact that one of those groups is unable to legally buy beer is something that the advertisers are willing to overlook.

Going beyond that problematic inconsistency, there are more aspects to the way these beer giants market themselves that deserves mentioning. Let us start with Coors Light, the "Silver Bullet that won't slow you down." For years, Coors Light has advertised itself as offering a refreshing brew that is easy to drink. The main way that the MillerCoors Brewing Company has done this is with a train that bolts from seemingly out of the blue, like a deus ex machina, to bring refreshment to those who are suffering. This train has roared through cities, racetracks, playing fields, and yes, even ski slopes. What this train demonstrates is that there is no place that is not suitable for a party—because every time the train arrives, left in its tracks are groups of happy imbibers with Coors Light in their hands.

Coors Light chose another avenue in the spring and summer of 2012. They did not drop the train but added another concept, a "super-can" coming from outer space to deliver beer to pleased recipients on the beach. While it is easy to ignore the question of who in space was making the beer or whether Coors Light is made from extraterrestrials, the concept deserving further scrutiny is that of the limited-edition cans for summer. What MillerCoors has tapped into is the collector idea, one that younger generations will identify with, having gone through Pokemon cards, Beanie Babies, and any of the goodies sold by the fast food chains.

The MillerCoors companion beer, Miller Lite, has adopted some other strategies in their advertising, most likely not to compete with Coors since the merger in 2007. One of their concepts was to question manliness and decision making in their 2010 commercials. These spots usually took place in a bar and featured a group of friends out drinking, with one oddball who seemed a bit clueless. As part of these commercials, Miller Lite touted their the new thing, the vortex bottle, that allowed for a smoother and faster pour (though many beer aficionados would query as to whether a smoother pour for a Miller Lite would improve its quality in any regard). What the commercials did was provide a 30-second comedy, laughable scenarios that would ingratiate Miller Lite with a young and hip crowd. Absurdist comedy is a growing phenomenon in advertising, and the alcohol companies have used it to their benefit.

The vortex bottle was then supplanted with the punch-top can in 2012. Once again, this development was promoted as a smoother way to pour one's Miller Lite. That notion is just subterfuge for what the punch-top can really is: a quick way to shotgun a beer. For the uninitiated, shotgunning a beer means drinking it as fast as possible, and by punching that second hole in the can, drinkers are able to do pull off this feat with alacrity. It should be noted that the core group that shotguns beers are those in high school and college, and these drinking accomplishments tend to occur at parties, commonly when someone is challenged. Once again, Miller Lite found a new way to connect with its target audience.

One of the most identifiable beer marketers is Budweiser (Bud) and Bud Light. Having placed their name on all kinds of sponsorships and advertised on what seems like everything at one time or another, it is not surprising that the company regularly places its two beers as top sellers. In the 1980s, the company grabbed incredible attention with their Bud Bowl ads that ran during a number of Super Bowls. Since then, the company has divided the two in noticeable ways, with Bud Light becoming the de facto beer of the younger crowd.

Bud Light, throughout the aughts, has used the absurdist comedy concept to sell their beer with much success. At one point, it was the "Whassup" gentlemen, which not only targeted the younger demographic, but also focused on black Americans. The fact that little else was said other than, "Whas-s-s-u-u-up," illustrates the lack of complex concept to push the beer; the fact that they proved as popular as they did is a different matter. Another one of their successful campaigns was the ads that featured Leon, the self-centered football player. In these ads, Leon would be asked to do something or comment on something and his response extolled an overt sense of self-involvement that fans often attribute to modern athletes. While these ads do not strike to the heart of party culture, their reference to football connects it to the overall bar-and-party culture that surrounds the sport on both Saturdays and Sundays.

In the latter part of the decade, Bud Light chose to go with the slogan "Here We Go." Each one of these ads presents a party culture. In one ad, a Bud Light deliveryman is carting the beer into an elevator, and shortly thereafter, the elevator becomes *the* place to party—indicating that it is Bud Light that truly gets a party started. A second example of this campaign has been that of another party where the host adopted a dog named Wego. The commercial depicts the dog being called repeatedly, "Here Wego," and the dog delivering Bud Light to the partygoers. In a move of strategic brilliance, Bud Light is sure to mention that viewers should support their local pounds and shelters. This statement at the end develops a connection with pet lovers and also harkens to the days of Spuds McKenzie, the bull terrier who was a spokes-dog for Bud Light in the 1980s. So not only is Bud Light the beer to get a party started, but it is also the beer that cares about dogs.

This party style of advertising, complete with its humor and ability to construct youthful, happy images, develops connections with late adolescents and twentysomethings. These beer companies have maintained top sales spots much in part due to their ability to market themselves thusly. Even Heineken has made use of this idea, showcasing that their beer exists as a pseudo ticket to the best parties. Of course, beer companies are not the only ones to use this strategy, as Bacardi rum and Captain Morgan rum have also found this method useful.

The Sophisticated Party

The use of the Sophisticated Party concept is not a new one. Hugh Hefner, the *Playboy* founder, may have used this tactic best to create his empire. In this category, there is a marked shift from beer selling to hard alcohol. Part of this shift has to do with sales. Throughout the early 2000s, beer sales have been sluggish, and marketers have recognized that the business class is looking for something more refined for their drinking pleasure. Because of this trend, advertisers have tailored their ads and messages for these groups. In this category, the big booze-fest is replaced with a quieter party experience, and one that appears to have an air of exclusivity. This discriminating party offers an air of elegance, with the underlying theme showing that these people are wealthy.

Two vodka companies spearhead this notion, Ketel One and Skyy. In Ketel One ads, handsome professional men are spotted ordering and drinking the vodka. What the viewer is supposed to identify is that these gentlemen have used their worldly and discerning tastes to order this vodka, which gives their selection gravitas. Included in one commercial is the added element of chivalry. In it, three dashing men are waiting for a taxi in the rain, showing a sense of responsibility by not driving, and as their cab arrives, three striking females exit the same club. The guys, with little hesitation, offer their cab to the ladies so they will not have to get soaked. Though the whole ad comes off a little contrived, the fact that these men show taste, act responsibly, and defer to these women offers a lot of positive messages to the potential consumer.

The Skyy vodka ads take the concept in a slightly different direction. For their settings they tend to use open sets and feature groups of beautiful people, not focusing solely on a small set. These model-esque people all express fun while dancing about in tight dresses for the women and tailored suits for the men. Once again, the viewer is left to connect that by drinking Skyy, one is invited to a beautiful-people party and that an erudite air will be part of the atmosphere. That no one is clowning around or does anything absurd illustrates this point. It should be mentioned that Absolut vodka also had a successful run of presenting itself as sophisticated in the 1980s and 1990s. They created an ad campaign that was based on drawings and photographs of their bottles, showing them to be art. In fact, the collection of these ads often travels the world showcasing the different creations.

Vodka is not the only alcohol that exists in this category, as beer again makes its presence known. Though Budweiser has become a beer targeted for an older audience, their ads have not featured a party culture in them for a few years. Instead, it is the recent ads for Dos Equis beer that have taken on an interesting slant. Featuring an ostensibly aristocratic older gentlemen, known as "the Most Interesting Man in the World," these ads have become both comedic and interesting. The viewer is sold the notion that this man can do almost anything and does these things with a casual aplomb, from riding horses, to spending time with dignitaries, to sport. But it is the tagline of the commercials that make them stand out: "I don't always drink beer, but when I do, I prefer Dos Equis." There are two ideas to be derived from that statement, the first being that this man is not always in the mood for beer, and the second being that when he is in the mood, it is Dos Equis he chooses. This decision making shows that Dos Equis is a beer that should be enjoyed when your sophisticated palette is looking for a brew. The overall message that comes across from these ads is that Dos Equis can be associated with pleasurable and interesting pursuits, and it is one to be enjoyed in moderation. The final take from these commercials is that this beer is what helps create a roving party, because wherever he is, something special is happening.

It should be noted that competitor Corona has long used a subtle and civilized marketing strategy for their beer. It often features a couple on a quiet, seemingly deserted beach. The ads are quiet and offer a sense of escapism, but rarely feature what could be considered a party. Perhaps the Keystone beer commercials offer the most unique take, as they blend both redneck and cosmopolitan sensibilities. In them a character with a mullet, wearing a trucker hat and usually a flannel shirt and jeans, helps attractive females out of difficult situations—some of those at parties. He then delivers his signature line, à la James Bond, when he looks in the camera and says his name: Keith Stone. The allusion to Bond and his erudite attitude while trapped in what seems to be a lowbrow persona creates an ironic take on the sophisticated concept.

The products discussed here are not the only ones to model this sophisticated concept of drinking. Tequilas, such as Avion and Jose Cuervo 1800, and some whiskeys have also done so, though their presence seems limited more to print ads then television. But these ads have also eschewed the party idea for one that is toned down and more individualistic, thereby representing a wholly different concept.

The Fitness Party

One of the emerging trends in beer sales is to tie the product to being active and living a healthy lifestyle. Though this idea may give the impression of being counterintuitive, it has not stopped advertisers from combining the two, and with success. It is not surprising that these two activities would meet. As Palmer examined, sports and alcohol have had a long-standing relationship, but it was based on the spectator experience, be it at the event, in a bar, or at home.[3] But the change to marry being active with beer crossed the line into new territory, and one that will most likely see continued development.

The beers that are most associated with this trend are those with scant calories, ones that sit below those in the light-beer category. Their names are also part of strategy, like Bud Select, Miller 64, and Michelob Ultra. That so few of these beers exist exemplifies the impression that this category is new and will be further exploited. Oddly enough, of the three beers mentioned, only two of them have prominent pushing.

Michelob Ultra seems to be the first to aggressively advertise its product, and it has done so with none other than Lance Armstrong as the prominent spokesperson for the brew. In the commercials, viewers are treated to watching Armstrong ride his bike, hike, and do other various activities with his companions. When the setting turns to night, we find Armstrong at a party surrounded by other fit people. The difference here between the Sophisticated Party and the Fitness Party is that those in the latter are dressed in a casual way that helps to manifest their attention to their bodies. It should also be mentioned that these people look a little more neat and tidy than those of the Big Party. By using a man who can be considered the paragon of fitness (doping allegations aside), Michelob Ultra created a world where their beer is comparative to that of Gatorade and allows for consumers to believe that it is healthy. While that leap could be considered large, it does, at the very least, create an idea of healthiness associated with the beer.

In a slight contrast, Miller 64 advertises its beer in a slightly different fashion. In the same way that Ultra uses the day-night dichotomy, so too does Miller 64. Similarly, Miller 64 uses the daytime as one for activities and getting work done. One of the differences that exist is that Miller uses more of the common man approach, not settling for one superstar, but a group of guys who are trying to maintain a modicum of fitness. That one of these men grimaces while in a yoga class typifies the style used. The sing-along limerick song that accompanies the commercial adds to this idea, avoiding any pop allusions or trendy chicness. The close of the ad is particularly telling, as these various men get together to enjoy their Miller 64s with, of course, some attractive women. Here is a tactical change from so many of the other products mentioned: the beer serves as a reward for trying to be fit.

As beer companies attempt to find ways to increase their sales and market share, one can expect to see these fitness beers gain more attention, possibly in the number of them that exist or more prominent advertising. What Michelob Ultra and Miller 64 have done is set a blueprint for how future advertisers may attempt to capitalize on the market.

The Unheard Alcopop Party

In the 1980s, wine coolers debuted and gained widespread recognition mainly through the Bartles & Jaymes commercials featuring two grandpa-like figures. Their success spawned continued evolution in this segment of alcoholic products, with drinks such as Zima, Bacardi Breeze, Smirnoff Ice, Mike's Hard Lemonade, and a line from Jack Daniel's, to name a few. The success of these beverages is based upon the mixing of sweet fruit and/or malt drinks with alcohol. The term alcopop acknowledges the concept that these drinks are akin to having a soda with alcohol mixed in, with the consumer not having to do any of the mixing.

Tax law changes in the late 1990s made wine coolers more expensive, which enabled those alcopops not based on wine to surge in popularity. Their growth, however, has never been something that would challenge beer or the hard liquors, and because of this challenge, alcopops have used a different strategy to reach their audience. With the exception of Mike's Hard Lemonade, which has a history of TV commercials, alcopops have been relegated to print ads.

That aspect has changed with the rise of the digital age. What alcopops have done is employed social media such as Facebook and Twitter to spread their message. As Sarah Mart has asserted, using these mediums actually makes it easier for these companies to connect with the younger target audience.[4] While this group still faces the problem of actually purchasing the alcopops, these kind of viral techniques develop a relationship with a generation that is comfortable in the digital world and will seek out the products. The fact that the drinks are sweet like a soda or fruit drink makes the relationship easier to consummate when underage drinkers actually do get their hands on the product. The thing that the viral campaign has done is create a digital party, as consumers are encouraged to "like" or "follow" a specific beverage. Thus alcopops may provide one of the more unique challenges with regard to its regulation and understanding its market.

The Wrap-Up Party

One of the dominant themes that exist throughout all of the alcohol advertising is that the target audience is men. At the Big Party, mainly men are featured, either doing dumb things or hanging out, with women as scenery. When one is at the Sophisticated Party, the women are objects to be held in high esteem and appreciated, like pieces of art. The Fitness Party focuses on men being and getting in shape but seems to assume that women are already in that state. The Alcopop Party is an evolving one, but can be expected to follow the parameters that seemed to have been set by the others.

That women are marginalized is not a unique or surprising concept, but the focus here is on the party culture, and it is a ubiquitous intention in the selling of alcohol. While there exists a complementary stream of advertisements, that of intimate and quiet settings, they lack the prevalence of the party theme. So no matter what group with which consumers may align themselves, the understanding is the same: buy this, and the party is about to begin.

Notes

1. Malcolm Gladwell, "Drinking Games," *New Yorker*, February 15, 2010, http://www.newyorker.com/reporting/2010/02/15/100215fa_fact_gladwell. In this essay, Gladwell looks at how culture and environment affect people's behavior when drinking. In doing so the author revisits a study from 1957 that has largely been ignored by Dwight Heath.

2. Emily Bryson York, "Coors Light Overtakes Budweiser as No. 2 Seller," *Chicago Tribune*, January 11, 2012, http://articles.chicagotribune.com/2012-01-11/business/ct-biz-0111-light-beer-20120111_1_budweiser-sales-benj-steinman-millercoors.

3. Catherine Palmer, "Key Themes and Research Agendas in the Sport-Alcohol Nexus," *Journal of Sport and Social Issues* 35, no. 2 (May 2011): 168–85.

4. Sarah M. Mart, "Alcohol Marketing in the 21st Century: New Methods, Old Problems," *Substance Use and Misuse* 46, no. 7 (May 2011): 889–92.

Bibliography

Cooke, Matthew. "Challenging a Culture of Alcoholism." Huffington Post, May 28, 2011. http://www.huffingtonpost.com/matthew-cooke/challenging-a-culture-of-_b_839376.html.

Engels, Rutger C. M. E., Roel Hermans, Rick B. van Baaren, Tom Hollenstein, and Sander M. Bot. "Alcohol Portrayal on Television Affects Actual Drinking Behaviour." *Alcohol and Alcoholism* 44, no. 3 (May 2009): 244–49.

Gladwell, Malcolm. "Drinking Games." *New Yorker*, February 15, 2010. http://www.newyorker.com/reporting/2010/02/15/100215fa_fact_gladwell.

Grube, Joel W. "Alcohol Portrayals and Alcohol Advertising on Television: Content and Effects on Children and Adolescents."*Alcohol Health and Research World* 17, no. 1 (1993): 54–60.

Mart, Sarah M. "Alcohol Marketing in the 21st Century: New Methods, Old Problems." *Substance Use and Misuse* 46, no. 7 (May 2011): 889–92. Academic Search Premier, EBSCOhost (accessed August 3, 2012).

Palmer, Catherine. "Key Themes and Research Agendas in the Sport-Alcohol Nexus." *Journal of Sport and Social Issues* 35, no. 2 (May 2011): 168–85.

York, Emily Bryson. "Coors Light Takes No. 2 Spot." *Chicago Tribune*, January 11, 2012. http://articles.chicagotribune.com/2012-01-11/business/ct-biz-0111-light-beer-20120111_1_budweiser-sales-benj-steinman-millercoors.

CHAPTER TWELVE

Break Time Is Game Time: A History of Super Bowl Advertising

Natalie Moses

Even before the NFL season starts, a fight for a different kind of Super Bowl glory rages on amongst the largest advertisers in the United States. Year after year, the game changes and different teams show up for battle, but the audience type is consistent. There are always the hardcore team fans that will not leave the couch for the duration of the game, the NFL fans that wait all year for this final showdown, and even a section that is ambivalent toward football but watches solely for the entertainment provided by the commercials. With that in mind, it is easy to see why this day is anticipated like Christmas morning for advertisers who put their best players forward and pay top dollar for just 30 to 60 seconds of playing time. These small spots have given names to rising companies, maintained momentum for iconic American brands, and provided pop-culture taglines since 1967.

A Super Evolution

Within just a few years after the first Super Bowl in 1967, the televised game became a national ritual. Today, one viewer in ten tunes in just for the ads.[1]

The Super Bowl was always an event that attracted large audiences, but the early years lacked today's viewership of epic proportions. A quick glance at Super Bowl I in 1967 compared to Super Bowl XLV in 2011 shows just how much the game has grown. The first Super Bowl was actually called the AFL-NFL World Championship Game and was the first and only to not sell out. It ended in a Green Bay Packers' 35–10 victory over the Kansas City Chiefs.[2] That year, 26.8 million viewers tuned in to CBS and 24.4 million tuned in to NBC to watch coach Vince Lombardi lead the Packers to glory. Again in 1968, 41.7 million viewers tuned in to NBC to watch the Packers defeat the Oakland Raiders, 33–14.[3] The commercials aired that year cost advertisers $37,500 for a 30-second slot, a rate that would steadily increase each following year.[4] Fast forward to Super Bowl XLV when the Vince Lombardi Trophy came back to Green Bay in 2011. The program attracted 111 million viewers, and 30-second commercials were sold at $3 million.[5] The 46-year journey from $37,000 to $3 million for 30 seconds is a colorful story in which the winners get their money's worth in ROI rather than in trophies and rings. Though there are many traditional events that are televised only once a year, why is this television event above all others an advertiser's dream come true?

The answer lies in the audience. It is the audience that sets the stage for this day to be "not only the crowning glory of American football," but the "Super Bowl of advertising" as well.[6] Advertisers see this as an elite social event, a place to "be seen and showcase their best."[7] After all, it is the most watched, most expensive, and most influential platform for major-league advertising there is.[8] The audience is standing by, allowing corporate America to compete for its money and doing so with open arms.

The audience size alone makes this event attractive for advertisers. From 2007 to 2010, the average audience size was 99 million viewers just in the United States.[9] In fact, 2012 was the third year for viewership to consecutively reach over 100 million.[10] That equals about 40 percent of American households.[11] Globally, the Super Bowl reaches 750 million viewers.[12]

The audience is not only massive but also diverse, making it even more appealing to advertisers. It is a great representative group of the American population, "a melting pot of every demographic and psychographic group in the country."[13] Where most sporting events reach the fan base of the two opposing teams, the Super Bowl attracts both male and female viewers of all ages, ethnic groups, and NFL team loyalties. Only 25 percent of the audience is the stereotypical middle-aged male football fan.[14] So, by putting out a single spot, a company reaches multiple demographics.

In addition to the audience being large and diverse, it is also more engaged than any other group. The Super Bowl "may be the only time when people talk about the ads *before* the event," with spots being released days ahead of time to generate hype amongst viewers and critics. This hype is effective, with 10 percent of the audience solely watching for the commercials. Rather than being the usual unwelcome annoyance, the commercials on game day actually attract viewers.[15] Over two-thirds of the audience actually pays significant attention to the commercials.[16] Out of those viewers, more than half discuss the commercials the next day.[17] The buzz about Super Bowl commercials continues past the next day and lasts weeks after the broadcast. CBS has even dedicated a show titled "Super Bowl's Greatest Commercial" to the best spots in past years.[18]

When reflecting upon the best spots, a few common threads have weathered the test of time. These commercials are, according to *The Super Bowl of Advertising* author Bernice Kanner, "often better entertainment, minute for minute, than what's happening on the field."[19] The experts at BBDO Worldwide, an agency that is a veteran when it comes to producing Super Bowl commercials, has stuck to this tried-and-true formula: tickle the funny bone, tug at the heartstrings, and toss in a surprise ending.[20] For example, a 2004 commercial by Goodby Silverstein & Partners that aired during Super Bowl XXXVIII captured all three of those aspects. It told the story of a lovable donkey that lived in the same barn as the majestic Budweiser Clydesdales. First, the heart of the audience aches for this unglamorous donkey that so desperately wants to pull the beer wagon with its beautiful roommates. Next, the audience gets a chance to chuckle as the donkey undergoes an audition and brays with all its might. Finally, a surprise ending shows that the donkey not only made the cut, but leads the Clydesdales in a festive beer parade.[21] This tasteful yet entertaining Budweiser spot meets all of BBDO's requirements and was praised as one of the stars of Super Bowl XXXVIII. Though heartwarming ads like the Budweiser Clydesdales have been crowd favorites, it is usually the humorous commercials that tend to succeed more widely. This is mostly because the Super Bowl is watched by large groups of people. In fact, the average Super Bowl party has 17 guests, which is more than the typical New Year's Eve party.[22] When large groups of people are together, they want to laugh rather than think. Another reason for the funny commercial's success may be that due to the high stress and tension of the game, viewers want a chance to let loose in between downs.[23]

Speculating why certain spots have flown where others have flopped is only one concern that advertisers face in creating a game-day advertisement. Looking to past decades provides insight on how the audience will react not only as entertainment-seeking viewers, but also as consumers. The following section highlights the best and worst Super Bowl advertisements per each decade as well as their impact and legacy in the world of game day commercials.

1967: A Tradition is Born

In 1967, no one could have imagined that Super Bowl Sunday would become a holiday so huge that even the commercials would be a spectacle.

The first Super Bowl was quite literally not a "super" event. At the time, it was simply called the World Championship game and was instituted as part of the huge merger agreement between the National Football League and the American Football League.[24] The history of the name proves that the media was always a large part of the Super Bowl. Though the father of the AFL, Lamar Hunt, wanted to call the bowl the "Super Bowl" as a result of his daughter playing with a super ball, NFL commissioner Pete Rozelle was not having it. It was not until two years later that the phrase "Super Bowl" was printed on a program, and the media declared the day "Super Sunday."[25]

In 1967, the most memorable role that advertising played in the World Championship was making Green Bay's head coach Vince Lombardi absolutely furious. The game was aired on both CBS and NBC for a total of 51.2 million viewers.[26] When the second half of the game commenced, a Winston cigarette commercial was still playing on NBC, forcing the referees to blow the whistle and have the Packers kick off again.[27] In the end the Packers were not harmed by it, because they defeated the Chiefs by 25 points.[28]

All programming debacles aside, the commercials that were aired during the first Super Bowl would elicit boos by today's audience standards for more reasons than one. In retrospect, these "awkward, amateurish, and interminable" spots were mostly 60 seconds, quite lengthy compared to the modern Super Bowl commercials that are generally only 15 to 30 seconds.[29] Some of the main advertisers, including Chrysler, RCA, R. J. Reynolds, and McDonald's bought time on both networks to reach a broader audience. The target audience that was kept in mind was not the diverse crowd of today but "the Archie Bunker man, back in the days when men were men," and that was evident in the content of the commercials.[30] For example, a Goodyear spot that centered on men's chivalry would most likely undergo extreme criticism for being sexist toward women if aired today. The damsel in distress, one that could not change her own tire and was not even strong enough to keep her hands on the steering wheel, was used to promote the Double Edge tire.[31] Besides Goodyear's Double Edge tires, some other commercials that aired in the World Championship of 1967 included: Haggar "Forever Prest" slacks that would stay "freshly pressed through heat and humidity"; American Airlines' new computer system that prompted smooth flying in every plane; Schaefer Beer, or "the one beer to have when you're having more than one"; Anheuser-Busch declaring the secret ingredient for Busch Beer is "just plain waiting"; and Tareyton cigarettes. Both Haggar and Tareyton then launched print campaigns that echoed their Super Bowl ads.[32] As far as commercials go, there were no standout or innovative spots during the first Super Bowl.

The year 1968 was a football rerun, the Packers repeated as champions in front of an audience of 41.7 million.[33] Yet another technical difficulty provided a memorable moment for Super Bowl commercials that year. For almost two minutes, 80 percent of television sets went black. The Newport cigarette spot that was supposed to be shown during that time was rerun later in the game to make up for the blackout.[34] A number of advertisers returned from the previous year, but this time around, the focus was placed on music. There were more jingles and pop songs, thus bringing more of an entertainment aspect to Super Bowl commercials. For instance, a Winston cigarettes jingle boasted, "Winston tastes good like a cigarette should," and Goodyear altered Nancy Sinatra's hit song "These Boots Are Made for Walking" to say their tires are "made for rolling, because Goodyear built them to."[35] In 1969, the antismoking movement was gaining momentum, and the National Association of Broadcasters cracked down on violence. That year saw fewer cigarette commercials and more cartoonish spots.[36] Though the 1960s ended with not much of a lasting legacy on Super Bowl advertising, the game was becoming more and more popular, setting the stage for future commercials to emerge as game-day legends.

1970–1979: The Creativity Begins

The 1970s were a time of "creative revolution" in the world of Super Bowl advertising.[37] Many commercials from this decade were so well loved that they were eventually remade. The year 1970 brought Super Bowl IV and marked the first majorly successful celebrity endorsement commercial in Super Bowl advertising. Chicago Bears' star Dick Butkus was the spokesman for Prestone antifreeze. As a linebacker, Butkus stated the tagline "because plugging holes is my business," and the pun seemed to stick.[38] Celebrity endorsements then quickly became a go-to selling point for Super Bowl advertisers. Not long after celebrity endorsement made it big off the field, another football star famously teamed up with Farrah Fawcett in 1973 for Super Bowl VII to introduce a sexy side to Super Bowl commercials. Joe Namath, quarterback for the New York Jets, exclaimed his excitement as he was "about to get creamed"—that is, get his face slathered in Noxzema shaving cream by Fawcett. That was not the only time Noxzema used sex to sell; they had also used Swedish model Gunilla Knutson dancing suggestively to a song called "The Stripper," daring customers to "take it all off."[39]

While some advertisers were using celebrities or sex in the early 1970s, Coca-Cola took a more conventional, feel-good theme. In 1972, the Dallas Cowboys crushed the Dolphins while Coke made history with a message of peace. A group of young adults from around the world, clad in their nation's traditional clothing, sang a message of world tranquility. Bill Backer of McCann-Erikson wrote the song after witnessing people coming together over Cokes on an international flight.[40] The lyrics sang: "I'd like to teach the world to sing in perfect harmony, I'd like to buy the world a Coke and keep it company."[41] The minute-long commercial cost $225,000 to make and quickly became "one of the most beloved commercials of all time."[42] The campaign reached around the world and ran successfully for six years. In 1990, for Super Bowl XXIV, some of the original singers were brought back together on the same hillside to recreate the spot.[43]

The year 1974 marked the beginning of a long time advertisement for Master Lock that was integral in creating an image for the product. The Master Lock became known as "blastproof" when a sharpshooter fires a bullet at the lock, and the lock remains intact.[44] This commercial, according to *Advertising Age*, is one of the "12 Spots That Changed the Game." It was so successful and influential because it proved that a simple image is sometimes the best choice. This demonstration of a lock holding strong even when shot "worked so well for the company that it ran the same spot for nine years."[45]

During Super Bowl IX in 1975, in addition to the Pittsburgh Steelers' Super Bowl–winning debut, a famous commercial that is still widely quoted today also made its debut. The tongue twister about McDonald's Big Mac listed the burger's ingredients in a difficult, but catchy way: "Two all-beef patties special sauce lettuce cheese pickles onions on a sesame seed bun."[46] The tongue twister remains a challenge.

The Steelers took the field again in Super Bowl X, but Ford stole the scene with its advertisement that truly brought an entertainment aspect to commercial time. To prove that Fords are built to last, the commercial showed scenes from the 1974 film *Mr. Majestyk*. These action-packed scenes centered on a late-1960s pickup that "took one tough beating."[47] The second advertisement that *Advertising Age* dubbed as one of the "12 Spots That Changed the Game" appeared in 1977 during Super Bowl XI. The commercial shows a monk finishing the backbreaking, laborious task of copying an ancient manuscript. Upon completion, the monk's superior asks for 500 more copies of the document. When the monk returns from a secret Xerox shop, the tagline of the commercial is dropped when his superior announces, "It's a miracle!" *Advertising Age* claims that the influence of this spot lies in the making fun of a religious sect.[48] Though disrespectful, it acted as a stepping-stone to some of today's more crude humor.

As far as Super Bowl advertising goes, the 1970s were full of stepping-stones. While the winners and losers were clear on the field, the best of the Super Bowl advertisements were mostly daring competitors. The sexy, racy Noxzema ads pushed the boundaries of appropriateness at the time, as did Xerox by poking fun at religion. These stepping-stone ads paved the way for even more outlandish commercial entertainment to come.

1980–1989: Legendary Spots

The Steelers started off the 1980s by winning their fourth Super Bowl title while one of the team's stars would leave his mark in the advertising game. Joe Greene, better known as "Mean Joe Greene," is a four-time Super Bowl champion and an NFL hall of famer.[49] However impressive these accomplishments are, he is equally famous for his 1980 appearance in a Coke commercial, which the *Los Angeles Times* called "one of the first truly memorable Super Bowl ads and exists forever in the lists of top ads ever."[50] In this famous commercial, the legendary rough player hobbles off the field, looking as mean as ever. An innocent child offers his hero a cold Coca-Cola, and Greene "reluctantly accepts."[51] After a sip, the player's entire demeanor changes to friendly as he turns and throws his jersey to the young fan, leaving him joyful. The spot ends with Coke's tagline "Have a Coke and a Smile." The shoot took three days, mostly because the boy was too starstruck by Joe Greene to remember his lines. The filming took place in a smaller high school stadium to make Greene seem even larger than life.[52] Coke's tagline fit perfectly. After all, if it could make the menacing Mean Joe Greene smile, it could make anyone smile. The popularity of this commercial was not easily forgotten and was even recreated twice—once in 2009 and again in 2012.

To the joy of Super Bowl advertisers, in 1982, viewership reached the highest numbers to date. Broadcast on CBS, 85.2 million tuned in for Super Bowl XVI when the San Francisco 49ers defeated the Cincinnati Bengals.[53] Not only did the viewership break a record, the price of commercials reached a record high (though a bargain by today's standards). At $324,300 for a 30-second spot, the price was just shy of 10 times the original cost 16 years earlier.[54]

In 1984, Apple singlehandedly "launched the era when Super Bowl ads became their own spectacle."[55] Written by Steve Hayden of Ogilvy & Mather, this iconic spot would fuel Hayden's career to later becoming vice chairman of the company.[56] In it, Big Brother is briefing a crowd of people enslaved in an Orwellian state. Out of the dark comes an athlete that hurls a sledgehammer at the screen. The ad shook the audience as it suggested revolution was in the air. The spot was released as Apple introduced its new Macintosh computer and was preparing to take on main competitor IBM. Why does *Advertising Age* file this as one of the 12 most influential commercials in Super Bowl history? "Super Bowl ads have always made us laugh. This one made us think."[57] This ad also told nothing of the computer that was about to be released, yet was instrumental in the success of the product. Though Apple was reluctant to release such a daring social statement, their worries were unfounded. The commercial reached 46 percent of American homes, driving 200,000 customers to view the Macintosh the next Monday, and 72,000 of those purchased the computer within the first 100 days. The commercial was named the Commercial of the Decade by *Advertising Age* and began a new era of integrated marketing communications.[58]

Riding on the success of their 1984 Super Bowl ad, Apple tried again to create a mini movie but failed miserably. The Lemmings' commercial for Macintosh Office featured a long row of "conformist executives" chanting "hi ho, it's off to work we go" as they marched unknowingly right off a cliff. Only one free thinker takes his blindfold off in time to change his path.[59] The suicide theme was not taken well, and Apple went into a slump. The company would not purchase Big Game airtime again until 1999.[60]

By 1986, the Super Bowl was considered the "ad Mecca," and it was known that these ads should be super exciting, dramatic, provocative, creative, and attention getting.[61] However, the hefty price tag of airtime started to turn advertisers away. Super Bowl commercial regulars like Northwestern Mutual and IBM sat out this game day, shorter 15-second commercials appeared, and many clients requested discounted spots during other programs as incentives to purchase. Instead, they got higher rates the next year, and the next. By 1988, 30 seconds went for $625,000.[62]

The 1980s ended with another San Francisco victory, while Budweiser created a different game. The "Bud Bowl" started in 1989 when Budweiser and Bud Light squared off in a football match that ran throughout the game.[63] This qualifies as one of *Advertising Age*'s game changers because it raised the idea of running an ad that lasts the whole game and "showed that an advertiser could devise something bigger around the Super Bowl than a couple of 30-second commercials."[64] Also in 1989, *USA Today* started the tradition of running a Super Bowl Ad Meter, crowning an American Express ad with Dana Carvey as the winner.[65] Though prices started to deter advertisers, this did not change the quality of entertainment in commercials or the draw of marketers to Super Bowl spots. Super Bowl advertising would continue to grow in price and influence.

1990–1999: Celebs, More Celebs, and Brand New Products

The 1990s focused heavily on celebrity endorsement and also marked the beginning of the Super Bowl as a "launching pad for new products."[66]

In 1994, celebrity endorsement reached an all-time high, with 43 out of 56 ads using stars to sell.[67] This was seen right from the beginning when Paula Abdul and Elton John sang a duet for Diet Coke in 1990. Though soda spots were musical and uplifting that year, in 1991, Coke discarded the lighthearted ads and somberly asked fans to recognize what was really important—the Americans serving in the Persian Gulf.[68] Coke was heavily criticized for this ad for appearing "phony and patronizing" and was considered a flop.[69]

Coke was not alone in its Super Bowl advertising slump. The whole country was experiencing financial difficulty, which affected sales for spots in 1992. Despite 42 advertisers paying $850,000 for 30 seconds that year, the spots took forever to sell during this recession. CBS was forced to offer deals and incentives to interested advertisers.[70] As the content of the commercials remained entertaining, viewers would never know there were problems behind the scene. Michael Jordan shone when he famously teamed up with Bugs Bunny in 1992 for Nike and again with Larry Bird in a hoop fight for a Big Mac in 1993. The Bugs Bunny spot, also called "Hare Jordan," served as inspiration for the film *Space Jam.*[71]

Anheuser-Busch took the next few years by storm without the help of celebrities. In 1995, the six-year favorite Bud Bowl commercials retired, only to introduce a new Super Bowl advertising legend in the form of swamp creatures. Three frogs, "Bud," "Weis," and "Er" comically croaked their names to form the word "Budweiser" and would continue to do so for years. Again in 1996, Anheuser-Busch released a legendary Ad Meter top five in which two cowboys witness the Budweiser Clydesdales playing a football game, complete with a horse-kicked field goal.[72]

Super Bowl XXXI brought something new to celebrity endorsement. Cindy Crawford appeared in advertisements twice during one Super Bowl, a rarity for celebrities. While her Pepsi commercial, where a newborn blows kisses to her and Tyra Banks, was a hit, General Motors ended up having to pull her Cadillac spot. She wore a princess dress with a daring neckline that offensively portrayed women.[73] In 1999, the decade closed with a spot by Monster.com that acted as a preview for the dot-com commercials that would take over the next Super Bowl. The decade closed with a black-and-white spot by Monster.com that featured children talking about their futures in a comical but depressing way. Instead of the usual children's dream of being an astronaut, they say things like becoming a "brown nose," wanting to claw their way to middle management, and even being forced into early retirement.[74] These career-doomed children by Goodby landed the agency the prestigious title of Agency of the Year from Adweek.[75] Why was this spot so influential? According to *Advertising Age,* "humor tinged with cynicism suggested that Super Bowl audiences were more sophisticated than anyone had dreamed."[76]

While superstars and sports legends graced the Super Bowl spots of the 1990s, the Gillette Sensor, the Nicoderm Patch, and Breathe Right nasal strips (to name a few) all owe their success to being launched during this time.[77] Though big names and product launches would never get old, Monster.com's 1999 spot acted as a preview for the new dot-com commercials that would take over the next Super Bowl.

2000–2012: Anything Goes Dot-Com

With the Internet becoming ingrained in the daily lives of Americans, the millennium brought a new wave of Super Bowl advertising. There were so many dot-com commercials that 2000 was nicknamed the "Dot-Com Bowl."[78] The 2000s saw the most emotional Super Bowl commercial in history, a few inappropriate years, new twists on old classics, and even fan-made spots.

Just because dot-com advertisers crowded the field in 2000 does not mean that they were successful, or even memorable. Just under half of the advertisers were for up-and-coming websites, but only 36 percent of viewers could name a single dot-com advertiser without help. Most were "Super Bowl virgins" hoping to score big like Apple's 1984 or Monster.com's 1999 spot, but failed to realize that "advertising here was just a down payment on a marketing plan that needed continuous cash flow to make an impact."[79] E-Trade's spot showed a silly dancing monkey, blatantly stated that they just wasted 2 million bucks, and asked the audience, "What are you doing with your money?" This, however, was no waste for E-Trade, as it is one of the few dot-com companies that ran ads that day and is still in business.[80] The dot-coms were not the only spots making scenes. Anheuser-Busch kindly added a new word to the American dictionary in 2000 with the debut of the long running "Whassup?" commercial.[81]

In 2002, Anheuser-Busch took a break from making people laugh and left a great many in tears with a tasteful and heartfelt tribute to the attacks on 9/11. The famous Clydesdales pull the beer wagon across the beautiful countryside. When they arrive on Liberty Island in New York, they stop to look at Ground Zero, and the team follows suit after the lead horse bows its head in respect.[82] That year, the choice between acknowledging the national tragedy or moving on with the usual funny spots was a tough choice for all advertisers.

For as appropriate as the 2002 Anheuser-Busch spot was, Super Bowl XXXVIII two years later was the exact opposite. With Janet Jackson's wardrobe malfunction and the potty humor in the commercials, the audience was surely entertained. Bud Light released one spot in which a horse literally had explosive gas in a woman's face, and another where a dog bites a man's crotch for a Bud. Though an object for critics, the fans loved these commercials, rating the crotch-biting dog as the best spot of the day.[83]

In 2007, Doritos changed Super Bowl advertising history by letting the fans compete to have their homemade commercials aired on game day. The winning spot featured a man that crashed his car while watching a beautiful woman eat Doritos. This made the top five on the Ad Meter with four Anheuser-Busch spots that each cost over $1 million to produce. The Doritos spot cost the makers $12.[84]

Two years later for Super Bowl XLIII, Crispin Porter + Bogusky remade the previously mentioned Mean Joe Greene Coke commercial with slight changes. In place of Mean Joe was Pittsburgh Steeler Troy Polamalu, and Coke Zero replaced original Coca-Cola.[85] Coke commercials are a good-luck charm for the Steelers, because they also won the Super Bowl that year. Also, in 2012, Downy obtained permission from Coke to make a parody in which a bottle of detergent and Amy Sedaris replace the refreshing beverage and the young boy. Sedaris tosses the bottle to the much older Mean Joe for something more important than quenching thirst—a clean jersey.[86] The commercial was more for laughs than the heartwarming original, but it gave the added bonus of nostalgia to the irony of Mean Joe Greene doing laundry.

In 2011, it was not a comical commercial that had the audience buzzing, but a lengthy two-minute spot by Chrysler that announced the return of the American auto industry. This spot coined the term "Imported from Detroit." With the price of commercials now around $3 million for 30 seconds, this spot proved that "anyone willing to spend big can shake up the typical Super Bowl marketing formula."[87] And it seems like these days, spending is all Super Bowl advertising is about.

A Bright (Expensive) Future

From the cheesy late-1960s jingles, to the daring 1970s spots, to the classics of the 1980s, and the celebrity-endorsed 1990s, spending big is the only theme of the 2000s. Whether companies are competing for Web traffic or product sales, the price is a nonissue. A Pepsi spokesperson said that "we almost can't afford not to advertise . . . it's no accident we've been doing this for 23 straight years."[88] The ROI generated from Super Bowl spots speaks for itself. Within one week of Super Bowl XLII in 2008, E-Trade saw a 32 percent raise in account openings, CareerBuilder saw 68 percent more job applications, Anheuser-Busch saw 21 million online ad views, and Audi experienced a 200 percent increase in Web traffic.[89] With these undeniable perks, it seems that the future of Super Bowl advertising is clear. Airtime will continue to get pricier as advertisers will continue to spend millions. The audience will surely lean forward in their seats for break time entertainment as long as the Big Game is played.

Notes

1. Bernice Kanner, *The Super Bowl of Advertising: How the Commercials Won the Game* (Princeton, NJ: Bloomberg Press, 2004), 1.

2. Robert Klara, "Super Bowl Ad Time Line I–XLIV," *Mediaweek* 21, no. 3 (January 24, 2011): 6, Academic Search Complete, EBSCOhost (accessed July 10, 2012).

3. Ibid.

4. Ibid.

5. David Bauder, "Super Bowl Ratings Record: Giants-Patriots Game Is Highest-Rated TV Show in US History," Huffington Post, February 2, 2012, http://www.huffingtonpost.com/2012/02/06/super-bowl-ratings-record-tv-giants-patriots_n_1258107.html.

6. Kanner, *Super Bowl of Advertising*, 1.

7. Ibid.

8. Ibid.

9. Klara, "Super Bowl Ad Time Line," 14–15.

10. Bauder, "Super Bowl Ratings Record," para. 1.

11. Kanner, *Super Bowl of Advertising*, 1.

12. Ibid.

13. Ibid.

14. Ibid.

15. Ibid., 3.

16. Ibid.

17. Ibid.

18. Ibid.

19. Ibid., 5.

20. Ibid.

21. Howard Davis, "Those Super Bowl Spots!" *Television Quarterly*, Spring 2004, 19.

22. Kanner, *Super Bowl of Advertising*, 3.

23. Ibid., 5.

24. Ibid., 13.

25. Ibid., 14.

26. Klara, "Super Bowl Ad Time Line," 6.

27. Kanner, *Super Bowl of Advertising*, 13.

28. Klara, "Super Bowl Ad Time Line," 6.

29. Kanner, *Super Bowl of Advertising*, 13.
30. Ibid., 15.
31. Ibid.
32. Ibid., 16.
33. Ibid.
34. Ibid.
35. Ibid., 16.
36. Ibid., 17.
37. Ibid., 13.
38. Klara, "Super Bowl Ad Time Line," 7.
39. Kanner, *Super Bowl of Advertising*, 19.
40. Ibid., 18.
41. Ibid., 17.
42. Ibid., 18.
43. Ibid.
44. Klara, "Super Bowl Ad Time Line," 7.
45. Brian Steinberg, "From Apple to Xerox: 12 Spots That Changed the Game," *Advertising Age* 83, no. 2 (January 9, 2012): 2–20, Academic Search Complete, EBSCOhost (accessed July 12, 2012).
46. Klara, "Super Bowl Ad Time Line," 8.
47. Ibid.
48. Steinberg, "From Apple to Xerox," 2.
49. Mean Joe Greene 75. http://meanjoegreene75.com/.
50. Patrick Kevin Day, " 'Mean Joe' Greene Re-Creates His Famous Super Bowl Ad." *Los Angeles Times*, February 2, 2012, http://latimesblogs.latimes.com/show tracker/2012/02/mean-joe-greene-recreates-his-famous-super-bowl-ad-for-downy -video.html (accessed July 15, 2012).
51. Klara, "Super Bowl Ad Time Line," 9.
52. Kanner, *Super Bowl of Advertising*, 19.
53. Klara, "Super Bowl Ad Time Line," 9.
54. Ibid.
55. Kanner, *Super Bowl of Advertising*, 3.
56. Ibid.
57. Steinberg, "From Apple to Xerox," 2.
58. Kanner, *Super Bowl of Advertising*, 28.
59. Ibid.
60. Klara, "Super Bowl Ad Time Line," 10.
61. Kanner, *Super Bowl of Advertising*, 33.
62. Ibid., 35.
63. Klara, "Super Bowl Ad Time Line," 11.
64. Steinberg, "From Apple to Xerox," 4.
65. Klara, "Super Bowl Ad Time Line," 11.
66. Kanner, *Super Bowl of Advertising*, 38.
67. Ibid., 48.

68. Klara, "Super Bowl Ad Time Line," 11.

69. Kanner, *Super Bowl of Advertising*, 41.

70. Ibid., 42.

71. Klara, "Super Bowl Ad Time Line," 11.

72. Bruce Horovitz, "20 Highlights in 20 Years of Ad Meter," *USA Today*, February 10, 2008, http://www.usatoday.com/money/advertising/2008-01-31-20th-super-bowl-ad-meter_N.htm (accessed July 17, 2012).

73. Ibid.

74. Steinberg, "From Apple to Xerox," 3.

75. Horovitz, "20 Highlights."

76. Steinberg, "From Apple to Xerox," 3.

77. Kanner, *Super Bowl of Advertising*, 41–48.

78. Horovitz, "20 Highlights."

79. Kanner, *Super Bowl of Advertising*, 157–58.

80. Horovitz, "20 Highlights."

81. Kanner, *Super Bowl of Advertising*, 59.

82. Klara, "Super Bowl Ad Time Line," 14.

83. Horovitz, "20 Highlights."

84. Ibid.

85. Eleftheria Parpis, "Coke Zero Remakes 'Mean Joe' Super Bowl Spot," *Ad Week*, January 27, 2009, http://www.adweek.com/news/advertising-branding/coke-zero-remakes-mean-joe-super-bowl-spot-98172 (accessed July 15, 2012).

86. Day, " 'Mean Joe' Greene Re-Creates His Famous Super Bowl Ad."

87. Steinberg, "From Apple to Xerox," 18.

88. Jeremy Mullman, Brian Steinberg, Jean Halliday, Natalie Zmuda, and Rupal Parekh, 2009. "Yes, the Super Bowl Is Well Worth \$3M a Spot," *Advertising Age* 80, no. 3 (2009): 1–37, Academic Search Complete, EBSCOhost (accessed July 27, 2012).

89. Ibid.

Bibliography

Bauder. David. "Super Bowl Ratings Record: Giants-Patriots Game Is Highest-Rated TV Show in US History," Huffington Post, February 2, 2012. http://www.huffingtonpost.com/2012/02/06/super-bowl-ratings-record-tv-giants-patriots_n_1258107.html.

Davis, Howard. "Those Super Bowl Spots!" *Television Quarterly*, Spring 2004, 16–20.

Day, Patrick Kevin. " 'Mean Joe' Greene Re-Creates His Famous Super Bowl Ad for Downy." *Los Angeles Times*, February 2, 2012. http://latimesblogs.latimes.com/showtracker/2012/02/mean-joe-greene-recreates-his-famous-super-bowl-ad-for-downy-video.html.

Horovitz, Bruce. "20 Highlights in 20 Years of Ad Meter." *USA Today*, February 10, 2008. http://www.usatoday.com/money/advertising/2008-01-31-20th-super -bowl-ad-meter_N.htm.

Kanner, Bernice. *The Super Bowl of Advertising: How the Commercials Won the Game.* Princeton, NJ: Bloomberg Press, 2004.

Klara, Robert. "Super Bowl Ad Time Line I–XLIV." *Mediaweek* 21, no. 3 (January 24, 2011): 4–15. http://search.ebscohost.com/login.aspx?direct=true&db=ufh &AN=57749847&site=ehost-live.

"Mean Joe Greene." Mean Joe Greene 75. http://www.meanjoegreene75.com/ (accessed July 12, 2012).

Mullman, Jeremy, Brian Steinberg, Jean Halliday, Natalie Zmuda, and Rupal Par- ekh. "Yes, the Super Bowl Is Well Worth $3M a Spot." *Advertising Age* 80, no. 3 (2009): 1–37. http://search.ebscohost.com/login.aspx?direct=true&db =ufh&AN=36269817&site=ehost-live.

Parpis, Eleftheria. "Coke Zero Remakes 'Mean Joe' Super Bowl Spot." *Ad Week*, January 27, 2009. http://www.adweek.com/news/advertising-branding/coke -zero-remakes-mean-joe-super-bowl-spot-98172.

Steinberg, Brian. "From Apple to Xerox: 12 Spots That Changed the Game." *Adver- tising Age* 83, no. 2 (January 9, 2012): 2–20. http://search.ebscohost.com/ login.aspx?direct=true&db=ufh&AN=70314185&site=ehost-live.

CHAPTER THIRTEEN

Contemporary Television Advertising: From Disney to the Kardashians

Leigh H. Edwards

Some of the most important trends in contemporary television advertising involve new ways in which advertising has become integrated into television narratives themselves. Given the rise of digital video recorders and viewers who routinely skip commercials, product placement is becoming increasingly more of a focus in television advertising. That product placement is often taking place at the level of plot. Corporate sponsors can now buy a seat at the story table, paying for input into how their products are integrated into specific storylines. In addition to new techniques of product placement, other important trends in television advertising involve methods such as transmedia storytelling, corporate synergy, mass customization marketing, and monetizing fandom practices.

The further integration of products into television storylines has generated new marketing practices and new narrative trends. In the past, a sponsor such as Coca-Cola would purchase product placement with a program such as Fox's *American Idol* (2002–), and the placement would involve judges sitting at their table sipping Cokes. More recently, that level of integration has risen, with, for example, entire segments in which host Ryan Seacrest interviews contestants while they sit in front of a Coke backdrop. The series also includes branded advertising in which contestants star in commercials for Ford, featuring music videos of the cast driving in Ford cars and singing.

Likewise, other series have incorporated corporate sponsors to a much more extensive degree than was previously evident in our contemporary era of television. Today, the products can drive the storylines. For example, NBC's drama series *Chuck* (2007–2012) was routinely on the edge of cancellation, but with a sponsorship by Subway, the series gained added life. The fast food franchise was incorporated into the program's plotlines by having the spy group headquartered beneath a Subway franchise (which replaced the previous setting, a yogurt shop). On NBC's *The Apprentice* and *Celebrity Apprentice* (2004–), the entire premise of the reality program is that contestants will complete tasks in which they are creating marketing promotions for corporate sponsors of the series, from designing new product campaigns for Walgreen's to staging events at Trump-owned properties or hawking Ivanka Trump's jewelry line. The overarching goal of that reality franchise is to advertise the Trump brand, and that goal prompts the program content.

This incorporation of advertising into program storylines is also evident in the trend of advertising itself becoming a theme and setting for television series. The AMC series *Mad Men* (2007–) is an obvious case in point, as it follows advertising executives on the Madison Avenue of an earlier era, using advertising as a backdrop for exploring the social and sexual mores of the 1960s. Other series have likewise dramatized the lives and careers of advertising executives, such as the short-lived NBC series *Free Agents* (2011), a romantic comedy about public relations executives at an advertising firm in Portland, Oregon (a series based on a British workplace sitcom). There, the newly divorced male and female lead characters begin dating each other while struggling with the increasing advertising pressures of new media and social networking. The TNT series *Trust Me* (2009) followed the exploits of a fictional advertising firm, focusing on tensions between the executives and the cutthroat competition for new accounts.

That thematic focus takes on an added dynamic on reality television because reality series promote actual products and brands as part of their narratives. On E!'s *The Spin Crowd* (2010), for example, public relations executives used reality shows to promote their clients' products and brands. Executive produced by E! reality star Kim Kardashian, the series starred Jonathan Chebon and Simon Huck and followed them as they expanded their own firm, Command PR, and represented stars like Kardashian and their brands. One episode tracked their efforts to help client Mario Lopez promote a self-tanner, while another found them scrambling to get some of their celebrity clients to appear on the red carpet for the launch of a candy line by a client company. The series promoted their celebrity clients, the products of their brand product clients, and it also promoted their PR firm itself. Chebon reported that an initial half-hour special version of the show, entitled *SPINdustry*, generated thousands of queries from publicists wishing to apply for a job at their firm.[1]

The series also promoted that television network itself as a brand. The Kardashians have been instrumental in changing the brand identity of the E! network. The network once focused on covering celebrity and entertainment industry news. Now, the success of the Kardashian reality shows has prompted E! to brand itself as the network that can create new reality stars, as evidenced by the comments of their executive vice president for original programming, Lisa Berger: "It has changed the face of E! We were a place to report on celebrity; we weren't a place to break and make celebrity, which is now the whole idea of the E! brand."[2] The Kardashian and Jenner family made over $65 million in 2010 alone, and their highly rated reality programs have included *Keeping Up With the Kardashians* (2007–), *Kourtney and Khloe Take Miami, Kourtney and Kim Take New York,* and *Khloe and Lamar.*[3] They have promoted products that they have signed on to endorse, such as QuickTrim, clothing and accessories for Sears and QVC, nail polish, cosmetics, a credit card, and their own fleet of clothing stores, Dash. The Kardashian franchise involves some extensive corporate synergy, as when *E! News* reports on their own network's reality stars, especially given that news anchor Ryan Seacrest is also the executive producer of the Kardashian franchise. Such synergy epitomizes what media scholar Eileen Meehan terms "excessive branding," where a company floods the market with branded product to such an extent that it marginalizes or entirely displaces nonbranded products.[4]

Another instructive example of "excessive branding" on television is a recent season of ABC's *The Bachelorette* (2003–), in which parent company Disney aggressively cross-promoted other entertainment properties. One episode had the star of the eighth season of this reality dating program, Emily Maynard, take her suitors to a special advance screening of Disney Pixar's animated film *Brave* (2012). In keeping with the film's themes, about a Scottish princess who wants to fight for her own destiny rather than being forced to marry a prince from a neighboring clan, the reality show episode has the men "fight" for Maynard's "hand" by taking part in Highland Games, just as in the film. Unlike the film, however, which has the princess take a feminist stance by entering and winning the competition herself in order to reject the suitors and avoid an unwanted arranged marriage, the TV episode has Maynard pick the suitor who performed the best to grant him a date and another chance to pursue her hand in marriage. The degree to which the episode exists as a piece of excessive branding for Disney is evidenced by the fact that the group is in Croatia at the time and the cast members continually comment on the fact that they are trying to play Scottish highland games in Croatia, which makes no sense to them. On *The Bachelorette* and *The Bachelor* (2002–), as well as on the spinoff series *Bachelor*

Pad (2010–), the programs brand themselves, featured products, and sponsors, and they even brand the reality characters themselves.

One way in which reality series brand characters is by creating storylines about who these cast members are by focusing on what they consume, i.e., their taste in everything from clothes to music to commodities. The reality television genre turns casts into characters and then turns them into brands. This dynamic creates some complex advertising practices, as a perhaps less predictable case study example from that season of *The Bachelorette* franchise can serve to illustrate.

When Dolly Met Disney

Dolly Parton, Disney, and *The Bachelorette*—what could bring this rather unexpected triumvirate together on television? Marketing. A recent episode of the ABC (under parent company Disney) franchise *The Bachelorette*, which took the reality TV dating show on a surprise trip to Dollywood and had the country doyenne serenade a couple on their date, epitomizes how key marketing techniques function on contemporary television.[5] The fact that viewers would certainly not expect Parton to come sauntering onto the set of *The Bachelorette*, and that the episode would be marketed as an incongruous "surprise trip," speaks to how the advertising is driving the plotline on this reality program, as is the case with much contemporary television. During the program's trip to Dollywood, Parton promotes her Dollywood theme park, sings one of her songs from the recent film soundtrack to her film *Joyful Noise* (2012), and she also sings a new song she wrote specifically for *The Bachelorette* star Emily Maynard and her date. The episode in question features aggressive crossover marketing with country music, which provides a helpful case study for corporate synergy as well as some unexpected transmedia storytelling. It also features some mass customization marketing as well as an instance of television's effort to monetize fandom practices like fan websites and blogs.

On *The Bachelorette* episode, the Parton sequences of cross-promotion are deeply integrated into the storyline and become key parts of the character development. The episode characterizes single mother Maynard by her love of Dolly, with Maynard rhapsodizing about how Parton was always her favorite singer, exclaiming that she has adored Parton ever since she was a child. During their tour through Dollywood, Maynard tries to explain to her date, race car driver Arie Luyendyk Jr. (who grew up in Holland and is not fully aware of the nuances of U.S. popular culture), why Dolly Parton is such an icon. When Parton later surprises them with the private concert just for them, Maynard says she "could die" right there, because she has realized her dream of meeting the singer. In intercut interviews, she talks about how Parton is so important to her and how much it meant to her that a prospective husband could share this experience with her. Her attachment to Parton becomes further a part of the storyline. As the season's narrative arc continues in later episodes, Luyendyk ends as the runner-up, and Maynard chooses a different suitor, Jef Holm, and becomes engaged to him. Maynard and her fiancé Holm could then meet only in seclusion until the show had aired, and the clandestine code name Maynard used for herself was "Dolly" and the pseudonym for Holm was "Dean," taken from Parton's husband's name.

In the Dollywood episode, the series creates a strong narrative for Maynard as *The Bachelorette*, fashioning a reality TV trope into what I have termed a "character narrative."[6] The narrative in this episode involves characterizing reality star Emily Maynard as a country music fan, creating an imaginative link between her and her hero, Dolly Parton, and engaging in a series of branding and cross-promotion moments, all of which further the narrative of *The Bachelorette*. A previous contestant on *The Bachelor* (season 15), Maynard was chosen by Bachelor Brad Womack, became engaged to him, and later broke off that engagement only to appear here on her own season of *The Bachelorette*. In this particular Dollywood episode, the cameras follow her on several outings that further her search for love. Some of these outings fit the typical reality dating show themes (tests for compatible interests, responses to stress, parenting skills, compatibility with friends). In her Charlotte hometown, four of her best friends interview the 16 remaining men (out of 25 suitors) and observe them playing with kids on a playground. On a one-on-one date with contestant Chris Bukowski, Maynard and her date don rope harnesses and climb the side of a museum building in downtown Charlotte and have a rooftop dinner, with Maynard assessing how well her suitor responds to stressful situations.

Yet other outings during this episode seem incongruous in this reality dating show setting, clearly dropped into the narrative to further a link to country music and product promotion. After the rooftop dinner, Maynard and Bukowski attend a Luke Bryan concert staged outdoors in downtown Charlotte. The opening sequence of the episode tries to emphasize a pastoral setting, with footage of horses grazing in pastures, speaking to the imagined pastoral links to country music (or a stereotypical iconography of country music). As Maynard prepares to go with Bukowski to the country music concert, a fan in the crowd watching them from below yells "We love you, Emily," underscoring Maynard's own celebrity status, since she has her own fans, and we see participatory fan culture literally staged on the show (making fans want to be interactive enough to go downtown and watch Maynard in public out on her dates for the program, many tak-ing pictures with their smart phones to post on social networking websites such as Twitter, Facebook, and Tumblr). As Maynard tells her date they are going to a Luke Bryan concert, she tries to establish a link to country music as a way of characterizing herself through her popular culture tastes. She tells him: "I remember the first night we hung out, you told me that you liked country music. One of my favorites is Luke Bryan." At the concert, the crowd gathers behind barricades, watching her dance with Bukowski as they listen to the short concert. From the stage, Luke Bryan sings his country hits, including "Drunk on You" and "Do I," while the crowd watches the couple who are watching the concert staged just for them. In an echo chamber of media fandom, the reality TV couple serves as fans for the singer, while the television fans who have appeared in person are fans for both the TV stars and the concert performer.

The episode's narrative here is furthering Maynard's characterization via her expressions of taste, but it is also furthering the show's marketing. The series continually links Maynard to country music and to NASCAR (con-stantly repeating the story that the father of her daughter is her late fiancé, NASCAR driver Ricky Hendrick, who died in a plane crash right before daughter Ricki was born). Each of these links becomes a cross-promotion opportunity, promoting Luke Bryan's music as well as NASCAR.

This emphasis on popular culture taste and targeted audiences also becomes an example of mass customization marketing, a prominent adver-tising trend in which products are customized for audiences but on a mass scale. An excellent example of this technique is when Amazon greets returning customers with suggestions for your "What You Might Like," which seem personalized to you but are actually generated by algorithms that designate lists for customers based on preferences and purchasing his-tory that customers reveal to the company. Each time customers share their tastes and preferences, companies further target their marketing to them. Media scholar Mark Andrejevic argues that the interactive nature of reality TV (which encourages audiences to use the Internet and smartphones to vote, comment, and express preferences about reality shows) becomes a way to get audiences to accept and even to seek out greater surveillance of them in practices like mass customization marketing—and also to get fans to perform their own marketing research on themselves. For Andrejevic, the democratic promise of the Internet becomes hijacked by corporate interests.[7] In the case of this mass customization marketing on this episode, the show is creating a profile for country music fans (who are also assumed to be NASCAR fans and Emily Maynard fans, or at the very least women who would want to buy the boots and dresses she wears). During the

Parton segments, Maynard continually remarks that most of the top songs on her iPod are Parton's, and the implication here is that the episode is her iPod come to life, i.e., her consumer tastes generate a reality TV story about her.

In the case of this Parton example, *The Bachelorette* becomes a transmedia text (or a story that unfolds across different media platforms in a coordinated way) in that episode because it is at that moment a TV episode that also has music content and links up to a theme park promotion. The episode goes beyond an earlier model of licensing or cross-promotion, precisely because Parton actually wrote a new song for the couple and sings it on the show. Dollywood itself is integrated into the storyline. Maynard exclaims that it is one of her "favorite places in the world," and then it becomes a sentimentalized site for her successful date with her suitor, footage to which the program continually flashes back later in the season because he is one of her finalists at the end. As the two lovebirds stand on a stage at Dollywood and listen to Parton singing to them, Parton sings her lyrics about finding "true love" and knowing that the person is right for them. Parton then meets with Maynard and talks with her about what she is looking for in a future husband, giving her advice on how Parton has kept her own long-running marriage to husband Carl Dean going for over four decades. Parton asks Maynard: "What are you really looking for in a guy?" Maynard replies: "That feeling that you just get when you know." Their exchange moves the storyline forward as Parton observes that Maynard and her date seem like a couple who could last. Maynard, meanwhile, gushes: "Dolly Parton is unbelievable." When Parton generates this content, both musical and otherwise, for the reality TV show, she extends the text into other media platforms. The cross-promotion of Dollywood and of Parton's music is a more familiar marketing strategy, but this moment of creating coordinated content for the show is new and different. Because it is so unexpected, it is an intriguing example of transmedia storytelling trends. Parton here participates in the world-building that *The Bachelorette* franchise is trying to create. Because Parton also sings to the couple her recent song from the movie *Joyful Noise*, a love song entitled "From Here to the Moon and Back," she is also simultaneously promoting both her album and that movie.

Having an ABC reality show film an episode at Dollywood featuring Parton's musical performance is a lively example of what Henry Jenkins terms "transmedia storytelling."[8] Multiplatform storytelling is a widespread media trend in which narratives are told across different formats, such as a television show that has webisodes, smartphone applications, music downloads, and even a film or a live musical tour (as in Fox's television series *Glee* [2009–], or an earlier example such as Disney's *Hannah Montana* [2006–2011], both of which have featured concert films and musical tours). Other prominent examples include the Harry Potter franchise (novels extended into films, an official J. K. Rowling website called Pottermore, and even a theme park, Universal's The Wizarding World of Harry Potter in Orlando) and *The Avengers* franchise (comic books taken into animated television, films, smartphone applications, and online games).

Jenkins argues that to succeed as a transmedia franchise, each text must contribute to the larger whole but also be able to stand alone; the story must create an entire narrative world that audiences wish to inhabit, one that is both encyclopedic and leaves enough narrative gaps for fans to fill in with their own interactive participation.[9] This participation can range from fan fiction to a phenomenon like the college Quidditch teams that have sprung up, with students playing their own real-life version of the fictional sporting game from the Potter franchise. The degree to which a transmedia story succeeds in enticing fans to want to engage in this dream of world-building can be seen in the strong reactions some fans had to James Cameron's film *Avatar* (2009). After seeing the immersive 3D film, some audiences saw it multiple times and wanted to "live" in that fictional world—so much that critics noted a phenomenon of audiences becoming depressed after the film because they wanted to live in the film's world rather in the real world, and they did not like returning to reality after their immersive filmgoing experiences. Critics have even termed it "Post *Avatar* Depression Syndrome."[10]

In *The Bachelorette* example, fans have many opportunities to interact with their favorite story across different media platforms. They can listen to the Parton song about Maynard's search for love as a text on a different media platform that has been coordinated and integrated with the TV series. They can read Maynard's online blog about her feelings during the episode, where she gives readers a window onto her reactions and her investment in Parton:

> I took Arie to one of my favorite places, Dollywood, and being from Holland, he didn't quite understand my obsession with Dolly Parton but he was still such a great sport about it all. The entire day was so perfect that I didn't think anything would make it more memorable, but as soon as I heard Dolly Parton's voice I could have died! I don't think I've ever been so shocked in my life!
>
> She has truly been one of my idols since I was a little girl, and I think every song on my "Top Played Songs" playlist on my iPod is a Dolly song. She couldn't have been sweeter or more down to earth, and I can't say thank you enough to her for making my childhood dream come true![11]

Maynard's blog emphasizes how the Dollywood trip fits into her self-image, her affiliation with Parton and country music, and her consumption of

Parton songs on her iPod, and it reinforces the way the series frames her as a character. It also uses Maynard's diaristic address to her fans to make them feel as if they are on this journey with their heroine, and they can experience what Maynard did not only by watching the episode, but by listening to the Parton songs. Maynard also uses imagines a familiarity with her audience, using an "everywoman" style of address that encourages the viewers feel as if they could be experiencing such an adventure, too.

Transmedia storytelling has become such a prominent trend in the entertainment industry that there is now a "transmedia" category in the Producer's Guild of America annual awards. There are transmedia companies in existence that focus on building content across film, television, comics, theme parks, music, the Web, online gaming, and mobile content. The trend has even sparked its own backlash, with some critics insisting that there is now too much of a focus on transmedia franchises in the entertainment industry.[12]

For television, this trend has particular significance, as the industry has begun envisioning each television show as an anchor for stories that cross into content for other media platforms, such as mobile episodes (or "mobisodes"), Web episodes ("webisodes"), online games, smartphone applications, and music downloads. The engine for this trend is how television has capitalized on new media developments as well as long-running fan behavior. As television scholar Jennifer Gillan has argued, television now imagines each series as a "multiplatform" or the basis for a coordinated array of texts in different media formats. Gillan argues that television adapted features like fan websites, monetizing preexisting fandom practices. She argues that these developments happened in two stages. In the first stage, in the 1990s, networks began fashioning TV series as platforms that could be used to promote other media (such as a fan website for a TV show, for example, the "Dawson's Desktop" website for the WB's *Dawson's Creek* [1998–2003]). In the second stage, in the 2000s, networks began thinking of a TV show differently, as an entire collection of networked texts, each of which can compel fans to jump along multiple different media platforms to look for the content they wish to consume (for example, in the fan-centered website for a TV series like *Heroes* [2006–2010]).[13]

Parton herself participated in earlier examples of transmedia storytelling with Disney, such as the Hannah Montana franchise. In the Disney channel's *Hannah Montana* television series, she appeared as the character "Aunt Dolly." Her television persona was similar to her Dolly Parton public persona, and she built on her autobiographical stories of being close friends with collaborator Billy Ray Cyrus and his daughter Miley (and having been asked by Cyrus to be his daughter's godmother, although she declined because she is gone so much of the time touring). Earlier, Parton actually had a Disney studios CBS-TV series that never aired, *Heavens to Betsy* (1994), which was to be the first network prime-time series for Disney MGM Studios, produced by Parton's Sandollar Productions in association with Touchstone Television. It was the first Walt Disney Studios television production to be produced at Disney MGM Studios. Parton wrote the soundtrack to the TV series, about a woman who had been a Las Vegas lounge singer but had a near-death experience and returned to her Tennessee hometown to make amends. Although the television pilot never aired, Parton turned some of that material into a TV movie, *Unlikely Angel* (1996).

The Dollywood Bachelorette example speaks to how multiplatform content is playing an increasing role in contemporary television advertising. The way such content targets audiences is distinctive as well. The TV industry, as Gillan has pointed out, now targets a broad audience (the traditional broadcast platform audience) as well as a narrowcast audience (smaller niche audiences drawn to multiplatform content, such as fans who might be inclined to play song downloads on their mobile phones). Advertisers enter into branded entertainment deals in order to capitalize on this new "narrowcast-broadcast" combination TV advertising model.[14] All of this advertising, of course, necessitates engaged fans who will interact with their favorite TV series, feeling a part of the world-building, whether that involves showing up to see the TV stars and be in an audience, or virtually participating by posting to social networking websites (reposting content or links) and building up fan networks.

These advertising developments speak to how television trends fit in with the larger media context.[15] Our own media era has been characterized by how media scholar Henry Jenkins describes "convergence culture," in which different media systems coexist and content flows over multiple media platforms. In this era, we witness new interactions between old media (which would include television, film, and books) and new media (by definition, media that uses interactive digital technology, which would include the Internet as well as "smart" mobile phones). Hence we see television shows with smartphone applications. Because of the interactive nature of this convergence culture, the way consumers and producers interact with each other is different as well, as consumers gain more of a voice and influence with the rise of participatory fan culture. Audiences thus start to become more active (surfing across different media platforms to find the entertainment content they desire). Jenkins also points to increased cooperation among media industries, different financing models, and grassroots-corporate media interactions that are novel and evolving. Providing historical context for our current convergence culture era, Jenkins highlights changes and innovations such as digitization as well as new cross-media ownership, dating from the 1980s (when we see media conglomerates buying up holdings from different areas of the industry, from music to comics, TV to computer games, and including other examples like film, websites, theme parks, newspapers, magazines, books, and even toys).[16] Thus, the kind of television advertising we see on everything from *The Bachelorette* to the Kardashians takes its place as part of this larger media convergence culture.

Notes

1. Christina Kinon, " 'The Spin Crowd' Showcases the Glitzy Side of Celebrity PR in a New Reality Show," *New York Daily News*, August 21, 2010, http://www .nydailynews.com/entertainment/tv-movies/spin-crowd-showcases-glitzy-side -celebrity-pr-new-reality-show-article-1.205215.

2. Judith Newman and Leslie Bruce, "How the Kardashians Made $65 Million Last Year," *Hollywood Reporter*, February 16, 2011, http://www.hollywood reporter.com/news/how-kardashians-made-65-million-100349.

3. Ibid.

4. Eileen R. Meehan, *Why TV Is Not Our Fault: Television Programming, Viewers, and Who's Really in Control* (New York: Rowman & Littlefield, 2005).

5. "Episode 803," *The Bachelorette*, ABC, May 28, 2012.

6. Leigh H. Edwards, " 'What a Girl Wants': Gender Norming on Reality Game Shows," *Feminist Media Studies* 4, no. 2 (Summer 2004): 226–28.

7. Mark Andrejevic, *Reality TV: The Work of Being Watched* (Lanham, MD: Rowman & Littlefield, 2003).

8. Henry Jenkins, *Convergence Culture: Where Old and New Media Collide* (New York: New York University Press, 2006), 8.

9. Henry Jenkins, "Transmedia Storytelling 101," *Confessions of an Aca-Fan: The Official Weblog of Henry Jenkins*, March 22, 2007, http://www.henry jenkins.org/2007/03/transmedia_storytelling_101.html.

10. Jo Piazza, "Audiences Experience Avatar Blues," CNN, January 11, 2010, http://articles.cnn.com/2010-01-11/entertainment/avatar.movie.blues_1_pandora -depressed-posts?_s=PM:SHOWBIZ.

11. Emily Maynard, "Emily Maynard Blogs: Meeting Dolly Parton and Confronting a Vampire Detector," *People*, May 29, 2012, http://www.people.com/ people/article/0,,20599218,00.html.

12. Andrea Phillips, "5 Lessons for Storytellers from the Transmedia World," Co.Create, http://www.fastcocreate.com/1680902/5-lessons-for-storytellers-from -the-transmedia-world.

13. Jennifer Gillan, *Television and New Media: Must-Click TV* (New York: Routledge, 2011), 2.

14. Ibid.

15. For a fuller discussion of these issues, see Leigh H. Edwards, *The Triumph of Reality TV: The Revolution in American Television* (Westport, CT: Praeger, 2013). See also Leigh H. Edwards, "Transmedia Storytelling, Corporate Synergy, and Audience Expression." *Global Media Journal* 12, no. 20 (Spring 2012).

16. Jenkins, *Convergence Culture*, 4–16. Jenkins cites political scientist Ithiel de Sola Pool's book *Technologies of Freedom* (1983) as the first to discuss the media convergence concept.

Bibliography

Andrejevic, Mark. *Reality TV: The Work of Being Watched.* Lanham, MD: Rowman & Littlefield, 2003.

Edwards, Leigh H. "Transmedia Storytelling, Corporate Synergy, and Audience Expression." *Global Media Journal* 12, no. 20 (Spring 2012).

Edwards, Leigh H. *The Triumph of Reality TV: The Revolution in American Television.* Westport, CT: Praeger, 2013.

Edwards, Leigh H. " 'What a Girl Wants': Gender Norming on Reality Game Shows." *Feminist Media Studies* 4, no. 2 (Summer 2004): 226–28.

Gillan, Jennifer. *Television and New Media: Must-Click TV.* New York: Routledge, 2011.

Jenkins, Henry. *Convergence Culture: Where Old and New Media Collide.* New York: New York University Press, 2006.

Jenkins, Henry. "Transmedia Storytelling 101." *Confessions of an Aca-Fan: The Official Weblog of Henry Jenkins.* March 22, 2007. http://www.henryjenkins.org/2007/03/transmedia_storytelling_101.html.

Kinon, Christina. " 'The Spin Crowd' Showcases the Glitzy Side of Celebrity PR in a New Reality Show." *New York Daily News*, August 21, 2010. http://www.nydailynews.com/entertainment/tv-movies/spin-crowd-showcases-glitzy-side-celebrity-pr-new-reality-show-article-1.205215.

Maynard, Emily. "Emily Maynard Blogs: Meeting Dolly Parton and Confronting a Vampire Detector." *People*, May 29, 2012. http://www.people.com/people/article/0,,20599218,00.html.

Meehan, Eileen R. *Why TV Is Not Our Fault: Television Programming, Viewers, and Who's Really in Control.* New York: Rowman & Littlefield, 2005.

Newman, Judith, and Leslie Bruce. "How the Kardashians Made $65 Million Last Year," *Hollywood Reporter*, February 16, 2011. http://www.hollywoodreporter.com/news/how-kardashians-made-65-million-100349.

Phillips, Andrea. "5 Lessons for Storytellers from the Transmedia World." Co.Create. http://www.fastcocreate.com/1680902/5-lessons-for-storytellers-from-the-transmedia-world.

Piazza, Jo. "Audiences Experience Avatar Blues." CNN, January 11, 2010. http://articles.cnn.com/2010-01-11/entertainment/avatar.movie.blues_1_pandora-depressed-posts?_s=PM:SHOWBIZ.

CHAPTER FOURTEEN

Infecting the Internet: The Influence of Online Viral Marketing Techniques on Public Opinion

Rekha Sharma

The marketplace of ideas is a metaphor for the role of communication in allowing societies to question and argue various points of view, hopefully accepting ideas of merit and rejecting notions that are harmful or of otherwise inferior quality. However, an interesting dimension of the marketplace allegory is the influence of parties possessing the ability to make their voices figuratively louder by seizing control of the communication process. Individuals or groups with enough resources could hawk their intellectual wares to enhance their personal gain, either through overt or covert persuasion.

History has provided ample evidence of obvious government propaganda and corporate advertising, but the impact of more subtle kinds of persuasion has yet to be fully understood. One such phenomenon is that of viral marketing, similar to word-of-mouth advertising, in which publicity is spread throughout a network of interpersonal channels.[1] Others have referred to viral marketing as "buzz" or "convergence marketing," describing essentially the same process of clients passing on information about a product or topic to other clients, leading to "explosive self-generating demand—or ruin."[2] But viral marketing involves more than a spike in popularity; it is the creation of trends, the initial push of an idea before its momentum increases naturally. The underlying premise of viral marketing is that the original message is artificially introduced into the communication system. Then it propagates itself through interpersonal or mass-mediated channels, just as a virus would infect and thrive in a living organism.

The use of stealth persuasion tactics such as viral marketing has raised interesting questions about the role of technology in manipulating the mass communication process. Specifically, the Internet, an electronic forum enabling interpersonal and mass communication simultaneously, has blurred the traditional distinctions between media types and the manner in which users seek and share information. The anonymity of users in online environments often creates ambiguity as to the credibility of sources and the veracity of messages. In this respect, technology has contributed to the complexity of communication by altering and filtering the information exchanged between senders and receivers.

Therefore, this chapter explores the potential consequences of viral marketing strategies in online environments via the use of e-mail campaigns, websites, blogs, and other kinds of electronic communication. The effects could extend to media outlets such as newspapers, television/radio stations, and magazines in their traditional forms and in their Web-based counterparts, perhaps augmenting the impact of interpersonal communication by spreading messages to mass audiences. With news coverage drawing more attention to the topic or product, the snowballing communication event could serve to sway overall public opinion. Because Internet technology is still evolving, much of this chapter will merely point out potential uses and hazards of viral marketing techniques. But the importance of the issue cannot be overemphasized because of its significance to the democratic process and the transparency of decision-making in societies around the world. After all, identifying the virus is a necessary precursor to developing resistance strategies and, in time, immunity to the infection.

Following a review of literature regarding the origins of viral marketing, I will present an overview of relevant communication theories having to do with opinion formation and the spread of information. Second, several corporate applications of electronic word-of-mouth advertising will provide a precedent for viral marketing techniques in political arenas. Third, an investigation of journalistic practices will elucidate possible avenues by which viral marketers could impregnate news agendas with slanted messages and assess whether audiences are susceptible or resistant to manipulation. Fourth, examples of electronic communication in recent campaigns will help uncover the role of viral marketing techniques in the political process.

What Is Viral Marketing?

Viral marketing has its origins in early multilevel marketing concepts, though it became a buzzword with the flourishing of Internet-based communication technologies in the 1980s and 1990s.[3] However, several pyramid schemes in the nineteenth century, in which operators persuaded an initial group of people to invest in risky schemes, operated in viral expansion loops.[4] Believing their gambles would yield high dividends, those people urged their friends and family to invest their money as well, and those people told their friends and family, and so on until the pyramid eventually collapsed because the operators could not pay the investors. Charles Ponzi, whose 1919 swindle gave us the term "Ponzi scheme"[5] to refer to the ventures of modern-day white-collar criminals such as Bernie Madoff, utilized viral communication.

In the 1920s, WearEver Aluminum Cooking Products found success with direct sales to women in rural areas who lacked access to department stores.[6] Other legitimate companies began to reach consumers in their homes and spread the word about their products via social networks in the following decades. Stanley Home Products augmented door-to-door sales in the 1930s when a customer provided a salesman access to her church group.[7] Tupperware relied on viral marketing techniques in the 1940s and 1950s, as sales agents—usually women—hosted parties in their suburban homes to promote food storage containers.[8] Mary Kay Cosmetics enlarged its pyramid of consultants and customers in the 1960s and 1970s.[9] Amway operated on a similar basis in the 1980s in selling a variety of products, and telecommunications provider MCI offered a "Friends and Family" plan in the 1990s to get customers to recruit their loved ones into the MCI calling circle.[10] Many Internet-based viral businesses (e.g., Hotmail,[11] eBay, MySpace, YouTube, Facebook, Twitter[12]) have sprung up in recent decades, creating multiple, overlapping social networks that have expanded rapidly.

Jay Conrad Levinson coined the term "guerilla marketing" in 1984, when as he said, "computers and printers were luxuries."[13] This idea of guerilla marketing hinged on the premise that companies need not spend exorbitant amounts on traditional media advertising if they could present their brands or products in creative, innovative ways.[14] It would allow advertisers to maximize frequency of ad exposure with minimal waste in their media planning budget.[15] Examples of guerilla marketing could include marking logos on pavement with chalk or stencil graffiti,[16] uploading videos, or identifying trendsetters and seeding messages to them to share with other people in their social networks.[17] Throughout the 1980s, guerilla marketing evolved to include "ambush marketing," which has been defined as legal or illegal attempts by an organization to associate itself indirectly with an event to gain media attention or other benefits typically reserved for the official sponsor of that event.[18]

However, "guerilla marketing" and "ambush marketing" are often synonymous with "viral marketing." Levinson described viral marketing as "digitized word-of-mouth," noting that popular ideas have always spread like epidemics, with each new user transmitting the message to others.[19] Seth Godin popularized viral marketing as an extension of guerilla marketing and permission marketing concepts from the 1980s, referring to people who spread viral messages as "sneezers."[20] When Godin released *Unleashing the Ideavirus* in 2000, he offered it for free as an e-book, encouraging readers to print it as many times as they wanted, forward the book as an e-mail attachment, or share hyperlinks with friends so they could download it themselves or purchase the hardback copy.[21] A decade later, millions of users had downloaded the book and thousands more had purchased the hardcover edition.[22]

Another key example of viral marketing was the promotion of *The Blair Witch Project*,[23] a 1999 mockumentary about student filmmakers researching a Maryland legend. To publicize the low-budget horror film, marketers started the rumor that the amateurish footage had been discovered, though the whereabouts of the students themselves were unknown. With fiction and fact intriguingly blurred, the film's official site attracted 75 million visitors in the first week of the film's release[24] and "spawned countless other websites, generating a cascade of chat room debate, as Web users passed around stories on the film. The early pioneers of word-of-mouth online created the benchmark for guerilla viral marketing campaigns."[25]

Viral marketing has been broadly defined as "any strategy that encourages individuals to voluntarily pass on a marketing message to others," and has been a low-cost and instantaneous way of propagating advertising via preexisting social networks, with the number of message recipients increasing exponentially under the right circumstances.[26] To better predict which ideas would "go viral," scholars and practitioners have analyzed qualities of the message, the communicators, and the networks by which a message may spread.

As communication scholars Richard R. Jurin, Donny Roush, and Jeff Danter explained, "In order to become virulent, a package has to contain a core message, but be swaddled in some coating—be it satire, shock, irony, or just plain funny—that gets it through the usual defenses of recipients."[27] Effective viral messages have been referred to as "sticky," or memorable enough to have an impact.[28] This is because as easy as it may be to share information in digital environments, it is equally easy to ignore a hyperlink or delete unsolicited messages. In an experiment testing viral e-mail transmission of tobacco prevention advertising, researchers concluded that their materials needed to be entertaining.[29] Otherwise, people would not be compelled to keep spreading the message.

One way to get past a person's advertising defenses is to launder the message through his or her relatives and acquaintances because people are less likely to ignore a message from someone they know.[30] Recipients often perceive the credibility of forwarded messages to be high because referral implies endorsement.[31] An added benefit of viral campaigns is that advertisers can follow electronic trails to see which ads attract which people or what may motivate a recipient to transmit a message to others.[32]

Theoretical Foundations

Researchers have asserted that online viral marketing is more advantageous than traditional word-of-mouth marketing because the Internet allows marketing information to be stored in multiple places for a long time and because people can pass on marketing messages at their own convenience or with a certain level of anonymity.[33] People from around the globe can communicate with one another, transcending physical dimensions of community, space, and time. With so many people contributing information, responding to one another, and monitoring discussions from the shadows of cyberspace, the Internet is an interactive form of mass media. Therefore, political and mass communication theories will provide a foundation for understanding the role of online viral marketing techniques in the formation of news coverage, and possibly, of public opinion.

Shaping Opinion: Agenda Setting, Inoculation Theory, and the Spiral of Silence

The agenda-setting theory of mass media was examined in a seminal study conducted by Paul Lazarsfeld during the 1940 presidential election and has since been applied in various contexts.[34] Although personal viewpoints and experiences would remain paramount in individuals' opinions and decisions, a body of research has emerged supporting the ability of news outlets to influence the salience of topics on the public agenda.[35] That is, individuals identified issues they deemed to be important, and those issues corresponded with topics that had received a good deal of media coverage.

Although critics have pointed out that such a correlation did not necessarily mean media coverage caused the public agenda, the evidence incontrovertibly established an association between news stories and audiences' perceptions of importance of certain content. Perhaps journalists simply pick up on trends and report on them. But in doing so, traditional media could still contribute to the perceived salience of topics by legitimizing opinions or drawing attention to issues, making people think about subjects rather than shaping a specific opinion. This link between media coverage and subsequent expressions of opinions has been termed "priming," wherein people draw upon information they consider salient when assessing topics.[36]

This theory raises the possibility that news outlets with Web presences could influence public opinion not only by shaping content in particular ways, but also by presenting an abundance of coverage of certain issues and people. Moreover, if journalists simply watch for trends in online communication, monitoring blogs or responding to electronic newsletters and e-mails, they could reinforce the salience of topics that were introduced into the public consciousness by viral marketers.

Viral marketing's epidemiological metaphor may also extend to inoculation theory. Just as an inoculation may prevent the propagation of a virus in an organism or population, inoculation messages may attenuate a viral message's impact on an individual and stop its spread through a communication network. This theory posits that inoculation messages may promote recipients' resistance to negative communication (e.g., political attack ads) by warning the receiver about the impending message and refuting it. The preemptive strategy weakens the persuasive power of the negative message, making the receiver less likely to change his or her attitudes or behaviors upon exposure.[37]

In a study of college students' resistance to the marketing efforts of credit card companies, researchers[38] found that not only do advertising messages spread virally, but messages designed to inoculate consumers against ads (i.e., warnings about the dangers of credit card debt) travel virally as well. Participants who received inoculation messages with strong counterarguments and strong refutations of those counterarguments reported they were more likely to tell other people negative things about credit card companies.

Along with agenda setting and inoculation theories, other research has established a connection between mass communication and individual opinion formation. In Elisabeth Noelle-Neumann's spiral-of-silence theory,[39] individuals develop a picture of what they perceive to be the public opinion, based on exposure to news coverage and interpersonal interactions. If these individuals believe their own opinion differs from the majority opinion, they will be less likely to voice their dissent. However, it was found that as people who believed themselves to be in the minority refrained from sharing their opinions, the perceived majority opinion could actually become the real majority opinion by default. As Noelle-Neumann explained, "The tendency of one to speak up and the other to be silent starts off a spiraling process which increasingly establishes one opinion as the prevailing one."[40]

The spiral-of-silence theory supports the notion that the Internet, a hybridized medium blending characteristics of mass media and interpersonal conversations, could allow viral marketers to create a perception of an artificial majority opinion, perhaps by launching websites, blogs, or e-mail campaigns about particular topics. As preferred viewpoints were spread from user to user or amplified by traditional mass media outlets, the perceived majority opinion would gradually receive more attention, with minority opinions languishing in obscurity.

Advertisers may initiate this process in multimedia viral campaigns by offering incentives to individuals who write testimonials. In an experiment regarding consumers' evaluations of products after being asked to write testimonials, researchers found that participants who tasted a product designed to be inferior were more likely to evaluate it favorably after writing a testimonial, but they evaluated it negatively if they felt they had been insincere about their testimonial.[41] Customers who blog or post videos about their brand experiences may exaggerate positive claims to gain prizes or because they think testimonials require puffery.[42] When those testimonials are used in ad copy or are amplified through TV commercials, consumers will only have been exposed to the positive claims.

Spreading the Word: Two-Step Flow, Diffusion of Innovations, and Social Contagion

Unlike viral epidemics that spread accidentally in nature, humans often communicate viral messages online purposefully and enthusiastically through the plethora of tools available for sharing opinions and information with other people.[43] The Internet's combination of mass and interpersonal communication implies that viral marketing techniques in a digital environment would make use of both channels. Therefore, the two-step flow of communication, with its indirect-effects view of media influence, could be important for understanding covert persuasive strategies. The theory states that certain individuals are considered "opinion leaders" regarding particular topics.[44] These opinion leaders tend to consume content from print and broadcast media, but impart information and opinions to other people—"followers"—via interpersonal interactions. Thus, media may shape or homogenize public opinion, but only indirectly.[45]

Diffusion of innovations[46] theory examines opinion leadership as a variable among many others in the adoption of new ideas. Everett M. Rogers defined diffusion as "the process by which (1) an *innovation* (2) is *communicated* through certain *channels* (3) *over time* (4) among members of a *social system*."[47] Researchers have sought to predict rates and patterns of diffusion on the basis of "network effects," or communication structures in a social network, which include the number and density of connections; "influencer effects" of those who have adopted an idea on those who have not yet adopted it; and "adopter effects," or characteristics of people who may adopt the idea or message—potentially becoming influencers themselves.[48] According to this theory, the advertiser would act as a "change agent,"[49] introducing its message to an "opinion leader,"[50] or a person who is able to influence others in his or her social network.

Social contagion, traditionally a theory of crowd behavior, has also been used to examine viral communication among mediated groups, focusing on how to seed messages most effectively in online social networks. Broadly, research has focused on "influentials," who keep up with developments and drive the adoption of ideas, and "imitators," whose adoption of ideas does not impact influentials.[51] Other researchers have differentiated people in online networks into three categories: (1) "hubs," or individuals who are connected to many other people; (2) "fringes," people with few connections; (3) and "bridges," people who link disparate subgroups together.[52] Conversely, Malcolm Gladwell,[53] a journalist specializing in matters of social psychology, identified three different types of people who are essential to word-of-mouth epidemics. "Connectors" are individuals who know many people in diverse social circles. "Salesmen" are people with the power to persuade others through eloquent verbal communication or charismatic nonverbal cues. "Mavens" share information not through an explicit wish to persuade, but because of a desire to help or educate. As academic researchers affirmed, people enjoy sharing and seeking information they perceive to be valuable, and individuals feel validated when others act on their recommendations.[54]

These theories support the effectiveness of viral marketing strategies by providing a logical link between sharing information through interpersonal and mass-mediated communication and the articulation of certain public opinions. But to understand viral marketing more directly, researchers should examine recent corporate ventures into Web-based advertising.

Corporate Exploitation of Viral Marketing Techniques

Viral marketing has been used in corporate settings to refer to word-of-mouth advertising of brands and products, especially in a digital context.

In implementation, viral marketing could take place via forwarded e-mails, listservs, blogs, chat rooms, bulletin boards, instant messaging services, or any other iteration of electronic communication that allows people to spread a particular message or advertisement to other users. In 2004, Microsoft developed the alternate-reality game *I Love Bees* to generate buzz over multiple online and offline communication channels (e.g., websites, e-mails, telephone messages) for the sci-fi video game Halo 2.[55]

Simply stated, viral marketing "is the process of encouraging individuals to pass along favourable or compelling marketing information they receive in a hypermedia environment; information that is compelling either by design or by accident."[56] This method of advertising could be more effective than direct marketing, and hence, more attractive to advertisers. Burger King put this philosophy to good use when it launched the Subservient Chicken viral campaign[57] to promote its Tendercrisp Chicken Sandwich. In line with the fast food chain's "Have It Your Way" message to customers, visitors to subservientchicken.com were able to control the actions of an actor in a chicken costume. The link to Burger King was subtle, but the site garnered millions of hits and lots of publicity.

By removing the company as the source of the message, viral marketing might reach consumers who otherwise might not have responded to corporate advertising. An egregious example of a corporation trying to seed advertising anonymously was when Sony Ericsson employed actors to approach potential customers as tourists and ask them to take their pictures with its latest cell phone camera.[58] Because the actors did not divulge that they had been employed to advertise the camera through these pseudo-social encounters, the recipients of the message did not even know they had been involved in a product demonstration.

Viral marketing usually requires little expense, involves voluntary testimonials, and can more accurately target messages to appropriate consumers who receive the messages from a trusted source such as a family member or friend rather than a company.[59] If messages come from people the consumers already know, users are less likely to disregard the content.[60] Furthermore, consumers may be less likely to recognize these types of messages as advertisements and might be less skeptical than they would be of a traditional TV commercial.[61]

Several companies have realized this phenomenon and have employed viral marketing to sell their products or improve their public image.[62] Walmart sent electronic messages to bloggers suggesting topics for postings, offering exclusive news updates about the company, or inviting them to corporate headquarters.[63] By communicating with bloggers, who might not be as responsible about source attribution as traditional journalists tend to be, the companies could influence opinion leaders who would legitimize the point of view stealthily introduced by the company. Readers of those blogs would then internalize the message or perhaps link to or reference the information in other online or face-to-face conversations.

Further evidence of the effective application of viral advertising was found in an analysis of Usenet discussion groups. In a study of online conversations and ratings for new TV shows in the 1999–2000 season, researchers[64] found that higher dispersion of messages was related to higher ratings for the programs. They explained that evaluations of a show's quality were being spread across online communities, consequently driving up ratings. They argued that their findings were strong enough to suggest a causal relationship, indicating that corporations should aim for dispersed buzz over concentrated buzz.[65]

Advertisers have adopted viral marketing in online environments without hesitation, heralding the Internet as a useful tool in tracking and measuring the previously imprecise impact of word-of-mouth communication. However, tech-savvy users might be more conscious of corporate marketing of products and brands, even when advertisements are sent along with the good wishes of a friend via e-mail or embedded in a favorite blogger's post. Furthermore, advertisers need to be aware of "mutations" or "self-generating viruses" that could mean negative publicity for a product, company, or brand.[66] Viral marketing could become more insidious, though, in its impact on traditional news outlets.

Creation and Consumption of Media Content

In spelling out *The New Rules of Marketing and PR*, David Meerman Scott counseled practitioners that "with careful nurturing over the news cycle and an awareness of traditional news media's and bloggers' roles in promoting ideas, [a] story can reach much larger audiences and help a smart organization to reach its goals."[67] Users who turn to online news sites or off-line newspapers, magazines, and radio or TV broadcasts might find themselves unwittingly exposed to virally marketed messages that gained enough momentum to warrant extensive media coverage. Because of its surreptitious nature, viral marketing could allow slanted messages to pass unchecked through traditionally credible journalistic filters by exploiting the practices and conventions of reporters, editors, and news directors.

W. Lance Bennett[68] noted that special interests in the government and in corporate lobbying groups could exploit journalistic conventions to influence news agendas. The author explained that entities wishing to plant stories in the media would craft messages that were simple, salient, credible, and framed within symbolism, drama, and themes appropriate to the occasion. Although viral marketing techniques could vary, a classic example would be the release of information through an anonymous source, also known as a leak. Benefits of this strategy would not only be that the original source could remain hidden, but that journalistic conventions would require that even if the source were to become known to the reporter, that reporter would protect the source's identity from public disclosure: "Because journalists must generally craft the story to make it appear self-contained and removed from its source, leaked stories can often be highly damaging to targeted opponents simply because the whole story and the politics behind it are not told."[69]

But viral marketing techniques could require less sophistication in electronic communication contexts. Bruce Garrison[70] found that over 75 percent of the reporters, editors, and news managers surveyed reported using e-mail to communicate with sources. They expressed some concerns about source authentication, security of communication, and reliability of information obtained through e-mail.

Blogs, an even newer form of electronic expression, have been recognized by some as a way for journalists to monitor public opinion and by others as an alternative to mainstream journalism. Research has shown an intermedia effect between blogs and traditional media, with bloggers criticizing mainstream media coverage yet linking to those news stories.[71] Traditional journalists, who often criticize bloggers for a lack of ethics and professional norms, have frequently relied on blogs for tips and information.[72] Such reliance on unfiltered information, though, could easily lead to the propagation of lies. Websites such as Wikipedia have recently come under scrutiny for publishing false and often damaging information because of a lack of editorial supervision.[73] In detailing how online communication allows for anonymous mudslinging, Philip N. Howard noted that during the 2000 U.S. presidential campaign, Republicans created websites such as gorewillsayanything.com and gorepollution.com, while Democrats developed iknowwhatyoudidintexas.com and millionaires forbush.com.[74]

As technology begins to change the value of editorial filtering in the minds of audiences and the line between alternative and mainstream media wavers through increased interdependence, the common markers of credibility will need to be reconceptualized. In a democratic society that has given media organizations the honorary title of the fourth estate of government, the impact of viral marketing on news agendas will undoubtedly affect the political decision-making process for potential voters.

Influence of Viral Marketing on the Political Process

Viral marketing has the dual effect of manipulating media coverage and crafting public opinion. In a study of newspapers and Internet bulletin boards during the 2000 general election in South Korea, two levels of the agenda-setting process were identified and analyzed.[75] First, newspaper coverage was found to influence users' opinions as expressed online. Second, the Internet bulletin boards influenced newspaper coverage. This interdependence of traditional media and online communication illustrates the potential impact of covert agenda-setting. Although media practitioners might not set out to create a public opinion about a particular issue, there are clearly mechanisms in place within credible news establishments and unstructured, Web-based discussions that allow for factions or special interest groups to direct the flow of information in political arenas through viral marketing techniques.

Thomas P. Lyon and John W. Maxwell discussed this political dimension of viral marketing as "astroturfing," essentially the creation of an artificial grassroots movement.[76] The researchers argued for passage of a bill that would demand full disclosure of corporate expenditures devoted to astroturf lobbying, wherein special interest groups attempt to persuade the government to enact favorable policies by employing public relations firms to pose as members of grassroots campaigns, engaging in such activities as operating phone banks and generating mail, petitions, or electronic communication.

Howard conducted ethnographic research of two companies that facilitate astroturfing via data mining of users' online behaviors, characteristics, preferences, and even their social networks.[77] This development of detailed "psychographic" profiles over the traditional "demographics"[78] emerged as part of a "hypermedia campaign" style of political communication that developed in the 1990s.[79] Hypermedia campaigns favor cheaper, targeted ads on the Internet rather than expensive TV ads broadcast to larger markets.[80]

Bill Clinton was the first president to use computer-mediated communication prominently in his campaign and his presidential administration.[81] Democratic presidential candidate Howard Dean also took advantage of the Internet during the 2004 primaries, but it was Barack Obama who showed real success with social media during his 2008 presidential election campaign.[82] Obama hired Facebook cofounder Chris Hughes to help organize an online grassroots campaign. With short, clear themes such as "Yes, We Can," amplification of his messages from musician Will.i.am and other celebrities who participated in a pro-Obama YouTube video, and a viral network of supporters willing to donate money and spread campaign messages, Obama was the first candidate to truly harness the political power of the Internet and its various communication channels.

Supporters of campaigns could be encouraged to pass on e-mail messages to undecided voters in a more interpersonal type of communication. This implementation of viral marketing of political platforms could overcome individuals' tendencies toward selective exposure to ideas already in line with their own opinions. It could also successfully target voters who would most likely ignore communication directly from the campaign but who would read messages forwarded by friends and relatives.[83] Passing along a carefully crafted message through viral marketing would also allow candidates to contact voters by proxy rather than engage in direct communication, which most candidates have avoided in previous campaigns because of the lack of control over how their responses would be interpreted and spread throughout the Internet.[84]

Future Research

Research on viral marketing and political campaigns should be updated in light of technological advances. Although lack of control would likely remain an issue for candidates considering the value of online interactions with potential voters, studies could show an increased use of blogs, chat rooms, and e-mails that have been crafted strategically. Campaign managers could adapt viral marketing techniques to distance the candidate from the source of the message; issues or opinions could be released covertly, appearing to be words of other voters. If enough momentum could be gained by spurring a dialogue spanning websites or by linking blogs and other forms of electronic expression, news agencies could unwittingly validate the information simply by covering the trend.

More research is also needed to understand how journalists have adapted themselves and their news-gathering practices in an increasingly digital information environment. Qualitative research could reveal greater cognizance of credibility issues and perhaps a clearer articulation of ethics policies regarding fact-checking and technology use in newsrooms.

Finally, communication researchers must examine what kinds of inoculation effects might mitigate viral marketing techniques. Studies should assess whether users have become knowledgeable enough about the interplay between corporations, government, and media to be skeptical of viral marketing strategies and, hence, more resistant to their effects. The potential problems presented here are perhaps worst-case scenarios, but scholars must realize the importance of investigating the role of technology in the democratic process. Online communication is a digital extension of human society, with many of the same benefits and evils of the analog world. However, technology frequently augments the dysfunctions of our own power structures and highlights our personal fallibilities. Therefore, viral marketing must be understood as a new method of persuasion and an added dimension of the complex network of human interaction.

Notes

1. David Godes and Dina Mayzlin, "Using Online Conversations to Study Word-of-Mouth Communication," *Marketing Science* 23 (2004): 545–60.
2. Angela Dobele, David Toleman, and Michael Beverland, "Controlled Infection! Spreading the Brand Message through Viral Marketing," *Business Horizons* 48 (2005): 144.
3. Shintaro Okazaki, "Viral Marketing: How to Spread the Word via Mobile Device," In *Marketing Metaphors and Metamorphosis*, ed. Philip J. Kitchen (New York: Palgrave Macmillan, 2008), 118–19.
4. Adam Penenberg, *Viral Loop: From Facebook to Twitter, How Today's Smartest Businesses Grow Themselves* (New York: Hyperion, 2009), 29–30.
5. Ibid., 30–31.
6. Ibid., 28.
7. Ibid.
8. Penenberg, *Viral Loop*.
9. Douglas Rushkoff, *Coercion: Why We Listen to What "They" Say* (New York: Riverhead Books, 1999).
10. Penenberg, *Viral Loop*, 13.
11. Jay Conrad Levinson, *Guerilla Marketing for Free: 100 No-Cost Tactics to Promote Your Business and Energize Your Profits* (New York: Houghton Mifflin, 2003), 52.
12. Penenberg, *Viral Loop*, 18.
13. Levinson, *Guerilla Marketing for Free*, 63.
14. Phillip Johnson, *Ambush Marketing and Brand Protection: Law and Practice*, 2nd ed. (New York: Oxford University Press, 2011).
15. Lin Zuo and Shari Veil, "Guerilla Marketing and the Aqua Teen Hunger Force Fiasco," *Public Relations Quarterly* 51 (2006): 8–11.
16. Megan Hicks, "Horizontal Billboards: The Commercialization of Pavement," *Continuum: Journal of Media and Cultural Studies* 23 (2009): 765–80.
17. Johnson, *Ambush Marketing and Brand Protection*, 7–8.
18. Ibid., 8.
19. Levinson, *Guerilla Marketing for Free*, 52.
20. Seth Godin, *Unleashing the Ideavirus* (Do You Zoom, Inc., 2000), www.sethgodin.com/ideavirus/downloads/IdeavirusReadandShare.pdf.
21. Ibid., 3.

22. Richard Guthrie, *Publishing: Principles and Practice* (Thousand Oaks, CA: Sage, 2011), 196.

23. *The Blair Witch Project*, directed by Daniel Myrick and Eduardo Sánchez (1999, Santa Monica, CA: Artisan Entertainment), motion picture.

24. Okazaki, "Viral Marketing," 119.

25. Guthrie, *Publishing*, 196.

26. Owen B. J. Carter, Robert Donovan, and Geoffrey Jalleh, "Using Viral E-mails to Distribute Tobacco Control Advertisements: An Experimental Investigation." *Journal of Health Communication: International Perspectives* 16 (2011): 698.

27. Richard R. Jurin, Donny Roush, and Jeff Danter, *Environmental Communication: Skills and Principles for Natural Resource Managers, Scientists, and Engineers*, 2nd ed. (New York: Springer, 2010), 151.

28. Malcolm Gladwell, *The Tipping Point: How Little Things Can Make a Big Difference* (Boston: Little, Brown and Company, 2002), 92; Chip Heath and Dan Heath, *Made to Stick: Why Some Ideas Survive and Others Die* (New York: Random House, 2007).

29. Carter, Donovan, and Jalleh, "Using Viral E-mails to Distribute Tobacco Control Advertisements," 706.

30. Ralf van der Lans, Gerrit van Bruggen, Jehoshua Eliashberg, and Berend Wierenga, "A Viral Branching Model for Predicting the Spread of Electronic Word of Mouth," *Marketing Science* 29 (2010): 348–65.

31. Adam Lindgreen, Angela Dobele, Michael Beverland, and Joëlle Vanhamme, "Viral Marketing," in *Marketing Metaphors and Metamorphosis*, ed. Philip J. Kitchen (New York: Palgrave Macmillan, 2008), 113.

32. Ibid.

33. Nur Undey Kalpaklioglu and Nihal Toros, "Viral Marketing Techniques within Online Social Network." *Journal of Yasar University* 24 (2011): 4112–29.

34. Maxwell McCombs and Amy Reynolds, "News Influence on Our Pictures of the World," in *Media Effects: Advances in Theory and Research*, ed. Jennings Bryant and Dolf Zillmann (Mahwah, NJ: Lawrence Erlbaum, 2002), 1–18.

35. Ibid.

36. Ibid.

37. Michael Pfau, Henry C. Kenski, Michael Nitz, and John Sorenson, "Efficacy of Inoculation Strategies in Promoting Resistance to Political Attack Messages: Application to Direct Mail," *Communication Monographs* 57 (1990): 25–43.

38. Joshua A. Compton and Michael Pfau, "Use of Inoculation to Foster Resistance to Credit Card Marketing Targeting College Students," *Journal of Applied Communication Research* 32 (2004): 343–64.

39. Elisabeth Noelle-Neumann, "The Spiral of Silence: A Theory of Public Opinion," *Journal of Communication* 24 (1974): 45–51.

40. Ibid., 44.

41. Terence A. Shimp, Stacy L. Wood, and Laura Smarandescu, "Self-Generated Advertisements: Testimonials and the Perils of Consumer Exaggeration." *Journal of Advertising Research* 47 (2007): 453–61.

42. Ibid.

43. Penenberg, *Viral Loop*, 13.

44. Elihu Katz, "The Two-Step Flow of Communication: An Up-to-Date Report on An Hypothesis," *Public Opinion Quarterly* 21 (1957): 61–78.

45. Ibid.

46. Everett M. Rogers, *Diffusion of Innovations*, 5th ed. (New York: Free Press, 2003).

47. Ibid., 11.

48. Zsolt Katona, Peter Pal Zubcsek, and Miklos Sarvary, "Network Effects and Social Influences: The Diffusion of an Online Social Network," *Journal of Marketing Research* 48 (2011): 425–43.

49. Rogers, *Diffusion of Innovations*.

50. Ibid.

51. Christophe Van den Bulte and Yogesh V. Joshi, "New Product Diffusion with Influentials and Imitators," *Marketing Science* 26 (2007): 400–421.

52. Oliver Hinz, Bernd Skiera, Christian Barrot, and Jan U. Becker, "Seeding Strategies for Viral Marketing: An Empirical Comparison," *Journal of Marketing* 75 (2011): 56.

53. Gladwell, *Tipping Point*.

54. Ted Smith, James R. Coyle, Elizabeth Lightfoot, and Amy Scott, "Reconsidering Models of Influence: The Relationship between Consumer Social Networks and Word-of-Mouth Effectiveness." *Journal of Advertising Research* 47 (2007): 387–97.

55. Okazaki, "Viral Marketing," 119.

56. Dobele, Toleman, and Beverland, "Controlled Infection!" 144.

57. Lindgreen, Dobele, Beverland, and Vanhamme, "Viral Marketing," 110.

58. Ibid., 111–12.

59. Dobele, Toleman, and Beverland, "Controlled Infection!"

60. Joseph E. Phelps, Regina Lewis, Lynne Mobilio, David Perry, and Niranjan Raman, "Viral Marketing or Electronic Word-of-Mouth Advertising: Examining Consumer Responses and Motivations to Pass Along E-mail." *Journal of Advertising Research* 44 (2004): 333–48.

61. Sonia Livingstone, "Debating Children's Susceptibility to Persuasion— Where Does Fairness Come In? A Commentary on the Nairn and Fine versus Ambler Debate," *International Journal of Advertising* 28 (2009): 170–74.

62. Michael Barbaro, "Wal-Mart Enlists Bloggers in its Public Relations Campaign," *New York Times*, March 7, 2006.

63. Ibid.

64. Godes and Mayzlin, "Using Online Conversations."

65. Ibid.

66. Douglas Rushkoff, *Media Virus! Hidden Agendas in Popular Culture* (New York: Ballantine Books, 1994), 14.

67. David Meerman Scott, *The New Rules of Marketing and PR: How to Use Social Media, Online Video, Mobile Applications, Blogs, News Releases, and Viral Marketing to Reach Buyers Directly*, 3rd ed. (Hoboken, NJ: John Wiley & Sons, 2011), 108–9.

68. W. Lance Bennett, *News: The Politics of Illusion*, 4th ed. (New York: Addison Wesley Longman, 2001).

69. Ibid., 132.

70. Bruce Garrison, "Newspaper Journalists Use E-mail to Gather News," *Newspaper Research Journal* 25 (2004): 58–69.

71. Thomas J. Johnson and Barbara K. Kaye, "Wag the Blog: How Reliance on Traditional Media and the Internet Influence Credibility Perceptions of Weblogs among Blog Users," *Journalism and Mass Communication Quarterly* 81 (2004): 622–42.

72. Ibid.

73. Jane Kirtley, "Web of Lies: A Vicious Wikipedia Entry Underscores the Difficulty of Holding Anyone Responsible for Misinformation on the Internet." *American Journalism Review*, February–March 2006.

74. Phillip N. Howard, "Digitizing the Social Contract: Producing American Political Culture in the Age of New Media." *The Communication Review* 6 (2003): 217.

75. Byoungkwan Lee, Karen M. Lancendorfer, and Ki Jung Lee, "Agenda-Setting and the Internet: The Intermedia Influence of Internet Bulletin Boards on Newspaper Coverage of the 2000 General Election in South Korea." *Asian Journal of Communication* 15 (2005): 57–71.

76. Thomas P. Lyon and John W. Maxwell, "Astroturf: Interest Group Lobbying and Corporate Strategy." *Journal of Economics & Management Strategy* 13 (2004): 561–97.

77. Howard, "Digitizing the Social Contract," 228.

78. Douglas Rushkoff, *Coercion: Why We Listen to What "They" Say* (New York: Riverhead Books, 1999), 198.

79. Howard, "Digitizing the Social Contract," 224.

80. Ibid., 214.

81. Douglas Rushkoff, *Media Virus! Hidden Agendas in Popular Culture* (New York: Ballantine Books, 1994), 239.

82. Penenberg, *Viral Loop*, 14–17.

83. Andrew Paul Williams and Kaye D. Trammell, "Candidate Campaign E-mail Messages in the Presidential Election 2004," *American Behavioral Scientist* 49 (2005): 560–74.

84. Jennifer Stromer-Galley, "On-line Interaction and Why Candidates Avoid It," *Journal of Communication* 50 (2000): 111–32.

Bibliography

Barbaro, Michael. "Wal-Mart Enlists Bloggers in Its Public Relations Campaign." *New York Times*, March 7, 2006.

Bennett, W. Lance. *News: The Politics of Illusion*. 4th ed. New York: Addison Wesley Longman, 2001.

The Blair Witch Project. Directed by Daniel Myrick and Eduardo Sánchez. 1999. Santa Monica, CA: Artisan Entertainment. Motion Picture.

Carter, Owen B. J., Robert Donovan, and Geoffrey Jalleh. "Using Viral E-mails to Distribute Tobacco Control Advertisements: An Experimental Investigation." *Journal of Health Communication: International Perspectives* 16 (2011): 698–707.

Compton, Joshua A., and Michael Pfau. "Use of Inoculation to Foster Resistance to Credit Card Marketing Targeting College Students." *Journal of Applied Communication Research* 32 (2004): 343–64.

Dobele, Angela, David Toleman, and Michael Beverland. "Controlled Infection! Spreading the Brand Message through Viral Marketing." *Business Horizons* 48 (2005): 143–49.

Garrison, Bruce. "Newspaper Journalists Use E-mail to Gather News." *Newspaper Research Journal* 25 (2004): 58–69.

Gladwell, Malcolm. *The Tipping Point: How Little Things Can Make a Big Difference.* Boston: Little, Brown, and Company, 2002.

Godes, David, and Dina Mayzlin. "Using Online Conversations to Study Word-of-Mouth Communication." *Marketing Science* 23 (2004): 545–60.

Godin, Seth. *Unleashing the Ideavirus*. Do You Zoom, Inc., 2000. http://www.sethgodin.com/ideavirus/downloads/IdeavirusReadandShare.pdf.

Guthrie, Richard. *Publishing: Principles and Practice.* Thousand Oaks, CA: Sage, 2011.

Heath, Chip, and Dan Heath. *Made to Stick: Why Some Ideas Survive and Others Die.* New York: Random House, 2007.

Hicks, Megan. "Horizontal Billboards: The Commercialization of Pavement." *Continuum: Journal of Media and Cultural Studies* 23 (2009): 765–80.

Hinz, Oliver, Bernd Skiera, Christian Barrot, and Jan U. Becker. "Seeding Strategies for Viral Marketing: An Empirical Comparison." *Journal of Marketing* 75 (2011): 55–71.

Howard, Phillip N. "Digitizing the Social Contract: Producing American Political Culture in the Age of New Media." *Communication Review* 6 (2003): 213–45.

Johnson, Phillip. *Ambush Marketing and Brand Protection: Law and Practice.* 2nd ed. New York: Oxford University Press, 2011.

Johnson, Thomas J., and Barbara K. Kaye. "Wag the Blog: How Reliance on Traditional Media and the Internet Influence Credibility Perceptions of Weblogs among Blog Users." *Journalism and Mass Communication Quarterly* 81 (2004): 622–42.

Jurin, Richard R., Donny Roush, and Jeff Danter. *Environmental Communication: Skills and Principles for Natural Resource Managers, Scientists, and Engineers.* 2nd ed. New York: Springer, 2010.

Kalpaklioglu, Nur Undey, and Nihal Toros. "Viral Marketing Techniques within Online Social Network." *Journal of Yasar University* 24 (2011): 4112–29.

Katona, Zsolt, Peter Pal Zubcsek, and Miklos Sarvary. "Network Effects and Social Influences: The Diffusion of an Online Social Network." *Journal of Marketing Research* 48 (2011): 425–43.

Katz. Elihu. "The Two-Step Flow of Communication: An Up-to-Date Report on An Hypothesis." *Public Opinion Quarterly* 21 (1957): 61–78.

Kirtley, Jane. "Web of Lies: A Vicious Wikipedia Entry Underscores the Difficulty of Holding Anyone Responsible for Misinformation on the Internet." *American Journalism Review,* February–March 2006.

Lee, Byoungkwan, Karen M. Lancendorfer, and Ki Jung Lee. "Agenda-Setting and the Internet: The Intermedia Influence of Internet Bulletin Boards on Newspaper Coverage of the 2000 General Election in South Korea." *Asian Journal of Communication* 15 (2005): 57–71.

Levinson, Jay Conrad. *Guerilla Marketing for Free: 100 No-Cost Tactics to Promote Your Business and Energize Your Profits.* New York: Houghton Mifflin, 2003.

Lindgreen, Adam, Angela Dobele, Michael Beverland, and Joëlle Vanhamme. "Viral Marketing." In *Marketing Metaphors and Metamorphosis,* edited by Philip J. Kitchen, 102–17. New York: Palgrave Macmillan, 2008.

Livingstone, Sonia. "Debating Children's Susceptibility to Persuasion—Where Does Fairness Come In? A Commentary on the Nairn and Fine versus Ambler Debate." *International Journal of Advertising* 28 (2009): 170–74.

Lyon, Thomas P., and John W. Maxwell. "Astroturf: Interest Group Lobbying and Corporate Strategy." *Journal of Economics and Management Strategy* 13 (2004): 561–97.

McCombs, Maxwell and Amy Reynolds. "News Influence on Our Pictures of the World." In *Media Effects: Advances in Theory and Research,* edited by Jennings Bryant and Dolf Zillman, 1–18. Mahwah, NJ: Lawrence Erlbaum, 2002.

Noelle-Neumann, Elisabeth. "The Spiral of Silence: A Theory of Public Opinion." *Journal of Communication* 24 (1974): 45–51.

Okazaki, Shintaro. "Viral Marketing: How to Spread the Word via Mobile Device." In *Marketing Metaphors and Metamorphosis,* edited by Philip J. Kitchen, 118–31. New York: Palgrave Macmillan, 2008.

Penenberg, Adam L. *Viral Loop: From Facebook to Twitter, How Today's Smartest Businesses Grow Themselves.* New York: Hyperion, 2009.

Pfau, Michael, Henry C. Kenski, Michael Nitz, and John Sorenson. "Efficacy of Inoculation Strategies in Promoting Resistance to Political Attack Messages: Application to Direct Mail." *Communication Monographs* 57 (1990): 25–43.

Phelps, Joseph E., Regina Lewis, Lynne Mobilio, David Perry, and Niranjan Raman. "Viral Marketing or Electronic Word-of-Mouth Advertising: Examining Consumer Responses and Motivations to Pass Along E-mail." *Journal of Advertising Research* 44 (2004): 333–48.

Rogers, Everett M. *Diffusion of Innovations.* 5th ed. New York: Free Press, 2003.

Rushkoff, Douglas. *Coercion: Why We Listen to What "They" Say.* New York: Riverhead Books, 1999.

Rushkoff, Douglas. *Media Virus! Hidden Agendas in Popular Culture.* New York: Ballantine Books, 1994.

Scott, David Meerman. *The New Rules of Marketing and PR: How to Use Social Media, Online Video, Mobile Applications, Blogs, News Releases, and Viral Marketing to Reach Buyers Directly.* 3rd ed. Hoboken, NJ: John Wiley & Sons, 2011.

Shimp, Terence A., Stacy L. Wood, and Laura Smarandescu. "Self-Generated Advertisements: Testimonials and the Perils of Consumer Exaggeration." *Journal of Advertising Research* 47 (2007): 453–61.

Smith, Ted, James R. Coyle, Elizabeth Lightfoot, and Amy Scott. "Reconsidering Models of Influence: The Relationship between Consumer Social Networks and Word-of-Mouth Effectiveness." *Journal of Advertising Research* 47 (2007): 387–97.

Stromer-Galley, Jennifer. "On-line Interaction and Why Candidates Avoid It." *Journal of Communication* 50 (2000): 111–32.

Van den Bulte, Christophe, and Yogesh V. Joshi. "New Product Diffusion with Influentials and Imitators." *Marketing Science* 26 (2007): 400–421.

van der Lans, Ralf, Gerrit van Bruggen, Jehoshua Eliashberg, and Berend Wierenga. "A Viral Branching Model for Predicting the Spread of Electronic Word of Mouth." *Marketing Science* 29 (2010): 348–65.

Williams, Andrew Paul, and Kaye D. Trammell. "Candidate Campaign E-mail Messages in the Presidential Election 2004." *American Behavioral Scientist* 49 (2005): 560–74.

Zuo, Lin, and Shari Veil. "Guerilla Marketing and the Aqua Teen Hunger Force Fiasco." *Public Relations Quarterly* 51 (2006): 8–11.

CHAPTER FIFTEEN

Web 2.0 and Mobile Internet Marketing

Peter Fontana

New York City's Times Square has played host to some of the biggest and brightest advertising in its 100-year history. But in 2010, the signs were metaphorically brightened further when it shared arguably the biggest stage in outdoor advertising with consumers. The brand was Corona, and their campaign grew their Facebook fan community by enabling users to submit a photo to be displayed on their billboard. In the city that was full of message-manipulating Mad Men 50 to 60 years earlier, this was truly a new advertising age.[1]

Like most periods of evolutionary history, eras are more gradual in reality than defined by exact dates. But it is largely accepted by industry observers that in the years following the dot-com bust at the turn of the century, consumer empowerment, new technologies, and eventual changes to advertising models for the Internet and mobile devices symbiotically delivered the era we have come to know as Web 2.0.[2]

The phrase Web 2.0, coined by software and media developer Tim O'Reilly during a conference in 2004, can be defined as the period when the Internet shifted from a largely publisher-content and user-consumption model, to one of universal creation and sharing.[3] It was at this time that new platforms increasingly marginalized broadcast marketing strategies and gave rise to new consumer expectations for two-way brand communication as well as free content supported by advertising. This evolution in marketing blurred the line between advertising and public relations, rewriting the rulebook for the benefit of brands and consumers alike.

O'Reilly's observations gave a name to this rise in consumer-generated media, but the era itself had already been in development for years, and some could argue, decades. Even now, it is debatable if we are still in the midst of this Web 2.0 era, or en route to the next. Whether the era is still upon us or passing us by, recording this history so close to the era itself presents the challenge of both relevancy and completeness when read five years or even one year from now. The reader will have to forgive these dated references and viewpoints and appreciate this writing as a snapshot of history as we knew it.

Advertising in this era largely evolved on the coattails of the Internet evolution, rather than with the progression. The initial failure of marketers to widely cash in on the first dot-com boom had left them skeptical of the Internet as an advertising channel. Marketers failed to harness the full potential of the social Web, as they saw only nominal success in extending traditional forms of broadcast advertising onto the new media channel. But, as brands discovered years after the dot-com bust, it was only their approach that failed, not the medium. Marketers simply did not know how to most effectively execute and construct a digital marketing mix within the new media channel.

In addition to early failures in monetization, the shift to a next-generation advertising was driven by an ever-growing user demand to connect to other people online. This democratic push gave rise to new platforms that turned traditional marketing on its head, where broadcasting mass messages was not only losing effectiveness, but in some cases threatened brands. Facebook founder and chief executive Mark Zuckerberg observed this evolution in advertising in a 2007 interview for the publication *Brand Republic*: "For the last 100 years, media has been pushed out to people, but now marketers are going to be part of the conversation."[4]

Marketers and advertising agencies were forced to change their executions from one-way communication to two-way, establish completely new forms of advertising, and, in the process, integrate their traditional forms of advertising on off-line channels such as television. New technologies, such as smartphones and tablets, pushed the relevance of the Internet channel to marketers as consumers became more easily accessible and more precisely targeted. But, as we will explore in this chapter, the industry was more reactive to this change than proactive.

From 1.0 to 2.0

Like all new mediums, the Internet as we know it did not start all at once, but in overlapping iterations, each evolving consumer-generated media.

Consumer-generated media (CGM) consists of the organic, unprompted consumer content in the form of opinions, comments, photos, videos, likes, shares, and other user-initiated actions.[5] Since the earliest days of the Internet, consumers were creating their own content and cultivating their own word-of-mouth communities around interest groups and brands.

While CGM has long existed, what has evolved and come to define the Internet is where and how it is created and exchanged, and its relationship to marketers. Having started with e-mail, chat rooms, and web pages, and followed quickly by instant messaging, search engines, and forums, the Internet extended in the Web 2.0 period to include blogging, social media, and mobile integration. Industry observers consider the start of this platform list to be in the era of 1.0 and the latter 2.0, but with CGM ever-present.

Earlier still, this online iteration of CGM was an extension of off-line consumer behavior. For example, brand communities have long existed and connected to share their collective passions and recommendations by word of mouth. Fans of Apple products have been connecting at conferences since the 1970s. Harley-Davidson claims their passionate fans have made tattoos of their logo second only to mom.[6] And at the onset of the Internet, the early popularity of chat rooms and forums allowed these people with similar interests to discuss everything from products to interests. For consumers, Web 2.0 was simply the evolution of this behavior.

Media theorist Douglas Rushkoff has observed this evolution as a correction to an old advertising adage that suggested content was king; instead, Web 2.0 showed that contact is king.[7]

Rise of the Consumer

The inherent social connection between consumers for brand affinity and recommendations was given license to expand globally just as our lives had become oversaturated with broadcast media that often overextended brand promises. The time was right for a revolution. Advertising through the 1990s had increasingly crept into consumers' lives with the rise of channels such as cinema advertising, mobile text-message advertising, and early Internet pop-up and banner advertising. The consumer had become inundated with broadcast messaging. As a result, its effectiveness was losing ground as consumers learned to skip or ignore the onslaught.[8]

The Power of Word of Mouth and Consumer Demand

Value propositions or brand promises made in these broadcast messages have always been trumped by user experience. If a brand does not deliver on its promise, it loses credibility and a consumer is unlikely to purchase the brand again. Negative experiences by a trusted colleague, friend, or family member carries a similar weight when that information is shared in the form of a recommendation. When this inner circle expanded to the global Internet, this word of mouth became increasingly powerful.

Mothers were among the first and continue to be among the top users of consumer-generated media for purchase recommendations, particularly when it deals with medical products, such as over-the-counter medications, or safety, such as child car seats and household cleaners. The popularity of mom groups has spawned sites such as Mumsnet, which provide open forums for advice exchanging among mothers including deal and coupon sharing.[9]

Taking this to the next level were the Generation Y teens of the 2000s who flocked to social media platforms to communicate, share photos, and express themselves on sites such as Hi5, Friendster, MySpace, Facebook, Twitter, LinkedIn, and many more.[10] New tools such as camera phones and video-sharing sites empowered consumers to pursue their creativity and share their message with worldwide access.[11] This generation was also among the first to grow accustomed to free content and information. Though illicit at first, such as the early Napster music downloading engine, it forced content providers to seek out new revenue models via embedded marketing.

Old Habits

But advertisers—accustomed to owning the message—were not quick to adapt to this consumer participation, instead extending tired broadcast strategies onto these platforms. As consumers drove the popularity of these new platforms, marketers were forced to shift Internet strategies from another broadcast medium to one in which the exchange was mutual.[12] As these communities evolved, consumers gained power, requiring brands to listen and provide users with better access. In a 2006 speech by Charlotte Otto, global external relations officer for Procter & Gamble, she recognized this shift in message delivery, saying, "Consumers own our brands. Consumers own our messages. Consumers own the conversation about how, where and if they invite our brands into their lives."[13]

Socially Awkward Advertisers

While seeds of this evolution were present in the earliest days of the Internet, advertisers took a different turn on the way to today's

Web 2.0 marketing, sometimes with disastrous results. Initially embraced as an extension to the off-line media mix, Internet advertising mirrored traditional, one-way communication executions such as banner advertising, pop-ups, and video spots.

But for better or worse, the Web was more measureable than offline channels driving stricter accountability for advertising dollars. The ability to prove success or failure of a media buy led to the development of scientific methods that automatically optimize broadcast ads for attributes like size, content, color, or the website of the ad based on user actions. Despite these efforts, response and conversion rates decreased year by year. Though still employed today for mass-reach and direct-response marketing objectives, these Web 1.0 executions did not match the social use of the Internet.

When social media platforms emerged, these same marketing strategies were employed but with enhanced targeting opportunities. In addition to optimizing based on consumer behavior, marketers were able to microtarget users based on self-declared interests listed in their social media profiles. Google has innovated heavily in this space, serving ads to users of their free tools. Today, someone using Google's full product range receives ads based on information from their Web searches, e-mail content, browser behavior, social media habits, and phone and tablet usage.

Brands struggled to find strong or lasting success on these platforms as they used social media as an extension of their broadcast messages.[14] In this oversaturated advertising marketplace, consumers processed these messages passively, peripherally, or ignored them completely. As marketers would later discover upon embracing two-way conversations, engagement prompted a more central processing of brand messaging and generated a positive brand experience.

The Blog Effect

Meanwhile, consumers were broadcasting their own messaging at an increased rate through the early and mid-2000s with a platform extension of early chat rooms and forums called blogs. Sites such as LiveJournal and Blogspot provided easy setup to produce blog content.[15]

While most marketers were not listening, other consumers were, as this CGM appeared in search engine results. This resulted in a shift in power from brands to peers who used the power of the Internet to research, connect, and share information.[16] Brand advertising claims, consumer experiences, and brand controversies could now easily be researched through Web searches of blogs and other user-maintained data sources, such as

Wikipedia. Marketing credibility in this evolved Internet age had become paramount.[17]

Traditional public relations responses to a brand crisis included attempting to control the message by reaching out to influential journalists or activists, but Web 2.0 empowered most anyone to become an influencer. Therefore, how and to whom to reach out was not immediately obvious.[18]

Dell's Worst Practice

One brand that was not quick to recognize the importance of these Web 2.0 influencers was computer manufacturer Dell when, in 2005, a blogger wrote of their negative consumer experience with the brand and it went viral. Jeff Jarvis, now professor at the City University of New York, and his *Dell Hell* blog posts chronicled his redemption of a Dell coupon to purchase what turned out to be a dysfunctional laptop, and his customer service struggles to obtain a refund.[19] Jarvis's accounts inspired other consumers to share their negative experiences about Dell. This eventually led to the creation of a community of anti-Dell consumers on the site IHateDell.net, which received so many visitors it rose among the top results in search engine results for the brand.[20]

Even as Dell continued to ignore these negative accounts and communities, Dell employees unofficially engaged with disaffected customers in an attempt to solve issues and connect consumers to help channels.[21] This led to the eventual creation of Direct2Dell, an official blog presence for the brand to listen and address customer service inquires in social media.[22]

In a retrospective interview with *BusinessWeek* in 2007, founder and CEO Michael Dell admitted the brand's early mistakes in Web 2.0: "We screwed up, right? ... These conversations are going to occur whether you like it or not, OK? Well, do you want to be a part of that or not? My argument is you absolutely do. You can learn from that. You can improve your reaction time. And you can be a better company by listening and being involved in that conversation."[23]

Marketers Share the Pulpit

Advertising evolved in Web 2.0 in part by embracing a half-century-old psychology concept known as the Hawthorne Effect, in which people feel empowered and flattered when their opinions are asked, driving further engagement, loyalty, and advocacy.[24] Shifting away from focusing exclusively on the broadcast strategy, brands fostered communities by starting corporate blogs, online customer service channels, and wider brand monitoring in social media in order to engage in two-way communication with consumers and build brand equity.[25]

Advertising Social Platforms

After learning the marketing pitfalls of the emerging Web 2.0 space, Dell further embraced social media with the launch of IdeaStorm. The platform allowed users to submit ideas and recommendations for existing and future product offerings. The result was both an engaged user community that felt empowered, and a valuable consumer feedback platform that was collected more cheaply than commissioning market research studies.[26] These new platforms, and later mainstream platforms such as Facebook and Twitter, provided advertisers with new ways to interact with consumers in a relevant and targeted way.[27] Messaging encouraged consumers to follow or subscribe to brand communities to receive content they could interact with and connect with fellow fans. Likewise, consumers could submit content on their own profile or that of the brand for community participation. When well executed, consumers shared advertising content, becoming advocates for the brand. This sharing of brand messages was not only effective, but it also cost far less than traditional forms of advertising.[28]

Purchase Reviews

In addition to engaging with these consumers on company-owned platforms, interaction became increasingly important on purchase sites that permitted point-of-purchase commenting. In the late 1990s and early 2000s, Amazon.com, Best Buy, and Circuit City were among the innovative leaders in the online purchase experience by providing both positive and negative user reviews on product pages to better inform consumers. Since these stores were not the manufacturer of the products, the review sections appeared credible, as it allowed consumers to make word-of-mouth recommendations.

After Dell's disastrous introduction into the consumer-empowered age, they too provided a consumer review section in an attempt to establish credibility. This allowed Dell to participate in the negative conversations, identify reoccurring product issues, and display rectification measures with consumers, such as money back or returns.[29]

Key Influencer Engagement

In addition to listening to influential consumers, brands began seeking them out in social media as a part of their marketing strategies. By

advancing public relations tactics used with journalism, brands began utilizing industry tools to identify their key influencers, to openly engage in
dialogue with them, and to encourage and amplify the positive while
responding to the negative.[30]

Red Bull, a brand with extensive events marketing and sponsorships, was
among the early adopters of this strategy by finding brand ambassadors online. By profiling and listening to potential influencers in their social media
presence, Red Bull recruited people who emulated their brand and who
were either already a part of a community, such as a college campus, or
could appear at events, such as sports games, and influence a crowd.[31]

Customer Service 2.0

As some brands needed to learn, Web 2.0 could empower customer relationship management (CRM) to a level of a public relations crisis; but it also
provided brands with an advertising opportunity to respond en masse and
provide customer service less expensively. No longer was a complaint isolated to a phone call between an operator and a consumer. The Internet
now served as a paper trail, searchable by any consumer, even years after
the incident. As a result, unattended complaints posed a threat. But this
searchability also streamlined the process for both the brand and the consumer, as common questions were now answered by search instead of
repeated customer service inquiries.

In addition, CRM efforts could be streamlined and more efficient digital
offerings.[32] Consumer inquiry outlets expanded to offer instant messaging
and forums, and replacing or supplementing expensive phone hotlines.
The onset of Web 2.0 social channels gave rise to another leading platform
in customer service: Twitter and Facebook. In recent years, brand community managers use company profiles to address customer service inquiries.

Twitter was the catalyst for this new channel, what is often referred to as social
customer relations management or sCRM.[33] Twitter was and still is the place
consumers turn to for real-time service inquiries and brand interaction due in
part to its accessibility. Twitter was among the first social platforms to use short
message service, or SMS, via text messaging on cell phones. Twitter messages
also required brevity, at a maximum of 140 characters, meaning messages could
be read and replied to in short order and en mass by customer service teams.

Seeking Out Conversations

But with the rapid growth of social media, the ongoing advertising challenge became wider social media listening, or finding these conversations

when they occur outside a brand's blog, Twitter, Facebook, or other owned platform.[34] This marketer need opened the door to a host of new research tools to isolate brand conversations in Web 2.0. These tools, such as Sysomos, Nielsen's Buzz Metrics and Radian6, provided marketers with a veritable Google for social media, using sophisticated Boolean search queries to isolate brand conversations.

Today, these tools are being furthered developed to interpret language better, such as emotional conversations and ever-more-accurate sentiment analyses to isolate positive and negative brand conversations. Market leaders in this innovative space, at the time of writing, include Crimson Hexagon and NetBase. Savvy brands began proactively seeking out customer service issues via social media monitoring based on consumer language and keywords and responding with the appropriate conversational advertising message.[35]

Web 2.0 Market Research

With this newfound CRM tracking, and its cost-effectiveness, advertisers soon saw uses for Web 2.0 to streamline their market research process. While at first, the measurement of consumer-generated media was considered by purists as only a subset of the larger sphere of consumer opinions, this quickly became the norm for directional brand measurement, as an increasing number of consumers in the 2000s researched and shared opinions online as a part of their purchase cycle.[36]

Prior to trackable CGM, unprompted, off-line word-of-mouth was coveted by market researchers but nearly impossible to track with any level of accuracy. Consumer opinions were largely gathered in artificial research studies in which responses were filtered, edited, and constrained by the pressure to say the right thing in a survey or focus group.[37] Now these opinions could be collected more often, and in their native environments where they were, in turn, more genuine.[38] The well of consumer feedback was and is ever-growing in CGM, allowing advertisers to craft strategies that can be more targeted and reactive to changes in consumer trends.[39]

Virtual Worlds

Native environment tracking has long been the model for ethnography research where consumers are observed and interviewed during their purchase process. A Web 2.0 parallel to this market research was found with the inception of virtual worlds such as Second Life and the teenager platform Habbo. Through both observation and direct engagement with users, insight began being derived into brand favorability and consideration as well as consumer behavior. Furthermore, the Internet's digital paper trail allowed perpetual data collection to feed back into strategies, and execute advertising back on these virtual world platforms as well as in the wider marketplace.[40]

Advertising Report Process and Metrics

This ongoing and streamlined market research process also had an impact on reporting in advertising. Even prior to the shift to CGM, brand managers and advertising agencies were seeking to regularly digest data sets across channels by shifting away from large presentation reports and toward streamlined one- or two-page reports often called dashboards or scorecards. With the digital nature of Web 2.0 and the tools used for reporting, these dashboards have become increasingly automated and updated for real-time tracking.[41]

This era has demanded new tracking methods, but further accountability models are still needed to prove the value of social media marketing. While brand experiences such as Dell have shown advertisers the price of not being a part of the social media space, the best practice to measure the return on that presence is still being developed. The environment of ever-emerging new platforms requires researchers to be equally nimble and creative in devising new ways to measure. At the time of writing, development continues for measuring Web 2.0's impact on sales and brand perception as well as the relationship to off-line media. Companies such as Nielsen, Arbitron, comScore, Millward Brown, and TNS Media Intelligence have been instrumental in measuring social advertising efficiencies and its impact on brand equity measures, including purchase intent, and increasingly return-on-investment modeling.[42]

An Industry in Transition

In order for brands to make the shift in advertising strategies in the Web 2.0 environment, personnel, agency structure, and marketing skills also required a transition. In 2008, industry research agency Forrester observed the need for this agency transition "from delivering push to creating pull interactions, and from orchestrating campaigns to facilitating conversations."[43] This shift required retooling skills, new platform education and integration, and efficiencies. The focus for messaging transitioned from delivering exclusively messages that contained content to creating shareable content that contained advertising messages.[44] This new advertising delivery required two-way conversation with consumers, more closely integrating advertising and public relations.

A New Kind of Agency

Without defined marketing standards for this uncharted territory, a blend of new thinking and risk taking was required. But marketers of the day honed the science of best practices rather than the art of innovation. These were aspects more typical of new companies or startups than large corporations or agencies.[45] Some industry observers suggest this was not entirely the fault of marketers who trained for another generation of advertising, and were attempting to fit emerging media into that mold.[46] In 2004, Harvard Business School professors John Quelch and Gail McGovern suggested marketers evolve with media. As such, they defined a "Super CMO" or super chief marketing officer, who would be more actively involved in integrated innovation and measuring results.[47]

Rapid innovation was not entirely a new concept, however. During the first Internet boom in the 1990s, the single, full-service agency model was divided as traditional or offline media agencies were not quick to adopt digital offerings. As a result, brands turned to new agencies with personnel specialized in digital needs. By the early 2000s, an agency was not considered full-service if it did not also do digital. With the emergence of Web 2.0 and mobile advertising, a similar trend has played out in which agencies have created social media divisions and a new kind of agency emerged, specializing in Web 2.0. These agencies blend innovative advertising and public relations personnel with social media evangelists and enthusiasts. In the spirit of full disclosure, this author has professional ties to one such agency, We Are Social, based in London.

Agency and Platform Collaboration

By the late 2000s, brands began supplementing their full-service agencies with these specialty agencies. In 2007, Nike wanted to develop a running shoe with a Web 2.0 angle to foster the active running community. The vision for this integrated campaign was deemed too advanced for their traditional agency, Wieden & Kennedy. While retaining their services for their broadcast strategies, Nike turned to R/GA who, along with Apple, developed the Nike+ campaign. In a blend of technological innovation and digital social marketing, they developed a workout tracker that connected to the user's iPod, and subsequently to a social microsite where consumers could share results, compare to athletes, and download workout music.[48]

The content with embedded advertising proved successful for Nike, as reported by *BusinessWeek* magazine in the aftermath of the campaign's initial success, "According to Nike's vice president of global brand management, 40 percent of the people who join the Nike+ community end up becoming Nike wearers."[49]

In contrast to the big splash Nike made into innovation, other brands started smaller. In 2006, JPMorgan Chase chose to advertise their new student credit card on Facebook, which was an all-student platform at the time. The relatively cheap promotion coupled with precise targeting made it a low-risk venture for the financial institution. The +1 campaign had a sponsored Facebook group and quickly grew to 34,000 members, which at the time put it among top pages such as American Eagle and Dave Matthews Band's Summer Tour group.[50]

The advertising agency model will continue to adapt and evolve in the ever-emerging Internet and mobile ecosphere.[51] And, as a footnote to the Nike+ example, today, Wieden & Kennedy is alive and well, offering integrated and innovative advertising solutions.

Off-line Integration and Migration

Web 2.0 changed consumer expectations content purchasing, access, and accountability as well as marketer expectations for measurement. As a result, off-line channels were forced to adapt, migrate, and integrate.

Free Content Generation

Especially among younger generations, people became increasingly accustomed to free content and information options. The teen population sought free sources initially out of necessity, due to the lack of funds to purchase. But this later bred a sense of foolishness to pay for something such as a magazine or newspaper when similar-quality content can be found online, free of charge.[52] This expectation extended to audio and video content as well. Initially manifesting as a veritable wild west of illegal downloading in the early 2000s, publishers coordinated to provide low-cost or even free content, supported by advertising.

Few of us think newspapers when we think of innovation, but the advertising and subscription medium was among the early adopters of Web 2.0 consumer participation media. Newspapers tapped into digital ad–based offerings in the 2000s largely to stay competitive with the free, instant information access of other Internet-only news sources; some have dropped their offline offering altogether, questioning the relevance of the term "newspaper." To maximize the profitability of advertising on free content sources, social functionality was a priority to increase advertising exposure. Even before some of today's leading social media platforms, articles contained comment sections revealing consumer opinions. As social integration continued, newspapers added share functionality in articles to tap into readers' social networks in order to drive more traffic.

For TV and movie content, the consumer options expanded from digital purchase on Amazon and Apple's iTunes to free access with advertising. Sites such as Hulu and Vimeo began providing streamable content with embedded video advertising, and share functionality on social media to encourage consumption. YouTube's model also empowered consumers to create video content and support with advertising for a monetary return. Although the advertising was still broadcast, the on-demand click forced users to centrally process the advertisement.

Advertising for music and radio has followed a similar pattern. While consumers could still purchase music from vendors such as iTunes, custom online radio stations with embedded advertising began allowing for free music listening. These platforms, such as Pandora and Spotify, innovatively allowed users to build libraries, share playlists with friends, and bring their music with them via smartphones or tablets.

Digital Integration

Despite this shift, as of this writing, TV has remained a viable off-line channel with expensive advertising placements as content continues to debut on the medium before it becomes available on digital platforms. This too, however, has become threatened in the Web 2.0 age of consumer empowerment with digital video recorders that allow for skipping ads.[53] As a result, innovative integration with two-way consumer strategies increased in the late 2000s. During the 2007 Super Bowl, advertisers such as Doritos, FedEx, General Motors, and Budweiser coupled their expensive advertising buys on TV with related content on their websites and blogs.[54] In the years since, an increasing percentage of off-line advertising began integrating digital components such as a website URL or social media profile to extend the consumer advertising experience.[55]

Raising the Measurement Bar

Web 2.0's landscape of highly trackable campaigns has raised demand for better off-line media measurement. For example, through the 2000s, survey-based ratings analyses for TV and radio have shifted to digital tracker devices created by companies such as Nielsen and Arbitron. Similar to collecting organic brand feedback in social listening, tracker devices allowed for a more genuine collection of media exposure, free from the bias and human error of the survey taker's memory of media consumption. Such innovations have also raised the accuracy of cross-platform measurement, aggregating and comparing broader media consumption habits.

All Politics Is Local—and Social

The power of consumer connection was transferred to voter connection during the 2004 presidential primary race in the United States when campaign advertising entered Web 2.0. Joe Trippi, campaign manager for Democratic candidate Howard Dean, organized a grassroots support team and fund-raising through a campaign website and e-mail outreach. These executions coupled with the support of the tech-savvy youth resulted in a donation sum exceeding $50 million through donations of $100 or less. This was a game changer for U.S. political campaigns as well as those of Europe, which took cues from these strategies to mobilize in the subsequent elections.[56]

The 2008 presidential campaign evolved these Web 2.0 advertising strategies with the Barack Obama campaign's savvy use of Twitter in the Democratic primary race against Hillary Clinton. Their use of anecdotal tweets encouraged community interaction, while follower growth was spurred by actively following would-be supporters who politely followed back; this grew their community to more than eight times the size of Hillary Clinton's. Each candidate fully embraced other social media channels as well, including Obama's successful "Yes We Can" YouTube video.[57]

Meanwhile, Along Came Mobile

Early mobile marketing evolved in relative isolation to the Internet but became integrated during this period of Web 2.0, as Web-enabled phones advanced to smartphones and tablets. The user experience with the Internet became device agnostic, with the onset of websites optimized for mobile and multiplatform games interfaced with social media.[58]

Direct-Response Advertising Roots

But prior to this integration, mobile marketing campaign executions were similar to direct e-mail strategies and exhibited the same two-way communication that eventually evolved in Web 2.0. Driven by the rise in

SMS or text message popularity in the 1990s and early 2000s, especially among teens, mobile carriers used customer data to target sponsored direct messaging via text including polls, contests, and coupons with response calls to action.[59] Although similar strategies were used in email marketing, SMS was cheaper and could be delivered on a mass scale, initially free from opt-out or antispam laws, and measurably more effective due to the ease of the user experience. Global statistics showed active mobile usage has always exceeded that of e-mail, with the phone largely kept on the user and checked more often. As a result, response time for text promotions was much faster than that of e-mail promotions. Better still, mobile phones already had a built-in payment system as they are connected to a user's phone bill.[60]

In the late 2000s, not-for-profits took note of this ease-of-use payment system for the user, by encouraging consumers to send money to help topical causes via text-to-donate campaigns. This was particularly successful in the aftermath of the 2011 Haiti earthquake, when the Red Cross raised $5 million in the first 48 hours.[61]

Offline Integration

Text-based voting extended to TV shows during the rise in reality show popularity. Among the first was the popular talent search program *American Idol* in 2002, where audience members participated in contestant outcomes. Off-line marketers saw this extension of the TV show experience as a CRM opportunity to gather teen viewer phone numbers for additional messaging later.[62]

The History Channel ran a successful execution of this kind in 2004, when they launched a new show entitled *Barbarians*. Profiling mobile numbers based on CRM data, text promotions for the show were sent to the appropriate target audience for the program. Over time, the History Channel promotions for shows such as *Decisive Battles* and *Command Decisions* became more measureable by encouraging audience participation by text for show reminders, contests, and games. Follow-up research showed 58 percent of consumers were more likely to watch the History Channel as a result of the promotions.[63]

Geo-Targeting, App Stores, and Games

Customer data also included global positioning technology, or GPS, which allowed marketers to better target text campaign executions with localized content. For example, mobile carrier Orange in the United Kingdom ran a campaign encouraging consumers to text a code to receive half-priced movie theater tickets. In response, the user received their voucher along with localized movie times at theaters in their area based on telephone number area codes.[64] As mobile technology evolved to include color interfaces and remote software updates, application stores began selling simple games through mobile carriers, and advertising soon followed. Among the popular early games was Snake on the Nokia phone platform. Advertising was targeted for app types and geography but were of a broadcast nature, similar to the Web 1.0 mass-reach advertising strategies.[65]

Driving the Web 2.0 Advertising Evolution

By 2006, Web-based social media platforms had begun to integrate with mobile devices, allowing users to publish text and even photo updates to their social profiles. As previously mentioned, Twitter was among the first to offer this, as their character limit was within limits set by mobile carriers, driving early adoption and mass usage. Facebook soon followed. But it would take a technological leap to fully realize the advertising potential of mobile social devices.

Smartphone popularity, from the mid-2000s to today, has fully integrated mobile marketing and Web 2.0 platforms while accelerating marketing opportunities. Brands began regularly creating their own applications, mobile gaming evolved, and social platforms created mobile versions. Within this, advertising has remained both direct-response executions and two-way communication campaigns utilizing Web 2.0 strategies.

Mobile's advertising legacy of direct response strategy extended to broadcast banner tactics with the onset of smartphones, but with the space's advantages of better targeting and quick access to purchasing. Mobile sites and applications began garnering revenue by employing advertising networks such as AdMob. Similar to Web 1.0 networks, AdMob connects mobile platforms with advertisers who buy relatively cheap inventory for either mass-reach or targeted banner messaging. Upon tapping these banners, advertisers began directing consumers to app stores or landing pages with a goal such as purchase, CRM signup, or redeeming a coupon. And because smartphones such as the iPhone are connected to a user's credit card information, purchases can be completed in a few screen taps.[66]

Mobile company Zynga has been among the market leaders in both ad-supported and for-purchase games on smartphones, employing Web 2.0 integration and incentive-based ads. Their popular Draw Something and Hanging with Friends games have integrated with consumer social media profiles to share content and challenge friends. These games started enticing users to view ads to increase a system of in-game currency, which can be redeemed for new features or items. For example, watching a 30-second advertisement earns the gamer coins, which they can trade for avatar swag. This consumer benefit earns revenue for Zynga, while advertiser messages receive a centrally processed exposure.

Social media platforms on mobile have evolved marketing opportunities on the channel, taking localized content targeting to another level. Consumers are now sharing content such as photos on Flickr and Instagram, videos on Tumblr, and links on Facebook through the ease of a pocket device. And with each upload, consumers who opt in are also telling marketers where they are through a process called geo-tagging, where the location of the upload is attributed to the social content. Combined with titles and descriptions, these tags allow advertisers to cater advertising and messaging to more relevant consumers.[67]

By aggregating consumer locations with interests via social profiles, marketers know more about consumers than ever before while engaging in two-way Web 2.0 executions. Platforms such as FourSquare began encouraging users to compete with friends for points by checking in to everything from museums and parks to retailers and restaurants, where advertisers can target them with coupons. Similarly, Groupon started capitalizing on user locations by offering locally targeted deals.[68]

Twenty-first-Century Barcodes

In a further integration between mobile and off-line marketing, the age of smartphones and cameras gave rise to a new generation of bar code: the quick response or QR code. Though largely standardized today, there have been several iterations of these codes and scanners since their invention in the mid-1990s by companies such as Microsoft, Denso-Wave, and Semacode.[69] Scanned with a smartphone camera from outdoor advertising such as subway ads, on restaurant menus, or via the backs of business cards, these unique codes drive consumers to additional online content in the form of websites, coupons, or other marketing. Unique codes have also ensured that the effectiveness of the off-line media placements can be individually measured.[70] At the time of writing, usage statistics continue to rise for QR codes especially among retail and tech advertisers. But long-term success and adoption is still to be determined.[71]

Modern Marketing Challenges

One hundred years ago, English businessman William Lever offered commentary on his advertising effectiveness when he said, "I know half my advertising isn't working; I just don't know which half." Lever's now iconic phrase pointed out the lack of research data in his time to effectively optimize marketing campaigns. The irony of the Web 2.0 era is that we are still challenged to answer this question due to having too much data, and with the added challenge of balancing consumer tracking and message control with credibility and trust.

Navigating this data storm requires the most appropriate tools that will aid in choosing the right media mix for a campaign. Equally as important is choosing measurement methodologies and defining benchmarks that mean success, including the elusive return-on-investment modeling of Web 2.0 marketing.

Innovation's Downside

With each Web 2.0 advancement, an opportunity is born for advertisers to explore creative executions, while a challenge is created for researchers tasked with proving the business worth. For example, today's text-based search tools are finding it challenging to measure Web 2.0 innovations such as picture-sharing site Pinterest. Compounding this challenge among researchers is that measurement solutions are sometimes perfected just in time to find the platform has fallen out of favor with the market.

This platform adoption can be dizzying for marketers as well, who must evaluate the longevity and potential of a new platform to decide if developing applications, building communities, and buying ad space are wise investments. Advertisers saw strong potential with social platform MySpace, prompting the 2005 sale to media mogul Rupert Murdoch's News Corporation for $580 million. While the platform remained among the top visited websites and produced successful spinoffs, a steady decline in popularity in the later 2000s resulted in the 2011 sale for just $35 million.[72] At the time of this writing, communities such as Tumblr are experiencing a resurgence and advertising monetization, while Google+ and its strong membership base has yet to convince advertisers that it can succeed in delivering two-way advertising messages.

Social Marketing Ethics

While Web 2.0 has empowered marketers to listen and respond for research purposes, it also enables marketers to essentially stalk users who speak negatively about a brand. Marketers have access to a consumer's entire social media footprint, if not set to private. Nothing is off the record in this digital world, and this loss in anonymity can also have disastrous consequences if your brand is, for example, a government where free speech is punishable by death.[73] But for marketers seeking to deliver positive brand experiences, this has resulted in self-enforcement of responsible best practices with the aim of keeping consumers' trust.

The Social Rumor Mill

And with this information access, social media can also be the consumer's fastest way to receive up-to-date information about news and brands; but it can also be the fastest way to receive up-to-date disinformation. In a health and safety example, during the 2011 London riots, a photo of the iconic London Eye during a fireworks celebration was repurposed as faux evidence that it had been set on fire and subsequently elevating the panic of the moment. Similar scenarios play out for brands, such as financial institutions, when news spreads of hackers tapping consumer databases and prompting a mob mentality to cancel accounts and run up customer service calls before a responsible account of the impact is reported. Without a layer of fact checking that a professional journalist would do, rumors can rapidly spread across the Twitter-sphere like screaming fire in a theater.[74] With today's ever-growing roster of Web 2.0 and mobile/tablet platforms, expanding measurement toolboxes, and whatever will come next in these emerging platforms, answering these challenges are arguably as much art and science as they were in Lever's day.

Advertising's Future History

The rapid rise in consumer power and the transformation of technology during the Web 2.0 era has reinvented marketing from the one-way communication advertising mainstay to a partnership of content cocreation, information sharing, and brand as well as CRM management. In a sector as fast-paced and innovative as the Internet, opportunities and challenges will continue for marketers in this space in the near future. Best practices will remain gray while investments will remain risky, pushing advertisers to be creative, nimble in trend observation, and bold in execution.

Advertising history in this era has taught the marketplace that to remain safe and stagnant in proven methods is to be left behind. And in a lesson from advertising's first go on the Internet, to find failure in marketing on a new medium is not always the failure of the medium, but sometimes of the advertising media.

Tim O'Reilly observed this media shift, among other Internet trends, when he dubbed the era Web 2.0. And just as Web 2.0 prompted an evolution from the Internet's early advertising to its current form, it is also a precursor to the next phase. And about that next phase, O'Reilly has already dubbed it Web Squared where a more seamless integration takes place between devices of the web experience.[75] By definition, we may already be there, or perhaps just on the cusp.

Perhaps we are outgrowing this Web 2.0 era and entering the next, an even brighter era of advertising. Ask me in 10 years, and until then, keep an eye on Times Square.

Notes

1. Ben Parr, "Corona's New Facebook Campaign Puts Your Face in Times Square," *Mashable*, October 12, 2010, http://mashable.com/2010/10/12/corona -lite-facebook/ (accessed May 1, 2012).

2. Douglas Rushkoff, *Program or Be Programmed: Ten Commands for a Digital Age* (New York: Or Books, 2010), 93.

3. Brian Solis, *Engage! The Complete Guide for Brands and Businesses to Build, Cultivate, and Measure Success in the New Web* (Hoboken, NJ: John Wiley & Sons, 2010), 111.

4. Alicia Buller, "Facebook Launches Ambitious Ad Scheme," *Brand Republic*, November 7, 2007, http://www.brandrepublic.com/news/765320/ (accessed May 1, 2012).

5. Pete Blackshaw, *Satisfied Customers Tell Three Friends, Angry Customers Tell 3,000: Running a Business in Today's Consumer-Driven World* (New York: Doubleday, 2008), 2.

6. Martin Thomas and David Brain, *Crowd Surfing: Surviving and Thriving in the Age of Consumer Empowerment* (London: A&C Black Publishers, 2008), 126.

7. Rushkoff, *Program or Be Programmed*, 93.

8. Blackshaw, *Satisfied Customers Tell Three Friends*, 4.

9. Ibid., 54.

10. Ibid., 52.

11. Thomas and Brain, *Crowd Surfing*, 121.

12. Blackshaw, *Satisfied Customers Tell Three Friends*, 10.

13. Ibid., 14.

14. Thomas and Brain, *Crowd Surfing*, 171.

15. Blackshaw, *Satisfied Customers Tell Three Friends*, 48.

16. Ibid., 61.

17. Ibid., 23.

18. Ibid., 163.

19. Thomas and Brain, *Crowd Surfing*, 43.

20. Ibid.

21. Ibid., 44.

22. Ibid., 46.

23. Jeff Jarvis, "Dell Learns to Listen," *BusinessWeek*, October 17, 2007, http://www.businessweek.com/bwdaily/dnflash/content/oct2007/db20071017 _27 7576.htm (accessed May 1, 2012).

24. Thomas and Brain, *Crowd Surfing*, 129.

25. Blackshaw, *Satisfied Customers Tell Three Friends*, 114.

26. Thomas and Brain, *Crowd Surfing*, 49.

27. Christopher Vollmer and Geoffrey Precourt, *Always On: Advertising, Marketing, and Media in an Era of Consumer Control* (New York: McGraw Hill, 2008), 82.

28. Thomas and Brain, *Crowd Surfing*, 128.

29. Blackshaw, *Satisfied Customers Tell Three Friends*, 94.

30. Ibid., 35.

31. Thomas and Brain, *Crowd Surfing*, 144.

32. Solis, *Engage!* 297–98.

33. Ibid., 301.

34. Blackshaw, *Satisfied Customers Tell Three Friends*, 92.

35. Ibid., 160.

36. Ibid., 58.

37. Thomas and Brain, *Crowd Surfing*, 169.

38. Blackshaw, *Satisfied Customers Tell Three Friends*, 8.

39. Vollmer and Precourt, *Always On*, 179.

40. Ibid., 75.

41. Ibid., 134.

42. Ibid., 115.

43. Mary Beth Kemp et al., "The Connected Agency," Forrester Research, February 8, 2008, http://www.forrester.com/The+Connected+Agency/fulltext/-/E-RES43875?docid=43875 (accessed May 1, 2012).

44. Vollmer and Precourt, *Always On*, 4.

45. Ibid., 15–16.

46. Ibid., 154.

47. Ibid., 10.

48. Ibid., 3–4.

49. Blackshaw, *Satisfied Customers Tell Three Friends*, 120.

50. Vollmer and Precourt, *Always On*, 41.

51. Ibid., 174.

52. Thomas and Brain, *Crowd Surfing*, 122.

53. Vollmer and Precourt, *Always On*, 36.

54. Blackshaw, *Satisfied Customers Tell Three Friends*, 103.

55. Ibid., 27–28.

56. Thomas and Brain, *Crowd Surfing*, 89.

57. Ibid., 101.

58. "Mobile Marketing 101," Quirk, http://www.quirk.biz/resources/mobile101 (accessed June 1, 2012).

59. Michael Baker, "Mobile Marketing's Evolution," iMedia Connection, March 25, 2005, http://www.imediaconnection.com/content/5337.asp (accessed May 1, 2012).

60. "Mobile Marketing 101."

61. Amy Feldman, "Haiti Earthquake Provokes Wave of Text Donations," *Bloomberg Businessweek*, January 14, 2010, http://www.businessweek.com/investor/content/jan2010/pi20100114_236518.htm (accessed May 1, 2012).

62. Thomas and Brain, *Crowd Surfing*, 174.

63. Baker, "Mobile Marketing's Evolution."

64. "Mobile Marketing 101."

65. Ibid.

66. Ibid.

67. Solis, *Engage!* 108.

68. "Mobile Marketing 101."

69. Ibid.

70. Ruben Corbo, "The Brief History of Mobile Marketing," *Garin Kilpatrick* (blog), August 19, 2011, http://garinkilpatrick.com/brief-history-of-mobile-marketing/ (accessed May 1, 2012).

71. Steve Smith, "QR Explosion: Retail and Tech Lead Among 2,300 Mobile Code Advertisers in 2011," *Mobile Marketing Daily*, February 28, 2012, http://www.mediapost.com/publications/article/168807/qr-explosion-retail-and-tech-lead-among-2300-mob.html (accessed May 1, 2012).

72. Andy Fixmer, "News Corp. Calls Quits on Myspace with Specific Media Sale," *Bloomberg Businessweek*, June 29, 2011, http://www.businessweek.com/news/2011-06-29/news-corp-calls-quits-on-myspace-with-specific-media-sale.html (accessed May 1, 2012).

73. Rushkoff, *Program or Be Programmed*, 83.

74. Ibid., 10.

75. Solis, *Engage!* 111.

Bibliography

Baker, Michael, "Mobile Marketing's Evolution." *iMedia Connection: Connecting the Marketing Community*. March 25, 2005. http://www.imediaconnection.com/content/ 5337.asp (accessed May 1, 2012).

Blackshaw, Pete. *Satisfied Customers Tell Three Friends, Angry Customers Tell 3,000: Running a Business in Today's Consumer-Driven World*. New York: Doubleday, 2008.

Buller, Alicia. "Facebook Launches Ambitious Ad Scheme." *Brand Republic*, November 7, 2007. http://www.brandrepublic.com/news/765320/ (accessed May 1, 2012).

Corbo, Ruben. "The Brief History of Mobile Marketing," *Garin Kilpatrick* (blog), August 19, 2011. http://garinkilpatrick.com/brief-history-of-mobile-marketing/ (accessed May 1, 2012).

Feldman, Amy. "Haiti Earthquake Provokes Wave of Text Donations," *Bloomberg Businessweek*, January 14, 2010. http://www.businessweek.com/investor/content/jan2010/pi20100114_236518.htm (accessed May 1, 2012).

Fixmer, Andy. "News Corp. Calls Quits on Myspace With Specific Media Sale," *Bloomberg Businessweek*. June 29, 2011. Accessed May 1, 2012. http://www .businessweek.com/news/2011-06-29/news-corp-calls-quits-on-myspace-with -specific-media-sale.html (accessed May 1, 2012).

Jarvis, Jeff. "Dell Learns to Listen," *BusinessWeek*, October 17, 2007. http://www .businessweek.com/bwdaily/dnflash/content/oct2007/db20071017_277 576.htm (accessed May 1, 2012).

Kemp, Mary Beth, Peter Kim, Jaap Favier, Kim Le Quoc, Evadne Cokeh, and Alice Bresciani. "The Connected Agency." Forrester Research, February 8, 2008. http://www.forrester.com/The+Connected+Agency/fulltext/-/E-RES43875 ?docid=43875 (accessed May 1, 2012).

"Mobile Marketing 101." Quirk. http://www.quirk.biz/resources/mobile101 (accessed June 1, 2012).

Parr, Ben. "Corona's New Facebook Campaign Puts Your Face in Times Square," *Mashable*, October 12, 2010. http://mashable.com/2010/10/12/corona-lite -facebook/ (accessed May 1, 2012).

Rushkoff, Douglas. *Program or Be Programmed: Ten Commands for a Digital Age.* New York: Or Books, 2010.

Smith, Steve. "QR Explosion: Retail and Tech Lead among 2,300 Mobile Code Advertisers in 2011." *Mobile Marketing Daily*, February 28, 2012. http://www .mediapost.com/publications/article/168807/qr-explosion-retail-and-tech-lead -among-2300-mob.html (accessed May 1, 2012).

Solis, Brian. *Engage! The Complete Guide for Brands and Businesses to Build, Cultivate, and Measure Success in the New Web.* Hoboken, NJ: John Wiley & Sons, 2010.

Thomas, Martin, and David Brain. *Crowd Surfing: Surviving and Thriving in the Age of Consumer Empowerment.* London: A&C Black Publishers, 2008.

Vollmer, Christopher, and Geoffrey Precourt. *Always On: Advertising, Marketing, and Media in an Era of Consumer Control.* New York: McGraw Hill, 2008.

CHAPTER SIXTEEN

This Boy's Bedroom: Product Placement, a New Masculinity, and the Rise of Geek Culture in the 1980s

John Kenneth Muir

Every student of advertising and mass communications likely remembers the infamous *E.T.—The Extra-Terrestrial* (1982) product placement story, a cautionary tale of golden opportunities missed. To recount it in brief, wunderkind movie director Steven Spielberg (*Jaws* [1975], *Close Encounter of the Third Kind* [1977], and *Raiders of the Lost Ark* [1981]), desired to feature a real brand of candy in his sentimental new sci-fi film, *E.T.*

Written by Melissa Mathison, the movie—originally to be called *A Boy's Life*—concerned a friendly alien marooned on Earth and cared for by a sensitive, lonely boy and child of divorce, Elliott (Henry Thomas). The PG-rated film contained no objectionable material save for some coarse language, specifically the notorious epithet "penis breath."

Thus, Spielberg actively sought the cooperation of Mars Incorporated. He hoped it would officially sanction the on-screen use of the company's popular chocolate sweet, M&Ms, in his uplifting genre narrative. However, in what might aptly be described as one of the most baffling and short-sighted corporate decisions of the past half-century, Mars declined to participate. It refused to license its famous product. Scrambling to find an alternative, Spielberg utilized a "little known confectionary brand"[1] from Hershey's called Reese's Pieces.

In the film, Elliott drops the little Hershey treats like bread crumbs to draw E.T. to his family's Southern California tract home. The Reese's Pieces nuggets thus serve as a tasty lure for the friendly, curious, and presumably hungry alien. And that lure is but a prologue to an equally sweet interplanetary friendship. When Spielberg's film for Universal Studios emerged as the highest-grossing film of all time in the summer of 1982, "resulting sales" of Reese's Pieces "spiked"[2] by a whopping 65 percent. And in less than a year's time, 800 cinemas in the United States stocked Reese's Pieces in their concession stands for the first time.[3]

As the legend goes, Hollywood and corporate America thus learned from this notorious exemplar of product placement strategy the valuable lesson of "synergy." Companies could invest big bucks in potentially successful film projects and in turn, their products would be featured—often prominently—in movies guaranteed wide release and plenty of press attention.

The strategy did not take long to catch fire. In the E.T. knock-off *Mac and Me* (1988), for instance, another alien visiting Earth could only continue to thrive in our atmosphere by drinking Coca-Cola and by eating the food served at McDonald's restaurants. The film's writers, Stewart Raffill and Steve Feke, reported that they were explicitly instructed to make McDonald's "integral to the plot."[4]

Steven Spielberg himself continued the trend he became cursed for initiating. One of the blockbuster films that he produced in the mid-1980s, Robert Zemeckis's *Back to the Future* (1985), reportedly featured more than 100 prominent examples of product placement,[5] thereby shilling, at least in the eyes of some, for Calvin Klein, Pepsi, Budweiser, Burger King, and other popular brands of the age. Today, modern audiences have witnessed the so-called "Spielberg method" of product placement in studio films amplified to steroidal levels, in both the James Bond films and *Transformers* films from Michael Bay, which relentlessly hawk tech products and General Motors cars, respectively.

Given such blatant and at times downright crass modern product placement, some concerned activists and scholars look back in anger. They blame Spielberg and E.T. for initiating a strongly negative and damaging trend in advertising methods. Their argument is that pervasive product placement has made it impossible to intuit where art ends and where commerce begins. Now every new release—even Academy Award–winning films—is out to sell you something.

However, just as a film's narrative and themes mirror important aspects of the society that created it, E.T.'s product placement campaign boasts a distinctive and specific context. By understanding that historical context properly, one can discern how Spielberg and his *E.T.* were actually part of a movement already in motion, and therefore involved in a burgeoning societal trend rather than acting as the mastermind instigators behind one.

Perhaps much more significantly, one can detect in some Spielberg-ian blockbusters of the 1980s, notably *E.T.*, that incidences of product placement often signify something more than premeditated, on-screen attempts to sell toys, candy, cars, comic books, or cigarettes to unsuspecting audiences. In fact, in a wide array of films from the early-to-mid 1980s, product placement actively reflects *a pro-social purpose*. The placement of specific products such as action figures remind children that they need not conform to rigid or preexisting societal standards. Implicit in that message is the belief that tolerance and diversity are virtues worth championing.

So while it is both convenient and understandable to gaze at *E.T.* as the apex of a long, slippery slope downward to a Hell of crass commercialism, ample reason exists to judge that product placement in some films represents part of a specific and *positive* argument about American society, and particularly the role of play and fantasy in a new brand of masculinity.

In short, a strong argument may be forged that product placement in the 1980s genre cinema actually gave rise to our modern geek culture, a world of intense media viewership, but also intense media participation. Today's geeks are, impressively, content creators as well as content consumers, and the films of Spielberg and his compatriots in the 1980s catalyzed this generational propensity. These directors accomplished this feat by choosing their avatars of product placement wisely, and also by selecting a particular venue for them that held importance and relevance—a suburban child's bedroom.

There You Go Again: Ronald Reagan, Deregulation, and the Media Marketplace

In November 1980, Ronald Reagan was elected the 40th president of the United States. Although the conservative, former governor of California received only a scant majority of the popular vote, 50.7 percent,[6] the Republican candidate romped over opponent Jimmy Carter in the Electoral College and exploited his widely perceived landslide victory as evidence of a mandate supporting his supply-side economic policies.

Perhaps foremost among those Reagan endeavors was deregulation in a variety of industries. While it is accurate to assert that widespread deregulation had begun under President Carter and congressional democrats in the late 1970s,[7] Reagan was nonetheless a fierce proponent of free markets and *generous* oversight. In accordance with his laissez-faire belief system,

President Reagan appointed in May 1981 Mark S. Fowler as chairman of the Federal Communications Commission. Like the new commander-in-chief, Fowler was an outspoken proponent of deregulation, and one who argued that television had, essentially, no social responsibility. Fowler famously declared, for instance: "The television is just another appliance—it's a toaster with pictures ... We've got to look beyond the conventional wisdom that we must somehow regulate this box, we must single it out."[8]

In practice, this hypothesis meant that the floodgates were now open in terms of allowing business interests to exploit television programming as an advertising venue. In 1982, the same year that *E.T.* premiered in theaters, children's television proved a prime target for deregulation. This drive promptly led to "program-length commercials for preexisting toys such as *He-Man* (1983) and *My Little Pony* (1984)."[9] Other toy-cum-children's-TV-shows of the era included *Transformers* (1984), *Challenge of the Gobots* (1984), *Thundercats* (1985), *G.I. Joe* (1985), *Jem* (1985), *M.A.S.K.* (1985), and *Silverhawks* (1986), to name just a few.

By 1987, the new wrinkle of "interactivity" was introduced in the TV program for Mattel's toy line, *Captain Power and the Soldiers of the Future*. Children could purchase their Captain Power spaceships at toy stores, and then, while watching videos or episodes at home, fire their vehicle's weapons at the television, thus creating a variety of audio responses such as explosions or laser blasts. On a primitive level by today's high-tech standards, this "interactivity" nonetheless equated to audience participation in the storylines.

Although activist groups such as ACT (Action for Children's Television) attempted to curb the new trend of TV properties based on toys because "very young children cannot distinguish between a commercial and the TV program that the ads interrupts,"[10] its best efforts failed. Fowler, a man who later repealed elements of the Fairness Doctrine, effectively removed any limitation on the duration and character of commercials in children's programs during his tenure. He once noted—again famously—that "the marketplace will take care of children."[11] By 1984, the FCC no longer regulated at all the content of television for toy and marketing tie-ins, "meaning that toys related to the show [*He-Man and the Masters of the Universe*] were available for purchase at the same time that the show was being aired."[12]

Given the widespread campaign of deregulation and philosophy of laissez-faire following President Reagan's inauguration in 1980, the critical appointment of deregulation advocate Fowler to the FCC in 1981, and the advent of products as programming shortly thereafter, Steven Spielberg's decision to include popular commercial products in his 1982 film *E.T.* hardly feels like the tip of the spear. Nor does it feel like the most blatant example of product promotion in the art of the day. At least in Spielberg's case, the creative desire to craft a meaningful and original narrative preceded any corporate plan to sell toys or other products.

However, *E.T.* may indeed represent the press's first collective recognition of the confluence of media and corporate interests. Still, it would be better viewed, instead, as part of the cultural and political context of the day, as part of a continuum that began with the election of Reagan and continued well into his second term and beyond. Similarly, it requires little effort to pinpoint many examples of product placement in children-oriented films in the years before *E.T.* was released. In Richard Donner's *Superman: The Movie* (1978), for instance, a box of General Mills' Cheerios cereal is visible amongst the idyllic "Americana"-styled décor of the Kent family farm. In the sequel, *Superman II* (1981), Lois Lane (Margot Kidder) visibly (chain) smokes Marlboros. Given these and other examples, notably an appearance of a Budweiser TV advertisement in Spielberg's own *Close Encounters of the Third Kind* (1977), it's virtually impossible to legitimately view *E.T.* and Reese's Pieces as the revolutionary initiator of the trend.

The Conventional Wisdom: Product Placement as Societal Evil

It is a *fait accompli*, perhaps, that product placement in motion pictures or on television is an egregiously bad thing; a craven attempt to market toys or other material possessions to children who, because of their innocence and lack of experience, cannot understand that they are being transformed into mindless consumers in order to drive profit for large, impersonalized corporations. Indeed, there are many movies—and good ones, too—that make this negative point quite ably. Tom Holland's horror film *Child's Play* (1988) is a delicious, point-by-point mockery of product placement, the TV-programming-as-advertisement trend sparked by Filmation's *He-Man*, and the 1983 Cabbage Patch toy craze.

On the latter front, there was a shortage of the popular Cabbage Patch dolls during the holiday season of 1983. Young boomer adults—who had once marched righteously for civil rights and protested the Vietnam War on campuses and on Main Street—were now middle-class parents. But they rioted in the 1980s instead to procure the "hot" toy for their indulged children. Black-market versions of the Cabbage Patch dolls fed this demand frenzy, and some independent "peddlers" even sold Cabbage Patch wares at incredibly inflated prices.

So, *did the marketplace care for the children?* Specifically, Holland's *Child's Play* critique of advertising on movies and TV involves a line of toys called

Good Guys Doll. These "Good Guys" boast their own Saturday morning program, toys, sugary breakfast cereal, fashion line, and even catchphrase: "I'll be your friend to the end." That catchphrase is an explicit promise to kids from toymakers—*You keep buying our stuff, and we'll keep taking your money.* The young protagonist in the film, Andy Barkley (Alex Vincent) runs afoul of the Good Guys products, however, when his particular doll turns out to be possessed by the spirit of a serial killer, Charles Lee Ray (Brad Dourif), or "Chucky."

The film's wicked point is that the commercial lure of owning *everything* in the Good Guy line has brought this particular boy, Andy, to the verge of his own destruction. After a time, such products seem to take on a monstrous life of their own, the film states, and their ubiquity means that no one can escape them. In his unappeasable desire to "have it all," Andy cannot see what ownership of Chucky means to his health, and even his life.

No doubt many parents of the age felt the same way about the Cabbage Patch Dolls, the Garbage Pail Kids, the Smurfs, and other ubiquitous toys. Yet, humorous satire of 1980s product placement and advertising trends notwithstanding, there is ample reason to suspect that in some cases, product placement efforts actually represented part of a consistent social message about diversity, tolerance, teamwork, and independence, especially in the hands of the most gifted artists.

But What Does a Kenner Yoda Doll Really Mean to a 90-Pound Weakling?

To further excavate this line of thought, one need only consider how certain nonathletic, cerebral-minded boys were viewed by American society in previous generations. One of the most famous print ads in twentieth-century history makes the point explicitly.

Exercise guru Charles Atlas advertised in comic books of the 1940s–1970s a scenario generically termed "the 90-pound weakling." In broad terms, the ad was always the same. A nice, skinny kid at the beach loses his beautiful girlfriend to a more muscular, more macho male and bully. The skinny boy then works out—in compliance with Atlas's exercise program, of course—becomes muscle-bound himself and wins back his lost girlfriend as well as the approbation of a multitude of beach onlookers. Might makes right; people respect physical strength.

Encoded, too, in this advertisement is the belief that a boy must grow up and become a certain kind of man. He must be athletic, muscular, physical, and able to win a fight against, essentially, a Schwarzenegger-like body builder. Or, as Alan Klein writes: "This sense of masculinity characterized men as having excessive need for status achievement and a lack of emotionality, interpersonally domineering tendencies and a need for independence, aggression, and anti-femininity."[13]

The concurrent work of psychiatrist Frederic Wertham in his 1954 treatise, *Seduction of the Innocent*, imposes further a sense of conformity upon youngsters, notably male children. Those who read comics, the good doctor argued, would be prone to an unwholesome life of crime and, worse, sexual deviancy.[14] In this setting, sexual deviancy equates to stereotypically effeminate or homosexual behavior. Many of the artists behind 1980s genre films, from Steven Spielberg and Joe Dante to George A. Romero and Stephen King, grew up under exactly this kind of restrictive home environment, a time immediately before Stan Lee and Marvel Comics began evidencing increased sensitivity to "teenage male angst."[15]

Thus in the 1950s, the commonly used phrase as "American as apple pie," meant, essentially, a diet of strict correspondence to adult notions about what represented appropriate adolescent male behavior and pastimes. Comic books, superheroes, science fiction, and horror were all looked down upon, by many, as "sissy" hobbies. Some young comic readers had to constantly worry that parents would discover their reading habits and toss their collections in the garbage. George Romero's *Creepshow* (1982) comments explicitly on this milieu in its wraparound narration, wherein a young boy mischievously uses voodoo to punish his father, who has thrown in the trash an edition of his favorite horror mag, the reflexively titled *Creepshow*. So this boy explicitly overturns the established order of the 1950s and its prevailing attitudes about masculinity.

Much of the product placement featured in films such as *E.T.*, Tobe Hooper's *Poltergeist* (1982) or Joe Dante's *Gremlins* (1984)—all produced by Spielberg—directly press the idea that comic books, monsters, aliens, and even the vocation of magic are not the obsessions of sick, deviant minds, but rather represent valid interests for growing, healthy young men. In *Salem's Lot* (1979), *The Funhouse* (1981), *Creepshow* (1982), *Poltergeist* (1982), *Gremlins* (1984), *The Stuff* (1985), *Invaders from Mars* (1986), *Neon Maniacs* (1987), *The Lost Boys* (1987) and *The Monster Squad* (1987), movie-brat nostalgia for the films of the 1950s, product placement and production design thus combine to create an atmosphere of acceptance of this "other" path for certain young men.

In virtually all these films, a young boy is featured as the protagonist, and his bedroom, replete with product placement in the form of toys, posters, and games, is prominently featured. By showcasing this room specifically, each film provides an example of how a boy can live; how he can choose to organize his most private place. It should be noted that this domain and sanctuary—a boy's bedroom—is critical in terms of adolescent development. Social scientists have likened the bedroom of adolescents to a "second skin" where a "teen surrounds himself or herself with objects that assist in the discovery process . . . where daydreaming and a construction of self from the inside out begin."[16] If a room is filled with toys from *Star Wars* (1977), games from Milton Bradley, or Aurora model kits of famous movie monsters, these items—these placed products—suddenly transcend consumer-ship or material possession and function as signifiers of that tender act of self-construction.

Many of the aforementioned films actively convey the idea that a love of such toys is not only appropriately masculine, but could literally prove life-saving. In Tobe Hooper's miniseries *Salem's Lot*, for example, a love of magic and monsters is important, because that is the "training" by which a person can detect the real vampire in his midst. When Mark Petrie (Lance Kerwin) is visited in his bedroom by friends transformed into menacing vampires (an example of conforming to a clique?), he immediately understands what they are, and that he is in mortal jeopardy. The reason why he survives, explicitly, is his love of horror, and that love is outwardly reflected in the production design of his bedroom, which highlight unique products such as model kits and movie posters.

Again, the appearance of toys in films like *Poltergeist* or *The Funhouse* is not merely self-reflexive homage to EC Comics or Aurora Models. It goes deeper than that. By featuring these bedrooms in these films—bedrooms filled with monster posters or models or action figures—artists make a point that a love of fantasy, sci-fi, or horror is in fact normal, and possesses value.

But the product placement is not simply about self-preservation, about defeating the twin monsters of conformity and accepted images of masculinity in American culture. In *E.T.*, especially, the selection of specific items for product placement involves a pro-social message about acceptance. For instance, in Elliott's bedroom, the audience sees commercially produced bed quilts and light switches—products again—featuring imagery of Marvel's the Incredible Hulk, a comic-book "monster" with good intentions but a fearsome physicality. Then, in short order, we are also introduced to Kenner action figures of Lando Calrissian, Hammerhead, Snaggletooth, Walrus Man, and other bizarre "beings" from the *Star Wars* cantina. There is also much discussion in the film of the *Dungeons and Dragons* (TSR) world, where goblins, elves, and other magical creatures exist in the imagination and act both alongside and against heroes. And E.T. even attempts to communicate with a human child wearing a Ben Cooper Yoda Halloween costume from 1980. He mistakes the boy for one of his own kind; a connection made possible, once more, by a commercially available product.

Cumulatively, the idea roiling under the surface of *E.T.* is that these pop culture influences and products actually *lead children toward an acceptance of what is different*, of what might seem terrifying on first blush, but which is actually merely different in appearance. Aliens, goblins, and monsters are people, too, says *E.T.*, and to understand them, we must look past their two-fingered "sucker"-type hands or other fearsome and strange differences. In countenancing these differences, young people can see that skin color and even sexual orientation fall under the same category, and aren't necessarily "bad" a priori.

E.T. purposefully asks audiences to accept that which is alternative or seems different, and judge it not by how it looks. The Hulk is a much more nuanced character than his green skin and monster muscles suggest. Chewbacca looks like Bigfoot, but is a loyal friend. Similarly, E.T. and Elliott develop a symbiosis, and so come to understand the *feelings* of one another. That process begins with products, first with Reese's Pieces, and then graduates to *Star Wars* action figures. Products join these two characters, and then bind them together over time. As Tom Shone writes, "It is with Elliott's *Star Wars* figures that Elliott first explains about life on Earth, and it is with Elliott's plastic wrap that E.T. explains where he comes from."[17] In the case of the action figures, Elliott is able to contextualize his world through play, and to share that world with someone of a vastly different stripe and origin.

No matter how different or alien someone may seem, they possess the same feelings that you do. That, too, is *E.T.*'s message, and it is conveyed primarily in two ways: where the journey of understanding one's self and others begins (in a boy's private sanctuary, his bedroom) and how it happens: in the deliberate product placement for Kenner, Marvel, Ben Cooper, and the mention of TSR's bestselling role-playing game. Those who highlight the Reese's Pieces product placement example miss the forest for the trees. There is actually multitudinous product placement in the Spielberg film, but the lion's share of the material actually transmits this sense of acceptance in differences. It is a deliberate rejection of the masculinity of the 1950s, in which no one wanted their child to be a comic-book-reading, 90-pound weakling.

By the 1980s, the dynamic was largely inverted, thanks to Spielberg and filmmakers of his age. *Star Wars* and *Star Trek* and superhero fans were becoming the norm, and they felt emboldened to make their lifestyle choice "known" because they had seen it modeled in the films of Spielberg and other movie brats. The upshot of seeing Elliott's bedroom, or Robbie Freeling's bedroom in *Poltergeist*—where Kenner toys, as well as Milton Bradley's Big Trak, are visible—is that a generation of American kids grew up understanding that it was okay not to be the same as everyone else, as someone's preconceived notion of what a man should be.

Did this message of accepting people who are different also bring large sums of money back to Steven Spielberg, George Lucas, and other film-makers who had cut marketing deals with toy companies? Absolutely, but in a capitalist society, the only thing better than a good cause is a good cause that turns a profit, some might say.

The Circle Is Complete: The Learner Is Now the Master

Buoyed by the examples of *E.T.*, *Poltergeist*, and other films that positioned *Star Wars* toys and other products right in the middle of the action, a generation has grown up to create its own art, often using products as a starting point. On YouTube, there are Lego movie presentations of *Star Wars* (*Lego Star Wars: The Quest for R2-D2* [2009]), *Indiana Jones*, and any other movie or franchise you care to name, by the dozen. The idea is that these toys—these products, again—are valid tools in the quest to artistically express one's self. In other words, "geeks are not just playing games, but try to make game content too. The geeks produce machinima, write fan-fiction, blog, etc."[18] In short, American society has seen since the *E.T.* generation of kids grew up an increasing acceptance of what older generations would have disparagingly termed "one's inner weirdo."[19]

Every year at the colossal Comic-Con celebration, Hollywood veritably bows down to geek culture, trying to work up enthusiasm for the next season's worth of genre film and television, and geek culture even now has its own sitcom, *The Big Bang Theory*. Ask yourself, who is "king" in this dynamic—the advertiser, or the geek? When conventions draw 60,000 fans per show and comic book sales exceed 300 million annually,[20] when character toys get licensed by toy companies for half a billion dollars, it is plain that the era of the geek has arrived as a powerful economic and cultural force.[21] Franchises that began as toy commercials in the 1980s like *The Transformers* have become the blockbuster obsessions of geeks today. The texts and mythologies of these films are no longer secondary to selling toys; they are coequal considerations for geeks.

Because the product placement deployed by Spielberg, Hooper, and other movie brats in the 1980s was positioned primarily in the bedroom, because it was used for social good in cases such as *E.T.*, it surely paved the way for the modern Geek Renaissance. This is a generation that expresses itself with nostalgia purchases on eBay and in blogs about cult movies. It is a generation that buys and reads comics. It is a generation that has turned the act of buying products into the act of contextualizing those products and considering what they represent and mean. "This Boy's Bedroom" of 1984 has become the toy-filled home office of Dad in 2012, and that's because Spielberg and his ilk taught Generation X that masculinity need not be defined narrowly and rigidly, and because their films showcased a safe place in which it was okay to display toys, and a domain in which those toys served as important ways of understanding values and morality.

Grown-up geeks today, from director J. J. Abrams to director Kevin Smith, have internalized the message and are today making movies for geek audiences. These movies sometimes reflect the works of Spielberg, as is the case of Abrams's *Super 8* (2011), where—surprise, surprise—one boy's bedroom (filled with model kits, games, trading cards, and poster) plays a crucial role in the story.

So the legendary Reese's Pieces *E.T.* story does not quite reveal the entire picture of how 1980s fantasy films harnessed the "synergy" of corporate product placement. The Hulk or Chewbacca are not mere toys, but avatars that carry meaning within their specific works of art, and which convey meaning. And by focusing product placement largely in the suburban bedrooms of adolescent boys, Steven Spielberg made it possible (and profitable) for a generation to expose its inner geek.

Notes

1. Jane-Marc Lehue, *Branded Entertainment: Product Placement and Brand Strategy in the Entertainment Business* (Philadelphia: Kogan Page Limited, 2007), 245.

2. Terry O'Reilly and Mike Temant, *The Age of Persuasion: How Marketing Ate Our Culture* (Berkeley, CA: Counterpoint; 2009), 89.

3. Martin Lindstrom and Paco Underhill. *Buyology: Truth and Lies about Why We Buy* (New York: Broadway Press, 2008), 45.

4. Kerry Segrave, *Product Placement in Hollywood Films: A History* (Jefferson, NC: McFarland and Co., 2004), 181.

5. Sorcha N. Fhlainn, ed., *The Worlds of* Back to the Future: *Critical Essays on the Films* (Jefferson, NC: McFarland and Co., 2010), 189.

6. Brian F. Schaffner, *Politics, Parties and Elections in America* (Boston: Wadsworth, 2008), 242.

7. William Greider, *Who Will Tell the People? The Betrayal of American Democracy* (New York: Simon & Schuster Paperbacks, 1992), 67.

8. "Voices of Reason—Excerpts of Interviews with Various Personalities from 1968 to 1998—Interview," *CBS Interactive Business Network Resource Library* December 1998, http://www.highbeam.com/doc/1G1-53260535.html (accessed June 25, 2012).

9. Juliet Schor, *Born to Buy: The Commercialized Child and the New Consumer Culture* (New York: Scribner's; 2004), 78.

10. Richard Campbell, Christopher R. Martin, and Bettina Fabors, *Media and Culture: An Introduction to Mass Communications* (Boston: Bedford/St. Martin's, 2012), 345.

11. William Kleinknecht. *The Man Who Sold the World: Ronald Reagan and the Betrayal of Main Street America* (Philadelphia: Perseus Books, 2009), 177.

12. Rhonda L. Clement and Leah Fiorentino, *A Child's Right to Play: A Global Approach* (Westport, CT: Praeger, 2004), 178.

13. Alan M. Klein, *Little Big Man: Body Building, Subculture and Gender Construction* (Albany: State University of New York Press, 1993), 235.

14. Robert C. Harvey, *The Art of the Comic Book: An Aesthetic History* (Jackson: University Press of Mississippi, 1995), 42.

15. Michael Flood, Judith Kegan Gardiner, Bob Pease, and Keith Pringle, eds., *International Encyclopedia of Men and Masculinities* (New York: Routledge, 2007), 77

16. Gail S. Fidler and Beth P. Velde, *Activities: Reality and Symbol* (Thorofare, NJ: Slack, 1999), 112.

17. Tom Shone, *Blockbuster: How Hollywood Learned to Stop Worrying and Love the Summer* (New York: Free Press, 2004), 135.

18. Lars Kornzack. *Geek Culture: The 3rd Counter Culture* (Aailborg, Denmark: Aailborg University; 2008). http://www.scribd.com/doc/270364Geek-Culture -The-3rd-CounterCulture.

19. N. K. Jemisin, Genevieve Valentine, Eric San Juan, and Zaki Hasan, eds., *Geek Wisdom: The Sacred Teachings of Nerd Culture* (Philadelphia: Quirk Productions, 2011), 21.

20. Barbara Kollmeyer, "Comic Publishers, Studios Enjoy Popularity of Superheroes," *Daily News/New York Knight Ridder Tribune News*, August 26, 2002, 1.

21. David Bloom, "Warner's Superheroes Suit Up for Toy Wars," *Daily Variety* 37 (July 15, 2002), 7.

Bibliography

Fhlainn, Sorcha N., ed. *The Worlds of* Back to the Future: *Critical Essays on the Films*. Jefferson, NC: McFarland, 2010.

Flood, Michael, Judith Kegan Gardiner, Bob Pease, and Keith Pringle, eds. *International Encyclopedia of Men and Masculinities*. New York: Routledge, 2007.

Jemisin, N. K., Genevieve Valentine, Eric San Juan, and Zaki Hasan, eds. *Geek Wisdom: The Sacred Teachings of Nerd Culture*. Philadelphia: Quirk Productions, 2011.

McBride, Joseph. *Steven Spielberg: A Biography*. Jackson: University Press of Mississippi; 2010.

Muir, John Kenneth. *The Encyclopedia of Superheroes on Film and Television*. Jefferson, NC: McFarland, 2004.

Segrave, Kerry. *Product Placement in Hollywood Films: A History*. Jefferson, NC: McFarland, 2004.

Shone, Tom. *Blockbuster: How Hollywood Learned to Stop Worrying and Love the Summer*. New York: Free Press, 2004.

CHAPTER SEVENTEEN

The Evolution of Product Placement: *South Park* and Guitar Hero

Patrick Mayock

[Stan's house, day. In the living room, Stan and Kyle stand before the TV with guitar controllers in their hands. Nine boys from class watch them from the sofa and the floor. A game starts up. Stan and Kyle immediately begin to play and the other boys begin to cheer them on. The song playing is "Wayward Son." Randy watches from the kitchen doorway]

Randy: [Walks up to Stan.] So you boys like this music, huh?

Kyle: Yeah, dude. It's Guitar Hero.[1]

Though it took Kyle, one of four animated adolescent protagonists of *South Park*, only 55 seconds to mention the name of the hit video game Guitar Hero during the episode, viewers tuning into the first airing of "Guitar Queer-O" on November 7, 2007, saw those familiar guitar-shaped plastic controllers from frame No. 1. It was not the first time Comedy Central's scathing satire opened with a clear tie-in to video game culture. The October 4, 2006, episode, "Make Love, Not Warcraft," featured an opening scene in which the boys' digital avatars were interacting within the World of Warcraft online universe.

But "Guitar Queer-O," for myriad reasons, seemed to resonate deeper with audiences. The timing of the episode, for one thing, could not have been better. Its original airing came only a few weeks after the release of "Guitar Hero III: Legends of Rock," the third main installment in the hugely successful video game franchise in which players hit colored buttons on controllers shaped like musical instruments to "play" along with famous rock 'n' roll songs. The game sold more than 1.4 million copies and grossed more than $100 million in its first week of release in North America. "Legends of Rock" sold another 1.9 million copies the following month, making it among the most successful video games launches in the past decade.[2]

Perhaps more than that, *South Park* creators Trey Parker and Matt Stone wove a narrative so inextricably tied to the video game that it transcended product placement and became a seamless thread in the plot. The storyline recounted the meteoric rise and devastating fall of Kyle and his friend Stan after their Guitar Hero prowess propelled them into the fast and loose world of rock 'n' roll. Call it a whip-smart spoof of VH1's *Behind the Music* for the video game age.

The resulting episode was also, in some ways, a spoof on traditional notions of what product placement can and should be. The term, which is commonly understood as a marketing strategy that "involves incorporating brands in movies (and other entertainment media) in return for money or for some promotional or other consideration,"[3] has evolved considerably over time. What first was conceived as a simple business transaction—an equitable exchange of payment for exposure—has become, in many cases, a means to more accurately depict the real world and the place of products and brands therein.

Product Placement: Past and Present

The origins of product placement are difficult to trace, as the term itself appeared more recently than did the practice. Indeed, several researchers point to examples during the early days of Hollywood in the mid-1940s and even as far back as the 1930s when the arrangement was known as exploitation, tie-ups, and tie-ins.[4] The former referred to publicity, such as contests or giveaways, that might generate attendance at motion pictures.[5] Tie-ins and tie-ups were used more interchangeably to describe "a cooperative venture between media maker and manufacturer, in which on-screen exposure of a product, offscreen endorsements by an actor, or a combination of on-screen appearances and offscreen endorsements were traded for paid advertising and unpaid promotions by the manufacturer."[6] The arrangement proved beneficial to all stakeholders; film producers received free props, while manufacturers gained access to captive audiences and the chance for their products to be associated with famous actors.[7]

One of the first documented instances of a movie star plugging a brand name on screen came in 1945, when audiences watched Joan Crawford drink Jack Daniel's liquor in *Mildred Pierce*. In the decades that followed, producers came to rely on product placement to subsidize the enormous production and advertising costs incurred when making and marketing their movies.[8] But the advertising practice was still conducted in a casual process governed by ad hoc decisions in which branded items were donated, loaned, or purchased at a discount for particular scenes.[9]

The era also gave rise to more explicit advertiser-funded programming on other media. The aptly named "soap operas," which debuted on American radio in the 1930s and by the end of the decade would represent some 90 percent of all commercially sponsored daytime broadcast hours,[10] were serialized dramas sponsored by household cleaning product manufacturers such as Procter & Gamble and American Home Products. The former, which established its own radio soap opera production subsidiary in 1940, produced the first network television soap opera in 1950, *The First Hundred Years*.[11] The show lasted only a month, but it paved the way for more successful P&G-sponsored entries, including *Search for Tomorrow* and *The Guiding Light*.[12]

Another successful radio-to-TV transplant was *The Texaco Star Theater*, a vaudeville relic comprising humorous—and often brash—skits from jack-of-all-trades entertainer Milton Berle with financial backing from petroleum giant Texaco. When the show made its debut on NBC-TV in September 1948, there were only a little more than 100,000 TV sets throughout the United States. The number would skyrocket sevenfold by the following year; two years later, there were 7.4 million more TV sets in use.[13] Advertisers quickly took notice of the proliferation of the medium and rushed to attach their names to programs. Along came *Hallmark Hall of Fame, Ford Startime, DuPont Show of the Month, GE Theater, Camel News Caravan, Bob Hope's Chrysler Theater, Gillette Cavalcade of Sports*, and *Kraft Music Hall*.[14] But as production and other costs escalated by 500 percent during the next decade and doubled again between 1959 and 1971, advertisers were forced to scale back and settle for 30- and 10-second commercial breaks and TV "specials" to peddle their products.[15]

Meanwhile, product placement on the big screen was just heating up. All it took was a pint-sized alien in 1982's *E.T.—the Extra-Terrestrial* to help launch the advertising practice into public consciousness. In what would become one of the movie's most famous scenes, the eponymous extraterrestrial followed a trail of Reese's Pieces to his new home. The candy-coated, peanut butter–flavored treats nabbed only a few minutes of screen time, but the cameo helped launch sales by 65 percent within three months.[16]

Perhaps the only thing more surprising than the success of that product placement was the fact that Hershey's competitor, Mars Company, passed on the offer. The script originally called for a breadcrumb trail of M&Ms, but the then-publicity-shy Mars declined to participate. *E.T.* coproducer Kathleen Kennedy turned to plan B, bringing in Hershey marketing executive Jack Dowd for a daylong negotiating session after the cameras already had started rolling. Dowd bit at the offer, agreeing to spend $1 million in a campaign to promote both the movie and Hershey's Reese's Pieces, which had entered national distribution only two years earlier.[17] "The movie was a hit, sales of Reese's Pieces increased dramatically, and to some the product placement industry was born."[18]

The box-office success of *E.T.* and the subsequent boon to Hershey's bottom line ushered in a wave of more proactive appeals to feature products and brands within the plots of big-screen blockbusters and small-screen serials. *Risky Business* famously revived Ray-Ban's Wayfarer sunglasses from extinction in 1983; all it took was a young Tom Cruise sliding across a hardwood floor wearing socks, underwear, and the stylish shades to move some 360,000 pairs—up from only 18,000 the year prior.[19] Cruise lent his commercial clout to a number of languishing brands in subsequent years, including another Ray-Ban sunglasses model, the Aviator, in 1986's *Top Gun* and then Red Stripe beer in the 1993 John Grisham thriller, *The Firm*; the latter saw sales in the United States increase by 50 percent.[20]

That same year as *The Firm* put moviegoers on the edges of their seats, classic movie candy Junior Mints landed a appearance in the TV comedy *Seinfeld*—and in the open chest cavity of a character on the operating table in one particularly iconic scene. Though no money exchanged hands between Tootsie Roll (Junior Mint's parent company) and *Seinfeld*—an arrangement not atypical for television, as it allows both advertiser and content creator to avoid the Federal Communications Commission's sponsorship identification rules[21]—the refreshing chocolate-covered mints played a prominent role in what would become one of the series' most memorable episodes.[22]

BMW scored two notable big-screen successes in the years that followed. The first came in 1995's *GoldenEye*, which featured a new James Bond, Pierce Brosnan, driving a new car, the BMW Z3 Roadster. The marketing coup—agent 007 had only driven Aston Martins in the franchise's previous 16 installments—cost the carmaker $3 million, but the investment generated $240 million in advance sales alone.[23] BMW's second turn came in the 2003 remake of *The Italian Job*, which featured a thrilling car chase with the automaker's Mini Coopers. Though the film was only a moderate success, it helped boost Mini sales by 22 percent year by year.[24]

General Motors found similar success when it contributed its Chevrolet Camaro to *Transformers* in 2007. Though the model featured in the film did not actually exist—it was tricked out with Autobot shields on the side panels and center caps of the wheels—the movie generated enough demand for GM to release it to real-life car buyers in 2009. By the end of the year, more than 60,000 units had sold.[25] It was not the first time the automotive group found success in product placement. Decades earlier, GM scored a high-profile turn for its 1982 Trans Am as a talking car in TV's *Knight Rider*. "With that one show, the Trans Am became one of the most desirable cars of the early 1980s."[26]

Product Placement Digitized

The steady string of product placement successes noted above is not meant to hide the litany of failures that have crashed and burned—or worse, went completely unnoticed—throughout the years. Nor are the more recent examples meant to convey a sense of consistency within the advertising world or the economic landscape that drives entertainment programming. On the contrary, there have been a number of seismic shifts in recent years that disrupted the value chain, forever changing the ways viewers consume content and the ways advertisements subsidize it.

One of the most influential in recent years was the rise of the digital video recorder, as embodied by poster child TiVo. Launched at the 1998 Consumer Electronics Show along with the less commercially viable ReplayTV,[27] the VHS successor revolutionized the way audiences watch TV, allowing them to digitally record, rewind, and pause live programming. More importantly, it diluted the value of the traditional 30-second television ads by allowing users to skip past commercials in recorded content.

ReplayTV actually touted that capability as a point of differentiation when it launched. Whereas TiVo users were forced to press a fast-forward button and manually hit play when a program returned from commercial break, ReplayTV users could skip ads through an automated service. A consortium of major networks quickly put the service on pause, however, claiming copyright infringement, among other charges.[28] The issue resurfaced more than nine years later when Fox and NBCUniversal filed suit against Dish Network to block its Auto Hop feature, which strips commercials from prime-time programming entirely.[29]

But how audiences skip advertisements is not as important as the simple presence of ad skipping in and of itself. With fewer eyeballs tuning in to commercial breaks, the value of those breaks began to diminish. This dynamic, coupled with general trends of audience fragmentation, created a greater need to catch would-be customers in their most likely habitats—noncommercial blocks of programming.

The subsequent increase in product placement was significant. Across 12 broadcast and major cable networks in prime time, there were 5,381 major product placements in 2010, up 22 percent from 2006.[30] Nowhere was the trend more pronounced than on reality TV, which showcased more than half of all broadcast TV product placements (4,664) during prime time.[31] A viewer tuning into Fox might see the snarky judges of *American Idol* quench their thirsts with Coca-Cola before crushing the dreams of yet another would-be pop diva, while on NBC the health-minded trainers on *The Biggest Loser* could be hocking anything from Brita water filters to Jennie-O lean ground turkey to Ziploc bags.

But the trend of infiltrating content with promotional pitches goes deeper, if not further back in time. Thanks to advances in technology, studios are now selling promotional spots in syndicated series by digitally altering old episodes with new products and brands. An episode of 20th Television's *How I Met Your Mother* that originally aired in 2006, for example, featured ads for the 2011 films *Bad Teacher* and *Zookeeper* playing on televisions or displayed in posters in the background of certain scenes. The goal: Wring more revenue out of the sitcom's already-lucrative syndication deals.[32]

Digitization has blurred the lines even further online, where entire Web series have been built around a product or brand. BMW's eight-part, short film series *The Hire* became the first high-profile, big-budget Internet marriage of advertising and entertainment when it debuted at the turn of the century. Each episode starred Hollywood actor Clive Owen—with a different BMW model—as a mysterious driver navigating his way through a labyrinth of high-octane obstacles with surgical precision.

The campaign was supported by TV, print, and Web ads, viral marketing efforts and aggressive public relations. Total production costs, according to estimates, hit nearly $15 million—a price tag that did not vary greatly from what a marketer like BMW would have paid for a major brand campaign at the time.[33] *The Hire* drew 787,000 unique visitors who spent an average of seven minutes at BMWFilms.com during May. A month later, the site drew 856,000 visitors who spent an average of 16 minutes.[34] Most importantly, it helped keep BMW sales booming. The automaker's U.S. sales in June hit 20,250 vehicles, up 32 percent from the year before.[35]

Though BMW eventually moved away from branded entertainment projects, citing ballooning costs associated with production and integration fees,[36] other companies eagerly threw their skin into the game. The short-lived FCU: Fact Checkers Unit from the equally short-lived NBC Universal Digital Studios, for example, essentially was a three-minute commercial for Samsung's Galaxy S smartphone.[37] Kmart provided wardrobes—not to mention funding—to produce Alloy Entertainment's First Day.[38] And AT&T showcased a different technology, some in only the development stages and unavailable to customers, in each eight-minute episode of Daybreak.[39]

Product Placement Goes Meta

In an ironic twist, product placement has become a cluttered outlet across all media—something the practice originally intended to avoid.[40] What is more, the oversaturation of the channel has made consumers more aware and thus more likely to resist persuasion.[41] What has not changed, however, is the need to subsidize the costs of content creation. Indeed, "advertising has traditionally provided about 70 percent to 80 percent of support for newspapers and magazines, and advertising or underwriting has entirely paid for broadcast TV and radio media."[42]

Several content creators have responded with intentionally self-aware treatments of product placement that are meant to downplay the accusations of "selling out" by bringing viewers in on the joke. NBC's Community, for example, made headlines when fictional Greendale Community College opened a Subway franchise in its cafeteria. The March 29, 2012, episode "Digital Exploration of Interior Design" featured a new student, fittingly named "Subway," who represented the collective humanity of the sandwich chain. The plot was as ridiculous as it was unique, and it generated considerable buzz on various blogs and media sites.

The king of self-aware, sales-related satire, however, is Community's neighbor in NBC's Thursday night block of comedies: 30 Rock. The Tina Fey–led lampoon of Saturday Night Live–style sketch shows has blatantly skewered a number of high-profile sponsors over the years. The show "has gained fame in ad-industry circles for an eyebrow-raising technique that . . . usually involves members of the cast making fun of the product or its TV-screen intrusion, often to resounding social chatter."[43]

One of the series' first notable forays was in the November 16, 2006, episode "Jack-Tor," in which Fey's character Liz Lemon argued with Alec Baldwin's Jack Donaghy over the merits of using product placement in the fictional sketch show T.G.S. with Tracy Jordan.

Liz: You're saying you want us to use the show to sell stuff?

Jack: Look, I know how this sounds.

Liz: No, Jack. We're not doing that. We're not compromising the integrity of the show to sell—

Pete: [Interrupts Liz after talking a drink from a prominently displayed bottle of Snapple.] Wow this is Diet Snapple?

Liz: [Pulls out her own bottle of Snapple.] I know! It tastes just like regular Snapple, doesn't it?

Frank: [Displays a half-drank Snapple bottle.] You should try Plumagranite. It's amazing.

Cerie: [Displays Snapple bottle and looks into camera.] I only date guys who drink Snapple.

Jack: Look, we all love Snapple. Lord knows I do. But focus here. We're talking about product integration.[44]

A year later, the show again tackled "product integration" head on when Fey's Lemon broke the fourth wall and addressed sponsor Verizon Wireless with a plea for cash.

Jack: These Verizon Wireless phones are just so popular I accidentally grabbed one belonging to an acquaintance.

Liz: Well sure. That Verizon Wireless service is just unbeatable. If I saw a phone like that on TV I'd be like, "Where is my nearest retailer so I can get one?" [Turns to camera.] Can we have our money now?[45]

The lampooning of product placement is by no means new, however. One of the most notable examples from the tombs of pop culture screened some 15 years before *30 Rock*'s debut in the hit comedy *Wayne's World*. In a single scene, stars Mike Myers and Dana Carvey break the fourth wall four separate times while shilling five different products.

Benjamin: Wayne, listen, we need to have a talk about Vanderhoff. The fact is he's the sponsor and you signed a contract guaranteeing him certain concessions, one of them being a spot on the show.

Wayne: [Holding a Pizza Hut box.] Well that's where I see things just a little differently. Contract or no, I will not bow to any sponsor.

Benjamin: I'm sorry you feel that way, but basically it's the nature of the beast.

Wayne: [Holding a bag of Doritos.] Maybe I'm wrong on this one, but for me, the beast doesn't include selling out. Garth, you know what I'm talking about, right?

Garth: [Wearing Reebok wardrobe.] It's like people only do these things because they can get paid. And that's just really sad.

Wayne: I can't talk about it anymore; it's giving me a headache.

Garth:	Here, take two of these!
	[Dumps two Nuprin pills into Wayne's hand.]
Wayne:	Ah, Nuprin. Little. Yellow. Different.
Benjamin:	Look, you can stay here in the big leagues and play by the rules, or you can go back to the farm club in Aurora. It's your choice.
Wayne:	[Holding a can of Pepsi.] Yes, and it's the choice of a new generation.[46]

Once an original, satirical stance, the "wink-wink" practice now has spilt throughout network television and film. Fake news anchor Stephen Colbert has emerged as one of the most prominent jesters on Comedy Central's *The Colbert Report* with several high-profile, intentionally cheesy pitches for Cocoa Puffs, Cheerios, Pringles, Bud Light Lime, KFC, Reddi-wip, Ensure, and others. And documentary filmmaker Morgan Spurlock addressed the proliferation of brands in *The Greatest Movie Ever Sold* using his characteristically honest, humorous approach.

Product Placement Gone "Mad"

Yet for all their coy and savvy, even the most self-aware product pushers are just that—pushers of product messaging who exchange their valuable on-air real estate for something in return. Thus, the means and the message do not matter; whether bringing audiences in on the joke or shoving a commercial down their throats, the aim is the same.

But this represents only a fraction of the brand exposure driven over "traditional" entertainment programming. If television or movies or the Internet are to convey any semblance of the recognizable world, they must invariably present some branded messaging at times, whether intentional or not. To strip all brands, logos, and advertisements from content would render much of it hollow and empty. A gritty New York City cop drama, for example, would have to blur out billboards and storefronts during car chases, during which no actual cars could be used so as not to film a certain make or model of automobile and characters would have to be naked so as not to be caught wearing certain clothing brands or labels. The attempt would be as impractical as it would be misguided. Indeed, research suggests audiences actually appreciate the realism of brand appearances because they can relate to what is familiar.[47] And not only do audiences appreciate them, but they are more likely to recall those realistic appearances when integral to the story or plot.[48] The Guitar Hero episode of *South Park* mentioned at the beginning of this chapter is a perfect example. The video game was as much a part of "Guitar Queer-O" as any walking, talking character, and audiences responded favorably. The show's use of product placement was rated as the most effective on television during 2007, according to iTVX, which measures brand marketing.

South Park has emerged as an interesting lens through which to study the evolution of product placement over the past 15 years. The animated program, which features aliens, imaginary characters, and other absurd plot elements, is about as far removed from reality as a show can get, and bands used in earlier episodes reflect this chasm. A season three episode, for instance, pondered the evils of "Chinpoko Mon"—a clear stand-in for Japanese import Pokemon. But as the show matured and became more sophisticated, so did its use of brands. Recent episodes have featured the likes of Nintendo's Wii gaming system, Apple's iPad, and video games such as Guitar Hero and World of Warcraft. Whether any of the products used were bred of actual product placement agreements is unlikely, as they were either used in compromising, less-than-favorable ways or were criticized openly in the plot. It is as if the brands in question, if not the practice of product placement itself, were hijacked, used by the show's creators to meet purely creative ends.

South Park's use of the tactic, while clearly apparent, is not pervasive. While a product might drive an entire episode one week, the next could feature no brand tie-ins at all. The same is not true for AMC's critical darling, *Mad Men*. The Emmy Award–winning drama's depiction of Madison Avenue advertising men during the 1960s and 1970s essentially hinges on products and brands. Without them, the series' characters would have nothing to do. Thus, each episode comprises not one but often numerous brand names, many of which are featured prominently in multiepisode narrative arcs. Among the household names to "go *Mad*": Lucky Strike, Kodak, Heinz, John Deere, Heineken, Cool Whip, and Howard Johnson.

Only a fraction of those, such as Heineken, were included as part of paid placement, however.[49] The majority is chosen by series creator and showrunner Matthew Weiner strictly to advance the show's narrative—much to the dismay of AMC. During a hiatus between *Mad Men*'s fourth and fifth seasons, the studio embarked in a very public dispute with Weiner over his use of products in the show, pushing him to subsidize costs by using more traditional placement agreements.[50]

Paying for placement might be the only way to ensure marketers' love versus loathing for the series. While *Mad Men* often celebrates consumerism by holding certain brand names in an almost saintly regard, its painstaking portrayal of the cutthroat 1960s advertising world requires some smearing as well. For every Hilton, which the drama affectionately portrayed as an awe-inducing white whale in the advertising world, there is a Lucky Strike or Jaguar. The former took its blows early on, with a season three storyline involving one of the cigarette company's executives sexually assaulting an agency art director and then demanding his termination. Jaguar is the more recent victim. Not only does *Mad Men* depict the company's automobiles as exceptionally unreliable—a critique that might have been warranted some 40 years ago—but it depicts their executives as slimeballs. During the May 27, 2012 episode "The Other Woman," the company's fictional head of its dealers association make his vote in an ad pitch contingent on having sex with office manager Joan Holloway Harris.

Mad Men's unpredictable depiction of brands mirrors the fragmented nature of product placement in general. For every portrayal of a product that serves as a legitimate driver of plot, there exists another, if not dozens, whose sole purpose is promotional. Some content providers blend the pitches seamlessly, while others are unapologetically blunt. But while approaches may vary, the trend is clearly heating up. Product placement is likely here to stay, growing in intensity as audiences fragment, economic models change, and the entertainment landscape becomes more competitive.

Naysayers need only look the 23rd installment of the James Bond franchise, *Skyfall*. Released in November 2012, the film set a product placement record with approximately one-third of its total budget, or $45 million, raised from companies wanting their brands displayed on the big screen.[51] The previous record was set by 2002's *Minority Report*, for which Lexus, Bulgari, and American Express together paid about $20 million to appear in the film.[52] That much is certain. Less so is at what point the promotional message begins to overtake the media.

Notes

1. "Guitar Queer-O," *South Park*, Comedy Central (New York: November 7, 2007).

2. Kris Graft, "Music Games Aren't Dead, Just Waiting to Be Reborn," Game/Life (blog), November 16, 2009 (6:50 p.m.), http://www.wired.com/gamelife/2009/11/music-game-sales/.

3. Pola B. Gupta and Stephen J. Gould, "Consumers Perceptions of the Ethics and Acceptability of Product Placements in Movies: Product Category and Individual Differences," *Journal of Current Issues and Research in Advertising* 19, no. 1 (1997): 37.

4. Jay Newell, Charles T. Salmon, and Susan Chang, "The Hidden History of Product Placement," *Journal of Broadcasting and Electronic Media* 50, no. 4 (2006): 576.

5. Ibid., 576.

6. Ibid., 577.

7. Ibid., 577.

8. Mary-Lou Galician and Peter G. Bourdeau, "The Evolution of Product Placement in Hollywood Cinema: Embedding High-Involvement 'Heroic' Brand Images," in *Handbook of Product Placement in the Mass Media: New Strategies in Marketing Theory, Practice, Trends, and Ethics*, ed. Mary-Lou Galician (Binghamton, NY: Best Business Books, 2004), 17.

9. Denise E. DeLorme and Leonard N. Reid, "Moviegoers' Experiences and Interpretations of Brands in Films Revisited," *Journal of Advertising* 28, no. 2 (1999): 71.

10. Robert C. Allen, "Soap Opera," Museum of Broadcast Communications, http://www.museum.tv/eotvsection.php?entrycode=soapopera (now defunct).

11. Ibid.

12. Alecia Swasy, *Soap Opera: The Inside Story of Procter & Gamble* (New York: Touchstone, 1993), 111.

13. Fred Danzig, "Uncle Miltie's Lasting Legacy," *Advertising Age*, 73, no. 16 (April 22, 2002): 28.

14. Ibid.

15. Ibid.

16. Galician and Bourdeau, "Evolution of Product Placement in Hollywood Cinema," 17.

17. Newell et al., "Hidden History of Product Placement," 590.

18. Ibid., 575.

19. Colin Leinster, "A Tale of Mice and Lens," *Fortune*, September 1987.

20. Dale Buss, "You Ought to Be in Pictures," *BusinessWeek*, June 1998.

21. Donnalyn Pompper and Yih-Farn Choo, "Advertising in the Ave of TiVo: Targeting Teens and Young Adults with Film and Television Product Placements," *Atlantic Journal of Communication* 16, no. 1 (2008): 50.

22. Stacy Conradt, "The Stories behind 10 Famous Product Placements," *Mental Floss*, April 6, 2008, http://www.mentalfloss.com/blogs/archives/13863.

23. Ibid.

24. Gail Edmondson and Michael Eidam, "BMW's Mini Just Keeps Getting Mightier," *BusinessWeek*, April 5, 2004, http://www.businessweek.com/magazine/content/04_14/b3877075_mz054.htm.

25. Daniel Bukszpan, "10 Successes in Product Placement," CNBC, June 3, 2011, http://www.cnbc.com/id/43266198/10_Big_Successes_in_Product _Placement.

26. Mallory Russell, "Here Are Some of TV's Most Successful Product Placements," *Business Insider*, March 14, 2012, http://www.businessinsider.com/here-are-some-of-tvs-best-product-placements-2012-3?op=1.

27. "Happy Blue Moon! TiVo Celebrates Its Birthday (A Little Early)," *Official TiVo Blog*, March 22, 2012, http://blog.tivo.com/2012/03/happy-blue-moon-tivo -celebrates-its-birthday-a-little-early.

28. Lisa M. Bowman, "ReplayTV Puts Ad Skipping on Pause," *CNET*, June 10, 2003, http://news.cnet.com/2100-1041_3-1015121.html.

29. Steven Musil, "Dish, TV Networks Duel over Ad-Skipping Feature," *CNET*, May 24, 2012, http://news.cnet.com/8301-1023_3-57441311-93/dish-tv -networks-duel-over-ad-skipping-feature/?tag=mncol;4n.

30. "Fact Sheet: U.S. Advertising Spend and Effectiveness," *NielsenWire* (blog), June 10, 2011, http://blog.nielsen.com/nielsenwire/media_entertainment/ fact-sheet-u-s-advertising-spend-and-effectiveness/.

31. "TV Dramas Account for Most Primetime Viewing, Timeshifting and Ad Spend," *NielsenWire* (blog), April 19, 2012, http://blog.nielsen.com/nielsenwire/ media_entertainment/tv-dramas-account-for-most-primetime-viewing-time shifting-and-ad-spend/.

32. Tanner Stransky, " 'How I Met Your Mother': Why Are Ads for New Movies in Old Reruns?" *Entertainment Weekly*, July 7, 2011, http://insidetv.ew.com/2011/ 07/07/how-i-met-your-mother-reruns-bad-teacher-zookeeper/.

33. Anthony Vagnoni, Jean Halliday, and Catharine P. Taylor, "Behind the Wheel," *Advertising Age,* 72, no. 30 (July 23, 2001): 10–12.

34. Ibid.

35. Ibid.

36. Jean Halliday and Marc Graser, "BMW Abandons Madison and Vine," *Advertising Age* 76, no. 40 (October 3, 2005): 10.

37. Eric Sullivan, " 'Fact Checkers Unite': NBC and Samsung's Spin on My Job," *Mother Jones*, August 17, 2010, http://www.motherjones.com/riff/2010/08/ fact-checkers-unit-nbc-and-samsungs-spin-my-job.

38. Sam Schechner, "Kmart's Web Series Stars Product Placement," *WSJ.com*, September 13, 2011, http://live.wsj.com/video/kmart-web-series-stars-product -placement/E27D5EA5-5B21-4AD4-87A4-BCB66E411B85.html#!E27D5EA5-5B21 -4AD4-87A4-BCB66E411B85.

39. David Castillo, "AT&T Product Placement Online," *Product Placement News*, June 2, 2012, http://productplacement.biz/201206024299/branded -entertainment/att-product-placement-online.html.

40. Ekaterina V. Karniouchina, Can Uslay, and Grigori Erenburg, "Do Marketing Media Have Life Cycles? The Case of Product Placement in Movies," *Journal of Marketing* 75, no. 3 (2011): 28.

41. Wei Mei-Ling, Fischer Eileen, and Kelley J. Main, "An Examination of the Effects of Activating Persuasion Knowledge on Consumer Response to Brands Engaging in Covert Marketing," *Journal of Public Policy and Marketing* 27, no. 1 (2008): 42.

42. Adam Thierer, "We All Hate Advertising, but We Can't Live without It," *Forbes*, May 13, 2012, http://www.forbes.com/sites/adamthierer/2012/05/13/ we-all-hate-advertising-but-we-cant-live-without-it/.

43. Brian Steinberg, "How '30 Rock' Pitched Kraft on Product Placement," *Advertising Age*, May 1, 2012, http://adage.com/article/tuning-in/30-rock-pitched -kraft-product-placement/234486/.

44. "Jack-Tor," *30 Rock*, NBCUniversal (New York: November 16, 2006).

45. "Somebody to Love," *30 Rock*, NBCUniversal (New York: November 15, 2007).

46. *Wayne's World*, directed by Penelope Spheeris (1992; Hollywood, CA: Paramount Home Entertainment, 2001), DVD.

47. DeLorme and Reid, "Moviegoers' Experiences and Interpretations," 77.

48. Cristel Antonia Russell, "Investigating the Effectiveness of Product Placements in Television Shows: The Role of Modality and Plot Connection Congruence on Brand Memory and Attitude," *Journal of Consumer Research* 29, no. 3 (December 2002): 313.

49. Diane Brady, "*Mad Men*'s Mixed Blessing for Marketers," *Bloomberg Businessweek*, May 30, 2012, http://www.businessweek.com/articles/2012-05-30/mad-mens-mixed-blessing-for-marketers.

50. "Irony Alert: 'Mad Men' Delayed Until 2012 . . . Over Advertising Dispute," *The Week*, March 29, 2011, http://theweek.com/article/index/213657/irony-alert -mad-men-delayed-until-2012-over-advertising-dispute.

51. John Harlow, "More Than a Word from 007's Sponsors," *Australian*, May 2, 2011, http://www.theaustralian.com.au/news/world/more-than-a-word-from -007s-sponsors/story-e6frg6so-1226047962752.

52. Ibid.

Bibliography

Allen, Robert C. "Soap Opera." Museum of Broadcast Communications. http://www.museum.tv/eotvsection.php?entrycode=soapopera.

Bowman, Lisa M. "ReplayTV Puts Ad Skipping on Pause." *CNET*, June 10, 2003. http://news.cnet.com/2100-1041_3-1015121.html.

Brady, Diane. "*Mad Men*'s Mixed Blessing for Marketers." *Bloomberg Businessweek*, May 30, 2012. http://www.businessweek.com/articles/2012-05-30/mad-mens -mixed-blessing-for-marketers.

Bukszpan, Daniel. "10 Successes in Product Placement." *CNBC*, June 3, 2011. http://www.cnbc.com/id/43266198/10_Big_Successes_in_Product_Placement.

Buss, Dale. "You Ought to Be in Pictures." *BusinessWeek*, June 1998.

Castillo, David. "AT&T Product Placement Online." *Product Placement News*, June 2, 2012. http://productplacement.biz/201206024299/branded -entertainment/att-product-placement-online.html.

Conradt, Stacy. "The Stories Behind 10 Famous Product Placements." *Mental Floss*, April 6, 2008. http://www.mentalfloss.com/blogs/archives/13863.

Danzig, Fred. "Uncle Miltie's Lasting Legacy." *Advertising Age* 73, no. 16 (April 22, 2002): 28.

DeLorme, Denise E., and Leonard N. Reid. "Moviegoers' Experiences and Interpretations of Brands in Films Revisited." *Journal of Advertising* 28, no. 2 (1999): 71–95.

Edmondson, Gail and Michael Eidam. "BMW's Mini Just Keeps Getting Mightier." *BusinessWeek*, April 5, 2004. http://www.businessweek.com/magazine/content/04_14/b3877075_mz054.htm.

"Fact Sheet: U.S. Advertising Spend and Effectiveness." *NielsenWire* (blog), June 10, 2011. http://blog.nielsen.com/nielsenwire/media_entertainment/fact-sheet-u-s-advertising-spend-and-effectiveness/.

Galician, Mary-Lou, and Peter G. Bourdeau, "The Evolution of Product Placement in Hollywood Cinema: Embedding High-Involvement 'Heroic' Brand Images." In *Handbook of Product Placement in the Mass Media: New Strategies in Marketing Theory, Practice, Trends, and Ethics*, edited by Mary-Lou Galician, 15–36. Binghamton, NY: Best Business Books, 2004.

"Guitar Queer-O." *South Park*. Comedy Central. New York: November 7, 2007.

Gupta, Pola B., and Stephen J. Gould. "Consumers Perceptions of the Ethics and Acceptability of Product Placements in Movies: Product Category and Individual Differences." *Journal of Current Issues and Research in Advertising* 19, no. 1 (1997): 37–50.

Halliday, Jean, and Marc Graser. "BMW Abandons Madison and Vine." *Advertising Age* 76, no. 40 (October 3, 2005): 10.

Harlow, John. "More Than a Word from 007's Sponsors." *Australian*, May 2, 2011. http://www.theaustralian.com.au/news/world/more-than-a-word-from-007s-sponsors/story-e6frg6so-1226047962752.

"Irony Alert: 'Mad Men' Delayed Until 2012 … Over Advertising Dispute." *The Week*, March 29, 2011. http://theweek.com/article/index/213657/irony-alert-mad-men-delayed-until-2012-over-advertising-dispute.

"Jack-Tor." *30 Rock*. NBCUniversal. New York: November 16, 2006.

Karniouchina, Ekaterina V., Can Uslay, and Grigori Erenburg. "Do Marketing Media Have Life Cycles? The Case of Product Placement in Movies." *Journal of Marketing* 75, no. 3 (2011): 27–48.

Leinster, Colin. "A Tale of Mice and Lens." *Fortune*, September 1987.

Mei-Ling, Wei, Fischer Eileen, and Kelley J. Main. "An Examination of the Effects of Activating Persuasion Knowledge on Consumer Response to Brands Engaging in Covert Marketing." *Journal of Public Policy and Marketing* 27, no. 1 (2008): 34–44.

Musil, Steven. "Dish, TV Networks Duel over Ad-Skipping Feature." *CNET*, May 24, 2012. http://news.cnet.com/8301-1023_3-57441311-93/dish-tv-networks-duel-over-ad-skipping-feature/?tag=mncol;4n.

Newell, Jay, Charles T. Salmon, and Susan Chang. "The Hidden History of Product Placement." *Journal of Broadcasting and Electronic Media* 50, no. 4 (2006): 575–94.

Pompper, Donnalyn, and Yih-Farn Choo. "Advertising in the Ave of TiVo: Targeting Teens and Young Adults with Film and Television Product Placements." *Atlantic Journal of Communication* 16, no. 1 (2008): 49–69.

Russell, Cristel Antonia. "Investigating the Effectiveness of Product Placements in Television Shows: The Role of Modality and Plot Connection Congruence on

Brand Memory and Attitude." *Journal of Consumer Research* 29, no. 3 (December 2002): 306–18.

Russell, Mallory. "Here Are Some of TV's Most Successful Product Placements." *Business Insider*. March 14, 2012. http://www.businessinsider.com/here-are -some-of-tvs-best-product-placements-2012-3?op=1.

Schechner, Sam. "Kmart's Web Series Stars Product Placement." *WSJ.com*. September 13, 2011. http://live.wsj.com/video/kmart-web-series-stars-product -placement/E27D5EA5-5B21-4AD4-87A4-BCB66E411B85.html#!E27D5EA5 -5B21-4AD4-87A4-BCB66E411B85.

"Somebody to Love." *30 Rock*. NBCUniversal. New York: November 15, 2007.

Steinberg, Brian. "How '30 Rock' Pitched Kraft on Product Placement." *Advertising Age*, May 1, 2012. http://adage.com/article/tuning-in/30-rock-pitched-kraft -product-placement/234486/.

Stransky, Tanner. " 'How I Met Your Mother': Why Are Ads for New Movies in Old Reruns?" *Entertainment Weekly*, July 7, 2011. http://insidetv.ew.com/2011/07/ 07/how-i-met-your-mother-reruns-bad-teacher-zookeeper/.

Sullivan, Eric. " 'Fact Checkers Unite': NBC and Samsung's Spin on My Job." *Mother Jones*, August 17, 2010. http://www.motherjones.com/riff/2010/08/fact -checkers-unit-nbc-and-samsungs-spin-my-job.

Swasy, Alecia. *Soap Opera: The Inside Story of Procter & Gamble*. New York: Touchstone, 1993.

Thierer, Adam. "We All Hate Advertising, but We Can't Live without It." *Forbes*, May 13, 2012. http://www.forbes.com/sites/adamthierer/2012/05/13/we-all -hate-advertising-but-we-cant-live-without-it/.

"TV Dramas Account for Most Primetime Viewing, Timeshifting and Ad Spend." *NielsenWire* (blog), April 19, 2012. http://blog.nielsen.com/nielsenwire/ media_entertainment/tv-dramas-account-for-most-primetime-viewing-time shifting-and-ad-spend/.

Vagnoni, Anthony, Jean Halliday, and Catharine P. Taylor. "Behind the Wheel." *Advertising Age* 72, no. 30 (July 23, 2001): 10–12.

Wayne's World. DVD. Directed by Penelope Spheeris. 1992; Hollywood, CA: Paramount Home Entertainment, 2001.

CHAPTER EIGHTEEN

Nike: Goddess of Victory, Gods of Sport

Danielle Sarver Coombs

Kobe Bryant and LeBron James. Cristiano Ronaldo and Wayne Rooney. Abby Wambach and Hope Solo. Tiger Woods. Lance Armstrong. Rafael Nadal. Roger Federer. Not only are these names among the most talented, successful, and famous athletes of the early twenty-first century, and not only are they sporting icons whose reputations likely will garner whispers of respect and admiration for long after their playing days are over. These athletes have achieved an ordination of excellence that is bestowed only upon those at the top of their games, those who set the bar for all who play with, against, and after them. These men and women represent Nike.

Named after the Greek goddess of victory, Nike Inc. is one of the biggest and best-known sporting apparel and equipment manufacturers in the world. Headquartered in Beaverton, Oregon, the company had total revenues of approximately $21 billion in fiscal year 2011.[1] Its products are some of the most sought after in the world, with professional teams clamoring for affiliation and teenagers hunting down the latest sneaker editions to show off to their friends. While Nike produces quality product, their profits and sales cannot and should not be attributed to product alone. Their shoes, uniforms, and outerwear often are not markedly different from competitive brands such as adidas and Reebok. Why, then, has Nike become the gold standard to which all others aspire? What sets them apart from their athletic-wear competition? What makes the best athletes in the world—the gods of their sports—want to sign on with Nike? In this case, it is not just about the product: it is about the brand.

A Brief History of Nike

Founded in 1964 as Blue Ribbon Sports by University of Oregon track and field coach Bill Bowerman and one of his runners, Phil Knight, the company originally served as the U.S. distributor for a Japanese brand of running shoes (Tiger). Bowerman, however, believed that he could design the shoes to be lighter, better, and faster, and he soon began testing his prototypes with his runners. In 1965, the pair hired Jeff Johnson as their first full-time employee. Johnson took over the marketing arm of the startup, taking photographs and creating materials that could be used to better sell their product. He also recognized the need to change the name, coming up with "Nike"—a tribute to the Greek goddess of victory[2]—as the preferred choice.

By the 1970s, the men behind the newly monikered Nike was ready to move on from their relationship with Onitsuka, the company behind Tiger shoes. After already making forays into shoe design and manufacturing, Bowerman and Knight were ready to shift their focus from serving primarily as a distributor and to become a shoe design and manufacturing company. With a newfangled outsole based on Bowerman's wife's waffle iron, the new Nike shoes were ready to launch in 1972, just in time for the U.S. Track and Field Trials held in Eugene, Oregon.

The Creation of the "Swoosh" in the 1970s

While Nike had the practical and tactical production elements ready to go, their new company still needed a logo. Instead of bringing on high-priced design firms, in 1971, Bowerman and Knight turned to Portland State University graphic design student Carolyn Davidson. Charging the heady sum of $2 per hour for her design work, Davidson presented the owners with a series of options. They selected what is now known as "the swoosh," but Knight reportedly did not fall in love with the basic design at first, allegedly saying: "I don't love it, but it will grow on me."[3] After originally invoicing Bowerman and Knight a total of $35 for her services, Davidson has since seen her compensation grown through stock options.

Despite Knight's initial uncertainty, the Nike "swoosh" is now considered "one of the world's most instantly recognizable logos."[4] Its iconic status and global prominence put Nike among the most elite of brands, and it is one of the few companies in the world that does not need to put its name alongside the logo. Over 40 years after the brand's and logo's inceptions, the "Nike name and swoosh are synonymous with what is 'hip' in youth culture. At the same time, Nike's products are part of the American mainstream."[5] Recognizable in any color and on any product, the swoosh stands for itself. The introduction of the swoosh, the Nike brand, and an innovative product in the 1970s marked the beginning of massive growth and success and were considered an industry leader by the dawn of the next decade.

"Just Do It": Advertising in the 1980s and Beyond

While Nike swooshed into the 1980s on waves of success, it began to lose market share by the middle of the decade. No longer the predominant sportswear manufacturer, Nike fought back with a new line of shoes endorsed by basketball superstar Michael Jordan. Smart endorsement deals and new footwear technologies stabilized the company, and they soon began to reattract core audiences. It was during this period that Nike's global advertising and marketing really began to take off. In 1987, the company launched the Air Max, a shoe that was the first to feature visible Nike Air bags. To market this product, the company created a television sport that used the original recording of the Beatles' "Revolution." Shot in what is now a recognizable Nike style, the ad cuts between shots of professional athletes (including John McEnroe) and amateurs, with quick close-ups of the Nike Air bags in action as a running shoe meets the ground.

Building off the success of the "Revolution" ad, in 1988, Nike launched what would become one of the longest-running and best-known brand catchphrases in advertising history: "Just Do It." This storied slogan is said to have emerged from an off-the-cuff remark by Dan Wieden, one of the founders of advertising agency Wieden+Kennedy, during a meeting with Nike executives. Looking at the Nike team with admiration, Wieden is reported to have said, "You Nike guys, you just do it."[6] The line was intended to represent the Nike culture, including "a willingness to take risks and just a touch of rebellion. It came to represent not just an athletic brand, but also a lifestyle that meshed easily with the popular culture of the time."[7] This new approach also allowed Nike to move beyond the somewhat cold and detached approach that defined previous campaigns. Instead, the "Just Do It" campaign "seemed to capture the corporate philosophy of grit, determination and passion, but also infused it with something hitherto unknown in Nike ads—humor . . . In a word, Nike is 'cool.'"[8]

This marked a significant shift. No longer was Nike simply selling athletic shoes that would help you play well; now, they were selling an attitude.

According to brand architect Scott Bedbury, Knight and his "cultlike vener-
ation"[9] of the company ethos inspired this campaign and the brand focus it
contained. Bedbury believes that "Nike was the first company that looked at
the brand as the organizing principle of the company. Everything had to
tie."[10] This was a "new religion of brand consciousness."[11]

During this period, Nike began to crystallize the key elements that would
represent their brand identity to the public: swoosh, "Just Do It," and relationships with high-profile, dominant athletes who embodied physical
and competitive excellence. By the onset of the 1990s, Nike was once again
on top of the industry. This position has not changed in the ensuing
decades.

The Gods of Sport: Nike and Global Superstars

From its earliest days as Nike, Knight and Bowerman recognized the
value of having elite athletes wearing—and representing—their product.
Nike's first recruit, Oregon running superstar Steve Prefontaine, was a
powerful advocate for the upstart company, appearing on their behalf and
promoting the "waffle" shoe to other runners. Although Prefontaine died
in a car accident in 1975 at the young age of 24, he remains an inspiration
for the company; Knight "has often said that Pre[fontaine] is the 'soul of
Nike.'"[12]

The success of Prefontaine's involvement with a fledgling Nike pointed
toward what would become one of their signature marketing strategies:
signing top athletes to endorse their products. They looked for the best:
the fastest, the most compelling, the ones whom you cannot stop watching
simply because they are so very, very much better than the rest of the field.
As mentioned earlier, basketball icon Michael Jordan—the player against
which all others are compared—and his "Air Jordan" sneakers stabilized
the company during Nike's economic woes of the early 1980s. Jordan and
his shoes, however, also marked Nike's first success in making inroads into
professional basketball. When Nike first signed Jordan, he was a "fresh new
face"[13] in the league. At the time, top National Basketball Association (NBA)
players—including legends Magic Johnson and Larry Bird—wore Converse. Knowing that those players were committed to another brand, Nike
made the bold choice of placing their bets on a young rookie from the University of North Carolina. They were not just asking for an endorsement,
however—Nike was thinking bigger by "considering creating and marketing a signature shoe around the player, and selling not just a piece of footwear, but an entire package of performance and personality."[14]

The risks were huge. At the time, there were very few mainstream African American stars in the United States, and the "idea of having a young black man sell shoes to white America was absurd. Let alone a young black man no one had ever met."[15] No one could guarantee Jordan's success in the pros, and no one could guarantee a product based on him would sell. But sell it did. Constructed in what would become its signature red-and-black color scheme, the Air Jordan was a massive hit. The brand and its visual "Jumpman" logo—a silhouette of a leaping Jordan, arms and legs spread wide as he stretches toward the hoop—have reached iconic status, even after Jordan's playing days drew closed. Since Jordan, Nike has continued to draw in some of the biggest names in the NBA, including LeBron James and Kobe Bryant. No longer is Converse the shoe of choice for professional basketball players; now, the best often are seen lacing up their Nikes.

Basketball is not the only sport in which Nike has made their name through association with the best and the brightest. The company has actively courted dominant athletes from around the globe, capitalizing on these associations to maximize the multinational appeal of Nike. Across almost all mainstream sports, Nike has relationships with the top-tier players. Some of the greatest names in recent tennis history are sponsored by Nike, including Andre Agassi, Rafael Nadal, Pete Sampras, Lindsey Davenport, Maria Sharapova, and Serena Williams. In golf, Tiger Woods and Michelle Wie wear the swoosh while playing in major tournaments. Lance Armstrong, one of the most successful bicyclists in the history of the sport, worked with Nike. In soccer, global superstars like Wayne Rooney (England), Carlos Tevez (Argentina), Ronaldinho (Brazil), Didier Drogba (Ivory Coast), Franck Ribery (France), Mesut Ozil (Germany), Park Ji-Sung (Korea Republic), Wilfred Bouma (Netherlands), Cristiano Ronaldo (Portugal), Fernando Torres (Spain), Olaf Mellberg (Sweden), and Landon Donovan (United States) are among the hundreds of men's national team players from around the world sponsored by Nike. While fewer in number, top female footballers are represented as well, including current American stars Alex Morgan, Megan Rapinoe, Hope Solo, and Abby Wambach. Nike picks the best of the best, and being signed by the brand is a mark of success for these athletes.

Nike's sponsorship deals often extend beyond individual athletes. The company has relationships with a number of elite national sports teams and organizations, including soccer (United States, Brazil, England, Portugal, and France, among many others), ice hockey (including Canada, Russia, and Ukraine) and India's cricket squad. Not surprisingly, Nike also works with some of the top clubs in the world in a range of sports, including soccer (Manchester United, Barcelona), baseball (Boston Red Sox, New

York Yankees), and American football (the entire NFL). For fans young and old, getting an official shirt for your team of choice often means buying a Nike product, and emulating the athletes on those teams means purchasing more from the same brand.

The Halo Effect? Nike and Athletes in Crisis

One of the basic tenets of corporate sponsorships and endorsements is that companies want to be associated with the positive characteristics of an athlete (or athlete, celebrity, etc.), but that often leads to a crisis when bad news leaks or—as is often the case—explodes. Unlike other major brands, however, Nike has a history of standing by players and organizations as they work through difficult periods. Tiger Woods, long considered an ideal brand spokesperson, fell hard and fast when revelations about his marital infidelity broke worldwide. While other brands with which Woods was associated severed their associations, Nike stood by their man.

Rather than sitting back and waiting for the smoke to clear, Nike created and ran a television spot to address Woods's situation head on. Using existing audio recordings of Woods's departed father and mentor, Earl, the ad had his father ask questions that felt relevant to the situation. In the latter part of the spot, Earl's voice-over asks: "I want to find out what your thinking was. I want to find out what your feelings are. And did you learn anything?" As his father's questions are posed, the camera zooms in on a remorseful-looking Tiger. Shot entirely in black and white, the spot was considered a strategic attempt at brand management for both Nike and Woods. In those 30 seconds, Tiger Woods—a sporting icon who had spectacularly fallen from grace—was humbled while being challenged to defend himself by a father who was no longer here to demand answers. As one commentator noted, "Nike has been one of the superstar golfer's most steadfast supporters in the wake of the image-shattering revelations of Woods' habitual infidelity, and now the company gets to justify its loyalty by also serving as Tiger's surrogate scold."[16]

This loyalty to athletes has been demonstrated repeatedly, with Nike maintaining relationships during and in the aftermath of athlete scandals and crises that often sent other brands running. The company publicly announced its continuing support of Lance Armstrong when he decided to no longer fight accusations of doping, English soccer player Wayne Rooney during a marital cheating scandal, and both Pittsburgh Steeler Ben Roethlisberger and Los Angeles Laker Kobe Bryant despite accusations of rape. Much like the characters of Greek mythology from which its name is drawn, Nike seems to recognize that there can be a dark side to the gods and that these athletes all too often will be found fallible. Unlike other brands, Nike's relationships with its athletes are not limited to celebrations and parades; instead, the company often demonstrates loyalty during the darkest hours of a player's career.

This loyalty extends past individuals. In November 2011, Jerry Sandusky, a retired assistant football coach who had worked under legendary head coach Joe Paterno at Pennsylvania State University for 30 years, was indicted (and later convicted) for child sex abuse. During the trial and the investigation around it, shocking revelations about Sandusky's use of Penn State facilities and events to lure and abuse young boys came to light. Questions immediately arose about what Penn State and, more specifically, Joe Paterno knew about Sandusky and these activities. Within days of Sandusky's arrest, Paterno's employment was terminated by Penn State. Less than three months later, Paterno passed away, his legend tainted by Sandusky and questions about what he did or did not know—and what he did not (but should have) done.

In the wake of the Sandusky scandal and ensuing fallout for Penn State and its once-storied football program, Nike opted to maintain ties. This loyalty in part can be attributed to the close relationship between Paterno and Knight, with the latter referring to Paterno as his "hero" in the wake of Nike cofounder Bowerman's death in 1999. During Paterno's memorial service in January 2012, Knight defended the coach and his memory, saying: "Whatever the details of the investigation are, this much is clear to me: There is a villain in this tragedy that lies in that investigation, not in Joe Paterno's response to it."[17]

Although Knight had defended Paterno during the coach's memorial service, the issuance of the Freeh Report later that year caused a change in tone. The result of an extensive investigation by former Federal Bureau of Investigation director Louis Freeh, the report indicated Paterno and senior Penn State administrators knew more, earlier than originally thought. While Nike continues its association with the university, Nike eventually did opt to remove Paterno's name from the child care center at its headquarters. In July, Knight issued the following statement:

> Throughout Joe Paterno's career, he strived to put young athletes in a position to succeed and win in sport but most importantly in life. Joe influenced thousands of young men to become better leaders, fathers and husbands. According to the investigation, it appears Joe made missteps that led to heartbreaking consequences. I missed that Joe missed it, and I am extremely saddened on this day. My love for Joe and his family remains.[18]

Although Nike is remarkably loyal to those with whom it has relationships, clearly some lines still cannot be crossed.

While athletes and teams form the cornerstone of Nike's paid activity, they have developed a tremendous proficiency for getting visibility at international sporting events—even when they are not the official sponsors.

Major Sporting Events and Ambush Marketing

Every four years, people around the globe stop during summer to focus attention on what arguably is the most high-profile sporting event in the world: the Summer Olympics. This prominence comes with tremendous value, and thus the sponsoring organization—the International Olympics Committee (IOC)—goes to great lengths to protect the associated brand and advertising space on behalf of its corporate partners. A substantial part of this responsibility is to prevent any unapproved brand activity, commonly referred to as ambush marketing. In ambush marketing, nonofficial partner brands use guerilla approaches to get their brand and their message to audiences without having to pay the exorbitant sponsorship fees. During the 2010 World Cup in South Africa, for example, 36 beautiful Dutch women wearing matching orange dresses—the color of the Netherlands team—were removed from a stadium and detained by police when it was discovered their dresses were received as promotional gifts from a Dutch beer firm, Bavaria.[19] The problem? Official sponsor Budweiser had exclusive rights to advertise beer within FIFA venues and, in order to maintain these lucrative deals, FIFA needed to ensure the paying brand is the only one represented.

During the 2012 Summer Olympics in London, the IOC took things even further in order to protect what may be the most protected brand in the world—the five interlocking rings—as well as the exclusivity of the official sponsors paying massive amounts of money to use the Games as an advertising platform. In the weeks leading up to the opening ceremony, so-called "brand police" traveled London to search out potential violations. These were easy to find, however, since "associated words" including such common terms as 2012, Games, London, and Summer. While one of these words alone would not trigger a violation, two of the words would.[20] Small businesses in London were required to take down signage, and IOC president Jacques Rogge had to issue a public statement saying "common sense would prevail" after London head organizer Sebastian Coe indicated that Pepsi T-shirts might lead to fans being barred admission to venues because Coca-Cola was a main sponsor.[21] While Rogge stepped back from this hardline stance, he firmly articulated the IOC's position: "Our position is very clear. We have to protect the sponsors because otherwise there is no sponsorship and without sponsorship there is no games ... (I)f there is a blatant attempt at ambush marketing by another company or by a group of people with commercial views, then of course we will intervene."[22] The reasoning behind this is clear from a corporate perspective. Brands officially associated with the Olympics pay top dollar to do so, with companies like McDonald's and Coca-Cola rumored to have coughed up $100 million each for the honor. With this kind of money at stake, the IOC takes brand protection very, very seriously.

Despite the considerable efforts of organizing committees and paying sponsors, Nike has managed to thwart all efforts to keep its brand off the global stage. During the Summer 2012 Games, it pushed the legal envelope further than ever before, creating a highly visible campaign featuring everyday athletes in cities and towns around the world—all named London. As one writer noted, "They're not actually saying the 2012 London Olympics, but subliminally and emotionally you can't avoid linking the brand to the city and, thus, the event. Oh, FYI, adidas paid around $60 million for their official brand status."[23] Further rubbing salt in adidas's wound, London mayor Boris Johnson read a recently written poem for the IOC that included the Greek word for victory—nike.[24]

Officially dubbed "Find Your Greatness," Nike's "other London" campaign relied on viral messaging and social media to connect with audiences. They created an active hashtag component that linked to its site and its commercials.[25] The tone of this campaign was clear: greatness is not just for the "gods of sport" described above. Instead, greatness can be found by any (and every) one of us. One of the most notable spots featured a 13-year-old boy from London, Ohio, identified only as Nathan. Unlike the elite athletes embodying physical prowess and fitness, Nathan was a heavy young man. The commercial opens with a figure in the distance as the camera keeps pulling away. As Nathan comes into the frame during his predawn jog, the voiceover begins: "Somehow we've come to believe that greatness is a gift reserved for a chosen few—for prodigies, for superstars—and the rest of us can only stand by watching." At the end of the minute-long spot, Nathan is directly in front of the camera, red-faced and huffing, barely lifting his feet off the ground as he pushes himself to keep going. The voice-over concludes: "Greatness is no more unique to us than breathing. We're all capable of it. All of us." The swoosh comes up with Nike's new instruction: Find Your Greatness.[26]

Linking the campaign back to Nike's traditional association with elite athletes, this tagline was echoed on the shirts distributed to and worn by the U.S. women's soccer team after their victory over Japan. Dominant throughout much of the tournament, the American women faced the team to whom they had lost in a penalty shootout during the previous summer's World Cup. When the final whistle blew, the U.S. women put on Nike shirts with the message "Greatness Has Been Found." In a rare marketing misstep, the women (and Nike) were criticized for the "smug, tacky"[27] slogan by critics from around the world, including the United States. As one writer noted, "I'm all for showing off the greatness of the United States and our sporting teams. At an Olympics, there's an easy way to do it: Stand on top of the podium while 'The Star Spangled Banner' plays. It gets the job done better than any marketing gimmick could."[28]

Nike's efforts during the games went beyond their "Find Your Greatness" marketing campaign, using a distinctive product to remind viewers—and athletes—of what Nike does best: build shoes that will help athletes perform at the top of their games. During the Olympics themselves, Nike product was everywhere. The Nike Volt shoe—instantly recognizable due to its neon yellow color—was visible throughout the track and field competition: "Indeed, in certain track and field events at the Olympic Games ... it appeared that nearly every runner wore the distinctive-colored shoes that were so bright, they might even glow in the dark."[29] By the end of the track and field events, over 400 runners wore the spectacularly identifiable shoes,[30] including British distance running hero Mo Farah.

In the wake of the 2012 Olympics, the August landing page for Nike's U.S. site blares "Game On, World" in large, bold font, touting how athletes can "get in the game with Nike+."[31] In the bottom left corner, Nike-sponsored superstars are presented in a group, each striking a pose indicating he or she is ready to play—and play tough—as part of the Nike+ Mission. LeBron James, Hope Solo, Rafael Nadal, former Olympic gymnast Shawn Johnson, Brazilian mixed martial artist Anderson Silva, and other elite athletes are there to "lead you through daily training sessions and challenges."[32] When you click through to the Mission section, you are invited to join and complete one of the Nike+ Missions across a variety of sports. As the Olympics campaign introduced, the company is promising that this is a way to find greatness: When the mission is completed, greatness is found.

Conclusion

Since the launch of the swoosh in the early 1970s, Nike has developed into one of the most successful brands in the world across all categories, not just footwear. Instantly recognizable, the company has married elite athletes—gods of sport—and a consistent brand voice to build audience loyalty. One of the most remarkable aspects of its marketing is that

Nike manages to be a brand behemoth without losing credibility among young people, a feat rarely achieved by mainstream companies. "When we consider that Nike's enormous profits come mostly from sales to young athletes, we can better appreciate the brilliance of the company's marketing schemes. Nike has learned not only how to discern but also how to define the tastes of the aspiring athletes to whom it appeals."[33] Walking the line between marketing genius and brand credibility can be incredibly difficult, yet Nike manages this with aplomb. As one commenter noted, "Nike managed the deftest of marketing tricks: to be both anti-establishment and mass market."[34]

As demonstrated by the 2012 Olympics, Nike dominates global sporting events even when it is not the official sponsor. The ubiquitous swoosh, recognizable products, catchy campaign taglines, and relationships with high-profile athletes have positioned Nike as the clear choice for elite athletes, and the brand's multinational appeal continues to make it a branding example that companies from all industries admire and emulate. Aptly named, Nike's continual dominance is a remarkable brand victory.

Notes

1. "Nike, Inc. Comments on Q4 2012 Revenue Guidance; Issues Mixed FY 2012 Guidance-Conference Call," *Reuters Finance*, March 22, 2012, para. 1, http://www.reuters.com/finance/stocks/NKE.N/key-developments/article/2511684.

2. Mark Hughes, "Logos that Became Legends: Icons from the World of Advertising," *Independent*, January 4, 2008, para. 16, http://www.independent.co.uk/news/media/logos-that-became-legends-icons-from-the-world-of-advertising-768077.html.

3. Ibid, para. 17.

4. Ibid, para. 15.

5. Carol J. Singley, "From Women's Movement to Momentum: Where Are We Going, Where Have We Been, and Do We Need Nikes to Get There?" *Journal of American Culture* 25, no. 3–4 (2002): 457.

6. Center for Applied Research, "Mini-case Study: Nike's 'Just Do It' Advertising Campaign," (Philadelphia: Center for Applied Research, n.d.), 1.

7. "Game-Changing Ads: 'Just Do It'—1988," CNN Money, n.d., http://money.cnn.com/galleries/2009/fortune/0908/gallery.iconic_ads.fortune/5.html.

8. CFAR, "Mini-case Study," 2.

9. Jay Tolson, "What's in a Name?" *U.S. News and World Report*, October 9, 2000, para. 7, EBSCOhost (00415537).

10. Ibid.

11. Jolie Solomon, "When Nike Goes Cold," *Newsweek*, March 30, 1998, para. 4, EBSCOhost (386516).

12. Nike, "History and Heritage," Nike.com, n.d., para. 8, http://nikeinc.com/pages/history-heritage#tab3-tab.

13. Dan Wetzel, "For Nike, Jordan Delivered the Goods and More," Yahoo! Sports: NBA, September 8, 2009, para. 10, http://sports.yahoo.com/nba/news?slug=dw-jordannike090709.

14. Ibid., para. 11.

15. Ibid., para. 11.

16. Adam B. Vary, "'Tiger Woods' New Nike Ad Features Late Father Asking 'Did You Learn Anything?' Okay, You Got Our Attention," EW.com: PopWatch, April 7, 2012, para. 4, http://popwatch.ew.com/2010/04/07/tiger-woods-new-nike-ad-earl-woods/.

17. Wes O'Donnell, "Phil Knight: Nike Chairman Justified in Defense and Tribute of Joe Paterno," Bleacher Report, January 27, 2012, para. 8, http://bleacher report.com/articles/1041642-phil-knight-nike-chairman-justified-in-defense-and-tribute-of-joe-paterno.

18. Brian Bennett, "Phil Knight Issues Statement on Joe Paterno," ESPN, July 12, 2012, para. 6–7, http://espn.go.com/blog/bigten/post/_/id/53036/phil-knight-issues-statement-on-joe-paterno, para. 6 and 7.

19. Aislinn Laing, "World Cup 2010: Police Arrest Women in Dutch Orange Dresses," *Telegraph: Sport: Football: Competitions,* June 16, 2010, para. 1, http://www.telegraph.co.uk/sport/football/competitions/world-cup-2010/7830319/World-Cup-2010-Police-arrest-women-in-Dutch-orange-dresses.html.

20. For a complete story, see "The 'Do's' and 'Don'ts' in Connection with the Upcoming London 2012 Olympic Games," Finnegan.com: IP Update, July 24, 2012, para. 13; "Using the Brand," London2012.com, n.d., para. 32, http://www.london2012.com/about-us/our-brand/using-the-brand/.

21. Associated Press, "IOC Prez Plays Down 'Brand Police,'" ESPN.com: Summer Olympics, July 21, 2012, para. 3, http://espn.go.com/olympics/summer/2012/story/_/id/8187217/2012-summer-olympics-ioc-president-jacques-rogge-plays-brand-police-london-games.

22. Ibid., para. 4.

23. Robert Passikoff, "Ambush Marketing: An Olympic Competition. And Nike Goes for Gold," *Forbes CMO Network,* August 7, 2012, para. 3, http://www.forbes.com/sites/marketshare/2012/08/07/ambush-marketing-an-olympic-competition-and-nike-goes-for-gold/.

24. Mark Byrnes, "Not an Official Sponsor, Nike Still Gets More Attention than Adidas at Olympics." *TheAtlanticCities.com,* July 26, 2012, http://www.theatlantic cities.com/politics/2012/07/not-official-sponsor-nike-still-gets-more-attention-adidas-olympics/2727/.

25. Mike Sweney, "Olympics 2012: Nike Plots Ambush Campaign," *Guardian: News: Media: Marketing and PR,* July 25, 2012, para. 6, http://www.guardian.co.uk/media/2012/jul/25/olympics-2012-nike-ambush-ad.

26. "New Nike Ad Demonstrates Greatness Is for Everybody," MSN.com: What's Trending, August 1, 2012, para. 1, http://now.msn.com/nike-debuts-new-viral-ad-find-your-greatness.

27. Chris Chase, "Backlash over Team USA's Nike Gold-Medal T-shirts," Yahoo! Sports, August 9, 2012, para. 1, http://sports.yahoo.com/blogs/olympics -fourth-place-medal/nike-gold-medal-t-shirts-were-tacky-vain-213051108 —oly.html.

28. Ibid., para. 8.

29. Randy Yagi, "Nike Volt Running Shoes Score Big at the 2012 London Summer Olympics," RunningShoesGuru.com: Featured, August 21, 2012, para. 2, http://www.runningshoesguru.com/2012/08/nike-volt-running-shoes-score -big-at-the-2012-london-summer-olympics/.

30. Deborah Arthurs, "The High Tech Trainers That Helped Mo Farah Speed His Way to Double Gold . . . Plus the KNITTED Marathon Shoes," *Daily Mail Online: Femail*, August 13, 2012, http://www.dailymail.co.uk/femail/article-2187649/ The-high-tech-Nike-trainers-helped-Mo-Farah-speed-way-double-gold-KNITTED -marathon-shoes.html.

31. Nike, "Game On, World," n.d., http://www.nike.com/us/en_us/ (accessed August 31, 2012).

32. Ibid.

33. Singley, "From Women's Movement," 457.

34. Solomon, "Nike Goes Cold," para. 4.

Bibliography

Arthurs, Deborah. "The High Tech Trainers That Helped Mo Farah Speed His Way to Double Gold . . . Plus the KNITTED Marathon Shoes." *Daily Mail Online: Femail*, August 13, 2012, http://www.dailymail.co.uk/femail/article-2187649/ The-high-tech-Nike-trainers-helped-Mo-Farah-speed-way-double-gold-KNITTED -marathon-shoes.html.

Associated Press. "IOC Prez Plays Down 'Brand Police.'" ESPN.com: Summer Olympics, July 21, 2012. http://espn.go.com/olympics/summer/2012/story/_/ id/8187217/2012-summer-olympics-ioc-president-jacques-rogge-plays-brand -police-london-games.

Byrnes, Mark. "Not an Official Sponsor, Nike Still Gets More Attention than Adidas at Olympics." TheAtlanticCities.com, July 26, 2012. http://www.theatlantic cities.com/politics/2012/07/not-official-sponsor-nike-still-gets-more-attention -adidas-olympics/2727/.

Center for Applied Research. "*Mini-case Study: Nike's 'Just Do It' Advertising Campaign.*" N.d. Philadelphia: Center for Applied Research.

Chase, Chris. "Backlash over Team USA's Nike Gold-Medal T-shirts." Yahoo! Sports, August 9, 2012, para. 1. http://sports.yahoo.com/blogs/olympics -fourth-place-medal/nike-gold-medal-t-shirts-were-tacky-vain-213051108 —oly.html.

"The 'Do's' and 'Don'ts' in Connection with the Upcoming London 2012 Olympic Games." Finnegan.com: IP Update, July 24, 2012, para. 13.

"Game-Changing Ads: 'Just Do It—1988.' " CNN Money, n.d. http://money .cnn.com/galleries/2009/fortune/0908/gallery.iconic_ads.fortune/5.html.

Hughes, Mark. "Logos that Became Legends: Icons from the World of Advertising." *Independent*, January 4, 2008. http://www.independent.co.uk/news/media/ logos-that-became-legends-icons-from-the-world-of-advertising-768077.html.

Laing, Aislinn. "World Cup 2010: Police Arrest Women in Dutch Orange Dresses." *Telegraph: Sport: Football: Competitions,* June 16, 2010, para. 1. http://www .telegraph.co.uk/sport/football/competitions/world-cup-2010/7830319/World -Cup-2010-Police-arrest-women-in-Dutch-orange-dresses.html.

"New Nike Ad Demonstrates Greatness is for Everybody." MSN.com: What's Trending, August 1, 2012, para. 1. http://now.msn.com/nike-debuts-new -viral-ad-find-your-greatness.

Nike. "Game On, World." N.d., http://www.nike.com/us/en_us/, (accessed August 31, 2012).

Nike. "History and Heritage." N.d., http://nikeinc.com/pages/history-heritage #tab3-tab.

O'Donnell, Wes. "Phil Knight: Nike Chairman Justified in Defense and Tribute of Joe Paterno." Bleacher Report, January 27, 2012, http://bleacherreport.com/ articles/1041642-phil-knight-nike-chairman-justified-in-defense-and-tribute -of-joe-paterno.

Passikoff, Robert. "Ambush Marketing: An Olympic Competition. And Nike Goes For Gold." *Forbes CMO Network*, August 7, 2012. http://www.forbes.com/sites/ marketshare/2012/08/07/ambush-marketing-an-olympic-competition-and-nike -goes-for-gold/.

Reuters. "Nike, Inc. Comments on Q4 2012 Revenue Guidance; Issues Mixed FY 2012 Guidance-Conference Call." *Reuters Finance*, March 22, 2012. http://www .reuters.com/finance/stocks/NKE.N/key-developments/article/2511684.

Singley, Carol J. "From Women's Movement to Momentum: Where Are We Going, Where Have We Been, and Do We Need Nikes to Get There?" *Journal of American Culture* 25, no. 3–4 (2002): 455–67.

Solomon, Jolie. "When Nike Goes Cold." *Newsweek*, March 30, 1998. EBSCOhost (386516).

Sweney, Mike. "Olympics 2012: Nike Plots Ambush Campaign." *Guardian: News: Media: Marketing and PR*, July 25, 2012. http://www.guardian.co.uk/media/ 2012/jul/25/olympics-2012-nike-ambush-ad.

Tolson, Jay. "What's In a Name?" *U.S. News and World Report*, October 9, 2000. EBSCOhost (00415537).

"Using the Brand." London2012.com, n.d., http://www.london2012.com/about -us/our-brand/using-the-brand/.

Vary, Adam B. "Tiger Woods' New Nike Ad Features Late Father Asking 'Did You Learn Anything?' Okay, You Got Our Attention." EW.com: PopWatch, April 7, 2012. http://popwatch.ew.com/2010/04/07/tiger-woods-new-nike-ad-earl -woods/.

Wetzel, Dan. "For Nike, Jordan Delivered the Goods and More." Yahoo! Sports: NBA, September 8, 2009, para. 10. http://sports.yahoo.com/nba/news ?slug=dw-jordannike090709.

Yagi, Randy. "Nike Volt Running Shoes Score Big at the 2012 London Summer Olympics." RunningShoesGuru.com: Featured, August 21, 2012. http://www .runningshoesguru.com/2012/08/nike-volt-running-shoes-score-big-at-the -2012-london-summer-olympics/.

CHAPTER NINETEEN

From Jumpman to Business Man: A Look at Michael Jordan as the Blueprint for Sports Advertising and Beyond

Phylicia McCorkle

The wee hours of the morning are not what you would expect for the normal gym shoe shopper. All across the country thousands of teens and adults alike stand in lines wrapped around malls and shoe stores as they await the stroke of 6:00 a.m. At 6:00 a.m., the doors will open, gates will rise, and avid "sneakerheads" will rush to get their hands on the latest release. The latest release being described happens to be that of six-time NBA champion and basketball icon Michael Jordan. As his many accolades precede him, the irony falls in that in some cases, those anxious Jordan shoe collectors have never seen the man behind the name play one single game. He has the ability to sell a shoe with his name even after his final retirement in 2003, with some never knowing exactly all that he has contributed to the game itself. This statement alone highlights the impact Michael Jordan has had not only on the court but off the court as one of the top advertising icons of our time.

The Man, the Athlete

As with other star athletes, this story has a humble beginning. Born February 17, 1983, Michael Jeffrey Jordan's life began in Brooklyn with his parents James and Deloris and three other siblings. Hardworking parents provided a stable foundation for a young Jordan even as James and

Deloris moved the family to Wilmington, North Carolina. North Carolina
has become synonymous with the makings of the future "Air Jordan" as
he cultivated his talents through many trials and tribulations.

High school is the prime opportunity for young aspiring athletes to
develop their skills over the course of four years. Jordan was no exception.
Laney High School proved to be the speed bump on his road to stardom.
During his sophomore year of high school, Jordan found himself cut from
the varsity basketball team. Such a decision would be a devastating blow
to anyone's self-esteem, and Jordan was no different. It has been told that
after being cut, Jordan devoted a majority of his free time practicing his
jump shot and other skills in order to be better prepared for next year's try-
outs. Such dedication paid off as the following year Jordan returned as a
taller, stronger player ultimately making the varsity team.

Upon entering the NBA, a young Jordan was destined to make a great
impact on the game. During his time at University of North Carolina, Jordan stood out as a key player for the team. His freshman year alone was
noteworthy as he made the game-winning shot against Georgetown to win
the NCAA championship.[1] Ironically, Jordan had never thought of attend-
ing the university, yet his impact was felt and much appreciated. The Tar
Heels became a force to be reckoned with during his time and continue to
be a strong college basketball program to this day.

In 1984, Jordan delayed his senior year in order to go professional. His
stellar resume at the University of North Carolina made him an ideal candidate for the NBA draft. As the third overall draft pick, Jordan went to the
then unsuccessful Chicago Bulls. At the time the Bulls were facing a losing
record and possible franchise termination. The owners and coaching staff
were not happy with the franchise's current state and sought a breath of
fresh air to recharge the organization. The recharge they needed was found
in Jordan himself. During his first season as a Bull, Jordan managed to show
his skills, although it would be a few more seasons before he truly shined.
In addition to being a new player to the league, Jordan was a part of the
1984 gold medal U.S. Olympic basketball team and would do so again in
1992 as a part of the "Dream Team." To top it off, Jordan was named Rookie
of the Year in 1985.

In 1988, Jordan found himself under the eye of a new coach, Phil
Jackson. After a major restructuring the Bulls picked up steam, making their
presence known in the NBA with a 55–27 record, the team's first winning
season since 1971.[2] The Bulls were a power team with a roster including
off-season draft picks Scottie Pippen and Horace Grant. On top of that,
Jordan became the only player to win both MVP and Defensive Player of
the Year in the same season. Such a feat emphasized his on-court skills

and power, making him a force to be reckoned with. This high-profile player did not go unnoticed by companies and brands alike. Soon, the world would be introduced to the Air Jordan himself.

Jordan and Nike

Philip Knight might be an unknown name, but his brand is recognizable. As a student-athlete, Knight was familiar with sport equipment and sought to create the best track shoe on the market. Starting off as a small idea, Knight sought to transform his dream into a reality. After a trip to Japan, the Blue Ribbon Sport company took shape on its journey to becoming a leading athletic shoe brand. Initial impressions were bleak as track athletes complained about the shoe make and quality. What Knight failed to take into account were the differences in climate between Japan and the United States, a huge factor in how athletes are able to perform. Many track athletes continue to train during the winter months. The original shoe cracked, split, and fell apart under the cold weather conditions of an American winter season. It was back to the drawing board as Knight soon developed his own technology and ideas toward track shoes, which soon helped propel his career and name to the forefront.

Today, Nike has become synonymous with high-performance, state-of-the-art, technology-infused athletic shoes and clothing. The name itself is derived from Greek mythology. Nike, the winged goddess of victory, was first mentioned to Knight by Jeff Johnson in the 1970s.[3] From that moment on, the name became official. In comparison, the name seems to have various connotations, and one can create their own interpretations. Nike, the goddess of victory, symbolizes all that the brand has become to this day. Many of the world's top athletes are featured wearing the brand in any way, shape, or form and rise to the top. Victory, and ultimately hard work, comes to those athletes draped in the clothing and shoes, but also to the brand and to Knight himself.

Upon entering the NBA, Jordan became a superstar. Other top athletic brands were considering using athletes as endorsers but were skeptical about entrusting their product to one athlete. However, Jordan was the biggest name, an untapped source of potential revenue and stardom. At the time, Jordan had offers from Converse and Adidas, both vying for the chance to use his likeliness to push their product to the next level. A determined Knight and other Nike executives wanted Jordan in their shoes. They sought a way to take the brand to the next level as aerobic shoes gained popularity, an area Nike failed to tap into. After a meeting in Oregon at the Nike headquarters and a little persuading from his agent, David Falk,

Jordan agreed to the $2.5 million over the course of a five-year contract.[4] Since then, Jordan and Nike have surpassed the $2.5 million mark, as Nike is a $10.7 billion company.

After Nike signed Jordan as the brand's new face, Knight sought to stretch advertisement and commercial creativity beyond imagination. A key component to the new take on Nike commercials was up-and-coming director Spike Lee. In 1986, Lee directed *She's Gotta Have It* starring himself as Mars Blackmon, an overzealous super fan eager to express his passion for Jordan.[5] Mars Blackmon highlighted and represented all fans at the time who could not believe such a basketball player possessed such skills and talents as Jordan. The first and subsequential commercials were successful as they showed clips of Jordan, who became known as "His Airness," performing amazing moves and dunks that only he could do. Fans were quick to accept the new advertising, especially that of Mars Blackmon. The dynamic between Lee and Jordan was infectious and, in turn, propelled the careers of both men forward. In 1989, Lee released the cult classic *Do the Right Thing*, a film highlighting the racial tensions in Brooklyn, New York, on a hot summer day. Lee's passion for Nike and Jordan shoes continued beyond the commercial and into his personal life as he is frequently spotted wearing one of many pairs of the coveted shoes.

The most influential aspect of the Nike and Jordan relationship lies in the shoes. Jordan's basketball skills were only trumped by his ability to jump high and complete dunks like never before. To capitalize on this, Nike sought to create and market a shoe specifically for Jordan. The Air Jordan 1, designed by Peter Moore, was the first in a long line of Jordan-inspired shoes. In April 1985, fans were able to purchase Air Jordan 1 for the first time. Young fans and adults alike clambered for the chance to own a pair of Air Jordan 1, the same shoe worn by their favorite NBA player. Over the course of a few days, stores across the country sold out of the shoe. In the first year, customers bought $130 million worth of Air Jordan shoes.[6] Jordan's status as the top NBA player along with his charismatic personality off the court helped sell the shoes from day one. In keeping with the momentum of the original Air Jordan shoe, Nike continued to design and sell other styles influenced by the man himself. Currently, there are 27 different Air Jordan–style shoes.

Brands Galore

Although Nike has been, and still is, Jordan's leading endorsement brand, other companies were eager to jump on the bandwagon in hopes of using his likeliness to experience the hype of "His Airness." Since his initial contract in 1985, Falk negotiated a seven-year contract for a guaranteed $18 million plus royalties on every shoe sold.[7] Offers for other brands poured in and the decision to endorse one over the other was solely based on strategy and image.

In 1991, Falk met with the director of sports marketing for Gatorade, Bill Schmidt, to discuss the possibility of Jordan endorsing Gatorade. The parameters were steep, as Coca-Cola was extremely interested in pursuing a deal with the most sought-after athlete in the world. At this time other entertainers and athletes were signing deals for $1 million to $2 million over the course of five years. Falk took it upon himself to leverage this information in order to receive the best deal for Jordan. After much deliberation, Coca-Cola was unable to meet the demands, allowing Schmidt to offer to Falk and Jordan a 10-year $13.5 million deal and the rights as the exclusive spokesperson for Gatorade.

Following the completed deal, a campaign was created around Jordan with the slogan "Be Like Mike. Drink Gatorade." Initial impressions were skeptical, as the company had never entrusted its product to one person. Gatorade prides itself on being a team-centered product, encouraging all members to be involved in their activity. In the end, the risk of giving Jordan exclusive spokesperson privileges proved to be successful. His young fans were anxious to drink the beverage in hopes of being like their favorite basketball player. Commercials featured Jordan himself playing basketball with kids followed by taking a break to enjoy his Gatorade. Along with commercials, a song was created incorporating the catchy slogan, which, in turn, pushed the brand forward with Jordan as its spokesperson. For months following the first airing of the commercial, kids could be heard singing along with the jingle, a sign the advertisement worked.

Other brands continued to offer deals to Jordan. Even a worldwide franchise such as McDonald's was no exception. McDonald's struck a deal agreeing to pay him $3 million a year. Jordan was featured in various McDonald's ads, with the first following the Bulls' 1992 NBA championship. Jordan was filmed stating he could "go for a Big Mac" while walking off the court at the end of the game.[8] It was only a short amount of time before the clip was used and broadcast across network television. In 1993, another major spot with the company featured Jordan and Larry Bird, fellow NBA player and Dream Team teammate, in a Super Bowl commercial entitled "The Showdown." The clip showed Jordan and Bird going back and forth in a game of horse, making shots in hopes of Bird winning Jordan's Big Mac but of course Jordan made every shot and yelled "nothing but net." This commercial is still considered to be one of the greatest Super Bowl commercials of all time.

A third big endorsement deal for Jordan came with Wheaties. Since 1924, the Minneapolis-based cereal company produced ready-to-eat, whole-grain flakes. Wheaties soon made its way into the sports world in 1933 with a simple ad in an old Minneapolis baseball field. Soon after "Wheaties—the Breakfast of Champions" was used to promote the brand and has gone on to embrace many of the greatest athletes of all time.[9] Because of his status within the NBA, Jordan was sought after, and in 1988, he became a brand spokesperson. Being a Wheaties spokesperson is significant, as only a total of six people have been chosen for the position, each representing the best of the best in their sport, never-ending leadership in charitable causes, and the time and effort put into helping America's youth.[10] Wheaties paid up to $3 million a year to Jordan during his time as a spokesperson.

Gatorade, McDonald's, and Wheaties account for only a few other brands Jordan has had the privilege of representing and endorsing. In addition, Oakley sunglasses, Wilson sporting goods, Rayovac batteries, and, in a more recent revamp, Hanes, have struck deals with Jordan to represent their brand. With Hanes, it can be said Jordan's brand has taken a more refined approach to endorsements. Although he has represented Hanes since 1989, his Hanes advertisements today seem to focus and highlight his impact on the older generation. Today, the Hanes "Bacon Neck" commercials feature him interacting with older actors who remember him from when they were a child. This change in tone emphasizes his new role as endorser that being to the audience that originally watched him play as a new and young NBA star. Tapping into this audience seems to be a strategy employed, allowing Jordan to remain visible to the advertising world and to target a different demographic that might be left out view from other endorsement deals.

Jordan's name and brand was even used within television and film with the debut of *Space Jam* in 1996. The film featured Jordan and a handful of other NBA stars who played against the MONstars to get back their talent. Jordan plays alongside the Looney Tunes characters in hopes of beating the MONstars. His reach extended beyond the food and beverage industry as he capitalized on his star status during his time in the NBA.

The Downside to New Releases

As Jordan's popularity grew, the need to own a pair of Air Jordan shoes created tension in some areas. Never before had an athlete's product caused violence as a result of fans attempting to purchase a pair of shoes. In the early 1990s, violence erupted at many stores as fans were injured, all in hopes of owning their own pair of their favorite player's shoes. It must be acknowledged that such violence was not the intended outcome of Nike or Jordan himself when releasing a new shoe. However, many shoes were released in urban areas with a lack of security and crowd control to prohibit such events.

Many critics argue the reason for such violence is in direct correlation to the high demand and low supply of the shoe. As hundreds of people wait in line for a single pair of shoes, store managers know they do not have enough for everyone. This, in turn, results in a mad dash to get the desired shoe at all costs. The probability of getting a pair of shoes is low, yet malls and stores have yet to find a way to inform customers of their supply. If stores found a way to let customers know inventory status, they might decrease the level of violence. This move would keep such violence from tarnishing both Nike's and Jordan's images.

In addition to the supply and demand, the cost is up for discussion. Depending on the number, most Air Jordan's range from $100 to $200 a pair. The high price for a single shoe is hard to comprehend, especially since so many young people are eager to wear the latest release. It becomes a matter of importance and whether or not owning every pair of Air Jordan's is beneficial in the long run. Ironically, fans continue to spend the money, disregarding the potential violence and financial loss as a result of purchasing a pair of shoes.

Jordan as the Blueprint

Jordan paved the way for future athletes to be used as high-profile endorsers for various brands and companies. Before him, no other athlete had been used in such a way to represent a brand. In 1998, *Fortune* magazine estimated that Jordan had generated more than $10 billion during his spectacular professional career in terms of increase in tickets sold, television advertising revenue, increased profits of products Jordan endorsed, basketball merchandising exploiting Jordan's figure, and his own films, businesses, and product lines.[11] At the time, such a large amount of money was unprecedented. To top it off, the amount of money he was paid in order to endorse all of the brands is what makes his rise as an advertising icon such an important factor in our understanding of athletic endorsement deals today.

With Jordan at the forefront of athletic advertising and endorsements, his road to success proves to be valuable. Before Jordan, other brands were in fact using and looking to continue their relationship with top athletes as a way to promote their product. The difference with Nike and Jordan lies within the athlete, so much so that in 1997, Jordan announced he was creating his own exclusive line of clothing. The brand, aptly labeled Jordan Brand, lacked the infamous Nike swoosh and "Just Do It" slogan. This created his own line of athletic clothing and shoes separate from the large brand that is Nike. It was projected the brand stood to gross $250 million in its first year. This number has been surpassed.

Since 1997, other top athletes have impacted their respective sport similar to that of Jordan. For example, Michael Vick, Derek Jeter, Terrell Owens, and Chris Paul have all endorsed and been a part of Jordan Brand since its launch. Although some are considered veterans in their sport, Jordan has used this to his benefit to leverage their existing fans in hopes of drawing them to his brand.

More recently, fresh and new athletes are being used in more innovative ways than ever before to push the brand and boundaries forward. For example, Miami Heat player Dwyane Wade and New York Knicks star Carmelo Anthony have each garnered their own shoe under the Jordan Brand. Both players even have their own clothing with individual logos representing their player persona. A new wave of basketball fans are eager to own the same shoes their favorite player wears on the court.

The key factor that should be taken away from Jordan as an advertising icon is the way in which athletes are being used today. LeBron James, Kevin Durant, and Kobe Bryant are three top players currently in the NBA. Their impact not only on the court but off the court is similar to that of Jordan during his career. Fans adore each player and are willing to support them by wearing what they wear. James, Durant, and Bryant each have their own brand within Nike. More recently, Kobe was given his own line of Nike products, the Kobe System, geared toward basketball and products intended to improve performance.

In 2003, LeBron James signed a seven-year, $93 million deal with Nike geared toward athletic apparel and shoes.[12] Since then another deal has been signed. In 2011, his shoe was the number-one basketball shoe on the market. Granted, teens are not waiting in line to purchase his shoe but his status is one to be reckoned with. In addition to Nike, LeBron has several other deals with companies such as McDonald's, Coca-Cola, State Farm, Upper Deck, and watch company Audemars Piguet. Each deal will allow the star to gross millions of dollars as he is deemed "the King." His popularity and skills are comparable to that of Jordan where both players are able to capitalize on their presence to increase their salary via endorsement deals like never before.

In addition to up-and-coming basketball players, other sports have found themselves giving way to outstanding athletes. For example, Serena

Williams has her own line of women's tennis clothing and equipment through Nike. She too has scored an endorsement deal with McDonald's along with Puma, and she has even extended her worth by becoming a part owner of the Miami Dolphins football team. Williams took the tennis world by storm and has not stopped as she continues to win countless titles. Her situation is slightly different as she has faced some hardships on her journey. It took time some time before being fully accepted as a top African American female tennis player, but once her skills superseded her race, she was unable to be stopped and has become a top earning female tennis player.

Along with Williams, Tiger Woods must be mentioned as a top athlete receiving endorsement deals. Although he faced trouble during his personal life resulting in several companies dropping him as an endorser, Woods continues to be another highly paid athlete based on endorsements. He, too, has products in his name through Nike Golf tapping into a younger generation and the African American community. EA Sports, NetJets, Tag Heuer, and Upper Deck stood by him during his crisis.

Baseball is a large sport industry in itself. Some of the top-paid athletes in the world play baseball including Derek Jeter for the New York Yankees. In 2006, *Forbes* magazine named Jeter the second-highest paid endorser in baseball, thanks to deals with Ford, Gatorade, Nike, Fleet Bank, and Visa.[13] His deals are some of the largest in baseball history, encouraging other brands to tap into other baseball players for additional endorsement ideas.

Jordan Today

Jordan's NBA career is a storied one, filled with triumphs and memorable moments. It must be noted over the course of his career, Jordan retired and reactivated his eligibility with the league on two separate occasions. On October 6, 1993, Jordan retired from the Chicago Bulls. During his retirement, Jordan played for the Birmingham Barons, the Chicago White Sox minor-league baseball team. His short-lived baseball career left him with a decent record consisting of three home runs and 46 runs scored. On March 18, 1995, Jordan returned to the Bulls and, in 1996, led the team in yet another championship winning season. In January 1999, he retired from the Bulls again, marking his last time ever playing for the franchise. Two years later, Jordan found himself on the Washington Wizards roster and played for the Wizards over the next two seasons. His presence on the team sold out games and brought a renewed sense of excitement from fans to the team. Ironically, his final retirement was the result of him being unable to transition and take full responsibility as owner of the team. This miscommunication left Jordan feeling used, ending his NBA playing career for the final time in 2003.

After two reactivations and a final end to his career, Jordan is still connected to the NBA. Most recently, Jordan became the first former player to become full owner of an NBA team. In 2010, he paid $275 million to purchase the Charlotte Bobcats.[14] In 2012, the Bobcats ended with the worst NBA season record in history. Although the team struggled during the season, Jordan has taken it upon himself to put forth necessary efforts in order for the team to move forward in upcoming seasons.

The ability to sell the latest shoe or beverage is easy when one is at the top of their game. Jordan played upon this notion, but he has also used his brand to give back to the community post NBA playing career. In 2001, the First Annual Michael Jordan Celebrity Invitational (MJCI) was held.[15] The MJCI is a golf outing event that seeks to raise money for select foundations and charities each year. Since its inception, MCJI has raised over $6 million for charity. Jordan utilizes his sport and entertainment connections to get top names to attend and participate in the outing each year. The 2011 beneficiaries included the James R. Jordan Foundation, the Make-A-Wish Foundation, the Nevada Cancer Institute, and Cats Care. A portion of the funds raised go toward each charity to help their individual cause.

Cats Care is Jordan's latest venture in hopes of giving back. As owner of the Bobcats, he realized the decision made by the previous owner to cut the community relations department hurt the team and fan morale. With Cats Care, players, coaches, and Jordan himself will travel to food pantries and soup kitchens to feed the homeless and hungry. In addition, a refrigerated Second Harvest Food Bank truck will be used as a mobile pantry for the poor in largely rural areas.[16] This act alone shows his determination not only to get the team back on track, but to help the surrounding community in need. NBA teams that put forth an effort to give back to the community represent a sense of pride and concern for the city while increasing the chance for future fan support.

Conclusion

Today, Jordan is a global legend and icon. It is almost impossible to flash his jumpman logo without some sort of reference to the man and the brand he created. From a young boy in North Carolina struggling to make his high school basketball team to a leading NBA player, Jordan's career has paved the way for future athletes in more ways than one.

Over the years critics, have found ways to criticize his life and actions. However, his image remains untarnished. Granted, Jordan has made business moves some believe to be out of the ordinary, but his impact on the world of athletic endorsements and advertising cannot be denied. Because of his status and impact on the game, his name continues to be used as a historical benchmark for young basketball stars on their journey to the top. Coaches and fans cannot help but use and reference his impressive resume. The only difference today is a little more explanation and maybe clips for added support might be used, as today's youngest generation is not as familiar with one of the greatest NBA players of all time.

Still, to this day, on any given release date, no matter the weather, price, location or potential for violence, "sneakerheads" alike wait in line for hours at a time anticipating their chance to purchase yet another pair of the coveted Air Jordan shoe. The number 23 has become synonymous with one single basketball player as the original NBA star. His efforts to give back to the community highlight his transition from NBA star to strategic businessman. A former force to be reckoned with on the hardwood alongside his captivating personality, Jordan continues to be viewed as the blueprint for future professional athlete advertising and endorsements.

Notes

1. "NBA Encyclopedia Playoff Edition," NBA.com, 2012. http://www.nba.com/history/players/jordan_bio.html.

2. Ibid.

3. Walter LaFeber, *Michael Jordan and the New Global Capitalism* (New York, NY: W.W. Norton & Company, 1999), 59.

4. Aaron Frisch, *The Story of Nike* (North Mankato, MN: Smart Apple Media, 2004), 24.

5. LaFeber, *Michael Jordan and the New Global Capitalism*, 59.

6. Frisch, *Story of Nike*, 24.

7. LaFeber, *Michael Jordan and the New Global Capitalism*, 65.

8. Ibid., 117–18.

9. "A Rather Humble Beginning," Wheaties.com, 2010, http://www.wheaties.com/pdf/wheaties_history.pdf (URL defunct).

10. Ibid., 6.

11. David L. Andrews, ed., *Michael Jordan, Inc.: Corporate Sport, Media Culture, and Late Modern America* (Albany: State University of New York Press, 2001), 44.

12. "LeBron Leads NBA's Endorsement All-Stars," Yahoo! Sports, 2011, http://sports.yahoo.com/nba/news?slug=ys-forbes-lebron_tops_nba_endorsements_060611.

13. "Top Athletes and Their Endorsements," CNBC.com, 2011. http://www.cnbc.com/id/43398070/page/1.

14. Viv Bernstein, "Jordan Has the Bobcats; Now It's Rebuilding Time," *New York Times*, March 18, 2010.

15. "The Michael Jordan Celebrity Invitational," mjcigolf.com, 2012, http://www.mjcigolf.com/general-info/default.aspx.

16. Mark Price, "Michael Jordan Seeks to Restore Charlotte Bobcats' Image," *Charlotte Observer*, February 18, 2012.

Bibliography

Andrews, David L., ed. *Michael Jordan, Inc.: Corporate Sport, Media Culture, and Late Modern America*. Albany: State University of New York Press, 2001.

Bernstein, Viv. "Jordan Has the Bobcats; Now It's Rebuilding Time." *New York Times*, March 18, 2010.

Frisch, Aaron. *The Story of Nike*. North Mankato, MN: Smart Apple Media, 2004.

LaFeber, Walter. *Michael Jordan and the New Global Capitalism*. New York: W. W. Norton & Company, 1999.

"LeBron Leads NBA's Endorsement All-Stars." Yahoo! Sports. 2011. http://sports.yahoo.com/nba/news?slug=ys-forbes-lebron_tops_nba_endorsements_060611.

"The Michael Jordan Celebrity Invitational." mjcigolf.com, 2012. http://www.mjcigolf.com/general-info/default.aspx.

"NBA Encyclopedia Playoff Edition." NBA.com, 2012. http://www.nba.com/history/players/jordan_bio.html.

Price, Mark. "Michael Jordan Seeks to Restore Charlotte Bobcats' Image." *Charlotte Observer*, February 18, 2012.

"A Rather Humble Beginning." Wheaties.com, 2010. http://www.wheaties.com/pdf/wheaties_history.pdf.

"Top Athletes and Their Endorsements." CNBC.com, 2011. http://www.cnbc.com/id/43398070/page/1.

CHAPTER TWENTY

Voter Disdain: Twenty-First-Century Trends in Political Advertising*

Michelle A. Amazeen

In 2004, nearly two out of three people contended that political advertising neither provided new information about presidential candidates nor was useful in contributing to their voting decisions.[1] More recently, in 2007, nearly three out of four people found political ads to be more confusing than helpful.[2] In the same survey of nearly 1,000 U.S. adults, one in three felt they could "hardly ever" trust what political candidates said in their ads, while just over half felt they could only "some of the time."[3] Yet in spite of the perceived uselessness of political advertising among the general public, as a proportion of the gross domestic product, increasingly more money is being spent on political campaigning.[4] During the 2008 presidential election, roughly $2.1 billion was spent on television ads by the candidates, political parties, and interest groups.[5] Television ad spending on just the broadcast networks for the 2012 presidential election was forecast to reach $2.8 billion.[6] Moreover, despite what people say in political polls, research has demonstrated that political ads can, indeed, influence the outcome of an election.[7] Alas, political advertising is here to stay regardless of the public's disdain for it. If "we are what we sell," it should not be any wonder why the public holds in contempt advertising that is unhelpful, is unbelievable, and serves the interests of voters minimally, if at all.

*The author would like to thank Michael Maynard for inspiring this article. Janet Byrne and Steve Haeckel also deserve thanks for their helpful comments on previous drafts of this chapter.

While considering the beleaguered voter, this chapter contemplates how political advertising trends are shaping American political life now and how they will continue to do so in the years to come.[8] The first trend considered is the shift in share of political voice that has occurred following campaign finance reform efforts. Whereas it was once candidate-sponsored ads which predominated in political advertising, that dynamic is changing. Aided by the *Citizens United* case, interest groups have been furthering their causes through increased political advertising. The ad strategies employed by these groups, together with those of other political actors, have played to the worst instincts of an evolving news media environment. Also to be explored is the inclination of an increasingly fragmented, polarized media to replay the most controversial, attack-oriented ads as part of their programming content to drive viewership. This phenomenon of ad amplification provides political advertisers with free air play while providing journalistic legitimization of their messages. The democratically unhealthy symbiosis between political advertisers and for-profit journalism perpetuates another trend to be addressed: negative advertising. As the share of political ad voice shifts in favor of independent groups, observers predict increasingly more negativity. Drawn to negativity, the mainstream news media are neglecting their historically important role of playing watchdog for the benefit of an informed electorate. As a result, inaccurate political claims proliferate, and citizens are disillusioned with the political process. Hope for improvement lies in an emerging trend toward independent fact-checking of ads. But if the trend in negative, factually suspect advertising cannot be reversed, society will increasingly suffer from a polarized, ill-informed discourse, disproportionately influenced by the interests of a wealthy minority.

Shift in Share of Voice

The most recent significant change in the political advertising landscape has come from the U.S. Supreme Court ruling in the *Citizens United* case.[9] In 2010, the court ruled in favor of allowing unlimited spending on political advertising by corporations and unions, thus effectively giving these entities the same political speech freedoms afforded to individuals.[10] As a result, more ads than ever before are originating not from candidates or political parties, but from outside interests.[11] This change has been addressed in the political science work of Christopher Hull, who observed that the share of political ad voice tends to follow deregulation.[12] Moreover, according to Dave Levinthal of the Center for Responsive Politics, ad funding from these outside interest groups had a determinative effect on the 2010 midterm elections. Also troubling is that many of these groups do not disclose the source(s) of their funding, so it is impossible for voters to determine the individual identities of who is influencing U.S. political elections. Candidates have increasingly become the target of attack advertising subsidized by organizations whose leaders (or donors) are unknown to the general public and thus cannot be held accountable. Increased interest-group spending may also signal a rise in the dubiousness of ad claims. Darrell West of the Brookings Institution has observed that questionable claims typically come from political groups independent of candidates.[13]

Another concern about the *Citizens United* ruling is that candidates become indebted to organizations that fund their campaigns rather than to the voters who elect them. Political scientist Thomas Ferguson offered an investment theory of party competition, which suggests that American politics has little to do with voter behavior because what really matters are the major investors in political campaigns.[14] Ferguson argued that voters generally do not or are not able to consider the substantive matters of legislative policies or their consequences. From Ferguson's perspective, politics is dominated by large investors who coalesce around the candidate best advancing their interests. "Blocs of major investors," he explained, "define the core of political parties and are responsible for most of the signals the party sends to the electorate."[15] In essence, money drives politics through the media attention, major endorsements, and the subsequent investors that it attracts. The *Citizens United* ruling has now legitimized this practice. Americans can expect increasing influence from organizations on both the political ads themselves and on the political narratives in the media.

Increase of Ad Amplification

Another trend shaping American political life is the growing phenomenon of ad amplification. Ad amplification is a term applied by political scientists Travis Ridout and Glen Smith to refer to unpaid media coverage of a political ad.[16] This phenomenon can be traced to Lyndon Johnson's "Daisy ad" from the 1964 presidential campaign. Even though the controversial spot aired only once as a paid ad, it was repeatedly rebroadcast in the news media, assuring it a wide audience.[17] Unpaid media coverage of political ads has become quite substantial and tends to focus on the more controversial comparative and attack-type ads.[18] The theoretical implication of ad amplification is a "political attack syndrome" akin to the "mean world syndrome" drawn from communication scholar George Gerbner's studies of television violence.[19] Rather than perceiving the world as more dangerous, negative political ads amplified in the news media cultivate voters to perceive political campaigning as more negative than it is in reality.[20] Thus, voter disdain is, in some respects, a result of frequent media focus on negativity.

Beyond simple ad amplification, by 2008, manipulation of news coverage was a common goal of political advertisers.[21] In scholarly terms, this is referred to as agenda building.[22] For example, political consultants serving both major campaigns during the 2008 presidential election freely noted the strategy of providing political ads to the media in order to influence news coverage. In reflecting upon the 2008 election, campaign strategists described the use of the press for the purposes of politics as "masterful."[23] Political consultants contended that their efforts to influence the news cycle were necessitated by the press' lack of focus on substantive campaign issues. For instance, Nicole Wallace, a senior advisor for the McCain campaign, stated, "In this campaign, people in the battleground states had a conversation for 15 months about how crappy the economy was. [By contrast] the national media only talked about it for the last six weeks."[24] A similar sentiment was expressed by Anita Dunn, chief communications officer for the Obama campaign. She argued that the ads they were running for voters "weren't covered because [the press did not consider them] interesting enough." Instead, the campaign provided their "idiotic press ads."[25] Ads were produced to drive news. "Print [interviews] does not drive news," explained Dunn. "Internet drives cable; cable drives networks. If you want a story in the *Post* or the *Times* to drive news, you have to consciously make it a news driver. *You produce an ad.*"[26]

The practice of announcing political ads to the media has become common in presidential campaigning, a notion referred to varyingly as "press ads," "phantom ads," or "vapor ads."[27] The purpose of these press ads is to achieve the free media coverage offered by ad amplification.[28] Political scientist Shanto Iyengar has noted that this well-established strategy involves political ads that may have aired only minimally in a small market or may never have aired at all (thus explaining the "phantom" and "vapor" labels).[29] The more controversial ads, he explained, can draw thousands of front-page news stories without the creators of the ads ever paying a dime in media costs.

The desirability of unpaid media coverage has an inverse correspondence with the low credibility of political advertising as evidenced in the introduction of this chapter. According to Gallup's annual professional honesty and ethics poll, people consistently rate advertising practitioners significantly lower than television and newspaper reporters.[30] It is this low credibility of advertising that necessitates media legitimation. West explained, "[t]he most effective [political] ads are those whose basic message is reinforced by the news media."[31] The attempts at political ad legitimation have their roots in the broader category of product and service advertising. As marketing experts Al Ries and his daughter Laura Ries have written, "Publicity provides the credentials that create credibility in the advertising."[32] Marketer

Sergio Zyman and coauthor Armin Brott have also noted that consumers are skeptical of advertising. "[B]ut when a piece of information is put out there by a supposedly neutral third party," they explained, "people are a lot more likely to believe it."[33] Thus, as the media environment becomes increasingly cluttered with commercial messages, journalistic attention lends credibility and legitimation to an ad message.

At the same time that commercial messages attempt to infiltrate programming and news content, the line between advertising and programming has blurred. Because of the predominant commercially supported media structure in the United States, ethical concerns about the ability of advertisers to exercise control over noneditorial programming content have arisen.[34] For example, it has been empirically demonstrated that magazines, particularly those targeting women, were significantly less likely to include articles about the dangers of smoking if they were reliant upon advertising revenues from cigarette manufacturers.[35] In similar fashion, political ads are being used to drive news content while offering lucrative revenue to television stations. Rather than investigating whether claims in the political ads are true, much of the attention given to political advertising by the news media falls within a game schema framework: exploring the campaign strategies behind the ads to explain which candidate is leading the race and which is falling behind.[36] Given all the staffing and resource cutbacks newsrooms have endured over the last decade, it is not that surprising that many journalists gravitate toward this readily available information subsidy with little consideration for its validity. Fact-checking ad claims is time-consuming and expensive and can anger staunchly partisan news consumers (when their candidate is criticized).[37] Fact-checking political ads also runs the risk of broadcasters losing a lucrative advertiser by metaphorically biting the hand that feeds them. An even greater risk is the liability to which broadcasters would expose themselves by pointing out false and misleading political ad claims, particularly as ads are increasingly originating from outside interest groups. If broadcasters continue to air inaccurate interest group ads after debunking the claims, stations may jeopardize their broadcast license with the Federal Communications Commission.[38] Thus, it is in the interests of broadcasters to use political ads to illustrate strategy-driven stories rather than examine whether the claims stand up to scrutiny.

Increasing Political Polarization

Another trend affecting the future of political advertising is the increase in partisanship and return to party-centric media. Since the mid-1970s,

Americans have become more partisan on matters of economics, civil rights, and moral issues.[39] The most recent data from the Pew Research Center confirm that as of 2012, there is a widening partisan divide in the political values shaping the public's fundamental beliefs.[40] Furthermore, the fragmentation of media audiences into specialized vehicles coupled with deregulation (such as abandoning the Fairness Doctrine) has facilitated the reemergence of partisan media vehicles.[41] Joining the opinion pages of the *Wall Street Journal* on the conservative side, programming such as Fox News has emerged along with talk shows hosted by Rush Limbaugh and Bill O'Reilly. Joining the *New York Times'* opinion pages on the Left are Air America, Rachel Maddow, and Keith Olbermann. Partisan media have arguably taken on the voter mobilization efforts once undertaken by the political parties. As scholars have noted, this is particularly true within the conservative opinion media establishment.[42]

The evolution of traditional television advertising has corresponded with media fragmentation. Where advertising was once perceived as 60- and, later, 30-second broadcast commercials separating programming content, today advertising is increasingly being integrated into the programming content. For some children's shows, advertisements have become the content (e.g., Transformers and Strawberry Shortcake).[43] The new reality in the practice of advertising is that advertising is more than 30-second commercials. It is any type of communicative message about a product or service.[44] While certain practitioners have attempted to deliberately delineate the domain of advertising narrowly, these limited definitions are often driven by a vested interest in protecting a marketing business that may specialize in a competing form of communication practice such as public relations.[45] Rather than proclaiming the death of advertising or conflating the discipline of advertising with technological platforms and delivery systems,[46] practitioners of the future are well advised to recognize what Zyman and Brott have written: Everything communicates. Everything is advertising.[47]

A similar progression can be argued in the rebirth of partisan media—in a world where program content has been commercialized, the infiltration of media vehicles by political ideology seems a natural extension. At its core, ideology is a philosophy about the important values in life and how the world ought to operate to maintain these ideals. Partisan media can be considered a guerrilla marketing approach in pursuit of building an agenda that makes a particular ideology seem commonsensical.[48] The future of political advertising will rely in part on effectively coordinating a strategic message across multimedia platforms while recognizing how to generate new media vehicles and take advantage of existing ones that are ideologically compatible. The danger, of course, is that compartmentalized sources of information may selectively present information that best serves an ideological cause. This in turn leads to distorted pictures of reality.[49] To the degree that partisan media conflict with an accurately informed electorate, until serious attention is given to promoting media that serve the public interest rather than political ideology, news and entertainment programming of the future will continue to cater to partisan interests.

A Landscape of Negative Political Advertising

The future of political advertising will also continue to include negativity. As polarization increases, it is likely that negative advertising will become even more prevalent. In his widely cited work on negative advertising, political scientist John Geer explained that increasing polarization means more areas of policy on which opponents disagree, creating more incentives to attack one another.[50] Defining negativity as "any criticism leveled by one candidate against another during a campaign," Geer tracked the prevalence of negative political ad claims between the 1960 and 2004 presidential elections and found evidence that negativity is on the rise.[51] Geer's research, however, looked only at candidate-produced ads. As the share of political ad voice shifts in favor of independent groups, observers predict increasingly greater negativity. Evidence from the 2008 election indicated that, indeed, independent groups were more likely to run attack ads than were the candidates.[52] The use of negative ads by independent groups was more pronounced in the 2012 presidential election.[53] Despite increasing negativity, however, Geer, among others, argued that criticisms of negative advertising have been overstated. In spite of their pessimistic tone, they argue, negative ads tend to offer more substantive policy content than positive ads.[54]

Many political observers use the term "negative" broadly to include varying degrees and types of attacks on an opponent. Some scholars have emphasized the importance of distinguishing between the types of attacks (whether an ad is exclusively attack-oriented versus offering a contrast between candidates) and whether or not attacks are accurate.[55] While Geer claimed that negative ads were more likely than positive ads to offer supporting evidence, it is problematic that he did not consider the accuracy of the evidence provided.[56] The emergence of independent fact-checking organizations such as FactCheck.org and PolitiFact.com now facilitates this effort. They represent neutral sources that have repeatedly confirmed that just because an ad offers evidence does not make the evidence true.[57] My own research offers empirical support that, among ads evaluated by fact-checkers during the 2008 presidential election, inaccurate claims were more likely to be contained in attack ads than in contrast or advocacy-type political ads.[58] Thus, while more substantive information is useful to the electorate, its utility only goes so far as its accuracy.

While negative campaigning has always been present in American politics, Geer argued that concerns about negative campaigning have been primarily driven by an increase in media attention to this phenomenon. Within the media coverage of candidates since 1960, a similar increase in negativity was noted by political scientist Thomas Patterson. And as negative media coverage has increased, so too have voter perceptions of candidates become increasingly negative.[59] Patterson explained that the political process became more reliant on the media in the wake of the McGovern-Fraser reforms following the 1968 presidential election.[60] As a result, wrote Patterson, "No candidate can succeed without the press. The road to nomination now runs through the newsrooms."[61] Thus, beyond the watchdog role of the press holding politicians accountable, the press was additionally tasked with the responsibility of informing voters to guide their nominating decisions. This new journalistic responsibility corresponded with a rise in what has been variously referred to as "game-schema," "horse-race," or "strategy-schema" reporting—interpreting who is leading, who is losing, and why.[62]

In essence, it is a combination of political pressures and marketplace pressures that has driven the prevalence of both horse-race reporting and negative advertisements. With less of a concern about offending partisans due to the fragmentation of media, neutral reporting seems to be waning. For its part, negative advertising can be argued as benefiting media owners in that journalism thrives on controversy.[63] It is, after all, the negative political ads that tend to draw coverage from the news media, a phenomenon with which political operatives are quite familiar.[64] As insinuated by the journalistic axiom "if it bleeds, it leads," controversy and sensationalism increase news viewership, which is reflected in higher ratings. With higher ratings, broadcasters can charge higher price points for advertising airtime. Even though political candidates are supposed to be charged the lowest advertising rate for a particular time of day, political interest groups and other industry advertisers will be charged the higher rate achieved with higher audience ratings. Thus, unless there is a change in the commercial structure of U.S. media, negative political advertising will continue to proliferate and influence how Americans perceive politics. Political practitioners get the free airtime they desire with negative advertising and journalists have provocative, readily available footage to fill airtime despite staff cutbacks in newsrooms across the United States.

Increasing Self-Regulation

In spite of growing concerns about the accuracy of political ad claims given the increased participation by interest groups, little in the way of governmental regulation is expected. It is unlikely even in cases of false political claims. As Day has explained, "false political speech is fully protected under the First Amendment as long as it is done without 'actual malice,' as defined in the *Sullivan* decision."[65] Actual malice would include being able to demonstrate that an ad claim was factually false as well as demonstrating a willful disregard of its falsity by the other candidate. Furthermore, even if broadcasters could be held responsible for libelous claims in the candidate ads they air, the principle of libel is not a particularly useful solution. Libel is an after-the-fact remedy rather than something that can be used to prohibit speech. Moreover, libel laws offer damage resolutions in terms of financial compensation, which does nothing to address an election loss resulting from disinformation.

Despite little oversight and enforcement of inaccurate political advertising content by governmental agencies such as the FCC, self-regulatory efforts have been expanding. One such effort includes the use of satire to hold media accountable. Painter and Hodges have noted a long line of press parodies, including Jonathan Swift's *A Modest Proposal* (1729), David Frost's television show *That Was the Week That Was* (1964–1965), *Saturday Night Live's* "Weekend Update" segment (1975–), the parody news organization the *Onion* (1988–), and television shows *Murphy Brown* (1988–1998), *The Daily Show* (1996–) and *The Colbert Report* (2005–).[66] Using *The Daily Show with Jon Stewart* as a case study, Painter and Hodges argued that Stewart holds broadcast media accountable by pointing out falsehoods, inconsistencies, and absurdities as well as satirizing the essence of broadcast news.

Another self-regulatory effort involves the political adwatching movement. Scrutiny of political advertising gained prominence during the 1992 presidential election.[67] Prompted by the notoriously deceptive attack ads from the previous presidential election of 1988, political adwatches were implemented by both broadcast and print reporters to police the ads for accuracy and fairness.[68] Adwatches were primarily designed to reduce the overall influence of inaccurate ads, promote the self-discipline of political ad creators, and enable corrective information to be disseminated to voters.[69] Despite the aspirations of adwatches, however, there have been questions about their effectiveness.[70] Nonetheless, some of the adwatchers remain steadfast that their efforts may have prevented the spread of political disinformation from being worse than it is currently.[71] While adwatching hit a low point during coverage of the 2000 presidential election, it has since been on the rebound particularly with the emergence of the online fact-checking organizations.[72]

Both PolitiFact.com and FactCheck.org are Web-based media vehicles that investigate the accuracy of claims made by U.S. political officials or candidates including those contained in political ads. Founded in 2003, FactCheck.org is affiliated with the nonprofit Annenberg Public Policy Center. It positions itself as a "consumer advocate" with a goal of reducing the amount of deception and confusion in U.S. politics.[73] PolitiFact was launched in August 2007 as an undertaking of the *St. Petersburg Times* to help readers "find the truth in politics."[74] In 2009, PolitiFact was awarded a Pulitzer Prize for National Reporting for its coverage of the 2008 U.S. presidential election.[75] In 2010, PolitiFact began to partner with newspapers in specific states, the first being the *Miami Herald*.[76] Since then, it has partnered with newspapers in seven additional states including Georgia, Ohio, Oregon, Rhode Island, Texas, Virginia, and Wisconsin. Thus, political adwatching does seem to be gaining momentum.

Other political observers advocate that it is time to revisit the idea of a national press council as a way of balancing freedom with responsibility.[77] Previous industry self-regulatory efforts went largely ignored by the press barons. Painter and Hodges contended that the 1947 Hutchins Commission's report suggesting an "independent agency to appraise and report upon the performance of the press" was disregarded, as was support for the National News Council, which operated between 1973 and 1984.[78] However, Painter and Hodges argued that the success of *The Daily Show* suggests that collaboration is possible. "There are forms of press criticism," they wrote, "that can hold the press accountable to the public while remaining acceptable to the press."[79] The collaborative inroads being made by PolitiFact.com with newspapers around the country further supports this notion.

Conclusion

As with product advertising, a significant challenge facing the practice of political advertising continues to be cultivating its credibility. With the new voices of corporate and union participants entering the political discourse aimed at persuading voters, efforts to legitimize the ad messages are proliferating. Whether it is tactics to achieve ad amplification or alignment with party-centric media, the increasing polarization of the United States suggests a political landscape filled with negativity. While there seems to be little in the way of institutional regulation that can effectively protect the public from false claims and distortions, self-monitoring efforts are under way. Despite the questionable state of commercial broadcasting and the general lack of watchdog adwatching, voters do have some respite from the proliferation of political disinformation: the adwatch organizations of FactCheck.org and PolitiFact.com. Yet overall we still seem to be selling the political process to moneyed interests that are increasingly influencing (if not taking over) the public's mass media systems in order to amplify their preferred messages. If we are what we sell, is it really any wonder why voters hold political advertising in such disdain?

To the degree that political advertising continues to be part of the media landscape, it needs to be held to the same accountability standards as programming content, particularly when it drives the news. This convergence of advertising with programming content—particularly news content—complicates the ethics and process of accountability. Can news media effectively perform its watchdog role while dependent upon advertiser revenues to sustain operations and while also dependent upon political newsworthiness to sustain audiences? To continue to disregard this paradox is a distortion of reality.

Even Theodore Levitt's defense of the morality of advertising was limited by "falsehoods ... purposeful duplicity, and scheming half-truths."[80] In comparing advertising to the same sort of distortions of reality offered by poetry and visual art, he concluded that "the issue is not the prevention of distortion. It is, in the end, to know what kinds of distortions we actually want."[81] To get beyond voter disdain, political falsehoods, duplicity and half-truths ought not to be in the future of political advertising. To truly serve the public interest, an undistorted look at the commercial support of U.S. news media is also in order.

Notes

1. CBS News, CBS News monthly poll #2, computer file, ICPSR version 4096 (New York: CBS News, Producer; Ann Arbor, MI: Inter-university Consortium for Political and Social Research, Distributor, May 2004).

2. CBS News, CBS News monthly poll, computer file, ICPSR version 23442 (New York: CBS News, Producer; Ann Arbor, MI: Inter-university Consortium for Political and Social Research, Distributor, April 2007).

3. Ibid.

4. Michelle Amazeen, "The Dole 'Godless Americans' Advert: Representations of the Unfaithful, Disloyal Villains," *Social Semiotics* 22 no. 3 (2012).

5. Bill Wheatley, "What Should TV Stations Do with All That Negative Ad Money?" Harvard's Nieman Watchdog Website, December 18, 2011, http://www.niemanwatchdog.org/index.cfm?fuseaction=background.view&background id=00597.

6. Marci Ryvicker, Daniel Bellehsen, Stephan Bisson, and Eric Katz, "SBGI and TVL: Best Positioned for 2012 Elections," *Broadcasting and Cable Equity Research* (New York: Wells Fargo Securities, January 5, 2012).

7. Ted Brader, *Campaigning for Hearts and Minds: How Emotional Appeals in Political Ads Work* (Chicago: University of Chicago Press, 2006); Greg A. Huber and Kevin Arceneaux, "Identifying the Persuasive Effects of Presidential Advertising," *American Journal of Political Science* 51 no. 4 (2007): 957–77; Richard Johnston, Michael G. Hagen, and Kathleen Hall Jamieson, *The 2000 Presidential Election and the Foundations of Party Politics* (New York: Cambridge University Press, 2004); Kate Kenski, Bruce W. Hardy, and Kathleen Hall Jamieson, *The Obama Victory: How Media, Money, and Messages Shaped the 2008 Election* (New York: Oxford University Press, 2010); Lynn Vavreck, *The Message Matters: The Economy and Presidential Campaigns* (Princeton, NJ: Princeton University Press, 2009).

8. Additional trends in political advertising are offered in Kenski et al., *Obama Victory*, particularly on early voting and microtargeting.

9. *Citizens United v. Federal Election Commission.* 558 U.S. 310 (2010).

10. Adam Liptak, "Justices, 5–4, Reject Corporate Spending Limit," *New York Times*, January 21, 2010, http://www.nytimes.com/2010/01/22/us/politics/22 scotus.html.

11. "Outside Spending," Center for Responsive Politics, http://www.open secrets.org/outsidespending/index.php (accessed March 20, 2011); Dave Levinthal, "Bad News for Incumbents, Self-Financing Candidates in Most Expensive Midterm Election in U.S. History," Center for Responsive Politics, November 4, 2010, http://www.opensecrets.org/news/2010/11/bad-night-for-incumbents-self-finan.html.

12. Christopher C. Hull, "Has Campaign Finance Reform Provoked Attack Ads? Modeling Candidate and Independent Group Negative Advertising" (paper presented at the 2007 Southern Political Science Association annual conference, January 4, 2007).

13. Darrell M. West, *Air Wars: Television Advertising in Election Campaigns, 1952–2008,* 5th ed. (Washington, DC: CQ Press, 2010).

14. Thomas Ferguson, *Golden Rule: The Investment Theory of Party Competition and the Logic of Money-Driven Political Systems* (Chicago: University of Chicago Press, 1995).

15. Ibid., 22.

16. Travis N. Ridout and Glen R. Smith, "Free Advertising: How the Media Amplify Campaign Messages," *Political Research Quarterly* 61, no. 4 (2008): 598–608.

17. Kathleen Hall Jamieson, *Dirty Politics: Deception, Distraction, and Democracy* (New York: Oxford University Press, 1992); Darrell M. West, "A Brief History of Political Advertising on Television," in *The Manship School Guide to Political Communication*, ed. David D. Perlmutter (Baton Rouge: Louisiana State University Press, 1999).

18. Erika Franklin Fowler and Travis N. Ridout, "Local Television and Newspaper Coverage of Political Advertising," *Political Communications* 26 (2009); Jamieson, *Dirty Politics*; Ridout and Smith, "Free Advertising."

19. George Gerbner et al., "The Demonstration of Power: Violence Profile no. 10," *Journal of Communication* 29, no. 3 (1979).

20. John G. Geer, *In Defense of Negativity: Attack Ads in Presidential Campaigns* (Chicago: University of Chicago Press, 2006); Jamieson, *Dirty Politics*; Ridout and Smith, "Free Advertising."

21. Kathleen Hall Jamieson, ed. *Electing the President 2008: The Insider's View* (Philadelphia: University of Pennsylvania Press, 2009). West, *Air Wars*.

22. Rita Colistra, "Shaping and Cutting the Media Agenda: Television Reporters' Perceptions of Agenda- and Frame-Building and Agenda-Cutting Influences," *Journalism and Communication Monographs* 14, no. 2 (Summer 2012).

23. Jamieson, *Electing the President*, 130.

24. Ibid., 145.

25. Ibid., 145.

26. Ibid., 141; emphasis added.

27. Jamieson, *Electing the President*, 130; West, *Air Wars*, 23.

28. Viveca Novak, "Context Included: Obama on Iran," FactCheck.org, August 27, 2008, http://www.factcheck.org/elections-2008/context_included_obama_on _iran.html (accessed July 27, 2009); Ridout and Smith, "Free Advertising."

29. Shanto Iyengar, "Election 2008: The Advertising," WashingtonPost.com, August 12, 2008, http://pcl.stanford.edu/press/2008/wp-2008advertising.pdf (accessed August 13, 2009).

30. "Honesty/Ethics in Professions," Gallup, 2010, http://www.gallup.com/ poll/1654/honesty-ethics-professions.aspx (accessed March 20, 2011).

31. West, "A Brief History," 27.

32. Al Ries and Laura Ries, *The Fall of Advertising and the Rise of PR* (New York: HarperCollins, 2002), xix.

33. Sergio Zyman and Armin Brott, *The End of Advertising as We Know It* (New York: John Wiley and Sons, 2002), 175.

34. Clifford G. Christians et al., *Media Ethics: Cases and Moral Reasoning*, 8th ed. (Boston: Pearson Education, Inc., 2009).

35. Ronald V. Bettig and Jeanne L. Hall, *Big Media, Big Money: Cultural Texts and Political Economy* (Lanham, MD: Rowman & Littlefield Publishers, 2003).

36. Jamieson, *Dirty Politics*; Thomas E. Patterson, *Out of Order* (New York: Vintage Books, 1994); Steven Waldman, *The Information Needs of Communities: The Changing Media Landscape in a Broadband Age* (Washington, DC: Federal Communications Commission, July 2011), 216, http://transition.fcc.gov/osp/inc-report/ The_Information_Needs_of_Communities.pdf. According to Waldman, a 2004 study cited by the FCC revealed that among over 4,000 local news broadcasts airing in the month before an election, only 8 percent even mentioned local races. When election coverage was provided, less than 1 percent of the stories critiqued the political ads that were inundating viewers.

37. Michelle A. Amazeen, "Blind Spots: Examining Political Advertising Inaccuracies and How U.S. News Media Hold Political Actors Accountable" (PhD diss., Temple University, 2012).

38. It is important to emphasize that *candidate*-produced ads receive broad constitutional protections and cannot be censored or otherwise altered by broadcasters even if claims are untrue. Ads produced by independent expenditure groups, however, do not enjoy these provisions and can be turned away by broadcasters if they contain inaccuracies. In fact, broadcasters are bound to provisions in the Communications Act of 1934. In exchange for their license, broadcasters must serve the public interest in part by taking care that the advertisements aired on their stations are not false or misleading. Amazeen, "Blind Spots."

39. Delia Baldassarri and Andrew Gelman, "Partisans without Constraint: Political Polarization and Trends in American Public Opinion," *American Journal of Sociology* 114, no. 2 (2008); Nolan McCarty, Keith T. Poole, and Howard Rosenthal, *Polarized America: The Dance of Ideology and Unequal Riches* (Boston: MIT Press, 2006), http://voteview.com/polarizedamerica.asp; Geer, *In Defense of Negativity.*

40. "Partisan Polarization Surges in Bush, Obama Years," Pew Research Center, June 4, 2012, http://www.people-press.org/2012/06/04/partisan-polarization-surges-in-bush-obama-years/.

41. Kathleen Hall Jamieson and Joseph N. Cappella, *Echo Chamber: Rush Limbaugh and the Conservative Media Establishment* (New York: Oxford University Press, 2010).

42. Ibid.

43. Susan Pearson, "Babes in the Marketplace: The Toy Industry Takes Over Saturday Morning Cartoons," *Multinational Monitor* 8, no. 9 (September 1987), http://www.multinationalmonitor.org/hyper/issues/1987/09/pearson.html.

44. Joe Cappo, *The Future of Advertising* (New York: McGraw Hill, 2003); Zyman and Brott, *End of Advertising.*

45. Ries and Ries, *Fall of Advertising.*

46. Roland T. Rust and Richard W. Oliver, "The Death of Advertising," *Journal of Advertising*, 23, no. 4 (1994).

47. Zyman and Brott, *End of Advertising.*

48. Most recently, Fox News aired what some have referred to as a four-minute anti-Obama attack ad. "Fox News Official Says Obama Video Was Unauthorized," *Wall Street Journal*, May 30, 2012, http://online.wsj.com/article/SB1000142 4052702303640104577437061876013318.html (accessed May 31, 2012). As reported in the *New York Times*, "The video had most of the hallmarks of a campaign attack ad, except that it was produced and paid for by a news network rather than a candidate or a political action committee." Brian Stelter, "Obama Video on Fox Is Criticized," *New York Times*, May 31, 2012, A16. For an example in the print media, see David Carr, "Newspaper as Business Pulpit," *New York Times*, June 11, 2012, B1.

49. Brooks Jackson and Kathleen Hall Jamieson, *UnSpun: Finding Facts in a World of Disinformation* (New York: Random House, 2007); Jamieson, *Echo Chamber.*

50. Geer, *In Defense of Negativity.*

51. Ibid., 23. Also see West, *Air Wars.*

52. Amazeen, "Blind Spots"; Erika Franklin Fowler, "Presidential Ads 70 Percent Negative in 2012, Up from 9 Percent in 2008," Wesleyan Media Project, May 2, 2012, http://mediaproject.wesleyan.edu/2012/05/02/jump-in-negativity/; Hull, "Has Campaign Finance Reform Provoked Attack Ads?"

53. Fowler, "Presidential Ads."

54. John G. Geer, "Assessing Attack Advertising: A Silver Lining," in *Campaign Reform*, ed. Larry M. Bartels and Lynn Vavreck (Ann Arbor: University of Michigan Press, 2000); Geer, *In Defense of Negativity*; Kathleen Hall Jamieson, *Everything You Think You Know About Politics . . . and Why You're Wrong* (New York: Basic Books, 2000); Michael Maynard, "Positively Negative: Arguments in Favor of Political Attack Ads" (paper presented at the Association for Education in Journalism and Mass Communications Annual Conference, Washington DC, August 9–12, 2007).

55. Jamieson, *Everything You Think You Know*; Kathleen Hall Jamieson, Paul Waldman, and Susan Sherr, "Eliminate the Negative? Categories of Analysis for Political Advertisements," in *Crowded Airwaves: Campaign Advertising in Elections*, ed. James A. Thurber, Candace J. Nelson, and David A. Dulio (Washington, DC: Brookings Institution, 2000).

56. At the time Geer wrote *In Defense of Negativity*, he felt it was too difficult to determine with any precision whether an ad was misleading calling such an effort a "murky task" (5) and "a very slippery slope" (49).

57. Research by Graves and Glaisyer has shown FactCheck.org and PolitiFact.com to be among the "elite" fact-checking organizations, drawing attention from centrists as well as from those on the left and right of the political ideology spectrum in relatively equal measures. Lucas Graves and Tom Glaisyer, "The Fact-Checking Universe in Spring 2012" (New America Foundation, February 2012), http://newamerica.net/sites/newamerica.net/files/policydocs/The_Fact -checking_Universe_in_2012.pdf.

58. Amazeen, "Blind Spots."

59. Patterson, *Out of Order*.

60. Because of the contentious Democratic Party nominating process in the 1968 election, the McGovern-Fraser reforms transferred nominating power from party insiders to voters. Patterson, *Out of Order*.

61. Ibid., 33.

62. Shanto Iyengar, Helmut Norpoth, and Kyu S. Hahn, "Consumer Demand for Election News: The Horserace Sells," *Journal of Politics* 66, no. 1 (2004); Jamieson, *Dirty Politics*; Patterson, *Out of Order*.

63. Patterson, *Out of Order*.

64. Fowler, "Local Television"; Jamieson, *Dirty Politics*.

65. Louis A. Day, "Political Advertising and the First Amendment," in *The Manship School Guide to Political Communication*, ed. David D. Perlmutter (Baton Rouge: Louisiana State University Press, 1999): 70–71; *New York Times Co. v. Sullivan*, 376 U.S. 254 (1964). This case was based upon a complaint by an elected city commissioner, L. B. Sullivan of Montgomery, Alabama. Sullivan claimed to have been libeled by statements in a full-page political ad carried in the *New York Times* on

March 29, 1960. While most allegations were deemed accurate, several were not true. John D. Zelezny, *Cases in Communications Law: Liberties, Restraints, and the Modern Media*, 6th ed. (Boston: Wadsworth Cengage Learning, 2011).

66. Chad Painter and Louis Hodges, "Mocking the News: How *The Daily Show with Jon Stewart* Holds Traditional Broadcast News Accountable," *Journal of Mass Media Ethics* 25 (2010).

67. Joseph N. Cappella and Kathleen Hall Jamieson, "Broadcast Adwatch Effects: A Field Experiment," *Communication Research* 21, no. 3 (1994); Michael Pfau and Allan Louden, "Effectiveness of Adwatch Formats in Deflecting Political Attack Ads," *Communication Research* 21, no. 3 (1994).

68. Cappella and Jamieson, "Broadcast Adwatch Effects," 343.

69. Pfau and Louden, "Effectiveness of Adwatch Formats," 326; Cappella and Jamieson, "Broadcast Adwatch Effects," 345; Jamieson et al., "Eliminate the Negative?"

70. While the experimental research of Cappella and Jamieson indicated that adwatches are effective at influencing attitudes about the fairness and importance of political commercials, what they do not do is facilitate accurate interpretation of political realities, particularly among less-educated audiences. In other words, adwatches can affect how voters interpret the ads themselves but do not effectively promote corrective learning or "political literacy." Cappella and Jamieson, "Broadcast Adwatch Effects," 359. Moreover, Pfau and Louden offered evidence of a "boomerang" effect whereby, under certain format conditions, voters exposed to an adwatch were actually more influenced by the ad than the critique of the ad. Pfau and Louden, "Effectiveness of Adwatch Formats," 326. Similarly, Simons, Stewart, and Harvey offered evidence that rhetorical criticism by commentators—akin to adwatches—is conditionally ineffective. Herbert W. Simons, Don J. Stewart, and David Harvey, "Effects of Network Treatments on Perceptions of a Political Campaign Film: Can Rhetorical Criticism Make a Difference?" *Communication Quarterly* 37 (1989). However, Jamieson and her colleagues maintain that when conducted properly, adwatches benefit citizens. See Kathleen Hall Jamieson, and Joseph N. Cappella, "Setting the Record Straight: Do Ad Watches Help or Hurt?" *International Journal of Press/Politics* 2, no. 1 (1997): 20–21; and Kathleen Hall Jamieson and Paul Waldman. "Watching the Adwatches," in *Campaign Reform*, ed. Larry M. Bartels and Lynn Vavreck (Ann Arbor, MI: University of Michigan Press, 2000), 106. Within the broader movement of fact-checking, Graves and Glaisyer conclude that the fact-checking is too new to generate conclusive evidence of its effectiveness. Graves and Glaisyer, "The Fact-Checking Universe," 18.

71. Kathleen Hall Jamieson, and Brooks Jackson, "Our Disinformed Electorate," FactCheck.org, December 12, 2008, http://www.factcheck.org/special reports/our_disinformed_electorate.html.

72. Justin Bank, "Newspaper Adwatch Stories: Coming Back Strong," Annenberg Public Policy Center, November 9, 2007, http://www.annenberg publicpolicycenter.org/downloads/political_communication/factcheck/20071109 _factcheckingjournalism/20071109_fcj_Newspaper_Report.pdf; Bob Papper, "TV Adwatch Stories: On the Rise," Annenberg Public Policy Center, November 9,

2007, http://www.annenbergpublicpolicycenter.org/downloads/political
_communication/factcheck/20071109_factcheckingjournalism/20071109
_fcj_TV_Survey_Report.pdf. Although see Graves, "The Fact-Checking Universe," 4, for less optimistic data on the growth of adwatching within the context of fact-checking more generally.

73. "About: Our Mission," FactCheck.org, http://www.factcheck.org/about/.

74. "About PolitiFact," PolitiFact.com, http://www.politifact.com/about/ (accessed March 24, 2010).

75. Bill Adair, "PolitiFact Wins Pulitzer" PolitiFact.com, April 20, 2009. http://www.politifact.com/truth-o-meter/article/2009/apr/20/politifact-wins-pulitzer/.

76. Aaron Sharockman, "PolitiFact Florida Turns 1!" PolitiFact.com, March 18, 2011, http://www.politifact.com/florida/article/2011/mar/18/politifact-florida-turns-1/ (accessed March 21, 2011).

77. Painter and Hodges, "Mocking the News."

78. Ibid., 265.

79. Ibid., 272.

80. Theodore Levitt, "The Morality (?) of Advertising," *Harvard Business Review*, July–August 1970, 85, 91.

81. Ibid., 92.

Bibliography

"About: Our Mission." FactCheck.org. http://www.factcheck.org/about/.

"About PolitiFact." PolitiFact.com. http://www.politifact.com/about/ (accessed March 24, 2010).

Adair, Bill. "PolitiFact wins Pulitzer." PolitiFact.com, April 20, 2009. http://www.politifact.com/truth-o-meter/article/2009/apr/20/politifact-wins-pulitzer/.

Amazeen, Michelle. "The Dole 'Godless Americans' Advert: Representations of the Unfaithful, Disloyal Villains." *Social Semiotics* 22, no. 3 (2012): 1–16.

Amazeen, Michelle A. "Blind Spots: Examining Political Advertising Inaccuracies and How U.S. News Media Hold Political Actors Accountable." Ph.D. diss., Temple University, 2012.

Ansolabehere, Stephen, and Shanto Iyengar. *Going Negative: How Attacks Shrink and Polarize the Electorate*. New York: Free Press, 1995.

Baldassarri, Delia, and Andrew Gelman. "Partisans without Constraint: Political Polarization and Trends in American Public Opinion." *American Journal of Sociology* 114, no. 2 (2008): 408–46.

Bank, Justin. "Newspaper Adwatch Stories: Coming Back Strong." Annenberg Public Policy Center, 2007. http://www.annenbergpublicpolicycenter.org/downloads/political_communication/factcheck/20071109_factcheckingjournalism/20071109_fcj_Newspaper_Report.pdf.

Bennett, W. Lance. "Inside the Profession: Objectivity and Political Authority." In *News: The Politics of Illusion*, 186–219. New York: Longman, 2006.

Bettig, Ronald V., and Jeanne L. Hall. *Big Media, Big Money: Cultural Texts and Political Economy.* Lanham, MD: Rowman & Littlefield Publishers, 2003.

Brader, Ted. *Campaigning for Hearts and Minds: How Emotional Appeals in Political Ads Work.* Chicago: University of Chicago Press, 2006.

Cappella, Joseph N., and Kathleen Hall Jamieson. "Broadcast Adwatch Effects: A Field Experiment." *Communication Research* 21, no. 3 (1994): 342–65.

Cappo, Joe. *The Future of Advertising.* New York: McGraw Hill, 2003.

Carr, David. "Newspaper as Business Pulpit." *New York Times*, June 11, 2012, B1.

CBS News. CBS News monthly poll #2. Computer file. ICPSR version 4096. New York: CBS News [producer]; Ann Arbor, MI: Inter-university Consortium for Political and Social Research [distributor], May 2004.

CBS News. CBS News monthly poll. Computer file. ICPSR version 23442. New York: CBS News [producer]; Ann Arbor, MI: Inter-university Consortium for Political and Social Research [distributor], April 2007.

Christians, Clifford G., Mark Fackler, Kathy Brittain McKee, Peggy J. Kreshel, and Robert H. Woods Jr. *Media Ethics: Cases and Moral Reasoning.* 8th ed. Boston: Pearson Education, Inc., 2009.

Citizens United v. Federal Election Commission, 558 U.S. 08-205 (2010).

Day, Louis A. "Political Advertising and the First Amendment." In *The Manship School Guide to Political Communication*, edited by David D. Perlmutter, 67–76. Baton Rouge: Louisiana State University Press, 1999.

Ferguson, Thomas. *Golden Rule: The Investment Theory of Party Competition and the Logic of Money-Driven Political Systems.* Chicago: University of Chicago Press, 1995.

Fowler, Erika Franklin. "Presidential Ads 70 Percent Negative in 2012, Up from 9 Percent in 2008," Wesleyan Media Project. May 2, 2012. http://mediaproject .wesleyan.edu/2012/05/02/jump-in-negativity/ (accessed May 22, 2012).

Fowler, Erika Franklin, and Travis N. Ridout. "Local Television and Newspaper Coverage of Political Advertising." *Political Communications* 26 (2009): 119–36.

Geer, John G. "Assessing Attack Advertising: A Silver Lining." In *Campaign Reform*, edited by Larry M. Bartels and Lynn Vavreck, 62–78. Ann Arbor: University of Michigan Press, 2000.

Geer, John G. *In Defense of Negativity: Attack Ads in Presidential Campaigns.* Chicago: University of Chicago Press, 2006.

"Honesty/Ethics in Professions." Gallup. 2010. http://www.gallup.com/poll/1654/ honesty-ethics-professions.aspx (accessed March 20, 2011).

Huber, Greg A., and Kevin Arceneaux. "Identifying the Persuasive Effects of Presidential Advertising." *American Journal of Political Science* 51, no. 4 (2007): 957–77.

Iyengar, Shanto. "Election 2008: The Advertising." WashingtonPost.com, August 12, 2008. http://pcl.stanford.edu/press/2008/wp-2008advertising.pdf (accessed August 13, 2009).

Iyengar, Shanto, Helmut Norpoth, and Kyu S. Hahn. "Consumer Demand for Election News: The Horserace Sells." *Journal of Politics* 66, no. 1 (2004): 157–75.

Jackson, Brooks, and Kathleen Hall Jamieson. *UnSpun: Finding Facts in a World of Disinformation.* New York: Random House, 2007.

Jamieson, Kathleen Hall. *Dirty Politics: Deception, Distraction, and Democracy.* New York: Oxford University Press, 1992.

Jamieson, Kathleen Hall. *Everything You Think You Know About Politics . . . And Why You're Wrong.* New York: Basic Books, 2000.

Jamieson, Kathleen Hall, ed. *Electing the President 2008: The Insider's View.* Philadelphia: University of Pennsylvania Press, 2009.

Jamieson, Kathleen Hall, and Joseph N. Cappella. *Echo Chamber: Rush Limbaugh and the Conservative Media Establishment.* New York: Oxford University Press, 2010.

Jamieson, Kathleen Hall, and Joseph N. Cappella. "Setting the Record Straight: Do Ad Watches Help or Hurt?" *International Journal of Press/Politics* 2, no. 1 (1997): 13–22.

Jamieson, Kathleen Hall, and Brooks Jackson, "Our Disinformed Electorate," FactCheck.org, December 12, 2008, http://www.factcheck.org/specialreports/our_disinformed_electorate.html.

Jamieson, Kathleen Hall, and Paul Waldman. "Watching the Adwatches." In *Campaign Reform*, edited by Larry M. Bartels and Lynn Vavreck, 106–21. Ann Arbor: University of Michigan Press, 2000.

Jamieson, Kathleen Hall, Paul Waldman, and Susan Sherr. "Eliminate the Negative? Categories of Analysis for Political Advertisements." In *Crowded Airwaves: Campaign Advertising in Elections*, edited by James A. Thurber, Candice J. Nelson, and David A. Dulio, 44–64. Washington, DC: Brookings Institution, 2000.

Johnston, Richard, Michael G. Hagen, and Kathleen Hall Jamieson. *The 2000 Presidential Election and the Foundations of Party Politics.* New York: Cambridge University Press, 2004.

Kenski, Kate, Bruce W. Hardy, and Kathleen Hall Jamieson. *The Obama Victory: How Media, Money, and Messages Shaped the 2008 Election.* New York: Oxford University Press, 2010.

Levinthal, Dave. "Bad News for Incumbents, Self-Financing Candidates in Most Expensive Midterm Election in U.S. History." Center for Responsive Politics. November 4, 2010. http://www.opensecrets.org/news/2010/11/bad-night-for-incumbents-self-finan.html.

Levitt, Theodore. "The Morality (?) of Advertising." *Harvard Business Review*, July–August 1970, 84–92.

Liptak, Adam. "Justices, 5–4, Reject Corporate Spending Limit." *New York Times*, January 21, 2010. http://www.nytimes.com/2010/01/22/us/politics/22scotus.html.

Maynard, Michael. "Positively Negative: Arguments in Favor of Political Attack Ads." Paper presented at the Association for Education in Journalism and Mass Communications Annual Conference, Washington DC, August 9–12, 2007.

McCarty, Nolan, Keith T. Poole, and Howard Rosenthal. *Polarized America: The Dance of Ideology and Unequal Riches.* Boston: MIT Press, 2006. http://voteview.com/polarizedamerica.asp.

Novak, Viveca. "Context Included: Obama on Iran." FactCheck.org. August 27, 2008. http://www.factcheck.org/elections-2008/context_included_obama_on _iran.html (accessed July 27, 2009).

"Outside Spending." Center for Responsive Politics. http://www.opensecrets.org/ outsidespending/index.php (accessed March 20, 2011).

Painter, Chad, and Louis Hodges. "Mocking the News: How *The Daily Show with Jon Stewart* Holds Traditional Broadcast News Accountable." *Journal of Mass Media Ethics* 25 (2010): 257–74.

Papper, Bruce. "TV Adwatch Stories: On the Rise." Annenberg Public Policy Center. November 9, 2007. http://www.annenbergpublicpolicycenter.org/ downloads/political_communication/factcheck/20071109_factchecking journalism/20071109_fcj_TV_Survey_Report.pdf.

Patterson, Thomas E. *Out of Order*. New York: Vintage Books, 1994.

Pearson, Susan. "Babes in the Marketplace: The Toy Industry Takes Over Saturday Morning Cartoons." *Multinational Monitor* 8, no. 9 (1987). http://www.multi nationalmonitor.org/hyper/issues/1987/09/pearson.html.

Pew Research Center. "Partisan Polarization Surges in Bush, Obama Years." June 4, 2012. http://www.people-press.org/2012/06/04/partisan-polarization-surges -in-bush-obama-years/.

Pfau, Michael, and Allan Louden. "Effectiveness of Adwatch Formats in Deflecting Political Attack Ads." *Communication Research* 21, no. 3 (1994): 325–41.

Ridout, Travis N., and Glen R. Smith. "Free Advertising: How the Media Amplify Campaign Messages." *Political Research Quarterly* 61, no. 4 (2008): 598–608.

Ries, Al, and Laura Ries. *The Fall of Advertising and the Rise of PR*. New York: HarperCollins, 2002.

Rust, Roland T., and Richard W. Oliver. "The Death of Advertising." *Journal of Advertising* 23, no. 4 (1994): 71–77.

Sharockman, Aaron. "PolitiFact Florida Turns 1!" PolitiFact.com. March 18, 2011. http://www.politifact.com/florida/article/2011/mar/18/politifact-florida-turns-1/ (accessed March 21, 2011).

Simons, Herbert W., Don J. Stewart, and David Harvey. "Effects of Network Treatments on Perceptions of a Political Campaign Film: Can Rhetorical Criticism Make a Difference?" *Communication Quarterly* 37 (1989): 184–98.

Vavreck, Lynn. *The Message Matters: The Economy and Presidential Campaigns*. Princeton, NJ: Princeton University Press, 2009.

West, Darrell M. "A Brief History of Political Advertising on Television." In *The Manship School Guide to Political Communication*, edited by David D. Perlmutter, 27–32. Baton Rouge: Louisiana State University Press, 1999.

West, Darrell M. *Air Wars: Television Advertising in Election Campaigns, 1952–2008*. 5th ed. Washington, DC: CQ Press, 2010.

Zelezny, John D. *Cases in Communications Law: Liberties, Restraints, and the Modern Media*. 6th ed. Boston: Wadsworth Cengage Learning, 2011.

Zyman, Sergio, and Armin Brott. *The End of Advertising as We Know It*. New York: John Wiley & Sons, 2002.

CHAPTER TWENTY-ONE

Branding the City: Place Marketing and Class Politics in Washington, D.C.

Timothy A. Gibson

American cities have always competed with one another for economic growth and investment. In the colonial period, for example, Philadelphia, New York, and Boston competed to dominate the Atlantic trade. Later, these same cities raced to build canals linking their ports with rivers in the resource-rich American interior, while still later, new cities out West struggled fiercely for settlers and rail terminals.[1] As many geographers and historians have noted, this inter-urban competition is at least as old as capitalism itself.[2]

Yet at the same time, there is indeed something remarkable about the current period. In an era of intensified international integration and trade, city leaders in the United States now confront a global competition for future economic growth.[3] Unfortunately, the reality is that there is only so much urban prosperity to go around. Some cities and regions will find a way to secure a disproportionate share of this growth,[4] while others, alas, will be consigned to cycles of poverty and decline.[5] For urban policy and property elites embroiled in this global competition, the stakes are enormous. Accordingly, city leaders around the world have cast about for strategies that might help attract the key drivers of urban economic growth—jobs, workers, investors, and tourists.

One strategy for jump-starting urban economic growth, oddly enough, is *advertising*; or, more specifically, the increasingly sophisticated strategy of *urban branding* or, as some scholars term it, *place marketing*. The logic of urban branding goes something like this: if a city's leaders can find a way to project distinctive images of urban vitality to key targets like investors and tourists, then maybe, just maybe, they can improve their chances of convincing these targets to invest in *their* city and not elsewhere.[6] For this reason, place marketing—defined as "promoting a place's values and image so that potential users are fully aware of the place's distinctive advantages"[7]—is now a fundamental feature of contemporary urban governance, and most cities have created (usually with a complex brew of private and public funds) an integrated network of trade, economic development, and tourism organizations devoted to the task of cultivating, projecting, and managing urban images.[8]

The practice of urban branding is a complicated one, however. Cities are not like sweaters. They are not empty vessels into which an infinite number of meanings can be poured. Cities have histories, and for many American cities, particularly in the industrial Midwest and Northeast, this history includes 50 years of disinvestment, population loss, and antiurban images in local and national media (think: local crime news).[9] None of this makes the job of selling the city any easier.

So that is the challenge. If the city's "brand" has been stigmatized over the last 50 years, it now needs to be "repositioned."[10] To this end, officials in most major cities pour substantial amounts of public money into marketing and advertising campaigns designed to spread the good news about their metropolis and attract tourists, shoppers, and corporate investment.[11] These institutionalized efforts to draw in both jobs and tourists are by now familiar and have been the subject of extensive research.[12]

Of particular interest in this chapter, however, are those marketing campaigns designed explicitly to attract new *residents* into the city. Can advertising—a tool that has long been used to lure city dwellers out to the suburbs[13]—be used to lure them back? Clearly, such campaigns are nothing if not ambitious. Convincing a tourist to invest in a weekend visit to your city is one thing. Convincing a suburbanite to buy an urban condo is something else again. More than likely the suburbanite has been raised on a steady diet of urban crime news.[14] More than likely they also have concerns about the schools, the taxes, and the quality of city services.

Still, if the challenges facing such promotional campaigns are significant, city leaders believe the potential payoff might be equally impressive. If we can convince even a small percentage of suburban residents to embrace the possibilities of city living, the logic goes, then we can broaden the city's tax base, improve the funding of public schools, inspire new retail and housing development, and, if it all comes together, spark a virtuous circle of economic growth that will benefit *all* city residents, rich and poor alike.

But can urban branding campaigns—particularly campaigns targeted to affluent suburbanites—achieve these lofty civic aims? On the whole, scholars are rightly suspicious of claims to represent the universal civic good. It is much more common that such claims to represent the universal public interest are in fact masking the pursuit of a narrower, special interest.[15]

In this spirit, this chapter therefore examines the political and economic tradeoffs, as well as the social costs and benefits, of the District of Columbia's "City Living, DC Style" advertising campaign—a campaign designed to sell a particular vision of city living to the greater Washington metropolitan area. Drawing on 11 in-depth interviews with campaign planners and housing advocates, a semiotic analysis of campaign messages, and two days of field research conducted at the campaign's signature "Expo" event, what we will discover is the emergence of a profound gap between planners' *promises* (especially to conduct an inclusive campaign that would yield benefits for all District residents) and the actual *performance* of the campaign itself. By offering an account of the campaign as it moved from conception to execution, this chapter will therefore argue that the workings of class power and privilege both structured the planning of the campaign and ultimately exerted powerful limits on the campaign's ability to achieve its civic goals.[16]

"City Living, DC Style"—Planning the Campaign

By all accounts, in the winter of 2003, Mayor Anthony Williams looked across the District of Columbia and liked much of what he saw. After decades of suburbanization, population loss, and economic disinvestment, signs of renewed life in the District abounded. The MCI Center had opened in downtown to great fanfare, marking the return of the NBA's Wizards to D.C. and sparking a flurry of retail investment nearby. Construction of a massive new convention center in Mt. Vernon Square was well underway for a 2003 opening, and a forest of construction cranes in neighborhoods adjacent to downtown marked the resurgence of the residential market.

In such times, mayors tend to think about legacy, and Williams was no . exception. Addressing dignitaries assembled to hear his second inaugural address, Williams thus issued perhaps his most ambitious policy goal to date: finding a way to attract 100,000 new residents to the District in the next 10 years. Growing the city, he explained, meant growing the tax base, which in turn meant better funding for services and schools. Population growth would thus be a win-win for everyone. "We must lure back residents who fled the city in the past," Williams told the crowd. "But not at the expense of those who today call the District home. We can do this. We will do this."[17]

Still, this would be no small task. Like many American cities, the District had been bleeding residents to the suburbs and beyond for decades.[18] After the end of World War II, the District could boast 750,000 residents. By the year 2000, that number would shrink to 570,000—all during a time when the regional population expanded exponentially. Although the population of the District had stabilized since the late 1990s, attracting 100,000 new residents over the next decade would require a dramatic turnaround from a 50-year slump.[19] At the same time, however, demographers were projecting that over 1 million residents would descend upon the Washington metro area during that 10-year span. So, as one planner put it, all the District was asking for was 10 percent of this future growth.[20]

But what *kinds* of residents could—or *should*—the District attract? This was actually a matter of some discussion in the early 2000s, particularly in the wake of an influential Brookings Institution report titled *Envisioning a Future Washington*.[21] Authored in 2001, this report looked ahead to 2010 and proposed two distinct city futures, each based on a different strategy for attracting new residents to the District. The authors called the first strategy the "adult strategy," and it rested on the goal of attracting young, childless professionals looking to live in a hip urban setting. The beautiful thing about these residents, the report noted, is that they are relatively wealthy but, being young and childless, do not demand much in the way of services (like schools and libraries). However, the authors noted, this "adult strategy" also carried some risks—chief among them the potential for a deluge of affluent (and disproportionately white) hipsters to widen the gap between rich and poor, thereby exacerbating "racial and class tensions" across the city.[22]

The second strategy—what the authors called the "family strategy"— would attempt to grow the city by attracting and retaining middle-income parents and their children. Pursuing this strategy, while having the advantage of broadening the District's middle class, would be far more challenging for city policy makers. It would require, the authors noted, "a much higher level of community-wide commitment and effort than the adult strategy" and would not succeed without "significantly improved public services" (including especially improved schools) at considerable expense to city budgets in the near term.[23]

In this context, the idea of developing an urban branding and advertising campaign to attract new residents took on special significance. Would city planners take the path of least resistance and use the campaign to pursue the "adult strategy"—that is, to attract an audience of affluent and young hipsters—potentially at the risk of exacerbating tensions over gentrification and class in the District? Or would they use the campaign to take the more challenging road and pursue Brookings' more resource-intensive "family strategy"? The city's place marketing campaign—eventually titled "City Living, DC Style"—would thus offer fascinating clues as to which strategy the mayor's office had decided to pursue.

Planning the campaign itself, however, would fall to Deputy Mayor Eric Price. Faced with the task of assembling a campaign team, Price drew on marketing experts in the mayor's office, and also on his contacts in the urban development community, including, importantly, the D.C. Marketing Center and the Downtown Business Improvement District (BID). Both organizations offered the city staffing support and supplemental funding, and, together with a private event-planning firm, Price's task force began to plan a marketing campaign that would reach out to suburbanites and convince them to "come home" to the District.

It is at this point—with the inclusion of business booster organizations—that the campaign's goals began to multiply and the campaign's targets began to narrow. The D.C. Marketing Center, for example, is a public-private partnership funded jointly by the District government and the D.C. Chamber of Commerce. As staffers explained, the D.C. Marketing Center attempts to generate jobs in the District by promoting the city's business climate to retailers, financial institutions, and other potential investors. For its part, the Marketing Center became involved in the "City Living" campaign as part of their larger commitment to attracting new retailers to the District. Like many large urban centers, the District had long suffered from a lack of national-chain retailers, who long ago followed the flight of middle-class residents to the suburban fringe. Drawing these retailers back to the city required convincing them not only that the District was attracting new residents, but that these new residents had money to spend. "Retailers follow rooftops, and average household income," as one Marketing Center official said.[24] In short, if the District's urban-branding campaign succeeded in drawing in new residents—particularly middle-class or upper-income residents—then the Marketing Center might make more headway convincing the Targets and Home Depots of the world that "city living" in the District was indeed for them.

The Downtown BID—an organization of downtown property owners and retailers—had its own motives for getting involved. In 2003, after decades of stagnation, things in the downtown residential market were heating up fast. Encouraged by a resurgent regional economy, residential developers had descended en masse upon once-vacant downtown lots. As a result, in just a few short years, the downtown residential market exploded from essentially zero in 1996 to over 5,000 units of upscale housing built or under construction by 2003. In fact, it was almost too much, too fast: approximately 2,000 of the units were scheduled to hit the housing market in a single two-month span in the fall of 2003. "We wanted to make sure we filled these units quickly," one BID staffer said.[25]

Why the rush? For development experts, the risk was clear. If these units remained vacant for too long, future residential developers might draw the conclusion that downtown was overbuilt and then steer clear. So it occurred to the Downtown BID that they might want to do some marketing "to tell people about the new residential development downtown." There was only one problem, as one BID staffer recalled. "We couldn't get our guys [BID members] to pay for it."[26] The developers and residential property owners within the downtown district basically told BID's staff that they were happy with their individual marketing efforts and did not feel the need to help fund a collective "come and live downtown" campaign—a campaign that might help their competitors as much as themselves.

For these reasons, when Deputy Mayor Price called the Downtown BID and the Marketing Center for help, it all seemed to click into place. The city needed 100,000 new residents to expand the tax base. The Marketing Center needed middle-to-upper-income "rooftops" to attract new retailers. The BID wanted to conduct a marketing campaign to absorb downtown's 2,000 new housing units. Maybe they could meet all their goals by working together to market "city living" to suburban audiences. How, as one planner put it, "could we get people excited about living in the District?" And, how could they channel this excitement toward a decision to relocate?[27]

Here we arrive at the crucial challenge facing campaign planners. If suburbanites, raised on a diet of local crime news and antiurban gossip, believed that violence raged on the streets, that the city was still run by a convicted drug user, and that there was no nightlife beyond the floodlit memorials, then why on earth would they come? In order to make the campaign a success, the planners therefore needed to address, even if obliquely, the long-term accumulation of negative imagery about the District.

Campaign planners thus set to work on a strategy. At the center of the strategy would be a giant housing Expo, to be held in late October 2003. At this Expo, visitors could wander from booth to booth and learn about the new apartment and condo developments coming on line. At other booths, mortgage brokers would be available to offer advice on financing, city planners would tell visitors about the city's distinctive neighborhoods, and housing officials would promote the incentives available for first-time homebuyers in D.C. The event could even feature a series of panel presentations on the District's up-and-coming "hip neighborhoods."

In addition, planners decided to develop a sophisticated, six-month-long advertising campaign, with two key goals in mind. First, all campaign messages would promote the Expo event to key market segments, and second, the campaign's messages and images would also promote something less tangible—the unique advantages of the urban good life. In this way, campaign ads would begin to offer alternative images of the District to the images of crime and dysfunction broadcast on the nightly news.

By June 2003, the official kickoff of the campaign, the basic framework was in place. Throughout the summer months, the planners would promote "City Living, DC Style" through targeted print, radio, and television advertising. These activities would culminate in the year's signature event: the City Living Expo held in late October 2003—just when those units in downtown were coming "on line."

At this point, one last crucial decision remained. What audiences would be targeted by the campaign? Would it be a more narrow appeal to young professionals and hipsters, or would it be a broader campaign focused on families and expanding the District's middle class? With limited funds, the task force focused immediately on what one planner called the "low-hanging fruit"—in other words, those market segments, identified through research, that were most open to the idea of moving and buying a home in the District.[28] Right away, as numerous planners conceded, this excluded families with kids. "Schools definitely are a concern for a lot of people," one planner said.[29] "We're not advertising, 'bring your children in here to go to school,'" agreed another, "because we wouldn't be honest with ourselves if we did that."[30] For this reason, the campaign crafted specific appeals for three major suburban audiences: young professionals, suburban commuters, and "empty-nesters" (parents whose kids have moved out).[31]

At the same time, it was in the selection of these target audiences that the class politics of the campaign was most clearly revealed. For instance, when asked if income played any consideration in the selection of target markets, a DC Marketing staffer said:

> Not in the sense that we were targeting any particular class of people, or anything like that. We were aware that the cost of real estate here is expensive, and so we, we were sort of looking for, I mean, we weren't targeting any particular income, but we knew that certain, that people that had jobs, that had money, would be more likely to, and so, you know, we were looking for like the dual income, no kids families that have more disposable income ... *What we were trying to do is to be practical about the market rate [residential] units that*

are here, who's going to buy them? Who's going to lease them? (Emphasis added.)[32]

Or, as another planner put it, "you know, we have all this housing on-line. We want to make sure that it gets picked up."

These comments are worth quoting at length not merely because they demonstrate the clear discomfort informants felt when confronted with the issue of income and class, but also because they illustrate how the motives of the campaign's private players—in particular the need to fill the "market rate units" (especially those high-end units located down-town)—profoundly shaped the actual performance of the campaign. By the summer of 2003, the primary goal of the campaign was not merely attracting 100,000 new residents of whatever kind. Fully in the realm of the "practical," the campaign's messages would instead focus on attracting only a particular *kind* of new resident—young, childless professionals who had the means to "pick up" the high-end, market-rate housing coming "on-line" downtown. In other words, by 2003, the city had chosen its future, and it would be based on precisely those residents at the heart of the "adult strategy," as laid out in the Brookings Institution's 2001 report.

The City Living Campaign: Ads and Events

The "City Living, DC Style" campaign was not a single text. It was instead a tightly articulated collection of texts that included everything from television, newspaper, and radio advertisements, to key chains and knick-knacks, to the "City Living" website and the weekend-long Expo itself. What unified this complex intertextuality was, of course, "the brand."[33] Campaign planners were quite determined to develop for the District a strong brand within the regional marketplace. As one planner put it, "it's just like marketing a pair of jeans."

> I'm sorry but it's true! It's no different. You market a pair of jeans by saturating people with your brand until they can't think of anything else to wear. This is just the same. We're going to saturate them with our brand until they can't think to live anywhere else ... It's my job to market this brand.[34]

In this way, the key challenge facing the District's campaign planners lay in associating with DC's urban brand a limited set of positive images that would not only illustrate the benefits of "city living" but would also make the District stand out as distinct from, and superior to, other brands (Arlington, Bethesda, Fairfax County) in the regional field.[35] The ultimate goal would thus be to create conditions in which a single encounter with the "brand"—even just the tagline "City Living, DC Style"—would evoke a consistent set of images about the urban good life.

For this reason, exploring the images of the urban good life produced by the campaign is the next step in this analysis. In short, given the planners' focus on upscale, childless suburbanites, it is important to examine how campaign texts and events wove implicit messages of class and race into their illustrations of ideal city living. In other words, how did the goals of expanding the tax base and filling upscale downtown housing with young professionals find expression within the images and messages of campaign texts?

Advertising Biking and Class in D.C.: "Morning Commute"

Let us explore these questions within the context of a print advertisement titled "Morning Commute." This was one of a number of ads produced in the same style, featuring a single black-and-white image with a spare line of text and the "City Living, DC Style" logo. In this particular ad, the image shows a bicyclist (we see only the bicycle and the biker's legs) wearing spandex shorts speeding along a bike-only pathway. The roadway, the foliage along the path, and the cyclist him- or herself (the gender of the cyclist is unclear) are a blur across the page, evoking connotations of speed and motion. Across the bottom of the ad, in lowercase, the text reads "morning commute." The focus on motion was quite intentional, planners said.[36] They were guessing that suburban commuters stuck in the nation's third-worst traffic might identify with a desire for motion, speed, and convenience.

So far, so good. But by choosing cycling to represent the ideal commute, planners positioned readers as "the kind of person" who might bike to work. This obviously excluded working families with children, which in itself is strategic given the campaign's focus on the professional and the childless. More subtly, however, the practice of cycling itself carries class connotations that, in the context of this ad, serve to address some potential audiences while excluding others. As Pierre Bourdieu writes, while working-class residents tend to participate in competitive team sports, the middle and upper classes tend instead to embrace individual sports like cycling, sailing, or skiing. This is not merely because the costs of participation in such sports can often exclude subordinate classes (especially in the case of skiing), but also because the performance of these activities has become invested with a moralistic discourse of health and exercise common among such class fractions. The body, within middle-class discourse, becomes something to be "worked upon" and sculpted as an external display of one's self-discipline and intrinsic worth. The goal of these individual sports is therefore not merely "winning," but something "higher"—the achievement of health and the display of this achievement to others.[37]

Perhaps not surprisingly, then, a look at the marketing demographics of cycling magazines reveals an audience skewed toward the middle to upper reaches of the class structure. *Bicycling* magazine, for example, reaches a relatively young subscription base (with two-thirds of its readers between 25 and 54 years of age), who command an annual average household income of $101,858.[38] In their relations with others, marketing surveys conducted by the magazine reveal a class segment accustomed to exerting influence and giving rather than receiving orders and advice. For instance, between two-thirds and three-fourths of subscribers say they are "independent thinkers who rarely follow the crowd," that "people rely on me for advice," and that they "influence the buying decisions of others."[39] In other words, by positioning the viewers as "the kind of person" who might cycle to work, the text implicitly addressed an upscale audience while at the same time subtly excluding those potential residents for whom a cycle to work holds little practical, cultural, or sensual appeal.

Moreover, the race of the cyclist was significant as well, at least in hindsight. This is not to allege that, by casting the biker as white, campaign planners were attempting to send a direct message about the racial future of the District. At the same time, if, as we have seen already, a love for cycling is not shared evenly across social class segments, the same is true when it comes to race. For example, recent research cited in the *Washington Post* suggests that biking is simply "not as popular with African Americans as it is with whites" and that most of the growth in bicycle commuting in the last 10 years has come from middle- and upper-income white men.[40] In fact, as I will discuss in greater detail below, bicycle commuting and bike lanes—both central features of the District's current revitalization plans—have become increasingly controversial symbols (particularly within the African American community) of gentrification and racial change within the District.

In this way, then, by mobilizing images of bicycling commuting in its campaign, planners were not really sending a message about race *relations*, per se—in other words, the message was *not*, in my view, the simple and crude: "white people are welcome here." Rather, the message was much more subtle. The ad subtly communicated, in short, that District of the future would cater to the particular tastes, needs, and lifestyles of young, affluent, and, yes, *white* professionals. *They* would set the city's cultural agenda from this point forward.

Reading the City Living Expo

As noted above, within the campaign, ads such as "Morning Commute" played a dual role. On the one hand, they were designed to present an image of city living that might appeal to the campaign's affluent targets. On the other hand, the lifestyle ads also had a more utilitarian purpose: drumming up attendance at the campaign's flagship event, the City Living Exposition, held on the floor of the Washington Convention Center. At this event, then, the public would be invited to participate in the performance of the campaign's über-text within which the District would attempt to close the deal with its preferred target markets.

What I present here, therefore, is my own reading of this über-text as I wandered the convention floor and engaged with some of the participants in the scene. Upon arrival, my first task was to pursue the booths themselves, representing all of the public and private organizations who paid a fee to rent space at the conventional hall. After browsing a bit, I began to conduct ad hoc interviews with exhibitors and patrons, focusing on those booths marketing condos and apartments. After all, these were the folks with whom the planners were most concerned. Would these new units—in downtown and elsewhere in the District—be "absorbed" quickly enough to sustain a good climate for real estate investment? In chatting with these firms, then, I was mostly interested in determining *who* these property developers were attempting to reach. Who was their "market"?

The PN Hoffman booth was my first stop. PN Hoffman is, as one representative told me, a residential developer that focuses mostly on "urban infill"—that is, the practice of buying a "property that is either vacant or under-utilized," razing it, and then constructing a new building in its place. When asked about her target market, she said, "it's the DC market. Professionals. Empty nesters. People moving to DC and who only plan to be here 2–5 years and who don't want to spend a lot of time maintaining a residence." These folks, she said, "want something new. New is a big deal ... They don't want the hassle of an older house." What PN Hoffman offers this market is therefore "premium" housing. "We do premium," she said. "I don't like to say luxury. But it's certainly high-end finishes like granite countertops, stainless steel appliances, and urban contemporary design. It's definitely high-end."

As I moved to other booths, this pattern of a focus on "premium" units for "high-end" markets continued. For instance, across from the PN Hoffman booth, two young salespeople presided over the MassCourt booth. Located downtown, at Massachusetts and Seventh Streets NW, MassCourt was at that time nearing completion. "[It's] really three separate buildings," the staffer described. "One loft. One traditional. One historic. The loft apartments are like nothing else in the District. They're going to have concrete floors, exposed pipes, loft ceilings. Very New York style. Very unique. I think people will love the amenities, the yoga room, the rooftop pool with spectacular views of the Capitol Building, [and] the rooftop track and fitness area." But how much would it cost to rent a two-bedroom apartment? She replied, "$2,033 [a month] for a two-bedroom."

After she had listed off the amenities and handed me promotional materials with images of young single people, in impeccable clothes, enjoying the yoga room and fitness area, I asked about the kind of "audience" she was trying to attract to her building. In reply I received a long, uncomfortable pause and then simply, "anyone, really." Later I would learn from another booth that real estate firms are forbidden by housing antidiscrimination laws to talk about the "kind of person" they want as tenants. For this reason, the question of "preferred target markets" asked sales staff to move into dangerous legal territory, and accordingly, few took the bait.

At the same time, however, it was equally clear in the developers' promotional materials that they were in fact aggressively marketing to a particular slice of the housing market, to a particular "kind" of person—in class terms at least, if not in terms of race or ethnicity. Let us be frank. Yoga rooms emphatically do not appeal to just "anyone." They appeal, as MassCourt's own marketing images attest, to college-educated, upward-climbing, young professionals whose particular stock of cultural capital includes both an appreciation of Eastern philosophical pursuits and a taste for haute couture—and virtually all the development booths at the Expo pitched residences targeted to this market segment.[41]

And so we arrive at the key contradiction within the Expo über-text. Despite planners' stated commitment to conduct an inclusive campaign (a promise made in almost every interview with campaign planners), almost all of the vendors pitched granite countertops, high-end amenities, and "hip" locations. And despite the claim that the campaign would show the public that "there are ways you can make living here an affordable reality,"[42] the text of the Expo contained little evidence that this "affordable reality" was either real or affordable.

"City Living, DC Style"—10 Years On

In 2010, the census revealed a startling turnaround in the District's population. For the first time in 50 years, the city grew by nearly 30,000 residents—not the goal of 100,000, to be sure, but still an impressive uptick nonetheless. Between 2010 and 2012, in fact, the District added another

15,000 additional residents—pushing the total increase to 45,000. Was the campaign in this way a roaring success?

Probably not. The "City Living" campaign more than likely had little or nothing to do with the District's twenty-first-century population gains. This is not a criticism of the campaign, which in my view was well conceived and executed. But, six months of moderate advertising exposure and a single housing expo do not magically reverse a 50-year population decline. For any plausible explanation, we must look instead to the long-term demographic and economic changes that push and pull large masses of people.

So why, then, is the "City Living" campaign worth remembering? In my view, what was most important about the campaign was not the (unanswerable) question, "Did it work?" but rather, what the campaign reveals about how city leaders were thinking about the future of the District at a crucial juncture in the city's history. After all, the question asked by the 2001 *Envisioning a Future Washington* report was essentially this: Which future will city leaders choose? Will it be a future of gentrification based on an "adult strategy" and a foundation of affluent twentysomethings? Or will it be a future based on the "family strategy" and the more daunting challenge of rebuilding a broad urban middle class? To its credit, the "City Living" campaign provided an emphatic answer. Bring on the young, professional hipsters. And then bring on gentrification, displacement, and a widening gap between rich and poor.

And bring it on, they did. In the nine years since the "City Living" campaign revealed the city's commitment to the "adult strategy," the District has indeed become younger, richer, and whiter. According to the census, the majority of newcomers to the District during this time were between ages 18 and 34,[43] and they were not rushing to have kids, either. In fact, the number of child tax exemptions claimed by District residents steadily fell over the same period.[44] The newcomers also had more money to spend on housing and amenities on average than existing residents, and their combined affluence has pushed the District's median household income up by $8,000 since 2000.[45] Finally, recent arrivals were far more likely to be white and Latino than black. As the *Washington Post* notes, almost 60,000 whites moved into D.C. between 2000 and 2009, representing an increase of nearly 30 percent. The Latino population also grew by double digits during this time.[46] This demographic shift—a shift subject to much discussion, as we will see below—has yielded a District that is, for the first time in decades, not majority-black.

The result of this influx of the young and affluent has been an utterly transformed social and economic landscape. Overall, average single-family home prices in D.C. spiked dramatically from $252,000 in 2000 to just over $415,000 nine years later, and the Great Recession has only slowed, not stopped, this growth.[47] The growth in apartment rents was even more dramatic during this time, with average rents more than doubling from $700 per month in 2000 to over $1,500 in 2009. Meanwhile, over 8,000 rental units were converted into condominiums in 2005 *alone*.[48] Overall, due to condo conversion and increasing rents, the District lost one-half of its low-cost rental units between 2000 and 2010.[49]

This is the statistical face of rapid gentrification, and its effects have been felt in different ways in different parts of the city. Some neighborhoods—especially those close to downtown and with easy access to federal jobs and nightlife (such as Columbia Heights, Shaw, Logan Circle, and Adams Morgan)—have seen a rapid turnover in residents and a jarring amount of redevelopment and change. Other neighborhoods, including some already-struggling, majority–African American neighborhoods in East Washington, have become even more distressed and poor over the past decade—the result, as one recent report argues, of low-income residents, displaced from gentrifying neighborhoods like Shaw, crowding into the city's remaining low-income neighborhoods in Southeast.[50]

In this way, if city leaders have reaped the benefits of the twentysomething "adult" strategy (including significantly increased funding for schools and services), they have also reaped the costs of this strategy—including especially increased social polarization along lines of race and class. For final evidence of this, you need look no further than the 2010 mayoral campaign and the fate of Anthony Williams's successor as mayor, Adrian Fenty.

In 2006, Fenty, a young, energetic African American city councilmember, won the mayor's office in a sweeping and historic win, where he prevailed in every council ward and won wide majorities of the both the black and white vote. Over the next four years, however, the economic and demographic changes brought by the District's rapid gentrification began to overwhelm his young administration. It did not help that his first-term agenda was full of quality-of-life initiatives aimed at making city spaces and neighborhoods more attractive and livable (rather than kitchen-table issues of jobs, health care, and unemployment). As it happens, in addition to a vigorous school reform initiative, Fenty focused with particular energy on building dog parks and paving miles of—you guessed it—new bike lanes. These initiatives quickly endeared him to affluent professionals in majority-white neighborhoods, but left black political allies and working-class constituents increasingly frustrated and feeling left out, especially as unemployment in some black and working-class neighborhoods reached nearly 30 percent.[51]

Fenty thus presided over, in the phrase of urbanists Stephen Graham and Simon Marvin, a "splintering city," with an increasing social gulf separating rich from poor, black from white.[52] Marshall Brown, a longtime African American political activist, spoke for many working class and African American residents when he put it this way: "The new white voters ... they want doggie parks and bike lanes [and not D.C. statehood or civil rights]. The result is a lot of tension. The new people believe in their dogs more than they do in people. They go into their little cafes, go out and throw their snowballs. This is not the District I knew. There's no relationship with the black community."[53]

When the next mayoral election arrived in 2010, Fenty's broad cross-race, cross-class coalition lay in tatters. While Fenty remained incredibly popular among white voters, winning 53 of 58 white-majority census tracts, his share of the black vote collapsed—indeed, Fenty won *only 10* of the District's 118 majority-black census tracts. The black vote thus swept his opponent, city council chairman Vincent Gray (arguably a more traditional, kitchen-table Democrat) into office.[54]

But Mayor Gray will undoubtedly face the same question as his young predecessor: How can you govern a splintered and divided city? The political challenge ahead thus seems clear. If, during the last decade, city leaders defined "City Living, DC Style" in a narrow, class-specific ways—in fact, as building a hip urban playground for young affluent professionals—and if this narrow vision of a future Washington has divided the city increasingly along lines of class, lifestyle, and even race, then Gray and his allies must find a way to broaden this vision. If they want to find their way back from the current splintered city, their vision for "City Living, DC Style" must become more inclusive and more focused on the needs of working- and middle-class families. City living, after all, works better when it works for all of us.

Notes

1. Edward Glaeser, *Triumph of the City: How Our Greatest Invention Makes Us Richer, Smarter, Greener, Healthier, and Happier* (New York: Penguin, 2011); Allan Pred, *Urban Growth and City Systems in the United States, 1840–1860* (Cambridge, MA: Harvard University Press, 1980).

2. James W. Carey, *Communication as Culture*, 2nd ed. (New York: Routledge, 2009); David Harvey, *The Condition of Postmodernity* (Oxford: Blackwell, 1989).

3. Saskia Sassen, *The Global City: New York, London, Tokyo* (Princeton, NJ: Princeton University Press, 1991); Dennis R. Judd and Todd Swanstrom, *City Politics: Private Power and Public Policy* (New York: HarperCollins, 1994); Manuel Castells, *The Rise of the Network Society*, 2nd ed. (Oxford, UK: Blackwell, 2000).

4. Castells, *Rise of the Network Society*.

5. Mike Davis, "Planet of Slums: Urban Involution and the Informal Proletariat," *New Left Review* 26 (March–April 2004): 5–34.

6. Richard Gruneau and David Whitson, "Upmarket Continentalism: Major League Sport, Promotional Culture, and Corporate Integration," in *Continental Order? Integrating North America for Cyber-Capital*, ed. Vincent Mosco and Dan Schiller (Lanham, MD: Rowman & Littlefield, 2001); David Harvey, "Flexible Accumulation through Urbanization: Reflections on 'Postmodernism' in the American City," in *Post-Fordism: A Reader*, ed. Ash Amin (Oxford: Blackwell, 1994).

7. Philip Kotler, Donald Haider, and Irving Rein, *Marketing Places: Attracting Investment, Industry, and Tourism to Cities, States, and Nations* (New York: Free Press, 1993), 18.

8. See Timothy Gibson, *Securing the Spectacular City*, especially chap. 4, for a description of some of these image-management activities.

9. Robert A. Beauregard, *Voices of Decline: The Postwar Fate of U.S. Cities*, 2nd ed. (New York & London: Routledge, 2003 [1993]); Timothy Gibson *Securing the Spectacular City: The Politics of Revitalization and Homelessness in Downtown Seattle* (Lanham, MD: Lexington Books, 2004).

10. John Hannigan, "Symposium on Branding, the Entertainment Economy, and Urban Place Building: Introduction," *International Journal of Urban and Regional Research* 27 (2003): 352–60; Gerry Kearns and Chris Philo, *Selling Places: The City as Cultural Capital, Past and Present* (Oxford: Pergamon Press, 1993).

11. M. Christine Boyer, "Cities for Sale: Merchandising History at South Street Seaport," in *Variations on a Theme Park*, ed. Michael Sorkin (New York: Hill and Wang, 1992); Kearns and Philo, *Selling Places*.

12. Richard Florida, *The Rise of the Creative Class* (New York: Basic Books, 2002); Dennis Judd and Susan Fainstein, eds., *The Tourist City* (New Haven, CT: Yale University Press, 1999); Kevin Fox Gotham, "Marketing Mardi Gras: Commodification, Spectacle, and the Political Economy of Tourism in New Orleans," *Urban Studies* 39 (2002): 1735–56; Stephanie Hemelryk Donald, Eleonore Kofman, and Catherine Kevin, eds., *Branding Cities: Cosmopolitanism, Parochialism, and Social Change* (New York: Routledge, 2009); Laikwan Pang, *Creativity and Its Discontents* (Durham, NC: Duke University Press, 2012).

13. Indeed, the very first advertisement on commercial radio, aired on New York's WEAF on 1922, promoted a new garden apartment complex in Queens (then considered to be a green suburb of crowded Manhattan). See Erik Barnouw, *Tube of Plenty* (New York: Oxford University Press, 1990).

14. Dennis T. Lowry, Tarn C. J. Nio, and Dennis W. Leitner, "Setting the Public Fear Agenda: A Longitudinal Analysis of Crime Reporting, Public Perceptions of Crime, and FBI Crime Statistics," *Journal of Communication* 53, no. 1 (2003): 61–73; Daniel Romer, Kathleen Hall Jamieson, and Sean Aday, "Television News and the Cultivation of Fear of Crime," *Journal of Communication* 53, no. 1 (2003): 88–104.

15. Pierre Bourdieu, *Language and Symbolic Power* (Cambridge, MA: Harvard University Press, 1991); J. B. Thompson, *Studies in the Theory of Ideology* (Berkeley, CA: University of California Press, 1984).

16. Sections of this chapter have previously appeared in Timothy Gibson, "Selling City Living: Urban Branding Campaigns, Class Power, and the Civic Good," *International Journal of Cultural Studies* 8, no. 3 (2005): 259–80; and Timothy Gibson, "City Living, DC Style: The Political-Economic Limits of Urban Branding Campaigns," in *Urban Communication: Production, Text, Context*, ed. Timothy Gibson and Mark Lowes (Lanham, MD: Rowman & Littlefield, 2004). These sections appear here with permission of Sage Publications and Rowman & Littlefield Publishers. The methodology of this article is inspired by Richard Johnson, "What Is Cultural Studies, Anyway?" *Social Text* 6, no. 1 (1987): 38–80.

17. Anthony Williams, "Mayor Williams' Second Inaugural Address: One City, One Future," http://www.dc.gov/mayor/speeches/speech.asp?cp=1&id=76 (accessed September 29, 2004).

18. Edward Glaeser, *The Triumph of the City: How Our Greatest Invention Makes Us Richer, Smarter, Greener, Healthier, and Happier* (New York: Penguin Press, 2011).

19. U.S. Census Bureau. "State and County Quick Facts: District of Columbia," http://quickfacts.census.gov/qfd/states (accessed September 14, 2004).

20. Interview, Deputy Mayor's Office, October 1, 2003. In addition, from this city's perspective, attracting new residents from the suburbs was about more than merely boosting numbers and repairing urban pride. New residents, particularly new homeowners, would expand the District's notoriously narrow tax base and provide much-needed revenue for improving city services and schools. Of course, most mayors would like a wider tax base, but in the nation's capital, the thirst for funds is especially acute. With acre after acre occupied by federal offices and foreign embassies, close to 40 percent of the District's geography is exempt from property taxes. Even worse, although nonresidents (read: suburban commuters) earn approximately two-thirds of all income in Washington, D.C., the U.S. Congress has prevented the District from applying a modest "commuter tax" that would recapture some of this income. The result of these unique restrictions is a District tax base that relies disproportionately on a narrow range of personal income and local business taxes, with the predictable result: although tax rates are relatively high, public services are chronically underfunded, and city budgets are more vulnerable to negative swings in the business cycle. Attracting more residents would therefore widen the tax base and spread the load of funding basic services among more citizens.

21. Carol O'Cleireacain and Alice Rivlin, *Envisioning a Future Washington* (Washington, DC: Brookings Institution, 2001), http://www.brookings.edu/~/media/research/files/reports/2001/6/cities%20ocleireacain/dcfuture.pdf (accessed June 20, 2012).

22. Ibid., 6.

23. Ibid., 7.

24. Interview, DC Marketing Center, October 8, 2003.

25. Interview, Downtown Business Improvement District, April 9, 2004.

26. Ibid.

27. Interview, Deputy Mayor's Office, October 1, 2003.

28. D. Nakamura, "Selling a Hipper Image: Marketing Campaign Seeks to Attract Upscale Residents," *Washington Post*, June 19, 2003, T10.

29. Interview, Deputy Mayor's Office, October 1, 2003.

30. Interview, TCI Companies, November 6, 2003.

31. A fourth target audience included current residents within the District. This audience was not featured in the advertising campaign; however, some booths at the Expo were designed with the needs of current residents in mind.

32. Interview, DC Marketing Center, October 28, 2003.

33. Kent A. Ono, and Derek T. Buescher, "Deciphering Pocahontas," *Critical Studies in Media Communication* 18, no. 1 (2001): 23–41.

34. Interview, Deputy Mayor's Office, October 1, 2003.

35. The use of the term "field" to indicate a domain of competitive struggle over finite resources (in this case, affluent residents) is derived from the work of Pierre Bourdieu. See especially Pierre Bourdieu, *Practical Reason* (Stanford, CA: Stanford University Press, 1998).

36. Interview, TCI Companies, November 6, 2003.

37. Pierre Bourdieu, *Distinction: A Social Critique of the Judgment of Taste* (Cambridge, MA: Harvard University Press, 1984), 214–15.

38. Rodale Publishers, *Bicycling: 2012 Media Planner*, accessed from the Internet June 26, 2012, http://www.brookings.edu/~/media/research/files/reports/2001/6/cities%20ocleireacain/dcfuture.pdf (accessed June 26, 2012; URL defunct).

39. Rodale Publishers, "About *Bicycling*/About *Mountain Bike*," http://www.bicycling.com/about us/0,3291,s1,00.html (accessed September 13, 2004; URL defunct).

40. Vanessa Williams, "Taking Their Place in the Bike Lane," *Washington Post*, July 11, 2011, C1.

41. There was one exception to this trend: the William C. Smith booth and the Parklands development. When asked about their target market for Parklands (a townhouse community in Southeast, a low-income and majority-black section of the District), the representative said, "[A]ffordable housing. Our market is affordable housing." So how much would a townhouse in Parklands cost? They were, in her words, "truly affordable" at $160,000 each. That she would describe these properties as affordable revealed much about the District's more general housing market at the time. Put simply, $160,000 (U.S.) is still a lot of money. According to the National Low-Income Housing Coalition, the median annual income for renting households in the District in 2003—the year of the Expo—was just under $33,000. At this income, the Fannie Mae Foundation estimates that the median renting household looking to buy in the District back in 2003 would only have been able to afford a $128,000 mortgage and a monthly payment of $990 a month—and this figure assumes that the buyers would have saved

$8,000 for a down payment and secured a lender at a 5 percent interest rate In other words, if Smith's townhouse developments were what passed for affordable housing within the Expo "text," then this effectively excluded more than half of all renters in DC in 2003.

42. Interview, Deputy Mayor's Office, October 1, 2003, previous two quotations.

43. Jonathan O'Connell, "DC's Growth Is Fueled by 20-Somethings. Can the City Grow Up with Them?" *Washington Post*, May 25, 2012.

44. Fannie Mae Foundation and the Urban Institute, *Housing in the Nation's Capital, 2009* (Washington, DC: Urban Institute, 2009), 7, http://www.urban.org/publications/1001340.html.

45. Carol Morello and Dan Keating, "Population of the District Soars Past 600,000," *Washington Post*, December 22, 2010, A4.

46. Ibid. This was matched by an outmigration of African American households during the same time period.

47. Fannie Mae Foundation and the Urban Institute, *Housing in the Nation's Capital, 2003* (Washington, DC: Urban Institute, 2003), 40, http://www.urban.org/publications/1000567.html; Fannie Mae Foundation and the Urban Institute, *Housing in the Nation's Capital, 2009*, 20.

48. Fannie Mae Foundation and the Urban Institute, *Housing in the Nation's Capital, 2006* (Washington, DC: Urban Institute, 2006), 37.

49. O'Connell, "DC's Growth is Fueled by 20-Somethings."

50. Fannie Mae Foundation, *The Poorest Become Poorer: A Report on Patterns of Concentrated Neighborhood Poverty in Washington, DC* (Washington, DC: Fannie Mae Foundation, 2003). The link between gentrification of some neighborhoods and concentrated poverty in others is argued in Fannie Mae Foundation and Urban Institute, *Housing in the Nation's Capital, 2003*.

51. Paul Schwartzman and Chris Jenkins, "Fenty Lost Black Vote, Then His Job," *Washington Post*, September 19, 2009.

52. Stephen Graham and Simon Marvin, *Splintering Urbanism: Networked Infrastructures, Technological Mobilities, and the Urban Condition* (London: Routledge, 2001).

53. Marc Fisher, "Does Culture Follow the Census?" *Washington Post*, April 11, 2011.

54. Schwartzman and Jenkins, "Fenty Lost Black Vote," A7.

Bibliography

Barnouw, Erik. *Tube of Plenty*. New York: Oxford University Press, 1990.

Beauregard, Robert. *Voices of Decline: The Postwar Fate of U.S. Cities*. 2nd ed. New York: Routledge, 2003.

Bourdieu, Pierre. *Distinction: A Social Critique of the Judgment of Taste*. Cambridge, MA: Harvard University Press, 1984.

Bourdieu, Pierre. *Language and Symbolic Power*. Cambridge, MA: Harvard University Press, 1991.

Bourdieu, Pierre. *Practical Reason*. Stanford, CA: Stanford University Press, 1998.

Boyer, M. Christine. "Cities for Sale: Merchandising History at South Street Seaport." In *Variations on a Theme Park*, edited by Michael Sorkin. New York: Hill and Wang, 1992.

Carey, James W. *Communication as Culture*. 2nd ed. New York: Routledge, 2009.

Castells, Manuel. *The Rise of the Network Society*. 2nd ed. Oxford: Blackwell, 2000.

Davis, Mike. "Planet of Slums: Urban Involution and the Informal Proletariat." *New Left Review* 26 (March–April 2004): 5–34.

Fannie Mae Foundation. *The Poorest Become Poorer: A Report on Patterns of Concentrated Neighborhood Poverty in Washington, DC*. Washington, DC: Fannie Mae Foundation, 2003.

Fannie Mae Foundation and the Urban Institute. *Housing in the Nation's Capital, 2003*. Washington, DC: Urban Institute, 2003. http://www.urban.org/publica tions/1000567.html.

Fannie Mae Foundation and the Urban Institute. *Housing in the Nation's Capital, 2006*. Washington, DC: Urban Institute, 2006. http://www.urban.org/publica tions/1001038.html.

Fannie Mae Foundation and the Urban Institute. *Housing in the Nation's Capital, 2009*. Washington, DC: Urban Institute, 2009. http://www.urban.org/ publications/1001340.html.

Fisher, Marc. "Does Culture Follow the Census?" *Washington Post*, April 11, 2011.

Florida, Richard. *The Rise of the Creative Class*. New York: Basic Books, 2002.

Gibson, Timothy. *Securing the Spectacular City: The Politics of Revitalization and Homelessness in Downtown Seattle*. Lanham, MD: Lexington Books, 2004.

Gibson, Timothy. "Selling City Living: Urban Branding Campaigns, Class Power, and the Civic Good." *International Journal of Cultural Studies* 8, no. 3 (2005): 259–80.

Glaeser, Edward. *The Triumph of the City: How Our Greatest Invention Makes Us Richer, Smarter, Greener, Healthier, and Happier*. New York: Penguin Press, 2011.

Gotham, Kevin Fox. "Marketing Mardi Gras: Commodification, Spectacle, and the Political Economy of Tourism in New Orleans." *Urban Studies* 39 (2002): 1735–56.

Graham, Stephen, and Simon Marvin, *Splintering Urbanism: Networked Infrastructures, Technological Mobilities, and the Urban Condition*. London: Routledge, 2001.

Gruneau, Richard, and David Whitson. "Upmarket Continentalism: Major League Sport, Promotional Culture, and Corporate Integration." In *Continental Order? Integrating North America for Cyber-Capital*, edited by Vincent Mosco and Dan Schiller. Lanham, MD: Rowman & Littlefield, 2001.

Hannigan, John. "Symposium on Branding, the Entertainment Economy, and Urban Place Building: Introduction." *International Journal of Urban and Regional Research* 27 (2003): 352–60.

Harvey, David. *The Condition of Postmodernity*. Oxford: Blackwell, 1989.

Harvey, David. "Flexible Accumulation through Urbanization: Reflections on 'Post-modernism' in the American City." In *Post-Fordism: A Reader*, edited by Ash Amin. Oxford: Blackwell, 1994.

Hemelryk, Donald, Stephanie, Eleonore Kofman, and Catherine Kevin, eds. *Branding Cities: Cosmopolitanism, Parochialism, and Social Change*. New York: Routledge, 2009.

Johnson, Richard. "What Is Cultural Studies, Anyway?" *Social Text* 6, no. 1 (1987): 38–80.

Judd, Dennis R., and Susan S. Fainstein, eds. *The Tourist City*. New Haven, CT: Yale University Press, 1999.

Judd, Dennis R., and Todd Swanstrom. *City Politics: Private Power and Public Policy*. New York: HarperCollins, 1994.

Kearns, Gerry, and Chris Philo. *Selling Places: The City as Cultural Capital, Past and Present*. Oxford: Pergamon Press, 1993.

Kotler, Philip, Donald Haider, and Irving Rein. *Marketing Places: Attracting Investment, Industry, and Tourism to Cities, States, and Nations*. New York: Free Press, 1993.

Lowry, Dennis T., Tarn C. J. Nio, and Dennis W. Leitner. "Setting the Public Fear Agenda: A Longitudinal Analysis of Crime Reporting, Public Perceptions of Crime, and FBI Crime Statistics." *Journal of Communication* 53, no. 1 (2003): 61–73.

Morello, Carol, and Dan Keating. "Population of the District Soars Past 600,000." *Washington Post*, December 22, 2010.

Nakamura, D. "Selling a Hipper Image: Marketing Campaign Seeks to Attract Upscale Residents." *Washington Post*, June 19, 2003.

O'Cleireacain, Carol, and Alice Rivlin. *Envisioning a Future Washington*. Washington, DC: Brookings Institution, 2001. http://www.brookings.edu/~/media/research/files/reports/2001/6/cities%20ocleireacain/dcfuture.pdf (accessed June 20, 2012).

O'Connell, Jonathan. "DC's Growth Is Fueled by 20-Somethings. Can the City Grow Up with Them?" *Washington Post*, May 25, 2012.

Ono, Kent A., and Derek T. Buescher. "Deciphering Pocahontas." *Critical Studies in Media Communication* 18, no. 1 (2001): 23–41.

Pang, Laikwan. *Creativity and Its Discontents* (Durham, NC: Duke University Press, 2012).

Pred, Allan. *Urban Growth and City Systems in the United States, 1840–1860*. Cambridge, MA: Harvard University Press, 1980.

Rodale Publishers. "About *Bicycling*/About *Mountain Bike*." http://www.bicycling.com/about us/0,3291,s1,00.html (accessed September 13, 2012).

Rodale Publishers. "*Bicycling*: 2012 Media Planner." http://www.bicycling.com/sites/default/files/uploads/2012_Bicycling_media_planner.pdf (accessed June 26, 2012).

Romer, Daniel, Kathleen Hall Jamieson, and Sean Aday. "Television News and the Fear of Crime," *Journal of Communication* 53, no. 1 (2003): 88–104.

Sassen, Saskia. *The Global City: New York, London, Tokyo.* Princeton, NJ: Princeton University Press, 1991.

Schwartzman, Paul, and Chris Jenkins. "Fenty Lost Black Vote, Then His Job." *Washington Post*, September 19, 2009.

Thompson, J. B. *Studies in the Theory of Ideology.* Berkeley: University of California Press, 1984.

U.S. Census Bureau. "State and County Quick Facts: District of Columbia." http://quickfacts.census.gov/qfd/states (accessed on September 14, 2004).

Williams, Anthony. "Mayor Williams' Second Inaugural Address: One City, One Future," http://www.dc.gov/mayor/speeches/speech.asp?cp=1&id=76 (accessed September 29, 2004).

Williams, Vanessa. "Taking Their Place in the Bike Lane." *Washington Post*, July 11, 2011.

About the Editors and Contributors

The Editors

Danielle Sarver Coombs is an assistant professor in the School of Journalism and Mass Communication at Kent State University. She received her undergraduate degree in media studies from Ohio University, returned there for a master's in international mass communication, and then earned her doctorate in mass communication and public affairs at Louisiana State University. A professional researcher by trade, Coombs worked as a brand consultant and researcher for Insight Research Group (now Insight Strategy) in New York. While there, she conducted brand studies and developed strategic insights for such clients as Payless ShoeSource, Gap Inc., Scripps Networks (HGTV, Food Network, Great American Country), and the American Museum of Natural History. Before this, Coombs was director of Election Research for Edison Media Research, the company responsible for conducting exit polls used by national media. Her research focuses primarily on the relationships between and among sports, politics, and branding, including extensive work on the trials and tribulations of England's Aston Villa football club and the National Football League's Cleveland Browns. Her work has been published in such journals as the *International Journal of Sport Communication*, *Sport and Society*, and *Public Relations Research*, as well as the edited volume *Soccer and Philosophy*. With partner Anne Cunningham Osborne, Coombs's current research agenda includes work on sports journalists in the United Kingdom and the experiences and performances of women as fans in the United States and the United Kingdom. With Bob Batchelor, Coombs coedited the Praeger three-volume collection *American History through American Sports*. Coombs is also editing a two-volume Praeger series on Internet culture with Jacqueline Marino.

Bob Batchelor is James Pedas Professor of Communication and executive director of the James Pedas Communication Center at Thiel College. A noted cultural historian, Batchelor is the author or editor of 24 books, including three volumes in Greenwood's Popular Culture through History series: *The 1900s*, *The 1980s*, and *The 2000s*. In addition, he edited the four-volume *American Pop: Popular Culture Decade by Decade*, the three-volume *Cult Pop Culture: How the Fringe Became Mainstream*, and the three-volume *American History through American Sports*. Batchelor has published articles in *Radical History Review*, the *Journal of American Culture*, the *Mailer Review*, the *American Prospect Online*, and *Public Relations Review*, as well as some 30+ book chapters.

Batchelor is the book series editor for two book series, Contemporary American Literature and Great Writers, Great Books, published by Rowman & Littlefield. He is a member of the editorial advisory boards of the *Journal of Popular Culture* and the *International Journal for the Scholarship of Teaching and Learning*. An active member of the John Updike Society, Batchelor is director of marketing and media for the John Updike Childhood Home Museum in Reading, Pennsylvania.

Batchelor's latest book is *John Updike: A Critical Biography* (Praeger, 2013). His next book will be the first in the Contemporary American Literature series, published in November 2013: *Gatsby: A Cultural History of the Great American Novel*. He is also writing a short biography of rock icon Bob Dylan. Batchelor received undergraduate degrees in history, philosophy, and political science at the University of Pittsburgh and earned his doctorate in English at the University of South Florida, where he studied with Phillip Sipiora.

The Contributors

Michelle A. Amazeen (PhD, Temple University, 2012) is an assistant professor of advertising at Rider University in Lawrenceville, New Jersey. She received her MS and BS in advertising from the University of Illinois at Urbana-Champaign. She has previously been an instructor in the Department of Advertising at Temple University where she taught courses on advertising ethics and media and society. Amazeen's career in the communications industry began by "selling air" and managing the student sales staff at WPGU Radio in Champaign, Illinois. Before returning to academia, she researched the effectiveness of advertising and marketing campaigns for companies including the Signature Group and Millward Brown. A post-midnight encounter with a brand equity scatter plot of toilet bowl cleaners led Michelle to reassess her professional aspirations. She now enjoys challenging herself and her students to critically evaluate our media and communications environments. Amazeen's research interests primarily involve advertising and disinformation. She has examined the prevalence of inaccuracies in political advertising and how political actors are held accountable for their claims. She has also explored the authenticity of strategic communication efforts in the mediated information environment including the alignment of corporate social responsibility campaigns with advertising. Her work has appeared in publications such as *Journal of Business Ethics*, the *Pennsylvania Communication Annual*, and *Social Semiotics*.

Brian Cogan is an associate professor in the Department of Communications at Molloy College in Long Island, New York. He is the author, coauthor, and coeditor of numerous books, articles, and anthologies on popular culture, music, and the media. His specific areas of research interest are media studies, music, fandom, punk rock, popular culture, comic books, graphic novels, and the intersection of politics and popular culture. He is the author of *The Punk Rock Encyclopedia* (2008), coauthor with Tony Kelso of *The Encyclopedia of Popular Culture, Media and Politics* (2009), as well as coeditor with Tony Kelso of *Mosh the Polls: Youth Voters, Popular Culture, and Democratic Engagement* (2008), which is about youth culture and political involvement. Cogan is also the coauthor, along with William Phillips, of the *Encyclopedia of Heavy Metal Music* (2009), and is the editor of a collection of essays, *Deconstructing South Park: Critical Examinations of Animated Transgression* (2011). He is also the coauthor/editor of two forthcoming books in 2013: the two-volume *Baby Boomers and Popular Culture: An Inquiry into America's Most Powerful Generation*, coedited with Thomas Gencarelli (2013); and *Everything I Ever Needed to Know About _____* I Learned from Monty Python *Including History, Art, Poetry, Communism, Philosophy, the Media, Birth, Death, Religion, Literature, Latin, Transvestites, Botany, the French, Class Systems, Mythology, Fish Slapping, and Many More!* cowritten with Jeffrey Massey (2013). He is on the editorial board of the *Journal of Popular Culture* and *Pop Culture Universe: Icons, Idols, Ideas* (ABC-CLIO), as well as the board of directors of the Media Ecology Association.

Kristin Comeforo is a professor of marketing communications at Berkeley College in New York City. Before teaching, she spent several years working in advertising, direct response, and trade marketing. She tweets and blogs about industry news as BrandDR. She received her PhD in communication from Rutgers University in 2009 where she concentrated in media studies. Her current research interests include LGBT images in mainstream advertising and how audiences envision the "gay" ad. She is a diehard New York Mets and New York Jets fan, and is often very sad.

Leigh H. Edwards, PhD, is associate professor of English at Florida State University. She is the author of *Johnny Cash and the Paradox of American Identity* (2009), *The Triumph of Reality TV: The Revolution in American Television* (2013), and *Dolly Parton and Gender Performance in Popular Music* (2013). Her work in popular culture and media studies has been published in journals such as *The Journal of Popular Culture*, *Film and History: An Interdisciplinary Journal of Film and Television Studies*, *Narrative*, *FLOW: A Critical Forum for Television and Media Culture*, *Journal of Popular Music Studies*, *Global Media Journal*, and *Southern Cultures*. She is on the Editorial Board of *Pop Culture Universe: Icons, Idols, Ideas* (ABC-CLIO) and is a staff writer for *PopMatters* (popmatters.com). Her PhD is in English from the University of Pennsylvania. Writing on topics ranging from rockabillies to Twitter, she focuses in particular on popular music, television, and new media.

Jason Flowers is a doctoral student at the University of Texas at Austin in the Advertising Department. His primary research interests focus on how brand communities function to inform and socialize consumers to the culture of a brand. He looks at the role brand communities have in reinforcing or weakening the social impact of brands. More specifically, he is interested in how communication flows within and through brand communities and examines how that communication affects consumer attitudes and influences purchasing decisions.

Peter Fontana is a curious researcher with 10 years of experience in commercial media, both as an analyst and a content provider. With a career that has followed the advertising trend from off-line research methods to digital and now social media, his passions lie on the forefront of emerging media and with the research creativity the space requires for new tracking development. Fontana's research experience includes perceptual and qualitative studies at the custom market research firm Edison Research in New Jersey, digital advertising and web analytics at New York ad agency Deutsch Inc., and social media analysis at the agency We Are Social based in London. Each opportunity has presented measurement challenges in method selection, modification, and creation. First in digital advertising and presently with social media, Fontana has focused on defining client-catered key performance indicators applicable to new spaces while integrating these new metrics into more traditional marketing business objectives. Most recently, his research has surrounded social brand equity measures, media mix model integration, and return-on-investment methods. Recognizing the difficulty in teaching this nimble subject and the need to educate tomorrow's marketing professionals, Fontana is a regular guest lecturer on digital measurement at Kent State University and Emerson College, his alma mater. Peter holds a master's in integrated marketing communication from Emerson in Boston, as well as a bachelor's degree in communication studies and journalism from the College of New Jersey. On the content side, Fontana's experience includes both news anchor and music DJ positions for terrestrial and Internet radio. Staying in touch with commercial media and actively participating in social promotion has allowed him to remain both current in the latest content trends as well as credible in understanding social media platforms as an analyst. In his spare time, Fontana is grounded by his pursuit of cultural literacy via travel and regular volunteer work for the HIV/AIDS cause. Fontana currently resides in Brooklyn, New York.

Timothy A. Gibson is an associate professor in the Department of Communication and a faculty affiliate in the cultural studies PhD program at George Mason University. His interests include critical media studies, the political economy of communication, and urban studies. He has published articles at the intersection of media and urban studies in a variety of communication and cultural studies journals. He is also author of *Securing the Spectacular City: The Politics of Revitalization and Homelessness in Downtown Seattle*, which explores issues of gentrification and urban poverty in Seattle during the 1990s, and coeditor (with Mark Lowes) of *Urban Communication: Production, Text, Context*.

Catherine E. Goodall, PhD, is an assistant professor in the School of Communication Studies at Kent State University. She teaches courses on persuasion, effects of the media, and health communication. She conducts research on processing and effects of health messages in the media, particularly product advertisements (for products such as alcohol, tobacco, food), news coverage of health risks and crises, and health public service announcements. Much of her work investigates the impact of alcohol advertising, and public responses to news coverage of alcohol-related tragedies. She has authored and coauthored over a dozen peer-reviewed scholarly research articles and contributed to four books and book chapters on these topics. Goodall received her PhD in communication from Ohio State University in 2009. She resides in northeast Ohio. During her free time, she trains, and competes in dog agility competitions with her three-time Master Agility champion, and nationally ranked Standard Schnauzer, Abby.

Norma Jones is a David B. Smith Fellowship recipient and doctoral student in the College of Communication and Information at Kent State University. Her research interests include popular culture, identity, and narrative. Specifically, Jones is interested in critically examining heroic narratives as related to cultural identities and representations of various groups in society. She is also collaborating with Bob Batchelor and Maja Bajac-Carter to edit two upcoming books focused on the exploration of heroines in media, popular culture, and literature. Additionally, she has contributed to the *Asian and Pacific Islander Americans* edition in the Great Lives from History series, *American History through American Sports* volumes, as well as popular press books regarding business management strategies and nontraditional student experiences. Earlier in her career, she spent more than a decade working in the media, as well as consulting for multinational companies in a variety of fields, including public relations, marketing, sales, high-end jewelry, and international telecommunications. Jones received her master's degree from the University of North Texas in communication studies, focusing on gender, race, and the mass media. Her bachelor's degree is also in communication studies, from the University of California, Santa Barbara.

Sarah LaCorte is from Wickliffe, a small town east of Cleveland, Ohio. She attended Kent State University where she studied advertising and marketing. She is fascinated by the world of advertising and loves discussing the effects it has on society. Her chapter in this book is of particular interest to her because the history of advertising cigarettes to women shows how powerful advertising is and how it can both shape and reflect the culture it is part of. When she is not contributing chapters to books, she can be found crafting, listening to NPR, or watching a good documentary.

Huston Ladner grew up just outside of Philadelphia, Pennsylvania, and attended the University of Miami, earning a bachelor's degree in English literature. Following graduation, he pursued his desire to play music, moving to Athens, Georgia, where he played guitar and bass for a number of bands. After realizing that that he would not become a rock star, he attended the University of Georgia, earning a master's degree in sports studies. His focus there was on the National Football League and the antitrust collusion surrounding the drafting of John Elway.

Ladner next moved on the University of Southern California where he enrolled in the master's of professional writing program, focusing on fiction. While there he also tutored student athletes and ran an audiobook store. A move to Mississippi ensued, where he obtained a master's in library and information science at the University of Southern Mississippi. His master's project examined the bibliometric publishing patterns of sport and culture. Soon after graduating, Ladner enrolled at the University of Hawaii–Manoa, in the American Studies department, where he is a PhD candidate. One of his academic interests is the examination of how NASCAR employs and exports southern identity to the rest of the nation. In addition, having lived in the South a number of years, Ladner continues to look at how the region creates what is commonly called southern culture. He has written for a variety of publications, ranging from local magazines to scholarly works. He continues to torment himself by being both a Philadelphia and a Cleveland sports fan, while also being one of the few Hawaii residents that follows NASCAR and hockey, while even giving some attention to soccer.

Patrick Mayock is the international news editor of HotelNewsNow.com, an online news resource for the global hotel industry. He was integral in the launch and continued development of the award-winning digital platform, which serves a worldwide audience of hotel owners, investors, operators and developers. Patrick also contributes to Metromix, a national network of city-specific entertainment websites. He earned a bachelor of science in journalism from the E. W. Scripps School of Journalism at Ohio University and earned his master of arts in media management at Kent State University. Patrick lives in Lakewood, Ohio, with his wife, Emily, and dog, Coraline.

Phylicia McCorkle, born and raised in Cincinnati, Ohio, earned a master of arts degree in journalism and mass communication program with a concentration in public relations at Kent State University. She received her bachelor of arts in communication from Bowling Green State University in 2010. A sports enthusiast, her future career goals involve working using her public relations skills within the community relations department of a major or minor league sports team. With a passion for giving back and helping others, her journey toward earning a master's degree with a public relations concentration has proved beneficial. As a graduate assistant her bevy of skills have expanded, providing a well-rounded and much needed learning experience for the bright future ahead.

Jennifer L. McCullough (PhD, The Ohio State University) is an assistant professor in the School of Communication Studies at Kent State University. Her research interests include the social and psychological effects of the mass media on individuals and the role interpersonal communication plays in altering these effects. In particular, she examines the role of the media and family communication in developing children and young adults' consumer competency. This includes research on the effectiveness of parental mediation strategies designed to mitigate the unintended effects of advertising content on young children.

Mitch McKenney is an assistant professor in the School of Journalism and Mass Communication at Kent State University. He joined the Kent State faculty in August 2008 following an 18-year career in newsrooms, including a decade at the *Akron Beacon Journal* and Ohio.com, where he supervised online news, features, politics, in-depth and crime news reporters. He previously was a reporter and editor for the *Palm Beach Post* in southern Florida and at the *Times-Union* in Rochester, New York. Among the courses McKenney teaches at the Stark Campus are journalism writing courses such as newswriting, media writing, fundamentals of media messages and the graduate-level reporting for mass media, as well as lecture courses such as mass communication and media power and culture. In the lecture courses he focuses on the First Amendment and where government intersects with media, so his ears perk up when federal and other agencies seek to put limits on media content or regulate advertising. He also puts an emphasis on taxpayer access to government records, including sunshine laws and open-records laws. He also has developed courses in journalism specialties such as international storytelling—which has taken students to China and India—as well as environmental reporting and citizen media. McKenney's research has included work on credibility of news sites, the effect of reader feedback on news coverage online, public records access, environmental coverage and international reporting. He also studies the use of newswriting techniques such as narrative and features section staples such as comics sections and religion pages. His bachelor's in journalism and master's in business administration are both from Kent State. He lives in Hartville, Ohio, with his wife, Kim, and their three children.

Natalie Moses grew up in Pittsburgh with her face behind a Harry Potter book. She loved reading so much that she developed a passion for writing well before teachers started giving writing assignments. In high school, she was heavily involved with the Newspaper Club and by senior year became president and editor-in-chief. By this time it was clear that Hogwarts would not accept her, so she decided on Kent State University instead. She is currently majoring in applied communications with minors in PR and media literacy. During her second semester at Kent State, she became a features reporter for the *Daily Kent Stater*, where she quickly found a niche in humor writing. Reporting has provided opportunities that she never imagined possible, such as interviewing stars of her favorite movies and being the first to write about rising local music artists. Above anything, Natalie wants to write stories that will someday inspire little bookworms just like J. K. Rowling did for her.

John Kenneth Muir is the author of over two dozen books of film and TV reference, including award-winners *Terror Television, Horror Films of the 1970s,* and *The Encyclopedia of Superheroes on Film and Television.* His popular blog, *Reflections on Cult Movies and Classic Television* (http://reflectionsonfilmandtelevision.blogspot.com) was selected one of the "100 Top Film Study" sites on the net in 2010, and he is also the creator of the independent web series, *The House Between* (http://www.thehouse between.com). In 2009, John appeared in the documentary *Nightmares in Red, White and Blue: The Evolution of the American Horror Film* along with horror legends John Carpenter, Larry Cohen, and Joe Dante. John's most recent books are *Horror Films of the 1990s* (2011) and *Purple Rain: Music on Film* (2012). He lives in Charlotte, North Carolina, with his beautiful wife and young son.

Isaac I. Muñoz received his doctoral degree from the Department of Advertising at the University of Texas at Austin. He holds a master of science in marketing from Texas A&M University–Commerce with a focus on international marketing and branding, as well as a bachelor of business administration in marketing from Texas Tech University. His primary research focus is consumer behavior via the amalgamation of account planning, qualitative methods, film studies and consumer culture theory. Other research interests include entertainment and university marketing, marketing strategy, and health literacy, especially within the Hispanic population. Muñoz has worked on account planning for accounts such as: General Mills, MillerCoors, the City of San Antonio, the University of Incarnate Word, Payless Shoe Source, Reynolds Wrap, the NBA, and Western Union. He is currently a customer insights manager in the Marketing Department at Southwest Airlines. He has presented his research at the American Academy of Advertising, the Texas Leadership Luncheon, the McCombs' Healthcare conference on innovative forms of communication, and Cross Cultural Business Research. He has also lectured at Texas State University, the University of Texas at San Antonio, and the University of Texas at Austin. Muñoz's research has been published in the *Journal of Advertising Education, Journal of Computer-Mediated Communication,* the ARF (*Advertising Research Foundation*), and is under review in other academic journals.

Heather Ann Roy (MA, Syracuse University, 2012) is a doctoral student at the University of Iowa in the Department of Communication Studies. Her research interests include rhetorical theory, gender studies, queer theory, critical cultural studies, and visual rhetoric.

Rekha Sharma (MA, MS, Kent State University) is a doctoral candidate in the School of Communication Studies in the College of Communication and Information at Kent State University. With a background in journalism and information use, her current research interests include the uses and effects of news, political media, and popular culture. Her dissertation will focus on government conspiracy theories about the presidency. Her recent publications have addressed the use of YouTube in the U.S. primary and general presidential elections. She has also published work examining the use of film in the articulation of ethnic identity, the impact of film on news agendas, political outcomes of infotainment, and messages about war in animated cartoons. Her academic articles have appeared in journals such as *Global Media Journal–Canadian Edition, Electronic News, Mass Communication and Society,* and in the anthology *War and the Media: Essays on News Reporting, Propaganda and Popular Culture.*

Index

DATE DUE	RETURNED